Powwow

Powwow

Edited by Clyde Ellis
Luke Eric Lassiter
& Gary H. Dunham

University of Nebraska Press : Lincoln and London

Set in Quadraat by Kim Essman. Book designed by Richard Eckersley. Printed by Edwards Brothers, Inc.

Library of Congress Cataloging-in-Publication Data
Powwow / edited by Clyde Ellis, Luke Eric Lassiter, & Gary H. Dunham.
p. cm. Includes bibliographical references & index.
ISBN-13: 978-0-8032-2960-0 (cloth: alkaline paper)
ISBN-13: 978-0-8032-6755-8 (paperback: alk. paper)
ISBN-10: 0-8032-2960-7 (cloth: alkaline paper)
ISBN-10: 0-8032-6755-X (paperback: alkaline paper)
1. Powwows – North America. 2. Indians of North America – Rites and ceremonies. 3. Indian dance – North America. I. Ellis, Clyde. II. Lassiter, Luke E. III. Dunham, Gary H.
E99.P86P68 2005 793.3'1'08997–dc22 2005013441

Contents

CLYDE ELLIS AND LUKE ERIC LASSITER

Introduction

Every weekend of the year Indian people gather in one place or another to share their dances and songs, renew friendships, and reaffirm their shared experiences as members of a tribe, organization, family, or community. Whether in large metropolitan arenas, university gymnasiums, small community buildings, or isolated rural dance grounds, the powwow has become a way for Indian people to remember their past, celebrate the present, and prepare for the future.

For some participants the lure of big money, huge crowds, and nonstop excitement at powwows like the Gathering of Nations, Red Earth, or Schemitzun keeps them coming back year after year. For others, smaller annual community dances – especially in the summer months – offer the chance for reunions of all sorts. Sometimes dances are held to raise money for a local Indian club's activities; other times it's to help those who need medical care. Sometimes a dance commemorates a significant event or person, and sometimes it offers thanks for a safe trip from far away. "Why do we dance?" pondered the late Derek Lowry, a North Carolina Tuscarora. "Well, how many reasons you got? Sometime it's for ceremony. Sometimes it's because I want to put on my getup and shake a leg. And sometimes it's because I want to remember my friends and family. And sometimes it's just *because*. You don't always need a reason, do you?"[1]

As the essays in this volume suggest, Indian people from all walks of life, from all kinds of communities, with all kinds of interests, see the powwow as a source of renewal, joy, strength, and pride. For them the powwow has become a singularly important cultural icon in their lives. Anchored in deeply respected traditions but clearly modified over the years by the shifting tides of identity and belief that have appeared in every Indian community, the powwow has become a dynamic source of expression.

But if powwows share common characteristics throughout Indian country – for example, most powwows have a Grand Entry, most begin and end with prayers and memorial songs, and Fancy dancers in Oklahoma look a lot like Fancy dancers in California – powwow culture exists in Native American communities in many different and diverse ways. As the essays in this volume suggest, individual communities have accommodated the powwow to their particular needs, purposes, and cultures in a variety of ways. Once widely considered an icon of a post–World War II Pan-Indian movement in which Native people seemed to be part of a homogenized, melting pot Indian culture, in fact powwow culture began as – and remains – a complicated amalgam of sources and practices reflecting both particular and generalized notions of identity. One of the central goals of this volume is to explore the contours and consequences of those sources and practices and to offer some insights into the complex world of powwow culture.

Far from being an example of a homogenized Indian culture, powwow culture, since it first appeared in the 1930s in the forms familiar to us today, has maintained clear ties to specific tribal and community ways and practices. It's true that most powwows follow a common template that participants instantly recognize no matter where they are, but local customs and ways inevitably frame dances as events that are situated in specific contexts with particular meanings.

Recalling his experiences as a young boy learning dances from his father, for example, Southern Cheyenne W. Richard West Jr. has written: "I have always considered dance to be among the most profound cultural expressions – for me personally – of what it is to be Cheyenne." Others feel the same way. "It's our way of life," says Billy Evans Horse, a Kiowa from Southwest Oklahoma. "It goes with us all the time," he continues, "every day." Haddon Nauni, a Comanche, put it this way: "This arena is our society. . . . Here you are with all of your people, your family. . . . If you do it the right way, it'll be a blessing in your life." On the Northern Plains, writes Lynn Huenemann, "dance and dance events – including the songs, dance dress, and gatherings of the people – are among the strongest overt expressions and measures of the perpetuation of Indian life and culture." In Alaska, notes Maria Williams, "music and dance have been renewed to accommodate the dynamics of the modern Native Alaskan world."[2] Understanding the powwow in all of its many forms and uses, then, compels us to see how this institution is put to different uses and offers us a way of understanding how, why, and with what consequences Indian people have negotiated change. With that in mind we have solicited essays on many different aspects of powwow culture in an effort to understand from historical, cultural, community, and personal perspectives what this phenomenon is about.

Because many of our authors examine powwows from very specific perspectives, they tend to reject the argument that powwows are primarily Pan-Indian in form and function, a point made with some force by James Howard in his seminal 1955 essay on Oklahoma powwow culture. Since then, Howard's interpretation has remained very influential. Convinced that post–World War II Indian identity was becoming increasingly generalized, Howard wrote that institutions like the powwow reflected a "process by which sociocultural entities such as the Seneca, Delaware, Creek, Yuchi, Ponca, and Comanche are losing their tribal distinctiveness and in its place are developing a nontribal 'Indian' culture."[3]

Indeed, the powwow's widely shared and copied practices, format, and clothing seemed to confirm the existence of this new, generalized Indian culture. And it's difficult to argue with the idea that powwows have helped to create a common ground that provides strong bonds between various Indian groups. Following Howard's lead Barre Toelken reminds us that at many powwows we would be hard pressed not to see "the existence of a growing body of custom, observance, belief, propriety, and awareness which have superceded [*sic*] the specific tribal customs that once underscored the differences (often the open enmities) among the participating tribes. The emergence of this larger body of custom and observance . . . is an indication that specific tribal identity is being reassessed by many Native Americans and being replaced by a powerful synthesis of related traditions that can articulate Indianness."[4]

With the benefit of time, however, it's clear that both Howard and Toelken overstated the case. Powwows can reflect "a powerful synthesis of related traditions," but as several of the essays in this volume attest, they also simultaneously encourage tribally specific and community-specific senses of identity as well. William K. Powers has noted with some irony, for example, that "it cannot be overemphasized that Pan-Indianism is simply a variation of acculturation and assimilation studies," which was reason enough for him to see it as a problematic, even misleading concept. "Although the idea that Pan-Indianism strives towards the creation of a new ethnic group, the American Indian, is novel and interesting," wrote Powers in 1990, "it is unlikely that this definition can be regarded seriously, given what we know about the distinctiveness and variety of American Indian tribal cultures."[5]

Thomas Kavanagh agrees and clearly demonstrates that many Southern Plains powwows maintain a close affinity with tribally specific practices and interests even as they also incorporate elements of powwow culture that are not Comanche in origin or use. While noting that the powwow's role in creating what Robert K. Thomas called " 'a new ethnic group' is partially correct," Kavanagh offers compelling evidence of how the same events also allow innovations that speak directly to tribally specific notions of identity. Writing in 1982 Kavanagh noted that "the Comanche pow-wow is part of a wider network of pow-wows, and although this network includes many different cultural groups, the version of the pow-wow sponsored by Comanches does not exploit an 'Indian' identity function at the expense of a Comanche identity. In fact, several recent innovations in the Comanche pow-wow explicitly strengthen its tribal identity functions. It is through the identities created by and through participation in the pow-wow that a tribal identity gains political power."[6]

Focusing on Comanche men's societies and descendants' organizations, Kavanagh observes that even at deeply intertribal events like Gourd Dances, Comanche organizations have adapted clothing and insignia that clearly signal their identity as Comanches. Members of the Comanche Gourd Dance group known as the Little Ponies, for example, wear distinctive pins as "a mark of identity." Similarly, the Gourd Dance outfits of the Comanche Indian Veterans Association include a red ribbon embroidered with the association's shield. "When a Little Pony dances," Kavanagh notes, "whether or not other Little Ponies are present, he can be identified as a Little Pony, and thus as a Comanche, by the distinctive insignia of the society." Worried about losing their tribal identity in the large world of the intertribal powwow, Comanches have seized on symbols that affirm their specific tribal identity. "The participants in pow-wows, particularly in Oklahoma," Kavanagh writes, "have realized that the symbols and signs through which they had identified themselves are now ambiguous and that those symbolic expressions of identity need tightening." Robert DesJarlait makes the same point in an essay on Northern Plains powwows when he notes that where powwow practices "strongly conflict with Ojibwe-Anishinaabe dance traditions . . . we need to make sure that our traditional powwows retain and express our tribal-centricity."[7]

Without denying that widely shared aspects of powwow culture exist across tribal, regional, and cultural boundaries, Powers, Kavanagh, DesJarlait, and others remind us that many communities use the powwow to assert a tribally distinct, rather than a generalized, sense of Indianness. As someone put it at a small dance in Oklahoma in summer 2003: "You know, I don't know anybody who goes to powwows and says 'I'm here representing my people – the ones from the Pan-Indian tribe. Even when I go to Red Earth or Gathering of Nations, you know what really gets me going? It's when one of those drums sings a Comanche song. I say to myself 'Hey, good, that's one of *our* songs. It comes from *my* world. And then I go out and I join in with all of those other dancers – Navajos, Crows, Poncas, Zunis, even non-Indians. I love to dance to all of that powwow music, but if it's one of our Comanche songs, it really reminds me of who I am and why I'm here. So that's what I'd say about this Pan-Indian stuff."[8]

Our collection begins with a series of essays on the history and significance of the powwow. As Clyde Ellis observes in his essay on the formative era of Southern Plains powwows in the late nineteenth and early twentieth centuries, powwows there reflected a wide variety of innovations and adaptations but they also continued to nurture particular tribal traditions. Patricia C. Albers and Beatrice Medicine make a similar point in their essay on Northern Plains dances. Based on more than three decades of fieldwork and participation, Albers and Medicine carefully discuss some of the most notable changes and adaptations in that region's powwows with special attention to the relationship between tribally specific and intertribal gatherings. In his wide-ranging discussion of early-twentieth-century Ho-Chunk powwows in the upper Midwest, Grant Arndt focuses on the increasingly public, performative aspects of early powwow culture there. Loretta Fowler concludes part 1 with a comparative essay on powwow culture among the Gros Ventre and Blackfeet tribes in Montana and the Cheyenne and Arapaho tribes in Oklahoma. Reminding us that powwows are best understood "in local contexts and as products of local histories," Fowler deftly explores how dances can reflect very specific needs and interests related to age, class, gender, and community.

In part 2 our contributors address how various groups negotiate the meaning of the powwow's symbols and practices, noting that if some traditions are similar from community to community, their meanings do not always follow the same trajectory. As these essays suggest, traditions and practices are constantly negotiated, even argued about, all with consequences that shape the powwow's meaning. These ethnographically based essays focus on and emphasize the power of experience to shape and express identity in the powwow world. In doing so they confirm what scholars of ethnicity have pointed out time and time again: ethnicity and identity are not narrowly situated within a group or a place or an event but are ever-changing, evolving, and negotiated processes.[9]

In his thoughtful essay on Lakota song and dance, R. D. Theisz employs a deeply collaborative framework with the late Severt Young Bear as they examine the powwow's role in regenerating culture and tradition among the Lakota people. In their comparative discussion of Omaha and Dane-zaa traditions,

Robin Ridington, Dennis Hastings, and Tommy Attachie echo Fowler's work by examining how two tribes with equally strong dance traditions ultimately evolved in completely different directions.

Two essays in the collection address specific roles of powwow participants. Daniel Gelo's informative, entertaining piece on powwow emcees gives readers an unusual perspective. Gelo observes that the authority accorded to emcees marks them as the key figures of the powwows, not simply the announcers. Kathleen Glenister Roberts's insightful essay on powwow princesses examines how powwow culture celebrates the roles of women as representatives of both traditional and contemporary values. Jason Baird Jackson concludes part 2 by discussing the relationship between Stomp Dance and powwows. Although they are typically regarded as separate worlds, Stomp Dances and powwows can often occupy the same ground (literally).

If it comes as no surprise that powwows reflect tribally specific and community-specific practices in places like North Dakota, New Mexico, or Oklahoma, should we be surprised to discover the same trend in, say, North Carolina and Virginia? Or among German hobbyists, New Agers, or gay and lesbian Native people? The answer for most of us is probably yes. Part 3 assesses some ways in which powwow culture has moved out of its Plains homeland and into some very unusual but revealing contexts. For example, the essay by Samuel R. Cook, John L. Johns, and Karenne Wood on Virginia's Monacans and Chris Goertzen's essay on North Carolina's Occaneechi-Saponis reveal that these southeastern Indians have eagerly appropriated powwows complete with Plains-style singing, clothing, and ritual.

But just when we think we've stumbled onto a textbook case of Pan-Indian powwows in the American South, these essays reveal that Indians there aren't taking up the powwow because they've bought into a generalized notion of Indianness; they do it because powwows affirm in concrete, tribally specific terms their status as Native people and also advance the various campaigns for political recognition by state and federal agencies.[10] As these authors suggest, a close look at these powwows reveals a complicated set of motivations in which tribally specific interests and needs are expressed through the borrowed institution of the Plains powwow. But, importantly, it's a lens that North Carolina and Virginia Indians use to sharpen, not generalize, the image presented to observers.

Part 3 also includes essays about powwow people who have been more or less invisible to American audiences. In what might be the volume's most provocative essay, Brian Joseph Gilley examines "Two-Spirit" powwows in the gay and lesbian community. "By holding their own powwow," he writes, "Two-Spirit people are revising notions of tradition to include the gender diversity historically prevalent in Native North America." Renae Watchman introduces us to Germany's vibrant, growing powwow culture and asks questions about identity, appropriation, and meaning. In her hands the discussion clearly suggests the power of powwow culture to cross boundaries and shape expression in the most unlikely places and ways. Lisa Aldred's discussion of New Agers examines one of the most hotly debated issues in the contemporary powwow world. The appropriation of powwows by the New Age movement has sparked predictably heated confrontations and has prompted attempts to prevent Indians and New Agers from attending one another's powwows. Using conversations with Indian people to frame her comments, Aldred offers a damning indictment of New Age appropriations.

In the end our goal is to draw attention to some of the differences and similarities from community to community and group to group and to help point the way toward a more systematic and nuanced cross-cultural understanding of powwows. As a start we could begin by replacing the term *Pan-Indianism* with *intertribal*, a term widely preferred by powwow participants themselves, and one that we believe more accurately describes both the common and negotiated ground of powwow culture. (As one powwow participant put it with a chuckle, "You know, when they sing at powwows, the emcee calls it a set of intertribal songs, not a set of Pan-Indian songs.") But understanding the powwow as both a community-specific and a cross-cultural institution means doing more than simply renaming things, so dropping "Pan-Indianism" won't necessarily produce more perceptive treatments.

Whatever influence this collection has, we are not so presumptuous as to believe that we have solved these larger interpretive issues in one volume. Like most collections this one is imperfect. But as the first of its kind focusing solely on powwow culture, we hope it will encourage more ethnographic and cross-cultural studies. Among the issues that remain to be more fully explored and discussed are powwow food and other folkways, generational differences, powwow politics and its relationship to community leadership, the use of technology in powwows, arena shows like the Gathering of Nations and Red Earth, university and college powwows, the powwow recording industry, and powwow narratives and other literatures. Thus our goal is not to cover all of the powwow's cultural practices, geographical regions, dances, or song styles but simply to spark interest in the powwow as something more than a set of generalized cultural practices.

NOTES

1. Derek Lowry, interview with Clyde Ellis, June 9, 2001, Greensboro, North Carolina.

2. W. Richard West Jr., foreword to *Native American Dance: Ceremonies and Social Traditions*, ed. Charlotte Heth (Washington DC: Smithsonian Institution Press, 1992), ix; Billy Evans Horse, quoted in Luke Eric Lassiter, "Charlie Brown: Not Just Another Essay on the Gourd Dance," *American Indian Culture and Research Journal* 21, no. 4 (1997): 97; Haddon Nauni, quoted in Morris Foster, *Being Comanche: A Social History of an American Indian Community* (Tucson: University of Arizona Press, 1991), 153; Lynn Huenemann, "Northern Plains Dance," in *Native American Dance*, ed. Heth, 125; Maria Williams, "Contemporary Alaska Native Dance: The Spirit of Tradition," in *Native American Dance*, ed. Heth, 167.

3. James Howard, "Pan-Indian Culture in Oklahoma," *Scientific Monthly* 81 (November 1955): 215. See also Howard, "Pan-Indianism in Native American Music and Dance," *Ethnomusicology* 71 (1983): 71–82.

4. Barre Toelken, "Ethnic Selection and Intensification in the Native American Powwow," in *Creative Ethnicity: Symbols and Strategies of Contemporary Ethnic Life*, ed. Stephen Stern and John Allan Cicala, 137–56 (Logan: Utah State University Press, 1991), 140.

5. William K. Powers, *War Dance: Plains Indian Musical Performance* (Tucson: University of Arizona Press, 1990), 87, 108.

6. Thomas W. Kavanagh, "The Comanche Pow-wow: Pan-Indianism or Tribalism," *Haliksa'i*, University of New Mexico Contributions to Anthropology 1 (1982): 12–13.

7. Kavanagh, "The Comanche Pow-wow," 18–19, 21; Robert DesJarlait, "The Contest Powwow Versus the Traditional Powwow and the Role of the Native American Community," *Wicazo Sa Review* 12, no. 1 (Spring 1997): 124, 126.

For other discussions of tribally distinctive dance practices, see *Native American Dance*, ed. Heth; Loretta Fowler, *Shared Symbols, Contested Meanings: Gros Ventre Culture and History, 1778–1984* (Ithaca NY: Cornell University Press, 1987); Luke E. Lassiter, *The Power of Kiowa Song: A Collaborative Ethnography* (Tucson: University of Arizona Press, 1998); William C. Meadows, *Kiowa, Apache, and Comanche Military Societies: Enduring Veterans, 1800 to the Present* (Austin: University of Texas Press, 1999); Benjamin Kracht, "Kiowa Powwows: Continuity in Ritual Practice," *American Indian Quarterly* 18, no. 3 (1994): 321–48; Clyde Ellis, "'Truly Dancing Their Own Way': Modern Revival and Diffusion of the Gourd Dance," *American Indian Quarterly* 14 (Winter 1990): 19–33; R. D. Theisz, "Song Texts and Their Performers: The Centerpiece of Contemporary Lakota Identity Formulation," *Great Plains Quarterly* 7 (Spring 1987): 116–24; Mark Thiel, "The Omaha Dance in Oglala and Sicangu Sioux History, 1883–1923," *Whispering Wind* 23 (Fall/Winter 1990): 4–17.

8. Clyde Ellis, field notes, July 2003, Stroud, Oklahoma.

9. See Dan Aronson, "Ethnicity as a Cultural System: An Introductory Essay," in *Ethnicity in the Americas*, ed. Frances Henry, 9–19 (The Hague: Mouton, 1976); Fredrik Barth, ed., *Ethnic Groups and Boundaries: The Social Organization of Cultural Differences* (Boston: Little, Brown, 1969); James Clifford, "Identity in Mashpee," in *The Predicament of Culture: Twentieth-Century Ethnography, Literature, and Art*, 277–346 (Cambridge: Harvard University Press, 1988); Robert E. Daniels, "Cultural Identities among the Oglala Sioux," in *The Modern Sioux: Social Systems and Reservation Culture*, ed. Ethel Nurge, 198–245 (Lincoln: University of Nebraska Press, 1970); George Devereux, "Ethnic Identity: Its Logical Foundations and Its Dysfunctions," in *Ethnic Identity: Cultural Continuities and Change*, ed. George De Vos and Lola Romanucci-Ross, 42–70 (Palo Alto CA: Mayfield, 1975); Cynthia K. Mahmood and Sharon L. Armstrong, "Do Ethnic Groups Exist? Perspectives on the Concept of Cultures," *Ethnology* 31, no 1 (1992): 1–14; Devon Mihesuah, "American Indian Identities: Comment on Issues of Individual Choices and Development," *American Indian Culture and Research Journal* 22, no. 2 (1998): 193–226.

10. For another discussion of this, see Patricia Barker Lerch, *Waccamaw Legacy: Contemporary Indians Fight for Survival* (Tuscaloosa: University of Alabama Press, 2004), especially chapter 8, "The Powwow Paradox." For other regionally based interpretations, see also Ann McMullen, "Soapbox Discourse: Tribal Historiography, Indian-White Relations, and Southeastern New England Powwows," *Public Historian* 18, no. 4 (1996): 53–74; and Clyde Ellis, " 'There's a Dance Every Weekend': Powwow Culture in Southeast North Carolina," in *Southern Heritage on Display: Public Ritual and Ethnic Diversity within Southern Regionalism*, ed. Celeste Ray, 79–105 (Tuscaloosa: University of Alabama Press, 2003).

PART I

History and Significance

CLYDE ELLIS

1. "The Sound of the Drum Will Revive Them and Make Them Happy"

For one weekend every August the Tulsa Fairground teems with thousands of people attending the Intertribal Indian Club of Tulsa's annual powwow, known as the IICOT Powwow of Champions. There's big money on the line in every category, and champion dancers from across the Southern Plains are there, joined by a large contingent of dancers from other regions who stop over at IICOT as part of the powwow circuit that hits its peak in the summer months. Billed as the second-largest powwow in Oklahoma after Red Earth, and voted the top large powwow for four consecutive years by *Native American Times* readers, the IICOT dance has gained a reputation as one of the region's best. For a small admission fee ($5 for the 2005 powwow – the club's twenty-eighth), visitors can take in some of the finest singing and dancing on the Southern Plains (as well as the tastiest funnel cake in northeast Oklahoma) at an event that captures every bit of the contemporary powwow's power and spectacle. Best of all they can do it in the air-conditioned comfort of a ten-acre indoor arena.[1]

Inside, visitors can browse several dozen booths whose sponsors offer everything from arts and crafts to information on bone marrow transplants in Indian country. Afternoons and evenings become a jumble of events filled by hours of dancing, giveaways, and contests. Neighboring tribes host afternoon Gourd Dance sessions, visiting princesses and other powwow royalty are introduced and given prominent seats at the head of the arena, families ask for time to hold giveaways to acknowledge friends and relations with goods and monetary gifts, and dancers of all ages rush back and forth from the bathrooms to check their look. Elders open each dance session by praying over the assembled throng in their native languages, sometimes slipping in the English words "Intertribal Indian Club of Tulsa," "Jesus Christ," and "weekend." Some of Oklahoma's most prominent powwowers serve as head dancers and head singers and lend status to a dance that, despite its prominence, must compete with other powwows for participants.

A tag team of informative and entertaining emcees – also stars on the circuit – keeps the pace up. In between contest rounds and intertribal dance sessions, the emcees announce upcoming powwows, encourage spectators to visit the vendors, tell an endless array of mostly bad jokes, and plug IICOT's bingo hall, golf tournament, dance troupe, and scholarship fund. Meanwhile, powwow staffers work the crowd selling raffle tickets for Pendleton blankets, art, jewelry, and the always popular 50/50 pot, in which the winner takes home half of the money generated by ticket sales for that contest (and instantly becomes the best friend of everyone in sight).

The crowds ebb and flow as the dance sessions run their course, but when the contest finals roll around during the evening sessions on Friday, Saturday, and Sunday, thousands of spectators, friends, and participants jam the arena to take it all in. "For me, IICOT is what powwowing is all about," one dancer told me while we waited between contests for a round of intertribal songs during which everyone could participate. "The family's here, we have a good time, and if we're lucky one of us will take home some money. My folks have been here from the start [1977], and one day maybe my kids will come back." And besides, he added with a smile, "Mom gets to go to the mall while we're here."[2] When it's over the participants pack up and head home before striking out for another dance the following weekend.

Drive four hours to the southwestern corner of the state, and you can take in a powwow that is markedly different but equally powerful. In a copse of cottonwood trees on an allotment south of Carnegie, the Kiowa Tiah-Piah Society (pronounced "tie-pay") hosts its annual Gourd Dance and powwow during the July 4th holidays. There are no admission fees, no hassles with city traffic, and no charges for parking. Not surprisingly this powwow has considerably fewer amenities than at the IICOT dance – no indoor, air-conditioned dance arena, no flush toilets, and no grandstands. On a good day the road to the encampment is equal parts thin gravel and mudhole, and the parking lot is a grass field that often resembles Indian country's version of gridlock. IICOT's air-conditioned comfort is replaced by the humid blast furnace that settles over the Southern Plains like a sodden blanket every summer. The heat can be brutal. Tipis, nylon tents, and all manner of campers compete for the limited shade, and groups of friends and relatives wait out the afternoon heat under tarps and small brush arbors before the dancing begins. Children play in the small creek that wanders through the grounds, and teenagers occasionally slip off to the car and sit in the air-conditioning or make the short drive up to the Sonic drive-in at Carnegie.

As at similar powwows, families have camped for years in the same sites, where they have erected permanent picnic shelters and cooking areas. Visitors looking for one camp or another are pointed in the right direction by people who know the camps as well as they know their own neighborhood streets. Because it's held a short drive from the nearest town, Carnegie (which barely qualifies as a crossroads in some folks' opinion), the Tiah-Piah dance ground evokes an older time for many participants who remember when dances were held out in the country, away from the hustle and bustle of city life. Like IICOT, the Tiah-Piah Society's dance is notable for its easy familiarity and welcoming atmosphere. Extended families use the occasion to reconnect, and there is also a sense of camaraderie that is unique to such gatherings.

Many people eagerly await the week of the dance, and they arrange vacation days so they can spend as much time at the camp as possible. Some arrive a day or two early and linger another day or so after the dance ends before packing up for the drive home. Participants spend considerable time visiting other camps, and the overall mood is less hurried than at large contest powwows. Moreover, the camp is knit together physically and emotionally by a sense of shared purpose that some say is different from the feeling they get at, say, IICOT or Red Earth. This is partly because many of the participants come from a handful of local communities dominated by a relatively small number of tribes, most notably Kiowas, Comanches, and Apaches. The host organization also draws the participants together in a number of ways. On the evening of the first dance session, for example, the entire camp is invited in groups of twos and threes into a large tipi where several men from the Tiah-Piah Society bless participants with cedar smoke and gifts of sage picked that morning from the surrounding hills. Visitors are welcomed, often find themselves invited to camps for meals, and invariably comment on how well they're treated.

The powwow arena is a modest, relatively small circular affair in an open field surrounded by dozens of parked cars, trucks, and vans. A plywood speaker's stand dominates the western side, and benches for the dancers mark the arena's outer edge. A more or less reliable lighting system cranks up after dark and lights the way to the dozen or so portable outhouses, parking areas, and camps bordering the arena. Otherwise, as one Kiowa woman told me with a smile when I returned a folding chair that I'd borrowed one night, "it's flashlight country, unless you *like* wandering around in the woods. Ayyy."[3] Unlike IICOT, where as many as six drum groups sing, the Tiah-Piah dance has a single drum under the control of an invited head singer and anywhere from a dozen to twenty men and women who come out to sing. A trader or two might set up a table, but the area around the dance ground quickly fills with dozens of folding chairs. No contests are held, unless a family or individual sponsors one to honor friends or relatives.

Like most powwows this dance is intertribal and draws heavily from communities in and around Carnegie, Anadarko, and Lawton. There's also a large, welcomed contingent of non-Indians, mostly from south of the Red River – "Texicans" to their friends in the Kiowa community. Here, as in Tulsa, people gather to celebrate shared experiences through song and dance that maintain preciously guarded ways of life. As at the IICOT powwow, the sense of a community gathering is palpable. "Here," one Kiowa woman told me, "I remember what it means to be a member of this family, this tribe of people. I wouldn't miss this for the world."[4]

The IICOT and Tiah-Piah dances occupy opposite ends of the powwow spectrum, but they don't cover the entire scene. On any given weekend, if you take I-40 east out of Oklahoma City and make the forty-minute drive over to the Kickapoo Tribal Complex near the small town of McCloud, just north of Shawnee, for example, there's a good chance you'll find a powwow being held for one cause or another. One Saturday it's a fund raiser for the Kickapoo Powwow Club's annual dance; another day it's a birthday dance, a memorial dance, or a wedding anniversary dance. On one particularly memorable occasion in 1994, several families hosted a dance on short notice and raised money to fend off the foreclosure of the property on which the Kickapoo chapter of the Native American Church holds its meetings. The sponsors raised several thousand dollars, saved a sacred place, and fed dinner to nearly two hundred people in the bargain. It was a good day's work by any measure.

A cook shack out back is always busy by the time dances begin at midafternoon or early evening, and a small concession stand in the community building/gymnasium/multipurpose room, where many dances are held, does a brisk business in soda pop and candy bars. Inside, three or four concentric circles of chairs ring the benches around a dance arena that on most nights is barely thirty feet wide. By the time the singers set up in the middle of the room, it's a tight fit all around. When a crowd fills the room – as it does for most dances – the cranky exhaust fans don't usually keep up with the heat and cigarette smoke.

When large crowds are expected, the dancing moves outdoors to a small field. The Kickapoo Powwow Club's annual dance in August, for example, is held outdoors – weather permitting – and resembles a cross between the IICOT and Tiah-Piah events. At the 2002 dance almost no one camped overnight, but several camp areas were set up where families ate, changed into dance clothes, and visited with friends. One small refreshment stand raising funds for a high school drama club did a steady business selling drinks, hot dogs, and Frito pies (a concoction of Fritos and chili smothered with soft cheese – it's a dietary disaster worth every penny), and renowned Pawnee silversmith Bruce Caesar had the lone crafts booth (cash and checks, please – no plastic). Orville Kirk – a well-known emcee on the powwow circuit – entertained the crowd with jokes, stories, and announcements, while constantly reminding us of the big news: "This year we got permanent lights! Can you believe it? No more lining up all those Indian cars and turning on the high beams after dark. Some guy today said he thought we'd put up Sun Dance poles, ayyyyyyy."[5]

Neither as large as IICOT nor as rurally located as Tiah-Piah, powwows at the Kickapoo complex are nonetheless cut from the same cultural fabric. Oriented around songs, dances, and events that have significance for all in attendance, powwows at McCloud are intensely meaningful, perhaps because participants and spectators are tightly knit by kinship and a sense of community that is also expressed daily in numerous ways outside of the powwow. Indeed, some people believe that the smaller the dance the better, in which case McCloud serves as the perfect environment. It's not that IICOT doesn't have an equally intense effect. It does – but many people who go to both kinds of dances often comment on how different that effect can be. At many small community dances, for example, singers and onlookers often outnumber the dancers (sometimes by three or four to one); at a dance like this, visitors can begin to discern the complexities of such gatherings.

From Crow Fair to the local school's Indian club fund-raising dance, powwows are a vital element in creating and maintaining contemporary Indian culture across the United States. My examples here are drawn from the Southern Plains powwow culture, with which I am most familiar, but similar scenarios play themselves out in every corner of the country. The same kinds of Oklahoma dances that I've described also occur with endless variation in Montana, Georgia, Texas, Arizona, Minnesota, Florida, Kansas, California, Pennsylvania, and North Dakota. Where there are Indian people, you can bet your bottom dollar these days there will be a dance of some kind. You can powwow in Pembroke, North Carolina; Columbus, Ohio; Laramie, Wyoming; San Francisco, California; Ames, Iowa; Richmond, Virginia; Columbia, South Carolina; and Yankton, South Dakota. Native American student organizations sponsor dances at Stanford University, Dartmouth College, the University of North Carolina at Chapel Hill, Brown University, Michigan State University, Harvard University, Oklahoma State University, and the University of New

Mexico, to name only a few. Urban Indian organizations from New York City to Seattle to Dallas to Minneapolis host annual dances, as do groups in the unlikeliest of places, including the Hickory, North Carolina, Powwow Club.

And it isn't only Indians who are powwowing. In the United States an energetic hobbyist movement comprised almost entirely of non-Indians puts on dances all across the country, including a biannual "National Powwow," with crowds that reach into the thousands. In Europe enthusiastic gatherings in Germany, England, and Russia feature dancing and singing copied directly from their American models. Toss in the New Agers, Boy Scouts, and assorted others who find something meaningful in powwow ways, and you have a culture that has spread around the globe.

Indeed, powwows are everywhere. A search using any standard Internet engine can pull up thousands of hits. Plugging "powwow" into my local university library's WorldCat search engine recently produced 529 hits on print and media sources, including "Melodies from a New England Pow-wow"; Charles Wakefield Cadman and Nelle Richmond Eberhart's 1918 opera *Shanewis*, which includes a scene at an Oklahoma powwow; and a reference to Jane Richardson's papers at the Newberry Library.

And it isn't just the library where things are getting interesting. When a story about a powwow in Apache, Oklahoma, appeared in *Southern Living* magazine in late 2002, it's safe to say that something strange was afoot. Or, to raise an equally interesting example, what are we to make of an international conference on powwows, performance, and nationhood in Native North America sponsored by the British Museum in February 2003? There, in the same building that houses the Rosetta Stone and the Elgin Marbles, an audience of several hundred Natives and non-Natives gathered for three days to hear two dozen presentations on everything from Two-Spirit powwows to the evolution of Fancy dancing. Or what of a annual gathering in central North Carolina sponsored by Boy Scouting's Order of the Arrow that for more than a decade has drawn upward of five hundred Boy Scouts to a weekend-long seminar on Indian culture, which concludes with a lively (some would say circus-like) powwow?

Since the post–World War II era, when it took on its now-familiar form, the powwow has become one of the most popular and visible expressions of the dynamic cultural forces at work in Indian country. Folklorist Barre Toelken, whose daughter is an accomplished dancer, describes the powwow as "one of the most rapidly growing expressions of ethnic awareness and identity to be found in the world today." He continues: "In the fullest sense of the word, dance *embodies* cultural attitudes which cannot readily be articulated today in other ways."[6] Clearly linked to prereservation societies, institutions, and practices but also molded by modern values and needs, powwow culture reflects a considerable fund of cultural capital. It is a deeply complicated institution, simultaneously binding people from different communities, tribes, and traditions together even as it enforces social and cultural codes and relationships that are connected to tribally specific practices.

It is important to note, however, that powwows are not uncontested events. Power, knowledge, and status are at stake, and for many people the powwow is a way to assert a claim to one form or another of those things. Powwow people readily, even eagerly, comment on the disagreements and struggles that are common in the powwow world. Song knowledge, for example, is hotly contested, for singing carries considerable prestige and power. Head singers exercise tangible authority at the drum and in their communities, as do emcees and other leading figures on the powwow circuit. Not surprisingly some of the disagreements are not all that earth-shaking, as in the case of a Sac and Fox woman who told me she was skipping the 2002 Kickapoo Powwow because she believed one of the singers had treated her children disrespectfully at another dance. "He don't need my help," she said. Other times the divisions signal more deeply felt fault lines, as when powwow associations or drum groups split because of internal disagreements and disputes.[7]

Yet, for the most part, observers and scholars alike tend to view the powwow uncritically, seeing it as an event that downplays hierarchy and power. The irony of this position is that powwows often tend to do exactly the opposite. Nonetheless scholars and others continue to embrace curiously narrow interpretations of the powwow's core meanings. Benjamin Kracht, for example, has employed Victor Turner's communitas theory to argue that Kiowa powwows erase hierarchy and ease rivalries and disagreements. In Kracht's estimation, these dances encourage a " 'timeless condition' created by rituals bringing together people from different social strata . . . [who] are worshiping in a social environment where the participants are social and cultural equals." This notion of the powwow as an institution that levels social and cultural distinctions has a long history. Writing two decades prior to Kracht, Jack Campisi suggested that at powwows "a strong appeal to brotherhood . . . at least for the few hours of the ceremonies, acts thematically to draw the assemblage together."[8]

Yet, as Mark Mattern notes in a recent essay on powwow culture:

> The powwow is often cited for its importance in contemporary Indian life as a constituent of tribal and Indian identity, and as a unifying force in Indian life. Although each of these testimonies may be true, each tells an incomplete story. Each downplays or ignores entirely the disagreements and conflicts that occur within the powwow grounds and that swirl around powwow performances. Each erases the multiple differences among Indians and implies that Indian identity and commitments are simply reinforced and reproduced through powwow practices, rather than debated, negotiated, and changed. Each also erases the constitutive presence of power and politics within the powwow arena.[9]

This debate runs like a thread through the history of the powwow. Some Indians, for example, criticized their kin who danced in the Wild West shows, while others objected to what they perceived as the powwow's challenge to Christianity. Still others thought that powwows were relics of a past best left behind. Today some critics are disdainful of powwow people, who they believe spend an awful lot of time building elaborate dance outfits and chasing contest dollars instead of devoting their time and energy to more serious things, such as political activism. Clearly the powwow does as much to divide Indian people as it does to unite them, and in this sense it is no different from many other contemporary social, cultural, religious, and political institutions in Indian country. Gaming, for example, or peyote also tends to prompt passionate debates about what constitutes legitimately "Indian" expressions.

Yet, whether understood as an intertribal or a tribally specific event, dancing often satisfies needs and obligations that are not adequately met any other way. Such is dancing's power that today many Indian people organize their lives around dancing and all that it represents. "We're a dancing people, always have been," the late Harry Tofpi Sr. once told me. A Kiowa, Harry grew up in the 1930s in Carnegie, Oklahoma, where he began attending dances at an early age. "God gave us these ways," he told me. "He gave us lots of ways to express ourselves. One of them is these dances. When I go to them, whatever they are – powwow, Gourd Dance, Black Legs, whatever – I'm right where those old people were. Singing those songs, dancing *where they danced*. And my children and grandchildren, they've learned these ways, too, because it's good, it's powerful."[10]

As Loretta Fowler has noted, because dance is a cultural construction, it has been "invented, discarded, reinterpreted . . . [and] adapted to new social realities."[11] And that has been one of its most enduring qualities. As they have done since the late nineteenth century, when reservations wrought great changes, Indian people use dancing to negotiate new social and cultural realities and protect tribal and community values. Seeking to ameliorate what many Indian people saw as the corrosive effects of unbridled individualism, industrialization, and capitalism, tribes turned again and again to practices that had sustained them for generations. And in many cases Indian people appealed to dancing, for it often captured in a unique way the practices, relationships, and beliefs with which they were reluctant to part. Historically crucial for its role in prereservation tribal political economies, by the twentieth century dance had emerged as a kind of permeable boundary in the search for stability and cultural continuity. Resilient and adaptable, it proved capable of reinforcing important ideals and values even as the context and expression of those things shifted.

The powwow's role in maintaining old ways and introducing new ones is compelling and clear. Whether as social, cultural, psychological, economic, or political statements, powwows have become one of the most powerful expressions of identity in the contemporary Indian world. Gloria Alese Young, whose unpublished dissertation on Oklahoma powwows has been the standard source for nearly two decades, writes: "The powwow is an event built on an overarching philosophy of 'Indianness' which serves to (1) integrate the members of many disparate cultures into, at a supratribal level, one identity based on a set of previously established stereotypes, (2) establish symbolic boundaries between kinds of people (Indian/non-Indians, conservative/modern) and geographical regions, and (3) raise the quality of life of its participants through improved mental health and social contacts."[12]

Although scholars often mention powwow culture in discussions of twentieth-century Indian life, there have been relatively few attempts to trace its history, evolution, and meaning. Given the enormous importance that powwow people attach to these events, the relative lack of attention to powwow history is curious. As Toelken notes, however, the reasons for such lapses are not especially surprising. Ritual and ceremonial dances have often been topics for research, he writes, but vernacular dance traditions like the powwow have been taken less seriously. Toelken suggests that contemporary powwow probably contradicts popular notions about "authentic" Indian culture, and non-Indians are therefore tempted to think of them as "a mishmash of leftover ideas no longer seriously functional in the world of the Indians."[13]

As the essays in this book suggest, however, there is much more to the powwow world than "a mishmash of leftover ideas." Powwow people invariably say that dancing is about more than what can be seen. "We have to take care of it, to pass it on to our children. It's our way of life," says Billy Evans Horse, a Kiowa. "It goes with us all the time, every day." Whether through the acknowledgment of kinship ties, the naming of children, or the appointment of ceremonial leaders, in many communities powwows are the central vehicle by which Indian people negotiate a shared identity and a common cultural fabric. Although hardly the only activity Indians use to address these issues, dance is widely perceived as particularly potent and emotionally satisfying for those who embrace it. "Music and dance are integral parts of the social and cultural life of the native peoples," writes Thomas Kavanagh. They constitute "the dynamic and creative expressions of Indian identity and pride, both for individuals and communities."[14]

For Theresa Carter, a Kiowa, powwow music is such a central part of her life that she cannot "imagine being without it. . . . It's part of our everyday life. . . . I get *tired* sometimes, and I *gripe*. . . . But, I need that music." She is not alone. At the 1996 Kiowa O-ho-mah dances in Anadarko, Oklahoma, one man recounted publicly between sobs how his most precious memories were of his mother, "who sang O-ho-mah songs to us kids while she did housework. I'll *always* protect these ways. My mom, my dad, all those old ones from a long time back – I can't ever forget how they loved this dance." For others, expressions of kinship and community define the powwow as an event that draws Indian people together in a profoundly meaningful way. The late Ron Harris, a Sac and Fox, saw powwowing as a vital cultural current: "The simplest way to keep the fires strong is to keep within the sound of the drums." Harry Tofpi told me that because Daw-K'ee, or God, had given him this way, he was obligated to protect it "the best way I know how."[15]

Protecting and practicing these ways have not always been easy to do. Dances were targeted during the reservation era as vestiges of an uncivilized life; the Indian Office denounced them as lurid spectacles that promoted everything from sexual licentiousness to pagan worship, and government officials energetically attempted to suppress them. The campaign against dancing began in earnest in the 1880s when public pressure mounted for a solution to the so-called Indian Question. Missionaries, agents, and local citizens who made it their business to stop dances were speaking a language that policy makers understood.

No one spoke with more assurance or urgency than secretary of the interior Henry Teller, whose 1883 annual report captured official Washington's mood. Writing with the certitude that was a hallmark of nineteenth-century policy makers, Teller clearly identified the greatest threat to assimilation: a "few non-progressive, degraded Indians," he declared, "are allowed to exhibit before the young and susceptible children all the debauchery, diabolism, and savagery of the worst state of the Indian race." And although debauchery, diabolism, and savagery came in many forms, first on Teller's list was "the continuance of the old heathenish dances." Such occasions, Teller assured his readers, "are not social gatherings for the amusement of these people, but, on the contrary, are intended to stimulate the warlike passions of the young warriors," including theft, rape, and murder. To rescue the tribes from barbarism, went Teller's reasoning, reformers had to compel Indians "to desist from the savage and barbarous practices that are calculated to continue them in savagery."[16] And that meant an end to Indian dances. But reformers and bureaucrats soon learned that influences largely beyond their control were reshaping dance cultures so that by the 1930s a new form of dance that was public, performative, and intertribal appeared all across Indian country.

At the same time that government agents were trying (and mostly failing) to destroy dance cultures, a series of influences began to shape and reshape dance by actively encouraging Indians to sing and perform. The various Wild West shows and traveling carnivals popular at the turn of the twentieth century are a case in point. Beginning in 1883 with Buffalo Bill Cody, by 1890 fifty different shows toured the United States, Canada, and Europe. Hiring hundreds of Indians precisely because they could dance, showmen such as Cody and the Miller brothers from Oklahoma eagerly sought out Indians who would, as commissioner of Indian affairs Thomas Morgan dourly expressed it, parade "with [their] war dances, paint, and blanket." Show Indians, he lamented in 1889, were "the lowest type of Indian." In Oklahoma the Miller Brothers 101 Ranch Real Wild West employed hundreds of Poncas, Osages, Kiowas, and Comanches between 1908 and 1916, while dozens of small-time sideshows and carnivals crisscrossed the region hiring Indians to do everything from dancing to bull fighting.[17]

The arena shows that Cody popularized appeared to be little more than Hollywood-style extravaganzas, but their influence on the powwow was significant in several ways. The Wild West's grand entry parade, for example, complete with galloping Indians and gun-toting cowboys, was a crowd pleaser that quickly found its way, in modified form, into powwows. No powwow worth its salt these days opens without a Grand Entry, often referred to as "the parade in." Evidence also suggests that modern contest powwows have roots in the auditions held by the Wild West shows, in which winners were paid for their performance and rewarded with contracts. Yet, as Moses has observed, the Wild West had deeper significance. Indians did not need to be dragooned into the shows; many of them eagerly signed on for reasons that included "money, travel, and adventure." Black Elk, notes Moses, enjoyed "the adventure of it all, in performing re-creations of brave deeds, and in getting paid for it." Walter Battice, a Sac and Fox who worked for the 101 Ranch Real Wild West, was more blunt about the attractions of working with a Wild West show. About the travel he commented, "You can bet I saw all the law would allow me."[18]

As Mark G. Thiel has noted, the shows also became a kind of surrogate for older forms of gathering: "Reminiscent of pre-reservation warrior customs, the commencement and conclusion of many show seasons became a time of celebration when contenders for employment, performers, and their friends and relatives gathered." Moses echoes these sentiments: "Ethnic identity need not be preserved through isolation, it may also be promoted through contact . . . [which] strengthened rather than weakened culture. . . . It would be wrong therefore to see the Show Indians as simply dupes, or pawns, or even victims. It would be better to approach them as persons who earned a fairly good living between the era of the Dawes Act and the Indian New Deal."[19]

Indeed, it is difficult to see them as dupes when, as Adriana Greci Green has noted, show Indians did as much as they did to control the context in which they performed. Far from being put on display as automatons, many Indians who participated in the Wild West saw their experience as a form of cultural capital. "For Lakota headmen," Green writes, "touring in the shows was a validation in the white world of their accomplishments as warriors." Moreover, returning show Indians "infused Omaha dancing with renewed vigor, incorporating a showier and fancier manner which they had developed to entertain audiences."[20] Dancing for pay revealed that the relationship between victimization and agency rested on complex negotiations and mediations in which an either/or paradigm had little meaning.

It should also be noted that by the mid-1930s, commissioner of Indian affairs John Collier had inaugurated what he intended to be a radical departure from previous policy. Committed to reversing the attack on tribal culture, Collier issued Circular 2970 on January 3, 1934, calling for the "fullest constitutional liberty, in all matters affecting religion, conscience, and culture" and requiring the Indian Office to show an "affirmative, appreciative attitude toward Indian cultural values. No interference with Indian religious life or ceremonial expression will hereafter be tolerated. The cultural liberty of Indians is in all respects to be considered equal to that of any non-Indian group."[21]

Regardless of the conditions under which Indian people maintained their dance traditions, the point is that they continued to dance, and they continued to adapt such gatherings to reflect the new social and cultural contours of the twentieth century. In some cases there was open and defiant resistance, as in the case of the Kiowa O-ho-mah, whose members continued to meet and dance despite intense pressure. Indeed, the Kiowa calendars record the *revival* of several dance societies in 1912 following the suppression of the Sun Dance and the issuing of individual allotments where, ironically, advocates found remote locales for dances beyond the immediate reach of agents. O-ho-mah members mounted an especially determined resistance to government bans. One Kiowa woman recalls her great-grandfather's testimony: "If you want me to give up my Ohomo ways you'll have to kill me. Death is the only thing that will keep me from Ohomo." An O-ho-mah song composed during this time tells O-ho-mah dancers: "Do not hesitate to dance; Go ahead and be arrested/jailed."[22]

Because resistance often left dancers and their relatives in harm's way, however, many responses were less confrontational. Thomas Kavanagh observes that on the Southern Plains, for example, the Omaha Dance (also called the Grass Dance or Crow Dance), which played a key role in the development of the powwow, emerged among the Poncas, Kaws, Omahas, Kiowas, and Pawnees in the late nineteenth century at about the same time as the Ghost Dance. The Ghost Dance waned in most places by the late 1890s, but the Omaha Dance became increasingly important among the Southern Plains warrior societies. Originally led by officers who wore regalia linked to society practices and offices, the dance included "ceremonial and ritual acts involving the heroism of war deeds, and an accompanying feast."[23] When the martial ethos of warrior societies began to fade in the late nineteenth century, however, the immediate societal purpose of the Omaha Dance eroded and its practice took on a more secular form and meaning. Among the Pawnees, Omahas, Poncas, and Osages, notes Kavanagh, the dance "dispensed with the crow belt while retaining much of the ritual and many of the officers of the Inloshka societies." Subsequently referred to as "Straight Dance," the new dance showed elements of the Midewiwin, also called the Drum or Dream Dance, and was notable for a revitalization ethos similar to that prophesied by the Ghost Dance.[24]

Other communities were also transforming the Omaha Dance. When government policies prevented young Kiowas and Comanches from earning war honors and the social and ritual prestige associated with them, for example, many dances and ceremonies were deliberately modified to keep them relevant and alive according to new cultural realities. Among other things, notes Kavanagh, "the exclusive right of the men's societies to participate was abandoned, and the ceremony was opened to all, including women." Moreover, the Kiowas and Comanches were introducing elaborate new dance clothes and styles with bustles worn not only on the back but also on the arms and neck. Color-coordinated beadwork harnesses, dyed long johns, long strips of bells, and large feather-crest headdresses completed the ensemble that shortly came to be called "Fancy Dance." In other communities women and young men who previously would never have taken part in the older forms of society dances now found openings that made them welcome to participate.[25]

Morris Foster argues that by the early twentieth century radically changing conditions in Comanche communities similarly constrained their ability to associate in traditional ways and necessitated new arrangements regarding "the public social occasions used for the purpose of community maintenance." Because public gatherings like dances constitute "a history of the organization and maintenance of the Comanche community," notes Foster, they are crucial in the negotiation of public and private codes of conduct that reflect ongoing change.[26] One kind of response began in summer 1906 with annual summer encampments that featured traditional dances. Quanah Parker, for example, is known to have hosted a series of such encampments at Cache between 1903 and 1908. These were often held at isolated allotments and were attended by fairly small numbers of participants. "Mostly, just the elders took part [that is, danced]. Just a few selected men, maybe five or six," said Tennyson Echawaudah. These encampments shortly became the locus of a revived Comanche dance tradition.[27]

Importantly, although the summer encampments were an attempt to revive prereservation rituals, in time they gave way to a new social and cultural order inside the Comanche community increasingly based on evolving forms of dance gatherings. As communities began to host annual encampments by the second decade of the century, these events reflected a growing generational and ritual schism in the community. Previously restricted from participating (probably because they lacked warrior status), once the prereservation generation began to decline in numbers and influence by the 1930s, many young Comanches gained prominence in the dance crowd as well as in the Native American Church. Dancing and the use of peyote, Foster notes, had once been "elements of the same belief system." Rising generations of younger Comanches, however, now assigned powwows a distinctly spiritual power and thus fostered the rise of "two distinct religions" in the Comanche community. As a result "powwows provided these younger Comanches with their first opportunity to participate actively in a Comanche-derived . . . form of gathering. . . . Dance gatherings, which previously had had a carnival atmosphere, became more solemn occasions in the late 1930s."[28]

Two simultaneous events seemed to be occurring. On the one hand prereservation warrior societies and their dance rituals maintained some of the power and utility that had previously made them so important. On the other hand, as dance traditions responded to new realities, the momentum that was helping to revive warrior society dances also produced a new kind of secular, social event increasingly referred to during the post–World War II years as the powwow. "Powwows are not unchanging continuations from the depths of time," writes Kavanagh. For that matter, neither were nineteenth-century dance traditions. Change kept these dances meaningful and relevant, and it was not long before they became the source of new cultural practices responding to new needs. "We don't do dances the same way as a long time ago," a Cheyenne man told me, "but we hold on to the ideas, the thoughts that those old people taught us." When the Kiowas revived the Tiah-Piah in 1958, for example, it was not as a veterans' society but as a dance open to all Kiowas – men and women, young and old. Dances remained important but evolved in response to new social, cultural, spatial, and ritual realities.[29]

Scott Bradshaw, an Osage-Quapaw, told Alice Anne Callahan that even though his great-grandfather would not recognize all of the elements of the contemporary Osage I'n-Lon-Schka, he would nevertheless understand its function. "The sense of family, the pride of heritage, the seriousness of the occasion, the humor of the moment," says Bradshaw, "are the same as they have always been when Indians gather."[30] The annual Ponca Powwow, held every year in early August at White Eagle, Oklahoma, is clearly not the same thing as the Ponca Helushka, which meets and dances on other occasions. Yet it is clear that Ponca Powwow is a psychologically and culturally vital part of contemporary Ponca life. That it is also "secular" does not in any way lessen its profound role in the Ponca community.

One of the most important influences in the evolution of the modern powwow is modern warfare. As noted above, martial valor was a critical factor during the prereservation era in attaining status and prestige, so the erosion of such opportunities rippled through the entire cultural fabric of tribes. Largely denied opportunities for warfare by the end of the nineteenth century, many warrior societies languished. Ironically, modern warfare helped encourage the creation of a new yet traditionally inspired warrior ethic. In the opinion of many powwow people, twentieth-century warfare is the critical link in the revival of many dances and rituals from the prereservation period. Indeed, the World Wars dramatically influenced both the form and purpose of dance. Drawn to the martial ethos that defined a great deal of their past, many Indian people saw participation in the nation's wars as both an obligation to be borne by loyal citizens and a validation of their continued allegiance to specific and honorable traditions. As a result the utility of dances, songs, and rituals previously associated with warfare reemerged with even greater force. Ralph Kotay, a Kiowa, told me that "this powwow thing really got going when our boys came home from overseas in World War II. Those service clubs got going and sponsored dances for those boys, and then it just took off."[31]

As William Meadows notes: "The impact of the war and the traditional protocol necessitating the honoring of returning veterans was simply too much for even the agency to suppress." Thus tribes hosted dances at which they blessed departing soldiers according to old rituals or gave returning veterans new names based on their wartime exploits. In addition to serving as occasions for reviving warrior society practices, these dances sometimes featured the display of battlefield trophies, a practice that caused predictably high levels of exasperation among officials. A 1919 Cheyenne dance in Canton, Oklahoma, for example, reportedly featured the display of a German scalp. At other dances participants displayed parts of enemy uniforms and weapons as in the old days and engaged in mock charges and battles against effigies in the form of the German kaiser. New songs made reference to modern enemies and extolled the valor of Indian doughboys, according them the status of warriors. The war years breathed new life into old rituals all over Indian country, and dances once again became crucial conduits for the expression of venerated ideals.[32]

By the 1910s, moreover, tribes began to assume control of dances in ways that an earlier generation of policy makers would have rejected. (This should remind us, as Harry Tofpi once told me, that Indians "didn't need a white man to tell them they could dance.")[33] In 1914 a Kiowa man named Red Buffalo retained an attorney to fight the Indian Office's attempts to suppress dances. The Pawnees went one better, asking their kinsman and noted ethnologist James Murie to consult the tribe's attorneys about the government's policies on dances. Weary of their agent's harassment, a collection of Pawnee chiefs wanted to know of "any law declaring that Indian dances are a crime, and if the

Indian Dept. can legally interfere with these religious dances and dances that are gotten up for pleasure." After heated exchanges among the Pawnees, their lawyers, and government officials, the Pawnee agent in Oklahoma grudgingly admitted in 1917 that there was "no way in which such dance[s] could be prevented upon land not upon Governmental jurisdiction."[34]

Jess Rowlodge, an Arapaho, was so incensed by the government's refusal to allow a Sun Dance to pray for the well-being of Indian soldiers during World War I that he simply went around the Indian Office. After being turned away by Oklahoma's congressional delegation, his U.S. senator, the commissioner of Indian affairs, the secretary of the interior, and President Woodrow Wilson, Rowlodge changed tactics and wrote to the national office of the American Red Cross. When that organization endorsed his request and helped to dissuade officials from barring the dance, Rowlodge noted with considerable pride: "I run over the President of the United States that time!"[35]

Luke Eric Lassiter observes that, whatever they did, dance people "continually thwarted the goals of the Indian office." And as Carol Rachlin has noted: "Even at the worst period of federal suppression," no ceremony was interrupted for more than two years. "Indian culture in western Oklahoma," she concludes, "never died. . . . Indians remained Indians." The same can be said of many other regions and communities where isolation, inept agency officials, and, most important, a keen determination to maintain control of their ritual and ceremonial institutions meant that Indians kept dancing. For the Apaches, writes Clifford Coppersmith, "always there was the Mountain Spirit Dance." In its various forms, Thiel reminds us, dance remained "perhaps the most viable surviving pre-reservation activity."[36]

As the years during and after World War II saw more and more dances, and as the increasing availability of automobiles and other forms of mass transit facilitated wider circles of travel, a burgeoning powwow culture began to take its currently recognizable form in communities all across the West. Urban Indians, for example, found common ground in an intertribal dance culture that encouraged the sharing of songs and dances. The late Elmer Sugar Brown, an Oto-Missouria who was a world champion Fancy dancer during the 1940s and 1950s, told me: "We went everywhere and learned all kinds of dance steps. People would say 'that guy Elmer Sugar Brown used nine or ten different kinds of tribes and steps in his dancing.' I learned a lot watching those other boys – Gus McDonald, Chester Lefthand, Steve Mopope, Reuben Snake – all them guys could really get after it. But I watched them. That's how I got to be world champion."[37]

Large contest powwows and all-Indian fairs like those at the Crow and Rosebud agencies, at Anadarko in Southwest Oklahoma, and at Wichita, Tulsa, Bismarck, and Macy were joined by dozens of dances all over Indian country. By the 1960s powwows had spread east and west to college campuses and large urban centers. Before long the powwow trail that had begun in Tulsa or Lame Deer included stops in Chicago, Nashville, Jacksonville, and Los Angeles. During the 1970s and 1980s large arena shows joined the national circuit at events like Albuquerque's Gathering of Nations, Oklahoma's Red Earth, Denver March, and Schemitzun in Connecticut. The powwow has gained a national audience in other venues as well; in April 2003, for example, NBC broadcast "The World of American Indian Dance," a one-hour special on powwows produced by Four Directions Entertainment, an enterprise of the Oneida Indian Nation.

Wherever we choose to look at powwows, the story has generous proportions. There's a youth movement in many places that has stamped its own brand on powwow ways, just as there are also communities where elders maintain influence no matter what the latest trends are. Tribes that never powwowed before have eagerly adopted it as a satisfying expression of culture, identity, and pride that ties them to other Native people. And whether the dance is a birthday powwow in Oklahoma, a homecoming powwow in Kansas, a graduation dance in South Dakota, a contest dance in Connecticut, or a small-time get-together in some crossroads reservation community, a shared sense of meaning and power connects these events.

It's not that powwows aren't without their problems; petty jealousies, bitter disagreements, and life's everyday disappointments are just as visible at powwows as anywhere else. But people go to powwows to have a good time – to listen to the songs, see their friends, eat a good meal, and reminisce about old times. The next time you're at a dance, listen to those old people sitting in their folding chairs, and chances are you'll hear them say, as one woman told me at the 2002 Sac and Fox Powwow, "You know, this is just the *best* place for me to be this evening. That music – it soothes me. Makes me forget my aches and pains. In my mind I see my dad out there again, hitting that drum."[38]

Pay attention to the children who come out for the first time in the arena, and listen to the family members who speak for them. "It's your *right* to have this way," said one man on behalf of his grandson at a small dance in Oklahoma that I attended a decade ago. "But you have to be careful with it. Take care of it. Respect it. Your people are here, in this arena. Be proud of it." Do that, and you'll know what Peter Le Claire, a Ponca, meant when he told Jim Howard: "It is said that anyone that is not well and feeling bad and anyone that is mourning, the sound of the drum will revive them and make them happy."[39]

NOTES

1. The Intertribal Indian Club of Tulsa's Web page (http://www.iicot.org) has links to the club's activities.

2. Clyde Ellis, field notes, August 1990.

3. Clyde Ellis, field notes, July 2000. In Indian country, "ayyy" is a teasing term often used to suggest irony or humor in everyday situations.

4. Clyde Ellis, field notes, July 2000.

5. Clyde Ellis, field notes, August 2002.

6. Barre Toelken, "Ethnic Selection and Intensification in the Native American Powwow," in *Creative Ethnicity: Symbols and Strategies of Contemporary Ethnic Life*, ed. Stephen Stern and John Allan Cicala (Logan: Utah State University Press, 1991), 138, 153, emphasis in the original.

7. Clyde Ellis, field notes, August 2002.

8. Benjamin Kracht, "Kiowa Powwows: Continuity in Ritual Practice," *American Indian Quarterly* 18, no. 3 (1994): 322; Jack Campisi, "Powwow: A Study in Ethnic Boundary Maintenance," *Man in the Northeast* 9 (1975): 44. For a reply to Kracht, see Luke Eric Lassiter and Clyde Ellis, "Commentary: Applying Communitas to Kiowa Powwows," *American Indian Quarterly* 22, no. 4 (1998): 485–91. For a recent account that emphasizes the role of the powwow as a positive form of generalized Indianness, see James Hamill, "Being Indian in Northeast Oklahoma," *Plains Anthropologist* 45, no. 173 (2000): 291–303.

9. Mark Mattern, "The Powwow as a Public Arena for Negotiating Unity and Diversity in American Indian Life," *American Indian Culture and Research Journal* 20, no. 4 (1996): 183.

10. Harry Tofpi Sr., interview with the author, May 2, 1996, Shawnee, Oklahoma.

11. Loretta Fowler, *Shared Symbols, Contested Meanings: Gros Ventre Culture and History, 1778–1985* (Ithaca NY: Cornell University Press, 1987), 9.

12. Gloria Alese Young, "Powwow Power: Perspectives on Historic and Contemporary Intertribalism" (PhD diss., Indiana University, 1981), 68. Young's dissertation is a well-written, comprehensively framed discussion. Sharp and insightful, it is the fullest account of powwow culture on the Plains. However, because it has never been published (and is now more than two decades old), it is not as well known as it deserves to be and its influence has been largely limited to scholars working specifically on dance history and culture. Anyone working on powwow culture owes a large debt to Young's research and analysis. Other sources that place the powwow

in a larger context are Dennis Zotigh, *Moving History: The Evolution of the Powwow* (Oklahoma City: Center for the American Indian, 1991); Tara Browner, *Heartbeat of the People: Music and Dance of the Northern Powwow* (Urbana: University of Illinois Press, 2002); and William Meadows, *Kiowa, Apache and Comanche Military Societies: Enduring Veterans, 1800 to the Present* (Austin: University of Texas Press, 1999).

13. Toelken, "Ethnic Selection," 138. General discussions of the contemporary powwow may be found in Clyde Ellis, *A Dancing People: Powwow Culture on the Southern Plains* (Lawrence: University Press of Kansas, 2003); Charlotte Heth, ed., *Native American Dance: Ceremonies and Social Traditions* (Washington DC: Smithsonian Institution Press, 1992); George P. Horse Capture, *Pow Wow* (Cody WY: Buffalo Bill Historical Center, 1989); David Whitehorse, *Pow-wow: The Contemporary Pan-Indian Celebration*, Publications in American Indian Studies (San Diego: San Diego State University, 1988); William K. Powers, *War Dance: Plains Indian Musical Performance* (Tucson: University of Arizona Press, 1990); William K. Powers, "Plains Indian Music and Dance," in *Anthropology on the Great Plains*, ed. W. Raymond Wood and Margot Liberty, 212–29 (Lincoln: University of Nebraska Press, 1980); Luke Eric Lassiter, *The Power of Kiowa Song: A Collaborative Ethnography* (Tucson: University of Arizona Press, 1998); Mark Mattern, "The Powwow as a Public Arena for Negotiating Unity and Diversity in American Indian Life," *American Indian Culture and Research Journal* 20, no. 4 (1996): 183–201; James H. Howard, "Pan-Indianism in Native American Music and Dance," *Ethnomusicology* 27, no. 1 (1983): 71–82; Young, "Powwow Power"; Kenneth Ashworth, "The Contemporary Oklahoma Powwow" (PhD diss., University of Oklahoma, 1986); Jimmy W. Duncan, " 'Hethuska Zani': An Ethnohistory of the War Dance Complex" (master's thesis, Northeastern State University, 1997); Judith Ann Jones, " 'Women Never Used to Dance': Gender and Music in Nez Perce Culture Change" (PhD diss., Washington State University, 1995); Stephanie Anna May, "Performance of Identity: Alabama-Coushatta Tourism, Powwows, and Everyday Life" (PhD diss., University of Texas at Austin, 2001); Joan D. Laxson, "Aspects of Acculturation among American Indians: Emphasis on Contemporary Pan-Indianism" (PhD diss., University of California–Berkeley, 1972); Susan Applegate Krouse, "A Window into the Indian Culture: The Powwow as Performance" (PhD diss., University of Wisconsin–Milwaukee, 1991); Ann Axtmann, "Dance: Celebration and Resistance, Native American Indian Intertribal Powwow Performance" (PhD diss., New York University, 1999); Victoria Eugenie Sanchez, " 'As Long as We Dance, We Shall Know Who We Are': A Study of Off-Reservation Traditional Intertribal Powwows in Central Ohio" (PhD diss., Ohio State University, 1995); Lita Mathews, "The Native American Powwow: A Contemporary Authentication of a Cultural Artifact" (PhD diss., University of New Mexico, 1999); Kathleen Glenister Roberts, "Giving Away: The Performance of Speech and Sign in Powwow Ritual Exchange" (PhD diss., Indiana University, 2001); Adriana Greci Green, "Performances and Celebrations:

Displaying Lakota Identity, 1880–1915" (PhD diss., Rutgers University, 2001); Sarah Quick, "Powwow Dancing in North America: The Formation of an Indian Identity through Expressive Culture" (master's thesis, University of Missouri at Columbia, 2001).

14. Luke Eric Lassiter, " 'Charlie Brown': Not Just Another Essay on the Gourd Dance," *American Indian Culture and Research Journal* 21, no. 4 (1997): 97; Thomas W. Kavanagh, "Southern Plains Dance: Tradition and Dynamics," in *Native American Dance*, ed. Heth, 105. Similar arguments have been made for other regions; commenting on Northern Plains powwows, R. D. Theisz argues that song and dance are crucial for post–World War II Lakota identity. See his "Song Texts and Their Performers: The Centerpiece of Contemporary Lakota Identity Formulation," *Great Plains Quarterly* 7 (Spring 1987): 116–24. In "The Omaha Dance in Oglala and Sicangu Sioux History, 1883–1923," *Whispering Wind* 23 (Fall–Winter 1990), Mark Thiel notes that "for generations the Omaha dance has been the most popular social and nationalistic celebration of the Oglala and Sicangu Sioux, thus serving as an obtrusive demonstration of tribal identity and cohesion" (p. 4).

15. Lassiter, " 'Charlie Brown,' " 75–76; Clyde Ellis, field notes, July 1996; Jeanne M. Devlin, "Oklahoma Tribesmen: Every Picture Tells a Story," *Oklahoma Today*, May–June 1991, 22; Harry Tofpi Sr., interview with the author, May 3, 1997, Shawnee, Oklahoma.

16. Report of the Secretary of the Interior, 1883, House Executive document no. 1, 48 Cong., 1 session, xi–xii; Francis Paul Prucha, *The Great Father: The United States Government and the American Indians*, 2 vols. (Lincoln: University of Nebraska Press, 1984), 2:646–47.

17. See L. G. Moses, *Wild West Shows and the Images of the American Indians, 1883–1933* (Albuquerque: University of New Mexico Press, 1996); L. G. Moses, "Wild West Shows, Reformers, and the Image of the American Indian, 1887–1914," *South Dakota History* 14 (Fall 1984): 193–221; L. G. Moses, "Indians on the Midway: Wild West Shows and the Indian Bureau at World's Fairs, 1893–1904," *South Dakota History* 21 (Fall 1991): 205–29; Joy S. Kasson, *Buffalo Bill's Wild West: Celebrity, Memory, and Popular Culture* (New York: Hill and Wang, 2000). On the Miller Brothers, see Michael Wallis, *The Real Wild West: The 101 Ranch and the Creation of the American West* (New York: St. Martin's, 1999); Ellsworth Collings and Alma Miller England, *The 101 Ranch* (Norman: University of Oklahoma Press, 1937); and Barbara Williams Roth, "The 101 Ranch Wild West Show, 1904–1932," *Chronicles of Oklahoma* 43, no. 4 (1965): 416–31.

18. Thiel, "The Omaha Dance," 5; Moses, "Interpreting the Wild West, 1883–1914," in *Between Indian and White Worlds: The Cultural Brokers*, ed. Margaret Connell Szasz (Albuquerque: University of New Mexico Press, 1994), 161, 172; Walter Battice, quoted in Moses, *Wild West Shows*, 180.

19. Thiel, "The Omaha Dance," 5–6; Moses, *Wild West Shows*, 188, 279.

20. Green, "Performances and Celebrations," 125–26.

21. Prucha, *Great Father*, 2:951; Kenneth R. Philp, *John Collier's Crusade for Indian Reform, 1920–1954* (Tucson: University of Arizona Press, 1977), 55–70.

22. Meadows, *Kiowa, Apache, and Comanche Military Societies*, 113–22 (quote at 121). The O-ho-mah song referenced here is often called the "Resistance Song" and contains words that translate as "Do not hesitate to dance! Go ahead and be arrested and jailed" (Clyde Ellis, field notes, Kiowa O-ho-mah Ceremonials, Anadarko, Oklahoma, July 1996; Luke E. Lassiter, telephone conversation with the author, July 30, 2002). At the 1996 O-ho-mah dance, one speaker reminded the crowd that "O-ho-mah *never* stopped dancing." At the 2002 O-ho-mah dance, the Resistance Song was rendered along with a detailed explanation by Mac Whitehorse, the society's bustle keeper, of the song's history and meaning.

23. Kavanagh, "Southern Plains Dance," 109; Lassiter, *The Power of Kiowa Song*, 80–98; James H. Howard, "Notes on the Dakota Grass Dance," *Southwest Journal of Anthropology* 8 (1951): 82.

24. Kavanagh, "Southern Plains Dance," 110. See also Young, "Powwow Power," 129–53.

25. Kavanagh, "Southern Plains Dance," 111; Nancy O. Lurie, "The Contemporary American Indian Scene," in *North American Indians in Historical Perspective*, ed. Eleanor B. Leacock and Nancy O. Lurie, 449–50 (New York: Random House, 1971); James H. Howard, *The Ponca Tribe*, Bureau of American Ethnology Bulletin 195 (Lincoln: University of Nebraska Press, 1995), 107–8.

26. Morris W. Foster, *Being Comanche: A Social History of an American Indian Community* (Tucson: University of Arizona Press, 1991), 30.

27. Foster, *Being Comanche*, 123. Foster cites three reasons for the resurgence of Comanche dancing: (1) concern among older Comanches for reviving traditional rituals, (2) the hiring of Comanches to perform at local civic functions and celebrations, and (3) requests by Comanches for surviving members of military societies to dance at intracommunity events. Reports of Quanah's dances are in "Indian Celebrations and Dances, 1874–1917," Records of the Kiowa Agency, Oklahoma Historical Society, microfilm KA 47; see also William T. Hagan, *Quanah Parker, Comanche Chief* (Norman: University of Oklahoma Press, 1993), 102–3.

28. Foster, *Being Comanche*, 126–27. Kracht makes a similar argument in a recent essay on Kiowa religion, in which he says that some older people believe that "powwows serve as a religion for the youth." Kracht, "Kiowa Religion in Historical Perspective," *American Indian Quarterly* 21, no. 1 (1997): 28.

29. Kavanagh, "Southern Plains Dance," 105; Clyde Ellis, field notes, July 1991; Scott Tonemah, interview with the author, February 8, 1988, Norman, Oklahoma; Lassiter, " 'Charlie Brown,' " 89.

30. Alice Anne Callahan, *The Osage Ceremonial Dance: I'n-Lon-Schka* (Norman: University of Oklahoma Press, 1990), 134.

31. Ralph Kotay, interview with the author, August 13, 2002, Apache, Oklahoma. The best recent discussions of American Indians and military service are Thomas A. Britten, *American Indians in World War I: At Home and at War* (Albuquerque: University of New Mexico Press, 1997); Alison R. Bernstein, *American Indians and World War II: Toward a New Era in Indian Affairs* (Norman: University of Oklahoma Press, 1991); Tom Holm, *Strong Hearts, Wounded Souls: Native American Veterans of the Vietnam War* (Austin: University of Texas Press, 1996), esp. 66–102; Tom Holm, "Fighting a White Man's War: The Extent and Legacy of American Indian Participation in World War II," in *The Plains Indians of the Twentieth Century*, ed. Peter Iverson, 149–67 (Norman: University of Oklahoma Press, 1985); Aaron McGaffey Beede, "The Dakota Indian Victory Dance," *North Dakota Historical Quarterly* 9 (April 1942): 167–78; James H. Howard, "The Dakota Victory Dance, World War II," *North Dakota History* 18 (1951): 31–40.

32. Meadows, *Kiowa, Apache, and Comanche Military Societies*, 122–26; "Indians Use Human Scalps in Dance," *American Indian Magazine* 7 (1919): 184; Britten, *American Indians in World War I*, 150–51.

33. Harry Tofpi Sr., interview, May 3, 1997.

34. See Ellis, *A Dancing People*, 106–9, for a discussion of the Kiowa and Pawnee cases.

35. Jess Rowlodge, interview with Julia A. Jordan, June 4, 1969, T-458, Doris Duke Oral History Collection, Western History Collection, University of Oklahoma, 8, 11, 13–14.

36. Lassiter, *Power of Kiowa Song*, 94; Carol Rachlin, "Tight Shoe Night: Oklahoma Indians Today," in *The American Indian Today*, ed. Stuart Levine and Nancy O. Lurie (Baltimore: Pelican Books, 1970), 171, 182–83; Clifford Coppersmith, "Healing and Remembrance: The Chiricahua and Warm Springs Apache Mountain Spirit Dance in Oklahoma," unpublished manuscript in the author's possession; Thiel, "The Omaha Dance," 5.

37. Elmer Sugar Brown, interview with the author and Sandy Rhoades, January 20, 2003, Tulsa, Oklahoma.

38. Clyde Ellis, field notes, August 1996, July 2002.

39. James Howard, *The Ponca Tribe* (Lincoln: University of Nebraska Press, 1995), 106.

PATRICIA C. ALBERS AND BEATRICE MEDICINE

2. Some Reflections on Nearly Forty Years on the Northern Plains Powwow Circuit

Powwows, celebrations, or "doings," as they are called in some vernaculars of reservation English, include any of a wide variety of get-togethers that focus on dancing but may also include honorings and feasts, parades and pageants, rodeos, gambling, and carnivals. The roots of Northern Plains powwows, as we know them today, are complex and multifaceted. They can be traced back to the Grass Dances and exhibition performances of the late nineteenth century (Mekeel 1932; Pettipas 1993, 107–25; Young and Gooding 2001). Until 1960 powwows were largely rural events, typically associated with reservation fairs, anniversary commemorations, and such holidays as the Fourth of July or Labor Day. As their popularity grew they became a regular, recurring summer feature of small reservation communities and the larger agency towns as well as a common event on the urban scene. Combining the old with the new, tradition with innovation, the powwow remains a dynamic event, renewing cultural identities, traditional values, and social ties important to many of today's tribal communities in the Northern Plains.

Notwithstanding the importance of powwows in the Northern Plains over the past century, a surprising lack of writing exists on their history or contemporary expression. Several books and articles addressing Northern Plains powwows and aimed at popular audiences and tourists have appeared in recent years (Anonymous 1978; Crummet 1981; Parfit 1994; Braine 1995; Contreras and Bernstein 1996; Marra 1996; Roberts 1995, 1998; White 1996). Scholarly publications, however, remain slim. Other than Samuel Corrigan's work (1970) on powwows among the Canadian Dakotas and George Horse Capture's book (1989) on the powwow overall, most writings about the Northern Plains focus on specific aspects of their performance, not on their presence as a total social phenomenon. Much of what has been written deals with the feasts and giveaways that are often held in conjunction with today's powwows (Weist 1973; Grobsmith 1979, 1981; Kehoe 1980; Schneider 1981; M. Powers 1991). Other works look at powwow song, dance, or dress (Howard 1960; W. Powers 1970, 1980, 1990, 1994; Hatton 1974, 1986; M. Powers 1988; Browner

2002). In this last category, special mention must be given to Severt Young Bear's splendid autobiography, *Standing in the Light: A Lakota Way of Seeing* (Young Bear and Theisz 1994), which includes important descriptive and interpretative information on powwow activities from the head singer of one of the region's most famous drum groups, the Porcupine Singers. But other than Corrigan's and Horse Capture's writings and a few recent studies of powwows in the neighboring Great Lakes region (Mattern 1996; Desjarlait 1997), very little has been written about any of these events in whole, much less about where they stand in a comparative, intertribal perspective.

We must admit that we've been part of the reason why so little has been published on the powwows of the Northern Plains. Nearly forty years ago, in 1966, we began a collaborative study of powwows in the Northern Plains. Since then we have attended, jointly or separately, hundreds of different powwows in every Northern Plains province and state sponsored by a wide range of tribal nations, including the Arapahos, Arikaras, Assiniboins, Crows, Dakotas, Lakotas, Ojibwes, Peigans, and Sarcees. Over all these years we have been sitting on our field notes and putting off publishing our material because there's always something new to track down in the ever-changing and expanding world of the powwow, such as tracing the sudden explosion and spread of jingle dresses and dancing in the late 1980s.

In 1968, however, we wrote a preliminary assessment of the material we had gathered separately and together on the powwows we had observed on the Northern Plains. We presented this information in a paper entitled "Patterns and Peripheries of Plains Indian Powwows" at the meetings of the Central States Anthropology Association. Because we never published that piece or any of our other work, we have decided here to revisit what we wrote back in 1968 to see how it has withstood the test of time given both the enormous changes and the persisting traditions we have witnessed in our many years together on the Northern Plains powwow circuit.

The Model

In our 1968 paper we offered a representational model for powwows that, in the era's functionalist mode of thinking, postulated that aspects of the form and even meaning of celebrations in the Northern Plains were related to the different kinds of social formations being articulated and activated in these events. Based on a preliminary evaluation of material we had collected between 1964 and 1968, we organized celebrations along a continuum. On one end were family feasts and doings that solidified close relationships within and among extended family groups. At the other end were the exhibitions sponsored by white communities at rodeos, fairs, or events focused on American Indian culture that fostered alliances across racial lines. The latter group included, as examples, All American Indian Days at Sheridan, Wyoming; the Calgary Stampede; the Sitting Bull Stampede at Mobridge, South Dakota; and the Days of '77 at Deadwood, South Dakota.

In between these extremes we identified two kinds of celebrations that we called the "in-group" versus the "Pan-Indian," or intertribal, powwow. In-group events were sponsored by "committees" from small reservation communities or voluntary associations (e.g., Omaha societies and veterans' associations) to support reciprocal relations between kin and friends in neighboring locales. The summer celebrations at Wakpala, Bullhead, and Little Eagle on the Standing Rock Reservation; the Lone Buffalo Club's doings at Tokio, North Dakota; and the summer powwows of the Sarcees on their reserve in Alberta or the Dakotas' celebration at Long Prairie in Manitoba were examples of in-group events in the late 1960s. By contrast, Pan-Indian, or what would be labeled today as "intertribal," powwows were sponsored by committees in agency towns to create and maintain ties across a wide region among diverse tribal populations. Crow Fair, Browning Indian Days, Rosebud Fair, Poplar Oil Celebration, and Fort Totten Days were examples of these events in the 1960s. Our representational model focused largely on rural areas; with some modification college and urban powwows could have been incorporated into this scheme as well.

In its essential contours our representational model remains valid in the world of today's Northern Plains powwows. The greatest changes we have witnessed over the past thirty-seven years have to do, on the one hand, with shifts in the relative support that certain kinds of celebrations receive and, on the other hand, with the sheer growth and diversification of certain powwow activities. Here we will first briefly discuss the celebrations on the extreme ends of our continuum and then compare the two kinds of powwows situated in the middle.

Celebrations at the Edges of the Continuum

The edges of our continuum are marked by two very different kinds of contemporary celebratory events: one rooted in longstanding tribal traditions and controlled entirely by Native peoples; the other linked to a world of commercial festivities under the direction of white-run civic organizations. These events are important because some of their interests and purposes have also entered, in varied ways, the conduct of powwow activity at the center of our continuum.

Family doings remain at the heart of contemporary celebratory activity in the Northern Plains. Held on their own or in conjunction with in-group and intertribal celebrations as well as Sun Dances and Native American Church meetings, family honorings and the feasts and giveaways that always accompany them remain as essential to the cultural vitality of today's tribal communities as they did four decades ago.

Today, as in the past, many different occasions lead families to recognize their members through ceremonial honoring, feasting, and giving. Some doings mark major life cycle transitions, including the naming of a child, the celebration of a young man's first successful hunt, and a fiftieth wedding anniversary. Others acknowledge special achievements of family members in military service, higher education, or any other position deemed worthy of special respect and acclaim. Other celebrations – appropriately identified as "farewell" or "return" doings – recognize changes in residential status. Occasionally, special family feasts and giveaways are also held to seek the prayers and support of others for a family member who is ill.

Whatever the occasion, family doings are sponsored by the close kindred of the person being honored. These relatives collaborate in preparing for the celebration, in cooking the foods for the feast, and in "collecting" a respectable selection of "donations" (an expression used among the Lakotas and Dakotas to describe the items offered at giveaways). In the 1960s and 1970s the most prestigious items given away included star quilts, shawls, war bonnets, Pendleton or Hudson Bay blankets, beaded apparel, and horses. Patchwork quilts, afghans, blankets, aprons, potholders, embroidered pillowcases, crocheted bags, and ribbon shirts and dresses were among the handmade items distributed, while yard goods, silk scarves, towels, and enamelware dishes were included in the given manufactured items. Various amounts of cash were also commonly distributed at these doings. All of these sorts of donations are still given today, although manufactured items now outnumber handmade gifts.

When held as independent events most family celebrations take place at a community hall, a church meeting room, a cemetery (in the case of memorial celebrations), or the home of the sponsoring family. Attendance at these celebrations is by special invitation, which is given either by word-of-mouth or through special postcards. As in the past an invitation carries with it an obligation of acceptance unless compelling circumstances prevent a guest's appearance. Guests include distant relatives, fictive kin, and friends with whom the family has special ties; respected elders; and other persons from the same or neighboring communities with whom the honored shares a special affinity. If the honoree is a military person, for example, veterans are invited to attend, and often the most respected elderly or "visiting" veterans function as special honored guests. In Lakota family celebrations held on the Standing Rock Reservation, special guests are seated at reserved places and served first, given the best selection of food, offered extras (e.g., candy bars, cigarettes, and soda pop) not available to other guests, and honored with the most prestigious giveaway donations.

The conduct of family doings varies considerably, according to not only the occasions for which they are being held but also the tribal settings in which they take place (Weist 1973; Albers 1974, 342–50; Grobsmith 1979, 1981; Kehoe 1980; Schneider 1981). Although feasting and gift giving always occur and prayers and speeches are invariably given on behalf of the honored, other features vary not only across tribes but also within the same tribe and community. The elaborateness of the feast and giveaway and whether the honoring includes singers and dancers, for example, tend to vary according to the means of the families hosting the celebration.

Notwithstanding the contexts of their performance and varieties of expression, family celebrations have endured remarkably in their overall purpose and conduct. These celebrations are firmly grounded in local cultural traditions, even when they involve allusions to Christianity. They remain important public occasions for giving speeches in Native languages and for demonstrating an allegiance to a particular family and its associated cultural identities. Today's family celebrations still follow culturally specific protocols that show respect for the person being honored, give prestige to the sponsoring family, and also extend recognition to the guests, whose very presence validates the significance of the occasion and the social relationships it maintains. Family doings also continue to acknowledge and uphold many strongly felt values, such as sharing and generosity.

At the other end of the continuum and in marked contrast to family doings are the exhibition celebrations. These celebrations are physically removed from indigenous settings, and – except in terms of some of their superficial appearances – are often culturally divorced from them as well. Exhibition powwows hearken back to the late 1800s when American Indians from various tribes in the Northern Plains were invited and paid to tour and perform in the popular Wild West shows of the era (Standing Bear 1975, 247–68; Deloria 1976; Slotkin 1976; Moses 1996). In later years the nation's railways and tourist operators began to establish permanent performance venues where local tribal groups became featured attractions at such places as Glacier National Park; the Great Northern Railway Station at Mandan, North Dakota; and the Duhamel Indian Pageant near Rapid City, South Dakota (DeMallie 1984, 63–71; Born 1994; Albers 1998).

Simultaneously, many white towns in the Northern Plains started to hold their own annual festivities to which they invited select Indian groups to participate in scheduled performances of War and Grass dancing, horse racing, and tipi building, among other activities. Scudder Mekeel (1932) described in great detail how certain Oglala leaders from the Pine Ridge Reservation were invited to organize groups every year to attend the celebrations in various white communities in the Black Hills during the 1920s and 1930s.

In the 1960s many towns in the Northern Plains still invited people from neighboring tribal communities to participate in their stampedes, rodeos, and fairs. Most of these exhibitions were sponsored, financed, and managed through the local Jaycees (Junior Chambers of Commerce) or other similar business and civic associations. Indian participation was invited and controlled by "hiring" certain individuals and families to participate in the "performances" and "exhibits" managed by the celebration boards or "committees," which were dominated by white businesspeople. In some instances one or two representatives from participating tribes also served on the boards but usually with limited decision-making powers. Generally speaking, the Northern Plains exhibitions of the 1960s followed a longstanding pattern in which white entrepreneurs put on "Indian shows" for white audiences.

These events were largely commercial undertakings designed to bring business and tourists to the communities who ran them. However, communities often underplayed the profit side of their gatherings. Even when pressed they emphasized the amusements and diversions, and the potential for creating "goodwill" and improved community relations with local Indian tribes.

At most of these exhibitions special camping areas were set up to accommodate the Indian performers, who were usually given daily distributions of meat and other food along with wages for their participation in particular performance venues. American Indian people were hired performers at these events, often receiving considerably less than whites did as entrants and contestants, even in commonly shared events such as parades. Nonetheless, Native participation in exhibitions like the Calgary Stampede was an important source of annual income for some families, who – in the 1960s – could earn more than $500 for their various performance activities. In a time when average family incomes rarely exceeded $3,000 annually, participation in the Stampede or other such exhibitions was a financially rewarding endeavor that many of these families jealously guarded.

At all exhibition powwows, tight schedules were followed in the various performance venues, which typically included parades, princess pageants, "grand entries," "intertribal" and "contest" dancing, "specialty" acts, beadwork demonstrations, and tipi exhibits at mock villages. Indian participants were registered, were required to follow dress and behavior codes, and were usually sequestered in spaces clearly separated from the "cowboys" and the crowds of "paying" spectators. Much of the protocol in these events, even the language of performance, was fashioned after the rodeo. Indeed, at some of these events, American Indian people participated simultaneously in competitive rodeo events as well as in the more culturally segregated parade and dance programs.

Over the years Indian participation in exhibition powwows waned in the Northern Plains. These celebrations are now much less important than they were four decades ago in the panorama of events that make up the summer celebration circuit. Space does not permit us to detail the transition, but the early 1970s represented an important turning point in the fate of tribal involvement in white-run exhibitions. It was a time when growing numbers of younger Indian people refused to participate because they considered the events demeaning and exploitative. At the same time, fearing political protests and "radical takeovers," many white communities stopped inviting Indian participation. Indeed, one of the largest and most popular exhibition powwows of the 1960s, All American Indian Days in Sheridan, Wyoming, ceased to exist. Others, such as the Calgary Stampede, continued to invite Indian participation but greatly downsized their so-called Indian attractions.

A few new exhibition powwows have been initiated in recent decades, but these represent a fairly minor part of today's powwow scene. The Plains Indian Museum's annual powwow in Cody, Wyoming, is interesting because even though it is sponsored by a white-dominated institution, it is organized and run by a committee made up largely of members from local tribes. The powwow reflects this influence and has more of the feel and flavor of celebrations held in tribal communities than of those run by non-Indian organizations.

Even though tribal participation in exhibition venues run by white entrepreneurs has declined dramatically during the past four decades, some of the competitiveness and commercialism associated with these events, and indeed a large part of their historic programming, has been co-opted by some American Indian communities in putting on their own intertribal powwows.

Celebrations in the Center

The greatest change we witnessed over the past four decades has taken place at the center of our continuum, in the divide between the in-group and intertribal, Pan-Indian celebrations, or what are now commonly known on the circuit as the "traditional" and the "contest" powwows, respectively.

In the sixties the most obvious differences between these two kinds of powwows were their size, their location, and the relative social distance of their participants. In-group powwows were small, intimate gatherings, numbering between 250 and 500 people, most of whom knew one another personally through close, longstanding ties of kinship and friendship. Guests who attended these doings from other locales were often specially "invited" through traditional patterns of etiquette. Guests sometimes came uninvited as acquaintances of families hosting the celebration but rarely came as strangers. (If they did happen to be strangers, as we were on some occasions, they heard about the celebration through the "moccasin telegraph.") Most attendees did not travel far, usually coming from nearby locales within a radius of fifty to one hundred miles of the host community, and most shared the same tribal background, unless an established pattern of intermarriage with members of other tribes existed, as in the longstanding ties between the Arikaras of White Shield, North Dakota, and the Dakotas at Fort Totten, North Dakota.

In the 1960s in-group powwows were located on private or community-held lands, where each year dance areas and campgrounds were cleared by volunteers from the communities or the associations hosting the celebration. New dance enclosures – "arbors" or "bowries" – were erected; covered with boughs of cottonwood, willow, or pine, they were often configured in a circle with the opening facing east. In other regions dance areas were rectangular and covered with canvas "big tops." By the early 1970s many small reservation communities were able to use tribal development funds to build permanent enclosures with speaker's stands, benches, and even bleachers, all of which are now standard at many in-group summer powwows.

Tipis and old-style wall (A-frame) tents, some housing cast-iron stoves, were a common sight on the campgrounds. Families often set up their camps during the week before the celebration to secure a location with shade and close to a water tap. Known throughout the region as "camping day," Thursday was the day visitors typically traveled from other communities to make their camps. Today more powwow-goers are employed, and they generally travel to a powwow and make camp on Friday evening. By the mid-1970s Coleman tents, propane stoves, and other contemporary camping gear replaced the old-style equipment. Tipis, however, still remained; in recent years their presence at these small, in-group events has grown.

Some of the in-group powwows remaining from the sixties have increased in size, doubling or even tripling their numbers. They now draw many urban families who use the occasion to make visits to their original homes; they also draw many "strangers" who come because the celebration has built a reputation as a good "traditional" event. In fact, a few of the in-group powwows, such as Sioux Valley in Canada, have grown so large that they might be better identified today as intertribal. And to the extent that some have also transformed themselves in other ways – for example, by embracing contest dancing over feasts and giveaways – they should also be reclassified.

By contrast the intertribal, or Pan-Indian, powwows of the 1960s were huge events with thousands of people in attendance. Although most ranged from two to five thousand attendees, some of the larger ones, such as Crow Fair, drew upward of ten thousand people. Many who traveled to these powwows knew one another as relatives, friends, or acquaintances, but an even larger segment were total strangers. These events were multitribal, drawing crowds from hundreds of miles away. In the sixties many were just starting to be advertised through mimeographed and printed posters circulating in local reservation post offices, trading posts, and tribal buildings, although most still attracted their followings as much by reputation and word-of-mouth as by advertising. By the seventies celebration committees started to sell metal buttons, bumper stickers, T-shirts, and baseball caps with their powwow logos as a way not only to advertise their events but also to raise money. Today full-page ads in national Indian newspapers, announcements on tribally run radio stations, and brochures produced by state tourism agencies advertise the big powwows. There are even books (Marquis 1974; Tiller 1992), marketed largely for tourists, that provide the dates and details of some of the larger, better-known powwows.

On the Northern Plains most of today's intertribal powwows are still held in agency towns on tribally owned campgrounds, which now have large, permanent, and sometimes elaborately built facilities maintained by employees of the tribal labor force. In the sixties campers at these powwows started to arrive equipped with the best and latest models of Coleman camping gear. We came in a VW bus, a novelty at the time, but by the late 1970s, pickups with camper shells and vans outfitted as campers were how people with means traveled in style on the intertribal powwow circuit.

Intertribal powwows have grown too. A few can now be called mega-powwows, regularly drawing crowds of more than twenty-five thousand people. These events attract a wide cross section of the American Indian public, including a growing, urban and wealthier middle class, some of whom travel by air and rented car and stay overnight at local motels (always fully booked on powwow weekends). Besides Crow Fair, one of the biggest powwows on the Northern Plains is Bismarck's International Powwow, which represents the increase in events sponsored by multitribal institutions in urban areas. Indeed, the largest powwows today are found not in rural settings but in cities, such as Denver, with large urban Indian populations.

In the sixties a significant divide existed between in-group and intertribal powwows in the sorts of events they emphasized, in the ways they were organized, in the cultural ambiances they created, and in their patterns of sociality. Today this divide has become even more pronounced than in the past.

For example, in-group powwows have always focused strongly on traditional styles of protocol, emphasizing honorings, donations, and giveaways, which generally take up most of the afternoon activities on Saturday and Sunday. In Lakota and Dakota communities, the powwow committees hold giveaways on behalf of the children who are elected to committee offices – a continuation of the traditional "hunka" relationship, whereby families held special honorings for a favored child. Giveaways are also held at these powwows in conjunction with naming ceremonies, memorials, and other honorings that mark special events, transitions, and achievements in the lives of individuals from local families. Today it is not uncommon for urban families to return home to use their community's summer powwow as an occasion to hold their own honorings, feasts, and giveaways.

At most of the in-group powwows in Dakota and Lakota communities, a special effort is made to acknowledge the presence of all the visitors during the committee giveaways. For example, the officers of the Lone Buffalo Club, an Omaha association at Spirit Lake, make special efforts to identify all of the visitors present from neighboring reserves and reservations, often conferring with one another before the giveaways start to make sure that every visitor personally receives a gift from at least one of the club's officers. In the community of Wakpala on the Standing Rock Reservation, each of the committee officers usually reserves a portion of their gifts for a "throwaway" in which all the visitors not previously called on and given gifts are invited to take an item from a bundle of donations placed in the center of the dance arena. There are other styles of gift giving too, but in all instances they reflect the desire of the officers to make everyone feel welcome and an integral part of the celebration's festivities.

In-group powwows still take great pride in feeding their visitors. Communities distribute "rations" of canned goods, bread, coffee (tea in Canada), and meats to the campers, and most prepare one or more full meals a day for their guests. Volunteers from the host community or representatives of a local voluntary association prepare the meals. Fry bread, boiled meats, soups, and fruit puddings are especially popular, and many committees today make a special effort to serve traditional, highly honored foods, including tongue and pemmican. The "kids' chow line," however, still serves pork and beans, hot dogs, cookies, and Kool-Aid.

In the past, honorings and giveaways were also held at intertribal powwows, with Saturday and Sunday afternoons devoted to these activities. Generally, however, the giveaways were limited to tribal dignitaries, committee officers, and special offices, such as princess and junior princess. These powwows placed less emphasis on honoring and donations, but the giveaways tended to be much larger and more elaborate. During the seventies, when reservation economies were beginning to grow and expand, the giving standards at giveaways escalated in ways reminiscent of nineteenth-century potlatching on the Northwest Coast. Instead of families donating one Pendleton and a dozen star quilts, as was customary in the 1960s, we began to see giveaways with more than a dozen Pendletons and up to one hundred star quilts in the mid-seventies. By the eighties, when many intertribal powwows began to devote more of their time and money to support competitive powwow dancing, some of these inflationary tendencies started to subside.

Some patterns of gift giving have also become less inclusive as the size of celebrations has grown. At the intertribal events families who host honorings and donations still acknowledge and give gifts to the visitors they know, but less effort has always been made at these powwows to include all of the visiting attendees in the cycles of gift giving. Generally, visitors unknown to the committees of the larger celebrations are given gifts as part of a generic class, such as, for example, when requests are made for all of the visiting "elderlies," "veterans," or "Jingle dancers" to come up and shake the hands of the honored and accept gifts from their families.

Similarly, some of the intertribal powwows make special efforts to feed their campers and visitors by preparing daily meals or rations, but many have never done so or no longer do so. In some instances preparing a feast for the visitors has never been a community tradition; in others it has simply become too costly to feed the growing numbers of powwow-goers. More typically, feasting at the large intertribal events was (and still is) the work of individual families who take it upon themselves to bring groceries to friends, relatives, and other special visitors or who invite these guests to their tent or home for prepared meals. In fact, much of the intercommunity gifting at these powwows also takes place in this way.

Another feature that separates the small, in-group from the large, intertribal powwows are the dance events. In the 1960s contest dancing took up much less space in the programs of the big events, and like the smaller powwows, the contests were interspersed with dances in which everyone could participate. By the 1980s contest dances had become a major focus at some of the larger powwows, filling entire afternoon and evening schedules from Friday through Sunday. The larger powwows also had "specials," a term applied not only to family honorings but also to specialty performances by Hoop dancers, visiting delegations of Maori from New Zealand, and similar attractions. These kinds of specialty events are still common today at some of the larger powwows, but they are rare at the in-group celebrations.

Thirty years ago contest dance events were generally restricted to the evenings. Although some powwows began their elimination contests during the previous evenings, equal time was still given to what are now known as the "intertribals" but which some announcers back in the sixties called the "free-for-alls" – meaning anyone who wanted to was invited to dance during a song. In this earlier era, competition categories were few and were based primarily on age and gender, while prizes were nominal – for example, $100 to $250 for first place in the men's category. Many of these powwows also had no "Grand Entries."

In the early 1970s this format began to change. First, competition grew among powwow committees over the size of the prizes they awarded. By 1972, for example, Fort Totten Days was announcing first-place prizes of $1,000 in men's competitions; in the 1990s the amount still escalated as tribes rich with gaming revenues pushed the winnings even higher. Second, contest categories were growing more and more diverse. Not only did the age divisions become more refined, with categories for "Tiny Tots" and "Seniors" being added, but contests were separated according to dance and music styles. Today, for example, junior women (ages twelve to eighteen) compete in a "Jingle," a "Shawl," or a "Traditional" category, while junior men enter the "Grass," "Fancy," or "Traditional" classes. Some of the powwows further subdivide these categories along regional lines and hold separate competitions for different regional, "Northern" and "Southern" styles of dancing.

The emphasis on contests and competition at the intertribal powwows also brought with it more regimentation. Preregistration became required for dance competitors. Grand entries became commonplace, and all contestants were required to join them in order to qualify for the dance competitions. Contest events are now rigorously scheduled, following clock time rather than "Indian" time. Complex point systems are used to judge dancers, with special people assigned to keep track of the scores and computers used to tabulate the results. Even dress codes are now the norm (e.g., no tennis shoes). What's next? Powwow committees hiring certified public accountants to manage their "purses"?

The growing size of powwow purses, which now commonly exceed $100,000, has been accompanied by the emergence of a professional occupational class associated with the powwow. We can now speak of "professional" powwow families, who spend much of their time on the circuit and are able to earn a decent living through their winnings in contest singing and dancing.

Professionalization is also apparent in other areas. Today well-known and respected announcers, judges, and arena directors are invited and paid to work at events far from their home communities; some are able to make a respectable living not only during the summer powwow season but also at the larger urban and college events generally held at other times of the year. Forty years ago announcers, judges, and arena directors generally came from the sponsoring community or one nearby; if they were "hired" from the outside, the amount for their services was nominal and consistent with the modest gifts given to the singers, dancers, and others who performed important roles in the powwow.

Many of the small powwows still raise their revenues through traditional means, soliciting donations by singing "house to house" or receiving them from local families who request a special honoring song at other community events and donate cash, a horse, or a side of beef for the next year's summer celebration. Past sponsors of small powwows also held raffles and bingos to raise money for their summer celebrations, but with the appearance of casinos on most reservations, this mode of fund-raising has declined. In the past, even the large intertribal powwows used these methods to gather the necessary resources to run their events. By the 1970s some powwow committees started to charge admission fees or relied on subsidies from tribal treasuries to support their doings. Many tribes now earmark a portion of the earnings from their tribal casinos for the big summer celebrations.

Dancers at the larger powwows now number in the thousands, and their outfits – commonly called "regalia" – are costly and elaborate. In the 1960s, for example, a Dakota teenage girl's powwow outfit typically consisted of a simple satin dress (sometimes remade from material in a prom dress purchased at a local rummage sale) that was worn with a beaded belt and a medallion often of an unmatching design. Fringed but undecorated wool shawls, beaded moccasins, and hairstrings were also part of the standard apparel. Today a girl's Fancy Dance outfit is carefully coordinated and accessorized, consisting of a long skirt with a matching blouse embellished in ribbons of contrasting colors, a shawl with elaborate appliquè designs along with fully beaded moccasins, leggings, belts, yokes, and hair wraps that often carry designs matching the shawl (see also W. Powers 1994 for a description of the typical Lakota costume).

Today's "star" dancers are now recognized over wide regions, some even nationally. The presence of these well-known and much admired artists adds to the prestige of an intertribal powwow, and some powwow-goers organize their summer itineraries to take in the powwows that their favorite dancers typically attend. We have been told that a few of the men now have white female groupies following them from one powwow to another. Some of today's most accomplished and talented dancers can earn thousands of dollars a year, not only from the prize monies they win in competition but from gifts they receive from appreciative members of the host communities where they dance.

Like the talented dancers, the drums and their singers travel cross-country to compete for the big purses. The number of drums at intertribal events has steadily grown from an average of ten in the sixties to as many as one hundred in the nineties. It is now reaching the point where there's barely enough space to accommodate all the drums; in the future, singers may well have to reserve drum seats in advance to participate in some of the more popular doings. Some powwow committees are responding to this pressure by permitting only invited singers to participate in their events.

Thirty years ago intertribal powwow circuits were more regionalized, confined to one or a few adjoining states and provinces. By the end of the seventies, however, they had crossed regions, with dancers, for example, from Yakima,

Washington, regularly showing up at Fort Totten Days in North Dakota. And by the nineties a high-stakes powwow circuit had emerged, with stops at the big urban events and the casino-supported ones in Connecticut, Minnesota, and California.

Songs, styles of singing and dancing, and regalia designs unique to particular tribes and regions are now crossing cultural boundaries more and more often. This is a result not only of powwow-goers traveling farther and to more places to attend well-known powwows but also of the adaptation of modern technologies to powwow activities. In the late sixties, when portable tape recorders became widely available, they were ubiquitous at powwows – with circles four and five people deep surrounding a popular drum to record the songs of its singers. Eventually, some powwows had to set rules to limit recording and the numbers of people standing near a drum. Video cameras are now allowing people to record pictures of the powwows they attend and share their film footage with people at home. Some communities, including Browning, Montana, now have their powwows simulcast on the local airwaves so that the homebound are able to see the event "live."

In the meantime many of the smaller, in-group powwows, and even some of the old intertribal powwows, have moved in the opposite direction. Thirty years ago most in-group powwows, like their larger counterparts, also had a night of competitive dancing but with token prizes rarely amounting to more than $25 or $50. Now many of the smaller powwows have turned away completely from contests to avoid the insidious distinctions, "bad feelings," and "bad medicines" that have been reported to surround the heated competition at some of the bigger ones. Instead, monies are raised to provide token cash gifts, or "gas money," for all the dancers and singers. Some of the small celebrations are now gaining reputations for putting on good "traditional" events and are attracting more participants who wish to experience the sociality and intimacy of an "old-style doings" rather than the glitter, bustle, and anonymity of the big powwow.

Four decades ago people decided to attend and support the small powwows over the big ones on different grounds as well. The "elderly" and more traditionally oriented families often preferred in-group gatherings, where they could visit and reminisce with friends and relations in a congenial, unhurried atmosphere; where they could experience the generosity and hospitality of hosts who knew how to feed and donate in the "old" ways; where they heard speeches in their native languages that extolled tribal values and virtues; and where they could humor one another in customary ways (including local announcers poking fun at their sisters-in-law). Today many young families are also returning to these celebrations, instead of taking in the big events, as a way of renewing their ties to family, community, and a sense of tribal tradition.

In the sixties many people viewed the intertribal powwows as spectacles, and they saw themselves as spectators who came to watch the festivities rather than participate in performances. They were drawn to the large powwows by their glamour and popularity, the reputation of their star dancers, and the many other attractions to be seen. They traveled from Fort Totten in North Dakota to Pine Ridge in South Dakota not because they knew or were related to anyone but because the event had an impressive reputation. Back then intertribal powwows were often held in conjunction with arts and crafts competitions, parades, and rodeos, where people also competed in various contest categories. In subsequent decades the powwows also included carnivals, staged rock-and-roll dances, and some even invited country-and-western singers like Johnny Rodriguez to perform. More and more concessions, selling everything from hot dogs and Indian tacos to baseball caps, music tapes, and crafts supplies, encircled the arena. These were places to see and be seen by new people, to make acquaintances who might become friends, and, for parents, to possibly introduce their children to potential spouses.

As we argued thirty years ago, the cultural texture of modern celebrations differs by tribe and region. Notwithstanding these differences certain underlying similarities not only reveal widespread processes of borrowing and sharing, which now span the entire continent, but also reflect the distinctive social identities and relationships that different sorts of powwows address. The small, in-group powwows still celebrate family ties and local community links within tribally distinctive discourses, whereas the intertribal powwows speak to a more broadly based, widely shared sense of identity in which relationships cut across tribally diverse communities to articulate a regional and, increasingly, a national culture of celebration among American Indian people.

Conclusions

During the past thirty years we have witnessed many changes on the powwow circuit. Although the four kinds of powwows we have identified here still exist, the white-run exhibitions have declined in numbers, support, and importance. The family-run celebrations still survive and flourish, standing at the heart of today's celebratory activity. The in-group and intertribal celebrations also persist and prosper, but as their new names – "traditional" and "contest" – imply, they have also become more differentiated and specialized. The in-group qua traditional powwows, whether small or large in size, are emphasizing old-style protocols and turning away from commercialism and competitive dancing. By contrast the intertribal contest powwows have become much more commercialized, regimented, and "professionalized" in relation to what they do and perform. They have also become more internally diverse. The proliferation of contest categories, for example, acknowledges the greater diversity of tribes and tribal influences ("Northern" and "Southern") represented at most of the larger intertribal powwows.

In the modern world, where Indian people of different tribal backgrounds constantly gather and interact, celebration activity provides a meeting ground, a common context for communicating diverse identities and understandings through a shared language of performance, honor, and respect. Some of what we see in powwows today reflects traditions that have survived over many generations, and this is especially true in the family and the traditional or in-group events. But we've also seen much innovation, especially in intertribal powwows. Some of this innovation reflects fads and fashions that have come and gone, but there are also indications of lasting change, which have resulted from wider transformations in the worlds in which American Indian people powwow.

Notwithstanding such change, celebrations remain an important source of pleasure and enjoyment in contemporary tribal communities. They provide apt settings for renewing old ties and making new ones; for honoring and respecting family, community, and tribe; for showing pride and accomplishment; and for expressing a sense of identity and belongingness among people with whom one shares a specific or general history.

It is also possible to look at powwows in other, more complex and elusive but often overdetermined ways as events having significant economic, political, and ideological values and consequences. Underlying, encircling, overriding, and even penetrating the more systemic, structural, and motivational properties of powwows, however, exists a kind of understanding that most scholars are loathe to acknowledge – that is, people partake of many things in life not simply for some ulterior reason or agenda, whether they are conscious of it or not, but for the sheer enjoyments they offer, for the good feelings they bring, and for the aesthetic pleasures they create. As many Dakota and Lakota have told us repeatedly over the years, powwows are "good clean fun."

REFERENCES

Albers, Patricia. 1974. "The Regional System of the Devil's Lake Sioux: Its Structure, Composition, Development, and Functions." Unpublished PhD diss., University of Wisconsin–Madison.

———. 1998. "Symbols, Souvenirs and Sentiments: Early Postcard Imagery of Plains Indians." In *Delivering Views: Distant Cultures in Early Postcards*, ed. Christraud M. Geary and Virginia-Lee Webb, 131–67. Washington DC: Smithsonian Institution Press.

Anonymous. 1978. "Powwows in 1978." *Sunset: The Magazine of Western Living*, May, 106–13.

Born, David. 1994. "Black Elk and the Duhamel Sioux Indian Pageant." *North Dakota Magazine of History* 61 (1): 22–29.

Braine, Susan. 1995. *Drumbeat, Heartbeat: A Celebration of the Powwow*. Minneapolis: Lerner.

Browner, Tara. 2002. *Heartbeat of the People: Music and Dance of the Northern Pow-Wow*. Champaign: University of Illinois Press.

Contreras, Ben, and Diane Morris Bernstein. 1996. *We Dance Because We Can*. Marietta GA: Longstreet.

Corrigan, Samuel. 1970. "The Plains Indian Powwow: Cultural Integration in Manitoba and Saskatchewan." *Anthropologica* 12 (1): 253–77.

Crummet, Michael. 1981. Crow Indian Fair. *Americana* 9 (3): 32–37.

Deloria, Vine, Jr. 1976. "The Indians." In *Buffalo Bill and the Wild West*, 45–56. Brooklyn NY: Brooklyn Museum.

DeMallie, Raymond J., ed. 1984. *The Sixth Grandfather: Black Elk's Teachings Given to John G. Niehardt*. Lincoln: University of Nebraska Press.

Desjarlait, Robert. 1997. "The Contest Powwow Versus the Traditional Powwow and the Role of the Native American Community." *Wicazo Sa Review* 12 (1): 115–27.

Grobsmith, Elizabeth. 1979. "The Lakhota Giveaway: A System of Social Reciprocity." *Plains Anthropologist* 24 (84): 123–32.

———. 1981. "The Changing Role of the Giveaway Ceremony in Contemporary Lakota Life." *Plains Anthropologist* 26 (91): 75–79.

Hatton, Orin T. 1974. "Performance Practices of Northern Plains Powwow Singing Groups." *Yearbook for the Inter-American Music Research* 10. Austin: University of Texas Press.

———. 1986. "In the Tradition: Grass Dance Musical Style and Female Powwow Singers." *Ethnomusicology* 30 (2): 197–221.

Horse Capture, George. 1989. *Pow Wow*. Cody WY: Buffalo Bill Historical Center.

Howard, James H. 1960. "The Northern Style Grass Dance Costume." *American Indian Hobbist* 71 (1): 18–27.

Kehoe, Alice. 1980. "The Giveaway Ceremony of Blackfoot and Plains Cree." *Plains Anthropologist* 25 (87): 17–26.

Marquis, Arnold. 1974. *A Guide to America's Indians: Ceremonials, Reservations, and Museums*. Norman: University of Oklahoma Press.

Marra, Ben. 1996. *Powwow: Images along the Red Road*. New York: Harry N. Abrams.

Mattern, Mark. 1996. "The Powwow as a Public Arena for Negotiating Unity and Diversity in American Indian Life." *American Indian Culture and Research Journal* 20 (4): 183–201.

Mekeel, Scudder. 1932. "A Discussion of Culture Change as Illustrated by Material from a Teton-Dakota Community." *American Anthropologist* 34 (2): 274–88.

Moses, L. G. 1996. *Wild West Shows and the Images of American Indians*. Albuquerque: University of New Mexico Press.

Parfit, Michael. 1994. "Powwow." *National Geographic* 185 (6): 88–113.

Pettipas, Katherine. 1993. *Severing the Ties That Bind: Government Repression of Indigenous Religious Ceremonies on the Prairies*. Manitoba Studies in Native History 7. Winnipeg: University of Manitoba Press.

Powers, Marla. 1988. "Symbolic Representations of Sex Roles in the Plains War Dance." *European Review of Native American Studies* 2 (2): 17–24.

———. 1991. *Dakota Naming: A Modern Day Hunka Ceremony*. Kendall Park NJ: Lakota Books.

Powers, William. 1970. "Contemporary Oglala Music and Dance: Pan-Indianism versus Pan-Tetonism." In *The Modern Sioux: Social Systems and Reservation Culture*, ed. Ethel Nurge, 268–90. Lincoln: University of Nebraska Press.

———. 1980. "Plains Indian Music and Dance." In *Anthropology on the Great Plains*, ed. W. Raymond Wood and Margot Liberty, 212–29. Lincoln: University of Nebraska Press.

———. 1990. *War Dance: Plains Indian Musical Performance*. Tucson: University of Arizona Press.

———. 1994. "Innovation in Lakota Powwow Costumes." *American Indian Art* 19 (4): 66–73.

Roberts, Chris. 1995. *Pow Wow Country*. Helena MT: American and World Geographic Publishing.

———. 1998. *People of the Circle*. Missoula MT: Meadowlark.

Schneider, Mary Jane. 1981. "Economic Aspects of Mandan/Hidatsa Giveaways." *Plains Anthropologist* 26 (91): 43–50.

Slotkin, Richard. 1976. "The 'Wild West.' " In *Buffalo Bill and the Wild West*, 27–44. Brooklyn NY: Brooklyn Museum.

Standing Bear, Luther. 1975. *My People the Sioux*. Lincoln: University of Nebraska Press.

Tiller, Veronica E., ed. 1992. *Discover Indian Reservations USA: A Visitor's Welcome Guide.* Denver: Council Publications.

Weist, Katherine. 1973. "Giving Away: The Ceremonial Distribution of Goods among the Northern Cheyenne of Southeastern Montana." *Plains Anthropologist* 18 (60): 97–103.

White, Julia. 1996. *The Pow Wow Trail: Understanding and Enjoying the Native American Pow Wow.* Summertown TN: Book Publishing Company.

Young, Gloria, and Erik D. Gooding. 2001. "Celebrations and Giveaways." In *Handbook of North American Indians*, vol. 13, no. 2, *The Plains*, ed. R. J. DeMallie, 1011–15. Washington DC: Smithsonian Institution Press.

Young Bear, Severt, and R. D. Theisz. 1994. *Standing in the Light: A Lakota Way of Seeing.* Lincoln: University of Nebraska Press.

GRANT ARNDT

3. Ho-Chunk "Indian Powwows" of the Early Twentieth Century

In 1908 the *Badger State Banner*, a weekly newspaper published in Black River Falls, Wisconsin, carried a front-page story on the "Great Pow-wow" being staged by the Ho-Chunk Wazijacis (then referred to as the Wisconsin Winnebagos) at their settlement six miles east of the city. The paper explained that the powwow "consisted of a series of dances, pony races, ball games, foot races, etc." and that the "main thing, of course, was the dancing." The Ho-Chunks had erected a large dance arbor (presumably of wooden poles with a pine-bough roof, as in later years), which contained a large drum with a half-dozen or so drummers "beating the drum with sticks in perfect time." Around the drum and singers circled the dancers; first a group of twenty or more women danced, "in perfect time and some of them wearing very elegant customs [*sic*] which would rival those of some of the society white people in richness and beauty." After the women came the men "decked in war paint of gaudy colors, and wearing fancy custumes [*sic*] that even excelled those of the [women] in dazzling beauty."[1]

The dances had attracted nearly three hundred Indian participants, many of them visitors from other Ho-Chunk settlements in the state but also including a delegation from the Winnebago Reservation in Nebraska. The paper reported that the dancing, as well as a set of athletic contests and "suttlers tents and ice-cream parlors," had attracted "the interest of many of our citizens, who drove out at intervals to witness the festivities." This white attraction to Indian ceremonial activities had been evident in the area for at least a decade, but the Ho-Chunks responded to it in an innovative way in the following years. At the next powwow, in 1909, they introduced a "new method of charging a fee for admittance to the grounds." The local newspaper noted with interest that this fee "acted rather as a stimulus than as a discouragement to the attendance of whites to witness the ceremonies, sports, games, and dances." On Sunday, a reported 150 to 200 people made the journey to the Ho-Chunk settlement, and "there would have been more had there been convenient conveyance at a moderate fee."[2] By 1939 Ho-Chunk people were spending most weekends in July and August traveling to Indian powwows, including one in Pittsville, Wisconsin; smaller one-time Indian powwows in other central Wisconsin towns; and the Stand Rock Indian ceremonial for tourists in the Wisconsin Dells, in addition to the Black River Falls powwow.[3]

This chapter examines the now largely forgotten history of these Ho-Chunk events, known throughout the period as "Indian powwows." Of central concern is the way Indian powwows combined Indian participation with a commercial orientation to non-Indian spectators. For just over a decade in the early twentieth century, this commercial orientation seems to have been viewed as compatible with the communal orientation. Eventually, however, the Ho-Chunks encountered difficulty maintaining the delicate balance between these two aspects of the powwow. The Indian powwow era of the early 1900s demonstrates the significance of some of the features of the powwows that emerged in Wisconsin, Oklahoma, and elsewhere in the second half of the twentieth century. It also helps identify the enduring dilemmas of Native American cultural performance in the public spaces of the United States.

The Ho-Chunk Wazijacis have lived in the lands now organized as Wisconsin since before first contact with Europeans in the early seventeenth century. The original Ho-Chunk polity is now divided into two federally recognized entities, the Winnebago Tribe of Nebraska and the Ho-Chunk Nation of Wisconsin. The Ho-Chunk people in Wisconsin descend from bands that resisted repeated attempts by the federal government to forcibly remove them from the state following the ceding of the tribal homelands in treaties negotiated between 1828 and 1837. They persisted as fugitives in marginal areas of central Wisconsin until special legislation passed in the 1870s and 1880s allowed them to take up homesteads. Following their organization of a tribal government in 1963, these homesteads became the foundation for six community regions in central Wisconsin, with a tribal headquarters established in Black River Falls.[4]

Even before they gained legal right to remain in Wisconsin, the "disaffected" refugee Ho-Chunk bands began to establish relations with the new Euro-American settlers. Ho-Chunk families came to rely on cash earned from seasonal agricultural labor to supplement subsistence hunting, trapping, and gardening, which became increasingly difficult as they were forced onto marginal lands deemed undesirable by white homesteaders. As the *Jackson County Journal* explained in a 1906 article:

> It is impossible for the Indians to make a living upon their land even with the assistance of their annuity. It becomes necessary for them to leave their homesteads the greater portion of the year and earn their living in other ways. It would seem the part of wisdom and the part of common sense upon the part of those in authority to encourage the Indians to get out and labor as industriously as possible during such seasons of the year as it is possible for them to obtain employment among the whites. Beginning with the ripening of the cranberries, there is a period of eight or ten weeks when for many years the Indians have been employed at what is often termed civilizing pursuits, the only time of year when any considerable number of the Indians are so employed. Picking cranberries, cutting corn, threshing, digging potatoes, husking corn, etc. During this time the Indians are scattered from Grand Rapids [later renamed Wisconsin Rapids] on the east to across the Mississippi into Minnesota on the west.[5]

The Ho-Chunks remained in a situation of "caste-like" poverty relative to their white neighbors throughout the twentieth century until their development of tribal economic enterprises in the 1980s.[6] The attitudes of white Wisconsin residents toward the Ho-Chunks were complex and often marked by ambivalence. While some settlers had actively supported the effort to remove them from the state, some even threatening to wage "a war of extinction" against their Indian neighbors if not appeased, others supported the Ho-Chunks' struggle to remain in the state throughout the same period. Historian Lawrence Onsager found that local white interference with the last major military removal effort in 1874 was a major factor in the federal government's decision to abandon removal efforts.[7]

The consolidation of a stable, hierarchical relationship between the Ho-Chunks and white residents of Wisconsin brought with it a significant change in white attitudes toward Ho-Chunk ceremonial activities. As late as the 1860s reports of Indian gatherings and "war dances" had set off so-called panics among settlers that frequently served as the rationale for renewed efforts at removal. By the 1890s, however, Ho-Chunk gatherings had become newsworthy only as subjects of local interest that often attracted white spectators. In 1895 the *Jackson County Journal* reported that an "Indian war dance" was in progress and that thirty or forty "Musquaquama [Meskwaki] Indians from Tama County [Iowa] were in attendance during the early part of the month." According to the *Badger State Banner*, "a large number of our citizens drove out

Sunday to witness the proceedings" and "some Kodak views were sprung on them." Later that month the *Banner* reported the arrival of a delegation of thirty Chippewas, who had been "royally welcomed" with a dog feast, ceremonial exchange of pipes, and formal speeches of welcome. Another delegation from the Chippewas was expected the following weekend to continue the dancing. Later, in October, the *Banner* noted that several Ho-Chunk groups had recently returned from Iowa, where they were attending "the big Indian meet and dance." The blasé reports of War Dances involving a number of Indian tribes suggest that local whites had lost their apprehensions regarding any possible threat from their Ho-Chunk neighbors.[8]

By the early twentieth century, local whites also came to perceive the Ho-Chunks, especially when engaged in traditional cultural activities, as living representatives of the romanticized "pioneer days" of the region, a time viewed with an increasing sense of nostalgia. When the town of Black River Falls organized a "homecoming" celebration in the summer of 1908 (just weeks before the Ho-Chunk powwow discussed above), one of the main attractions set up downtown was an Indian village. The *Banner* promised visitors, especially "Old settlers" returning for the homecoming, that the Indian village would be their "only opportunity . . . for another glimpse of Indian life . . . as many knew it to be in earlier days, [and] to renew their acquaintance with the red men they knew years ago." For the Ho-Chunk people the staging of the Indian village at the Black River Falls homecoming seems to have been simply a local venue at which they worked for the same local entrepreneur, Thomas Roddy, who organized their performances elsewhere.[9]

Charles Round Low Cloud, author of an Indian news column in the Black River Falls *Banner-Journal* during the 1930s and 1940s, wrote in an August 19, 1939, column (in his characteristically nonstandard voice) that "the Indians powwow when first beginning they don't call that, they used called Homecoming at Winnebago Reservation, Nebraska."[10] The Black River Falls Indian powwow originated around the turn of the century and, as Low Cloud indicated, was introduced by the Nebraska relatives of the Ho-Chunk Wazijacis. The Nebraska homecoming was either based on or influenced by the Heylushka, or Grass Dance, society. In the decades before the homecoming celebration had been brought to Wisconsin, the festivities had been made more elaborate; the Nebraska Ho-Chunks had, according to Low Cloud, "added inside some different perform, men, women, boys and girls races, or horse race and . . . they add all kinds dances."[11]

The growing popularity of the Heylushka society in the late nineteenth century is generally attributed to its ability to preserve the values and ceremonies associated with indigenous warrior customs in the absence of actual warfare. In the case of the Ho-Chunk community, however, Heylushka warrior dances continued to act as forums for warrior publicity of a very traditional sort. The writings of Sam Blowsnake, one of Paul Radin's main consultants and author of the autobiography *Crashing Thunder*, illustrate that, at least in 1903, the War Dances could serve as moments of community participation organized around strikingly traditional ideas about such performances. Blowsnake described a 1903 war expedition in which he led three friends in a raid to murder a Potawatomi man living in a neighboring Wisconsin county. He explained that the motivation for the expedition was their desire to earn the right to wear the head ornaments denoting achievement in war at Heylushka dances held at the Nebraska reservation. While Blowsnake's 1903 war expedition was an unusual manifestation of the Ho-Chunk warrior ethos at the time, it suggests that participation in Heylushka and other warrior-related cultural events in the early twentieth century were something other than survivals of a moribund culture.[12]

Long before Sam Blowsnake and his friends set out on their war expedition, they had worked as show Indians, and Sam had been one of the Ho-Chunks who helped stage the Ho-Chunk Indian Village on the Midway at the Chicago World's Fair of 1892–93. Ho-Chunk peoples had participated in an early example of "Indian show business" long before they ever participated in the Heylushka and other transitional cultural activities. The first documented Ho-Chunk commercial cultural performance for a white American audience occurred in 1828, during their very first diplomatic trip to Washington DC in the wake of the so-called Winnebago War of 1827. On the afternoon of November 28th, the day before they were to meet with President John Quincy Adams, the delegation staged what local papers labeled a "war dance" on the common between the White House and the Potomac River. Local spectators were charged a dollar apiece for admission to a performance, which included a "discovery dance, a mock battle and the rejoice dance."[13]

The Ho-Chunks did not explore the economic possibilities of similar performances until soon after they won the right to continue living in Wisconsin. By the 1880s a number of Ho-Chunk individuals had begun to work as show Indians in circuses and Wild West shows. The *Banner* reported in the 1880s that twenty local Ho-Chunk individuals had joined Casey's Wild West Show in Philadelphia and were traveling with it around the country. In 1893 thirty Ho-

Chunk dancers and their families traveled to Chicago's Columbian Exposition, setting up a camp and an Indian village exhibition on the Midway just east of the Chinese Theater. In 1897 the local troop played lacrosse for fairgoers at the Iowa State Fair in Dubuque, and the next year they staged an "Indian show" at Camp Douglass and journeyed to Minneapolis for an exhibition at the Minnesota state fair.[14]

Despite their long history as show Indians, the Ho-Chunks resisted early attempts by local whites to observe their local community ceremonies and gatherings. A cartoon created by Ho-Chunk artist David Goodvillage around the turn of the century shows an iconic Indian brave using a knife to scare two local whites away from the Black River Falls "powwow" and yelling, "You two white-faced got no business here." Such attitudes had evidently begun to change by the early twentieth century. In 1905 the *Banner* reported that "quite a number of white people from the city went out to see the sport," when the Ho-Chunks staged their annual "Homecoming" gathering. The *Banner* also reported that the Ho-Chunk organizers of the event had explained their intention to remodel the activity "after the model of the white-man's track meet." As already noted, by 1908 the Ho-Chunks had arranged for "sutlers" to sell refreshments to the visitors, and in 1909 they began to charge white spectators a fee to enter the grounds and witness the dancing.[15]

Coverage of the 1909 powwow drew attention to what contemporary white observers understood to be problems in the effective commercialization of the powwow. The correspondent for the *Banner* argued that "the Indians have a pretty poor idea of business" because they had done little to make the powwow's program convenient for potential white spectators. The powwow would, the *Banner* noted, "have been a more popular resort for the whites than it proved to be the past week had people been enabled to get any advance information as to the program." Some of the whites had gone out to the powwow and "staid [*sic*] a good portion of the day without witnessing anything but the beating of the tom tom." This lack of a clear and convenient schedule of events undermined all the other efforts the organizers had made. The *Banner* argued that "the fact that they charged admission to the grounds, got out admission tickets, and announced that the tickets would be on sale at the drug stores" proved the fact that the Ho-Chunk organizers had wanted white "spectators." The problem with their planning, according to the *Banner*, was that it had been "impossible for prospective patrons to ascertain anything doing worth the while to go and see. The revenue from admissions of white people would be considerable at these gatherings if it could be ascertained when the big events would take place." Local residents suggested that the city provide support to move the next powwow to the Jackson County Fairgrounds. Local businessmen believed the move would allow the Ho-Chunks to "pick up a good many more quarters" but noted with some evident frustration that it was "doubtful [that] they would accept."[16]

The frustration of the white observers may reflect their tendency to associate the Ho-Chunk Indian powwow with other commercial amusements, including Wild West shows and Indian exhibitions at fairs. The Ho-Chunks' decision to charge visiting non-Indians an admission fee to attend the powwow could also be interpreted as an invitation for non-Indians to participate in the powwow rather than to simply watch it as passive spectators. According to the published account of the early Indian powwows, the leaders of the powwow took care to explain to their white guests what was happening at the event. The *Banner* had noted in its report on the 1908 powwow that the "manager of ceremonies," George Monegar, had explained to white spectators that the powwow dances were held to "work . . . up the enthusiasm bringing about" the gifts of "articles of Indian value" from the Indian audience for the dance. These gifts, the paper reported, "represented days of labor and expenditure of considerable money." The implication could be drawn that whites themselves, in paying admission to the powwow, were being given the opportunity to become something more than voyeurs who stood outside Indian society; they were being invited inside to socialize and perhaps to begin to behave like human beings in their dealings with their indigenous neighbors.[17]

Whatever the goals of the decision to charge an admission fee for the powwow, accounts of the 1908 and 1909 powwows reveal a basic conflict between community and commerce facing the Ho-Chunk people as they attempted to organize new forms of cultural performance. Central to the conflict was the difference in participation frameworks and role expectations that Indians and whites brought to such events, encouraged by their divergent understanding of the implications of the commercial aspect of Indian powwows. The 1908 *Banner* articles indicate that some whites of the time considered themselves "patrons" of the Ho-Chunks and felt that their payment of an admission fee justified demands that the event satisfy their expectations for a good show. As long as whites expected powwows to conform to the pattern of other commercial entertainment forms, it would be impossible for the whites to fulfill their duties as "guests" at an Indian community event. The divergent demands of Indian participants and white spectators set up an internal conflict that would eventually all but destroy the Indian powwow.[18]

By the 1920s the Ho-Chunk people had added two other major sites for "Indian powwow" performances to their homecoming powwow near Black River Falls. The second major location in which Ho-Chunk prototypical powwow performances developed was the Wisconsin Dells, south of Black River Falls and near another of the main Ho-Chunk settlement areas in the state. A nineteenth-century leader of the Ho-Chunks, Yellow Thunder, had obtained a homestead near the Dells in the 1840s, which the tribe used as a refuge during the height of the removal efforts. The Dells had long been one of the most important tourism destinations in the region, due in large part to the work of photographer Henry Hamilton Bennett, whose photographs packaged the region's distinctive rock formations into a set of popular images. Stand Rock was one of the most visually distinctive formations in the Dells, and one of Bennett's most popular postcard images. It became the site of Ho-Chunk dances for tourists around 1918.[19]

While local stories circulated about Ho-Chunk people holding dances below the dam at the Dells as early as 1878, the new Indian performances began as an outgrowth of the already popular steamboat rides through the Dells. One local white entrepreneur, "Captain" Glen Parsons, recalled that around 1918, when he was piloting a boat for the Dells Boat Company, many tourists would ask him questions about Indians. Seeing an opportunity to make some extra money, he approached a Ho-Chunk acquaintance named Russell Decorah to see if he could put together some sort of Indian exhibition for the tourists. Decorah found about fifteen dancers and began to clear brush from what would become the Stand Rock ceremonial location. Phyllis Crandall-Connor, who managed the Stand Rock Indian ceremonial in 1939, identified Winslow White Eagle as the person who thought up the idea for the ceremonial. Crandall-Connor had heard that White Eagle felt that the Ho-Chunks "could make some money by showing the dances to the Whites" and that he had arranged with Parsons to have the Dells Boat Company stop their tours at Stand Rock. There Ho-Chunk dancers presented some of their dances and then passed the hat among the spectators for donations. Once established, the ceremonial rapidly became one of the most popular attractions at the Dells, expanding from an event lasting only five days in 1918 to twenty days in 1919 and then to thirty days by 1920. By 1928 an estimated twenty thousand people attended the powwow during its two-month season.[20]

The third major Indian powwow in the first half of the twentieth century took place in Wood County, east of the main Ho-Chunk powwow in Black River Falls in Jackson County. The powwows in the area shifted location during the early twenties, starting in Wisconsin Rapids (1921), then moving to Dexterville (1923–24), and then ultimately to Pittsville (1925–). Local "friendship" gatherings held at the Ho-Chunk and Potawatomi settlements had attracted both Indian delegations and white interest in the years prior to the introduction of the Indian powwow. These gatherings were described in local papers as "semi-religious" events held for the renewal of friendships. A giveaway at the 1922 friendship gathering included "fancy bead work of belts, scarves, shoulder straps, sashes, etc." and a reported twenty-seven ponies. Such details suggest that the friendship ceremonies were probably ceremonies associated with the Drum religion.[21]

The *Pittsville Record* reported that the impetus for the transformation of the friendship dance into a powwow had come from the Wisconsin Rapids chamber of commerce and "twelve councilmen of the Indians." These councilmen were "Chief George Carriman, Andrew Black Hawk, Sam Little Soldier, Dan Bear Heart, Chief Alex Lone Tree, Chief Young Swan, E. Wilson, Bill Short Horn, Tom Walker, Ray White, Fr. Lincoln, and Jim White Pigeon," with Albert [Yellow] Thunder as "legal interpreter." Lone Tree and White were identified in another contemporary article as the major Ho-Chunk forces behind the creation of the powwow, "backed by the local Chamber of Commerce." One key non-Indian involved in promoting the early Wood county powwows was a local entrepreneur named Ed Keenan. Keenan put on exhibitions with a local Indian baseball team, among other colorful enterprises, and local residents credit Keenan with the decision to organize a powwow in Dexterville. The transformation of these Wood county friendship gatherings into Indian powwows may be the root of the idea I encountered early in my fieldwork that the Ho-Chunk people had invented the powwow by "secularizing" the Drum religion, although powwow performance in the Black River Falls area also shows Drum Dance influence. By the mid-1920s, civic leaders in Pittsville had noted, in the words of the *Pittsville Record*, that "powwows have been held all round us at Dexterville, Hemlock Creek, and at the county seat [Wisconsin Rapids]."[22]

Although Ho-Chunk Indian powwows seem to have pioneered the form, by 1920 a network of quasi-ceremonial, quasi-commercial Indian performances could be found in Native communities throughout the upper Midwest. The Meskwaki Nation, living near Tama, Iowa, developed powwow activities in the second decade of the twentieth century; when the Meskwaki Nation held their annual powwow in 1916, over a thousand people paid admission to the gathering, earning the organizers an estimated $2,000. East of the Ho-Chunks the Menominee Nation had made the annual agricultural fairs encouraged by the Bureau of Indian Affairs into Indian powwow–like events by 1919. To the north the Lac Court Oreilles Ojibwas staged a "Homecoming celebration" on June 19, 1919, for soldiers returning from World War I. Following the Corpus Christi procession, a banquet for forty-six returned Indian servicemen was held with a "Victory dance" conducted in full regalia. The next year dances were staged throughout August by the Hayward area publicity association. They also performed dances at the Fourth of July celebration.[23]

By the early 1920s Ho-Chunk Indian powwows generally lasted three or four days, beginning on Friday evening and finishing Monday evening. The central dances presented were "war dances" (probably drawn from Heylushka society dances) with a set of additional dances presented over the course of the weekend. The *Banner-Journal* advised its readers in 1922 that "the best of the dancing is always given on Sunday evening, when the squaw [*sic*] dance, medicine dance and the war whoops are featured." In 1917 the schedule for the powwow noted that the morning (9:30–noon) of both Friday and Saturday would be devoted to "Indian Ceremonies and Dances," the afternoon to "Green Corn" and "war dances," and the evening to "squaw dance" and "some other interesting Indian dances, like Fish, Goose, and Indian soldier Dance." Sunday was generally similar in its program, beginning with War dancing in the morning and continuing in the afternoon, along with an afternoon lacrosse game and an evening of women's dance and other special dances. Monday featured more War dancing in the morning and afternoon as well as foot races, another lacrosse game, "and other interesting contests and ceremonies" The Wood County powwows of the early and mid-twenties resembled the Black River Falls powwow of the same period, although at first they featured "friendship dances" every afternoon and evening rather than "war dances." Similar special interest dances were offered, including the Chicken, Brave Man, War, Swan, Snake, Green Corn, Victory, Squaw, Over Sea, Calumet, and Feather Dance.[24]

An important feature of Indian powwows both at Black River Falls and in Wood County was athletic competition, including events similar to those introduced into the homecoming powwow by 1905. The *Banner* assured its readers in 1920 that "besides the dances, there will be horse races, foot races, and athletic contests by men, women, boys, and girls." In the 1920s these powwows often still featured an exhibition game of lacrosse ("Indian lacrosse") but more commonly included baseball games pitting the local Indian team against white teams from the surrounding communities. The games, the most significant competitive element in these early powwows, were usually held on Sunday afternoon, when the dancing in the dance arbor was stopped and, in the case of the early Wood county powwows, the crowd was led to the ball field for the game.

In contrast to the Black River Falls and Wood County powwows, both based in part on a preexisting ceremonial gathering, the Dells ceremonial came to focus on the special dances and lacked most of the activities that characterized the morning and afternoon portions of the other Indian powwows. The first part of the Dells ceremonial consisted of what the ceremonial program from the 1920s described as "Old Indian Dances." These included Ho-Chunk War, Green Corn, Swan, Young Maiden's, Snake, and Scout Dances. Ho-Chunk women danced the Swan/Wild Goose Dance, and Ho-Chunk singers were reputed to have a repertoire of ninety-nine songs to accompany it. Also included among the exhibition dances were the non-Ho-Chunk "Eagle dance" and "Flute ceremony," both identified as Pueblo dances. The second part of the Stand Rock program began with a series of historical tableaus, beginning with a historical reenactment of the "meeting of the Jesuit Father Marquette and the Winnebago Indians at Portage, Wisconsin, in 1673." There were also tableaus entitled "The Story teller," "The Warrior, Squaw and Papoose," "Peace Pipe," "Trail's End," "Bringing home a Bride," "The Basket Maker," and the "Tom-Tom player." The second part of the program also featured a series of individual performances showcasing "the modern Indian." The pageant performance concluded with "a beautiful patriotic tableau." At the end of the tableau the entire assemblage "gave thanks to the white man" as one performer sang the "The Star-Spangled Banner" and "a huge American flag [was] unfurled on the side of the cliff."[25]

The program of the Stand Rock ceremonial illustrates what the pressures of a commercial orientation to a white audience could do to the form of the Indian powwow. The ceremonial solved many of the problems with Indian powwows mentioned in the 1909 critique of the Black River Falls homecoming. The ceremonial created a presentation of dance and music that started and stopped at definite and convenient times and was organized internally in a way that conformed to white preferences. Yet this move reveals one of the major pitfalls accompanying the commercialization of Indian performances. In becoming more readily consumable, the Stand Rock ceremonial ceased to become a space of encounter in which whites could relearn ways of interacting with their Indian neighbors. Instead, the model of Indian performance at the Dells transformed Ho-Chunk performers into actors, playing themselves in terms imposed on them by the expectations of their audience.

The Black River Falls homecoming powwow remained under the control of the Ho-Chunk community throughout its history. In 1914 Will Winneshiek and Thomas Thunder were the fair chiefs. Thunder was a frequent leader of the Black River Falls powwow throughout the 1920s, a period during which he also acted as an entrepreneur organizing dances at powwows and fairs held elsewhere in the region.[26] Thunder was the promoter for the 1927 powwow, with James Swallow as treasurer and John Black Hawk as secretary. Charles Winneshiek was elected chief of the 1931 powwow. Although the exact significance of powwow committee roles in the early twentieth century is unclear from existing accounts, the leadership roles of Thomas Thunder and of various members of the Winneshiek family are understood by the present generation of Ho-Chunks as extensions of the duties of the Thunder and Winneshiek families as chiefly lineages. Contemporary community remembers members recall that Thunder would spend an entire year collecting horses, blankets, and other valuables to give away at the powwow. The generosity of the giveaway and the free meal provided to participants at the powwow are also manifestations of the "Heylushka way." After Thunder's death John Winneshiek took on the role of chief at the powwow in the 1950s and 1960s and also became the publicly recognized traditional chief of the Ho-Chunk Nation, an office that a member of the Winneshiek family continues to fill today.[27]

The powwow officials actively promoted the powwow to local residents. In 1912 Frank Big Soldier, "the general manager of the powwow," made a special trip to the offices of the *Banner* to "invite . . . the white people as well as the Indians to come and see the big sport." In 1914 Thomas Thunder stopped by the newspaper office "and requested us to tell all the White folks of the State of Wisconsin that the Winnebagoes will hold a fair for about a week commencing August 15th at the well known ground about six miles east of the city." In 1920 the *Banner* announced that the Ho-Chunk powwow officials were out distributing handbills announcing the powwow during the week before it began.[28]

By the 1930s local Wisconsin communities had become aware of the prospects of publicity and profit it was possible to obtain by staging Indian performances. In 1930 the Tomah *Monitor-Herald* ran an article on the success of the Pittsville powwow. They reported that "from a meager beginning the pow wow had grown into an annual event of state-wide interest, bringing to that little town a great number of people each year to witness the Indian ceremonies." Pittsville also illustrated the financial promise of Indian performance, having "as a result of these annual pow wows . . . a beautiful park valued at more than $10,000 . . . paid for by the attendance at these pow wows." The powwow had helped "to put that little town on the map" and to bring "many dollars to its citizens, which might otherwise never find their way into those channels." The article also noted the benefits to Native performers at the Pittsville event, who "have prospered through this arrangement and are making well off articles which they sell to tourists who are attracted to that community through the advertising the pow wows have provided." The *Monitor-Herald* chastised its readers for their failure to follow Pittsville's example, noting that "some time ago this paper . . . carried a suggestion for an Indian village for this community, to be maintained throughout the summer months as something unusual to attract stranger to Tomah." They observed that although many had admitted the "value of such an institution, there has never been anything more done about it and the project simply withered and died." They emphasized that the idea was still "worth considering."[29]

Tomah was not alone in considering the potentials of the Pittsville model of Indian performance. A number of local communities either held their own powwows or attempted to do so. In 1932 Charles Round Low Cloud reported in his "Indian Mission" column that La Crosse was organizing an "Indian Pageant pow-wow" at Wigwam Beach Park on August 19, 20, and 21, "both afternoon and evening" in a natural amphitheater cleared from a sloping hillside. Low Cloud also reported that "Wautoma fair wants some Indians to dance at fair grounds." By 1930 Indian powwows had become the newest form of Indian show business, available to civic boosters in towns throughout the area.[30]

Pittsville remade the Indian powwow into an event linked to civic boosterism. Civic leaders replaced Native community leaders as organizers of the powwows. The *Pittsville Record* claimed that civic leaders were able to give powwows "a better grade of advertising and a more systematic manner of doing it." In Pittsville the promotional system included the distribution of handbills as well as banners and stickers for cars and picture postcards distributed by the Wisconsin Rapids Oil Company. No one acknowledged that the Ho-Chunk powwow committee for the Black River Falls homecoming powwow had pioneered many of these promotional techniques years earlier.

The Pittsville powwow was the clearest example of an Indian powwow appropriated almost completely by a non-Indian community. The local newspaper, the *Pittsville Record*, served as a voice for the powwow organizers and addressed the citizens of Pittsville on their behalf. It called for town residents to give the powwow their "undivided suppor[t] and co-operation," and to tolerate the visitors the powwow would bring into the community. "The crowd will not be local," it explained, and would be "bringing with them customs and ideas peculiar to the localities in which they live" that "may not be considered 'just the thing' in our community and we must make allowances for them." It proclaimed: "We, the people of Pittsville and of the Pittsville district, can well afford to stand for some inconveniences for the glory of Pittsville and for the benefit of the park. We are not asking our good citizens to be imposed upon, but to make allowances for the crowd – the jam – that will be here Saturday and Sunday."[31]

As the Pittsville powwow became increasingly non-Indian in leadership, its identity as an Indian event was eroded in the name of entertainment. The *Pittsville Record* declared: "While . . . the Indian still holds an interesting place with the average White American . . . the pow-wows given at Pittsville are encouraged with the idea always of giving the public something new in this class of entertainment." The Pittsville powwow's organizers soon introduced novel attractions to supplement what Pittsville came to call "the Red Man's portion of the pow-wow." These additional attractions included merry-go-rounds and Ferris Wheels "for the delight of the children" and as many other novelties as could be readily arranged. The *Record* promised visitors: "These [*sic*] won't be a dull moment. There will always be something to do and see." The specialty attractions at the Pittsville powwow included an exhibition of fancy roping by "Chief Bear Face," an "Oklahoma Indian." Mary Red Eagle, "heralded from coast to coast, and a favorite at Hollywood," performed songs at the park bandstand. By the end of the 1930s the specialty attractions brought in to "to balance the program" included an escape artist, a tap dancer, and a "chair novelty act." The Indian dancing at the powwow, bringing the "constant tum-tum [*sic*] of the Indian drum" served to "lend fascination to the weirdness of it all." By this point the Pittsville powwow had clearly become more of a carnival that featured Indian dancing than an Indian community gathering open to white visitors.[32]

Even though contemporary newspaper accounts assured potential customers for the Stand Rock Indian ceremonial that "the program is staged by the Indians no white people participating," the ceremonial itself was closer to the Pittsville model in having non-Indians play formative roles in its organization. In 1929 the Crandall family and Wisconsin Dells Boat Company took over running the ceremonial. Glen Parsons leased new land and set up a second attraction where Ho-Chunk performers could stage an "Indian festival" in June and July. The Stand Rock ceremonial, "sponsored every season by the Dells Boat Company," began in late June and was to continue until September 3. It had grown to be one of the chief attractions at the Dells. The stars of the ceremonial included Chief Silvertongue, "a tenor of supreme quality"; Chief Evergreen Tree, "an impersonator of birds and animals that has no equal"; Little Moose, "a dramatic reader of a type hardly ever seen"; and Blue Bear, "a baritone singer with a voice as clear as crystal." According to Phyllis Crandall-Connor the prominent places given to these performers caused resentments among Ho-Chunk performers.[33]

Even when reduced to the status of hired performers, the Ho-Chunks still exercised some control over the Pittsville and Stand Rock performances. Ho-Chunk performers made decisions about which dances in their cultural repertoire would be performed at each venue. When a Pathe News crew from Chicago came to the 1927 Pittsville powwow to film the event for a newsreel that the Pittsville promoters hoped would "go out into the world heralding the Indian show at Pittsville," the Ho-Chunk performers protested and stopped the filming. And in 1938 Phyllis Crandall-Connor admitted to Leo Srole that her plans to expand the ceremonial at the Dells had run into resistance from the Ho-Chunk dancers, who would agree to perform only a portion of their repertoire of ceremonial dances for a white audience.[34]

The Dells was a unique site for Indian performance, and while similar pageants developed elsewhere in time, it was the Pittsville powwow that exerted a more tangible influence on Indian powwows in the state. The Pittsville powwow was such a alluring example of the promise of Indian powwows for promoting local communities that even the Black River Falls powwow was almost co-opted by civic boosters. In 1937 the Black River Falls powwow was staged in Merrillan, a small town not far from Black River Falls; by 1938 Merrillan officials were taking the lead in promoting the event. The Merrillan news column in the *Banner-Journal* reported that "Mayor Hendrix and Alderman Erickson of the 37th ward" had been seen around the area distributing powwow advertising. Ultimately, the Merrillan powwow became established as a second event for several years, but the original Ho-Chunk powwow endured as the only one of the Ho-Chunk Indian powwows that continued to be truly organized and controlled by the Ho-Chunk community.[35]

The Black River Falls homecoming powwow was nonetheless affected by the developments at Pittsville and Stand Rock. The *Banner-Journal* wrote in

1926 that the management of the powwow had promised that the powwow that year would feature a novel display of "the Charleston [, by] Alex Lonetree and Dan Bear Heart . . . in war paint and feathers." A noted Ho-Chunk performer, "White Wing" from Wittenberg, "a professional entertainer [who] has traveled extensively with the Orpheum circuit and on the stage [and] has made quite a name for himself as a singer, actor, and poser" was announced as a "stellar attractions." Yet they seemed to resist some of the development at the other Indian powwows. The *Banner-Journal* reported that the powwow organizers intended to make "every effort" to "furnish good, clean amusement to the visitors" but also assured readers that they would be "adhering [to] the Indian costume and custums [*sic*] as closely as possible."[36]

By the 1930s the Indian powwows had lost the delicate balance between the demands of Indian participants and those of white spectators characteristic of the earliest powwows in Black River Falls. The host-guest model of the early Black River Falls powwows suggested that the powwow could be a place where white people learned to interact with Indian people in more human ways, but the later performer/performance model emphasized, and even essentialized, the differences between Indian and white.

Yet, for all the changes they introduced into the form and goals of the Indian powwow, even the Pittsville and Stand Rock performances could serve Ho-Chunk performers as sites for cultivating community, albeit a community limited to Indians. Newspaper accounts of the Pittsville powwow reported that many Indian delegations arrived early "for the purpose of visiting before the regular ceremonies of the pow-wow commence." The *Record* explained in one report that "generally, the delegations are headed by the chiefs, or 'head men' of the tribes, although there is occasionally a stray family or even a stray Indian arriving. As a rule, however, they arrive in squads, and as they arrive they are assigned quarters about the grounds by Indians who have this matter in charge." The delegations arrived early, it was explained, to "come to pay their respects to local chiefs and friends of years gone by. They expect to meet their companions here and have a regular Indian visit before the big doings commence. Presents of wampum belts, headgear, and shoulder straps are already being made. Buckskin wear is another article of exchange and in the earlier days before the advent of the automobile, ponies were considered a highly prized article of gift."[37]

There were also reports of delegations at most of the major Indian powwows. The *Pittsville Record*, reporting on the 1925 Pittsville powwow, said that the Ho-Chunks had "sent out invitations" to many tribes, including "the Sioux, Fox, Osage, Pottawatomies, Chippewas, Odanas and the Cherokees, from all parts of the Mississippi Basin and the Midwest," and the powwow included delegations from "the Osage of Oklahoma, the Sax [*sic*] and Sioux, of the Crow reservation, Chippewas, from Coeur de Ray [*sic*], Winnebagoes and Pottawatomies from Nebraska and Wisconsin." A featured event at the 1939 Merillan powwow was the presentation of a drum to the Ho-Chunks by the Ojibwas in recognition of their "mutual friendship."[38]

The establishment of the camps at the Wisconsin Dells ceremonials indicates the extent to which the camps surrounding the Indians powwow could create a space for traditional ideas of collective social space. Glen Parsons recalled that when the Ho-Chunks had set up their camps at the Stand Rock ceremonial, and later at his own trading post, they had organized themselves according to traditional ideas about the spatial distribution of clans. The rule was that "whenever laying out a village to wait first for the man closest to the Chief's clan [Thunder] to put down his house." When Parson's village was built in 1937, the people insisted on waiting until Scott Mokey selected a site, and when setting up the Stand Rock camp, they waited for Tom Thunder to "settle" first. Once the Thunder clan had established its lodge, "the Bear clan was [then] to select a site to the north, Thunder to the east, Bird clan to the south, Deer clan to the west, with the closest relatives to the chief nearest to the chief's dwelling." Parson's account provides some insight into the famous diagrams of Ho-Chunk villages collected by Paul Radin in the early twentieth century and published in his book *The Winnebago Tribe.*[39]

Yet, at Pittsville and Stand Rock, even such authentic moments of community for Indian performers were marketed to white audiences as enticing objects to be consumed. The promoters of the Pittsville powwow advertised the powwow as a chance "to study the Indian as he is at home in peace – the barbecue of whole beeves, the teepees, the papooses, the squaws, bucks – everything pertaining to Indian life in camp." Parson's Indian village advertised that the performers were "housed in habitations built after the same plan as used by these Indians during their wild state, so that visitors to the village can see just how the aborigines lived before they were disturbed by the white man." The possibility of cross-cultural and cross-racial community had been supplanted by yet another spectacle, one that reduced Indian performance into another venue in which whites could reaffirm their differences and distance from Indians.[40]

By the 1940s the conflict between commerce and community in the three main Ho-Chunk Indian powwows had reached a climax. According to anthropologist Nancy Oestreich Lurie, the Ho-Chunk powwow near Black River Falls was discontinued during the years of World War II because members of the community had come to disapprove "of attempts to commercialize the gathering." Work in wartime industries left little time or economic need for commercial performance. Ho-Chunk performances at the Dells (Stand Rock) ceremonial were also marked by conflict. Phyllis Crandall-Connor told Leo Srole in 1938 that she was "sure that none of [the Ho-Chunk dancers] really believe that we make no profit out of the Show."[41]

With communal control of the most commercialized versions of the Indian powwows lost, Ho-Chunk performers began to complain that they were being exploited. In the late 1950s dancers at the Dells investigated the possibility of a lawsuit against the operators of the Stand Rock Indian ceremonial, charging that the conditions of their employment were intolerable and exploitative. Some outside groups consulted by the Ho-Chunk performers noted that if the Ho-Chunks could unite as a group, they could probably close down the ceremonial, since it would be economically unfeasible to "import Indians to fully staff the show." While the operators of the Stand Rock ceremonial never replaced Ho-Chunk performers, the promoters of the Pittsville powwow did, employing Chippewa performers from Hayward's Historyland attraction when the Ho-Chunks asked for an increased fee for powwows in the late 1940s. In both locations Indian powwows had become little different from other forms of white-controlled Indian show business.[42]

The creation, spread, and eventual decomposition of the Indian powwow provides an important historical context for analyzing the emergence of the "modern" powwows of the second half of the twentieth century. The Ho-Chunk community revived their Black River Falls powwow following World War II, eventually moving it to Labor Day weekend. They also added another annual powwow on Memorial Day weekend, one designed to honor Ho-Chunk veterans of the American military. Ho-Chunk people continued to dance at the Stand Rock Indian ceremonial in the Dells but came to Black River Falls for the powwow because, as the *Banner-Journal* explained, the local powwow "serve[d] as a special family gathering for many of them." Both the Labor Day and Memorial Day powwows were open to white visitors but no longer charged them an admission fee, instead collecting "a free will offering . . . to help defray the cost of the lights, loudspeaker equipment, etc. as well as to pay for the food for the dancers." The new form of Ho-Chunk powwows subordinated the earlier emphasis on encouraging non-Indians to attend the powwow, but it was not possible to escape their presence entirely.[43]

The Indian powwow offers an important lesson in the challenges of attempting to reconcile commerce with community. The issues that originally led the Ho-Chunk people to create the Indian powwow combined with those that arose as they lost control over its subsequent development to provide a context for Ho-Chunk participation in the development of the modern intertribal powwow. That development, signaled by introduction of intertribal dance contests, represents the next chapter in the Ho-Chunk people's local history of powwow performance.

ACKNOWLEDGMENTS

I would like to thank George Garvin, Nancy Oestreich Lurie, Myrtle Long, Cara Lee Murphy, William Hiles, Nancy Pollack, Gladys Jones, Mary I. Murray-Woods, Matthew Mason, Raymond D. Fogelson, Terry Straus, Laura Graham, Jodie Byrd, and my parents, Janet and Paul Arndt, for their assistance and/or encouragement during my research and writing of this article. I would also like to thank the staffs of the Wisconsin State Historical Society Library, the Iowa State Historical Society Library in Iowa City, the Chicago Historical Society, the Jackson County History Room, and the Monroe County Historical Society for their help.

NOTES

1. "Great Pow-wow by the Indians," *Badger State Banner*, August 27, 1908.

2. "Great Pow-wow by the Indians," *Badger State Banner*, August 27, 1908; "Redskins Have Heap Big Time," *Badger State Banner*, August 19, 1909.

3. For a description of the circuit, see Charles Round Low Cloud, "The Indian News" (column), *Banner-Journal* (Black River Falls WI), August 19, 1939.

4. See Nancy Oestreich Lurie, "Winnebago," in *Handbook of North American Indians*, ed. William C. Sturtevant, vol. 15, *Northeast*, ed. B. G. Trigger, 690–707 (Washington DC: Smithsonian Institution, 1978). On the removal era, see Lawrence W. Onsager, "The Removal of the Winnebago Indians from Wisconsin in 1873–1874" (master's thesis, Loma Linda University, 1985).

5. *Jackson County Journal* (undated clipping ca. 1906).

6. For a report on the conditions of the Ho-Chunk community (in 1960) mentioning their "caste-like" position of poverty in Wisconsin, see Helen Miner Miller and Nancy Oestreich Lurie, *Report on Wisconsin Winnebago Project: Contribution of Community Development to the Prevention of Dependency* (Washington DC: U.S. Social Security Administration, 1963).

7. Onsager, *The Removal of the Winnebago Indians.*

8. *Jackson County Journal*, August 8, 1895; "Indian War Dances," *Badger State Banner*, August 29, 1895; *Jackson County Journal*, September 4, 1895; *Badger State Banner*, October 17, 1895.

9. "To [sic] Good Attractions," *Badger State Banner*, July 23, 1908.

10. Low Cloud gained nationwide attention for his distinctive voice. For biographical details and selections from his columns, see William Leslie Clark and Walker D. Wyman, *Charles Round Low Cloud: Voice of the Winnebago* (Park Falls: University of Wisconsin, River Falls Press, 1973).

11. Low Cloud, "The Indian News" (column), *Banner-Journal*, August 19, 1939.

12. Paul Radin, "The Autobiography of a Winnebago Indian," *University of California Publications in American Archaeology and Ethnology* 16, no. 7 (1920); Sam Blowsnake, *Crashing Thunder: The Autobiography of an American Indian*, ed. Paul Radin (New York: Appleton, 1926).

13. Blowsnake, *Crashing Thunder*; Louise Phelps Kellogg, "The Winnebago Visit to Washington in 1828," *Transactions of the Wisconsin Academy of Sciences, Arts, and Letters* 29 (1935): 351–52.

14. "Indian Villages at the World's Fair," *Badger State Banner*, June 1893; "Return as Freaks: Descendants of Chicago's Original Settlers Come to Town," *Chicago Daily Tribune*, July 1, 1893; *Badger State Banner*, September 16, 1897; *Badger State Banner*, August 4, 1898; *Badger State Banner*, September 8, 1898.

15. "The Winnebago Grand Annual," *Black River Falls Banner*, July 2, 1905; "Great Pow-wow by the Indians," *Badger State Banner*, August 27, 1908; "Redskins Have Heap Big Time," *Badger State Banner*, August 19, 1909.

16. "Indians Lack System," *Badger State Banner*, August 26, 1909.

17. "Great Pow-wow by the Indians," *Badger State Banner*, August 27, 1908.

18. Nancy Oestreich Lurie discusses some of the differences in the way Native peoples such as the Ho-Chunk conceptualize money in her article "Money, Semantics, and Indian Leadership," *American Indian Quarterly* 10, no. 1 (1987): 47–63.

19. Steven Hoelscher, "A Pretty Strange Place: Nineteenth Century Scenic Tourism in the Dells," in *Wisconsin Land and Life*, ed. Robert Clifford Ostergren and Thomas R. Vale, 424–49 (Madison: University of Wisconsin Press, 1997).

20. Glen Parsons and Phyllis Crandall-Connor were interviewed (separately) October 12, 1938, by Leo Srole, a field worker from the University of Chicago (Special Collections, the Regenstein Library, the University of Chicago); "Indian Ceremonial Big Event at Stand Rock," *Kilbourn Weekly*, July 11, 1929.

21. "Big Pow-wow at County Seat Town," *Pittsville Record*, August 4, 1921; "To Have Heap Pow-wow," *Pittsville Record*, June 13, 1925; William Hiles Sr. and Sheryl Hiles, *Yellow River Pioneers* (Amherst WI: Palmer Publications/Pittsville Historical Society, 1987).

22. "Big Pow-wow at County Seat Town"; "To Have Heap Pow-wow"; Hiles and Hiles, *Yellow River Pioneers.*

23. "Indians Prepare for Corn Dances," *Gladerook (Iowa) Northern*, July 29, 1921, Iowa State Historical Society Clippings File; "Indian Fair Next Week," *Shawano County Advocate*, September 9, 1919; "Keshena Fair Drawing Record Crowds," *Shawano County Advocate*, September 18, 1919; "Indian Fair Next Week," *Shawano County Advocate*, September 7, 1920; *Sawyer County Record*, June 26, 1919; "Indian Dances a Big Success," *Sawyer County Record*, August 10, 1919; "Grand Celebration, Hayward Wisconsin, July 5th," *Sawyer County Record*, June 10, 1920; "Big Indian Powwow at the Trading Post," *Sawyer County Record*, September 16, 1920; Nancy Pollack, interview with the author, July 2001, Lac Courte Des Oreilles, Wisconsin.

24. *Badger State Banner*, August 24, 1922; "Indians to Have Dance," *Badger State Banner*, August 9, 1917; "Indian Pow Wow Well Attended," *Marshfield Herald*, August 29, 1924.

25. Chief Za-Za-Mo-Ne-Ka ("He Who Walks Alone") [Glenn Parsons], "The Indian Ceremonial Dances at the Dells" (descriptive program, State Historical Society of Wisconsin Pamphlet Collection Pam 57-2060); Phyllis Crandall-Connor, interview with Leo Srole, October 12, 1938; "Indian Ceremonial Big Event at Stand Rock," *Kilbourn Weekly*, July 11, 1929.

26. *Badger State Banner*, August 17, 1922; *Badger State Banner*, August 24, 1922. See also, among many mentions of Thunder's role in other Indian powwows, his organizing of a group from Hunter's Bridge to put on a powwow at the fairgrounds in Galesville, Wisconsin, in 1933, as discussed in Charles Round Low Cloud, "Indian Mission" (column), *Banner-Journal*, August 23, 1933; *Galesville Republican*, August 24, 1933.

27. "Heap Big Injun Says Fair: To Be Held at Reservation, Beginning August 14th," *Badger State Banner* (undated clipping ca. 1914); *Banner-Journal*, August 17, 1927; "Indian Pow-Wow a Success," *Banner-Journal*, August 20, 1930; "Indian Pow-Wow Successful," *Banner-Journal*, August 9, 1933; Myrtle Long, interview with the author, March 24, 2005; George Garvin, interview with the author, March 24, 2005.

28. "Winnebagoes to Have Big Dance," *Jackson County Journal*, August 15, 1912; "Heap Big Injun Says Fair"; "Winnebagoes Will Celebrate," *Badger State Banner*, July 29, 1920.

29. The (Tomah) *Monitor-Herald* article was reprinted in the (Black River Falls) *Banner-Journal* as "Indian Pow Wows Net Town $10,000," June 18, 1930.

30. Low Cloud, "Indian Mission" (column), *Banner-Journal*, August 17, 1932 (in this column, Low Cloud appears to be quoting a press release for the event); Low Cloud, "Indian Mission" (column), *Banner-Journal*, September 14, 1932.

31. "Be Good to Our Visitors," *Pittsville Record*, August 13, 1925; "Help Advertise the Pow-wow," *Pittsville Record*, July 22, 1926; "Welcome to Pittsville," *Pittsville Record*,

August 4, 1927; "Best Pow-wow Ever – Record for Year 1927," *Pittsville Record*, August 11, 1927.

32. "Annual Pow-wow Again Proves Successful," *Pittsville Record*, August 10, 1939; " 'All Ready' for Big Pow-wow Here This Week End, Aug. 4, 5, 6," *Pittsville Record*, August 3, 1939; "Annual Indian Pow-wow Will Start on Friday," *Pittsville Record*, August 11, 1938.

33. "Capt. Parsons Will Put on Show at Van Hill," *Kilbourn Weekly*, May 30, 1929; "Indian Ceremonial Big Event at Stand Rock," *Kilbourn Weekly*, July 11, 1929; Crandall-Connor, interview with Leo Srole, October 12, 1938.

34. "Best Pow-wow Ever – Record for Year 1927," *Pittsville Record*, August 11, 1927; Crandall-Connor, interview with Leo Srole, October 12, 1938.

35. "Annual Winnebago Pow-wow," *Banner-Journal*, August 4, 1937; see also news item in the August 4 and 11, 1937, editions of the *Banner-Journal*.

36. *Banner-Journal*, August 18, 1926; *Banner-Journal*, August 25, 1926.

37. "Indians Are Gathering for Pittsville's Big Show," *Pittsville Record*, August 4, 1927.

38. "Indian Powwow, Aug. 14, 15, 16, 17," *Pittsville Record*, August 13, 1925; "White Cloud, Survivor of Custer's Last Stand," *Pittsville Record*, July 29, 1926; "Many Indians Here – More Arriving Daily," *Pittsville Record*, August 5, 1926; "Merrillan Indian Pow Wow," *Banner-Journal*, August 9, 1939; Charles Round Low Cloud, "The Indian News" (column), *Banner-Journal*, August 19, 1939.

39. Parsons, interview with Leo Srole, October 12, 1938; Paul Radin, *The Winnebago Tribe* (1923; reprint, Lincoln: University of Nebraska Press, 1990).

40. "Heap Indian Pow-wow to Be Held at Pittsville, Aug. 4–5–6–7," *Pittsville Record*, July 28, 1927.

41. Nancy Oestreich Lurie, "The Winnebago Indians: A Study in Culture Change" (unpublished PhD diss., Northwestern University, 1952), 275n13; Crandall-Connor, interview with Leo Srole, October 12, 1938.

42. The labor situation at the Dells is discussed in archival materials from the Illinois-Wisconsin Friends Committee for American Indians, State Historical Society of Wisconsin; "Final Arrangements for Indian Pow-wow," *Pittsville Record*, July 24, 1947; "Large Crowds Attend Celebration in City," *Pittsville Record*, August 7, 1947.

43. "Hundreds See Thunderbird Lodge Dedication," *Banner-Journal*, May 31, 1961; "Big Labor Day Week End Pow-wow," *Banner-Journal*, August 30, 1961; "Pow Wow Memorial Day," *Banner-Journal*, May 23, 1962; "Winnebagoes Announce Two-day Pow-wow," *Banner-Journal*, August 29, 1962.

LORETTA FOWLER

4. Local Contexts of Powwow Ritual

The powwow is possibly the most important community ritual on the Plains. Viewing the powwow in its ritual and symbolic dimensions reveals the wide range of ways the powwow affects individuals and communities and allows them to act on their social and cultural world. Here I will draw on a large literature on ritual symbolism (see Kertzer 1988, 1–14, for a summary) to explore the powwow historically and ethnographically as a ritual process. As culturally and socially standardized and repetitive action wrapped in a web of symbolism, ritual – having both cognitive and emotional effect – builds individuals' confidence in themselves, in others, and in their local tribal community.

The multivocality and condensation properties of powwow symbols help explain how tribal social and symbolic forms coexist with those common to several tribes and, although stimulated by intertribal developments or diffusions, how they can help revitalize local institutions or can work to precipitate innovations compatible with those traditions. Powwows are expressions not merely of tribal identity but, rather, of a wide range of identities. They are a vehicle not only for creating unity or resource distribution but also for prompting political action, including struggles over leadership and challenges to the status quo (see Fowler 2002, 326–28). Powwow ritual both creates a context for the expression of modern identities, values, and interpretations of the past and is a means by which social cooperation and emotional bonding occur. The powwow is used by participants to effect sociocultural change and to challenge the status quo, for in the context of powwow ritual, change is made culturally and socially acceptable.

Powwows are held at least annually in tribal communities, and these gatherings attract the entire tribal membership (enrolled and nonenrolled, local resident and nonresident), regardless of economic circumstances, religious affiliation, or political alliances. A powwow provides individuals and families with a large audience as they try to establish identity or introduce change. Interpreting just how these rituals do cultural and social work requires that they be understood in local contexts and as products of local histories. This chapter explores powwow (and associated community dance) ritual by comparing the Fort Belknap reservation in Montana with the Cheyenne and Arapaho community in Oklahoma. I worked on Fort Belknap from 1979 to 1984 and in Oklahoma from 1984 to 1994.

The federal government established a reservation in northern Montana by executive order in 1874 for the Gros Ventres and their Blackfeet allies, but a permanent agency was not opened for the Gros Ventres until 1878. The Gros Ventres had been friendly toward the United States, in large part because their Sioux enemies were targets of U.S. military action and their territory had not been invaded by settlers. This reservation was reduced in 1888 to a tract on the Milk River forty by twenty-six miles, which Gros Ventres shared with Upper, or westernmost, Assiniboines. At the time of reservation settlement the Gros Ventres were wealthy in horses, and men strived to be "prominent" by generously distributing horses, cattle, and other property. The two tribal medicine bundles were the focus of much religious activity as individuals made prayer sacrifices in property and body (through fasting) to these sacred pipes.

Men belonged to Star and Wolf moieties and, with the help of their families, used moiety dances as an opportunity to be generous to members of the other moiety. The Assiniboines were viewed as rivals for political influence with federal officials and for limited agency supplies, so a quest for primacy on the reservation began to preoccupy Gros Ventre leaders just as success in war and raiding against enemies once did.

At the beginning of the twentieth century, the men's moieties were reconstituted as residence-based moieties (based on a north-south division of the Gros Ventre area of settlement), whose ceremonics provided outlets for public generosity and Grass Dance rituals, which were originally "owned" by the Wolf moiety and which involved the recounting of war exploits. These moiety ceremonies helped perpetuate Gros Ventre identity and the values of prominence and primacy until the 1930s, when the reservation entered a period of economic decline not reversed until the 1960s. The reservation was not allotted until 1922, and Gros Ventre leaders succeeded in preventing any reservation land from being declared surplus and subsequently put up for sale. Today about a thousand Gros Ventres and a thousand Assiniboines live on the reservation; the enrolled membership of the two tribes is more than four thousand (Fowler 1987, 14, 54–55, 57, 61–62, 65–66, 69–71, 76, 79, 84–85, 100–102, 199–201).

Post-1977 powwow ritual at Fort Belknap was the major component of a general cultural revitalization movement led by "youths," that is, individuals born between 1930 and 1955. During the relocation era in the late 1950s and early 1960s, many Gros Ventres left the reservation for distant urban areas. They raised their children in cities where the civil rights movement and American Indian militancy in the 1970s were particularly active. Those who stayed on the reservation had been brought up by an older generation of Gros Ventres who did not transfer ritual knowledge and who urged their children to focus on making a good living rather than perpetuating the rich Gros Ventre ceremonial life characteristic of the early twentieth century. The youths, then, who were raised in either the reservation or urban tradition, grew up not participating in Gros Ventre religious ceremonies or moiety dances. Those on the reservation had an opportunity to use veterans' benefits and War on Poverty funds in the 1970s to attend college in Montana, where they came in contact with youths from other reservations (Crow, for example) who had participated in tradition-based ceremonies in their home communities. This was the era of Native American pride (the "Indian boom," as it is sometimes described), and these youths returned to Fort Belknap determined to "revive" old traditions. They focused on the Milk River powwow. The youths who grew up in cities became involved in the American Indian Movement or were influenced by it. They participated in demonstrations against the federal government's policies and were also inspired by the new emphasis on respect for Native traditions. Attracted by self-determination projects at Fort Belknap in the late 1970s and early 1980s, they also came to the reservation determined to revitalize traditional ways of life. Powwows became the vehicle of sociocultural change (Fowler 1987, 102–3, 144–46).

The Native American pride movement was problematic for Gros Ventre youths because the elderly people who knew the ritual activities and supporting system of knowledge and who were considered qualified to pass this knowledge on to subsequent generations in the early twentieth century had declined to do so. Through vision experiences primarily, they had determined that Gros Ventre prosperity lay in adopting Catholic ritual. The youths, then, did not have elderly mentors to whom they could apprentice themselves to learn the "traditions" they wanted to revive. Instead, they revitalized ritual life at Fort Belknap by initiating new rituals in the context of powwows that drew on collective memories, apprenticeship to ritual leaders from other tribes, and new skills they had acquired as members of the "educated" generation (Fowler 1987, 142–44).

The youths who based their revitalization effort on experiences in Montana reorganized the Milk River powwow, that is, the Assiniboine dances at the agency. The gathering also became known as the Indian Days powwow. The symbols of Gros Ventre tradition were drawn from the Northern Plains Grass Dance – both the Assiniboine ceremony and the Gros Ventre rituals that were part of the Gros Ventres' community life at Hays during the early twentieth century. They transformed this symbolism to reflect contemporary goals and values and used it to build broad community support for the revitalization process.

The Milk River powwow drew on an older dance tradition. Assiniboines living around the agency on the northern sector of the reservation held Grass Dances during the early twentieth century. Some Assiniboines had purchased the ceremony from the Crow Society of the Sioux before the Assiniboines settled on Fort Belknap reservation. This society performed miraculous feats, helped the needy, cured the sick, and kept order. When the original members of the Assiniboines' Crow Society died, their regalia was buried with them. In about 1900, Assiniboine elders reorganized the society, making new regalia and modifying the duties originally assumed by the society. This new society danced at the agency at Christmas time and after the Sun Dance in the summer, dramatizing and recognizing war exploits. There were seventeen offices – four belt wearers, a forkman, two whipmen, four singers, one or two announcers, and four women with war bonnets (the latter four positions were added following instructions received in a vision by an Assiniboine man). In the late 1920s or early 1930s, the American flag was incorporated into the dance and gathering, and the man annually chosen to take care of the flag became the de facto leader of the event. Later a woman (the flagwoman) was chosen as well. Other changes in the offices also occurred. "Bumming" sticks were circulated among families, the receipt of which obligated them to donate food for the gathering. The last Sun Dance was held in 1952, and the summer dance subsequently was poorly attended. The winter dance had also lost participants by then, so that by the 1960s only a few families attended (Fowler 1987, 161–63).

The Hays Dance was started about 1902 in the Gros Ventre settlement in the southwest section of the reservation. At this time Gros Ventres organized a Christmas-week dance. The Grass Dance had been obtained from the Assiniboine about 1875, then modified to conform to Gros Ventre understandings and values. In the early 1900s the older men were Grass dancers; they performed during the dance while the younger men took responsibility for accumulating food for the event. Modeled after events on Crow Reservation, the north-south moiety system was organized as well, and the two moieties competed to see which group could accumulate the most donations and recruit the most dancers. Elders selected a men's chief and a women's chief to manage the preparations. A meal was prepared the night before the dance for families who had experienced a death that year; this symbolized the end of their mourning period and their reentry into society. Bumming sticks were circulated. The moieties organized giveaways (the distribution of property to honor someone).

The elderly Grass dancers selected younger men to perform in the ritual, giving them permission to wear a belt or dance with a whip. Use of the regalia required the generous distribution of property. Gradually, offices were added and participation in the dance became more broadly based. Men's offices included four chiefs, two belt keepers, two whipmen, a fork keeper, four singers, a drum keeper, a spoon keeper, two announcers, two war bonnet keepers, and a whistle keeper. There were also posts for women: two women chiefs, two war bonnet keepers, and two whip women. Individuals facing a personal crisis could vow that in return for supernatural aid they would help sponsor a Grass Dance. Lavish distribution of property when offices were transferred or when the holders of these positions acted publicly, the hierarchical ordering of the offices, and an association of supernatural sanction with some acts of office holders were features of the twentieth-century Grass Dance. By the late 1930s the celebrations had become less elaborate, and they ceased completely by the late 1950s as a result of outmigration and economic decline (Fowler 1987, 85–87, 157–61, 267n57).

The new Milk River powwow was organized each year by a committee of officers, whose duties were loosely modeled after the Grass Dance organization. Innovations were accepted by people at Fort Belknap because the new social forms were interpreted as traditional custom – that is, old meanings were assigned to new symbolic forms. The Indian Days powwow began with a "grand entry" parade of the dancers who had entered contests and the local organizers (the committee) of the powwow. Veterans hoisted the American flag. Contest dancing, interspersed with dancing to Grass Dance songs by all those who wished to participate, was followed by the selection of the committee for the next year's powwow. The officers for the new year were chosen by those of the preceding year, and officers were socially obligated to have a giveaway in which they distributed property to those attending the powwow. Offices were gender-specific, as in the Grass Dance. Men's offices included flagman, secretary-treasurer, drum keeper, two whipmen, and cultural advisors. Women's positions were flag bearer, head cook and cook's helpers, princess and attendants, and junior princess and attendants (Fowler 1987, 163–72).

Various phases of powwow ritual were associated with traditional religious ideas. Some elements once considered secular were assigned sacred status, as were some elements that were once sacred in a different context. The eagle staff was regarded as sacred, and some ideas associated with the tribal sacred pipes had also become associated with the staff – for example, taking hold of a pipe had once obligated a person to meet a request or fulfill a vow, and the staff served the same function. In fact, newly selected committee members were picked out of the crowd by a man carrying the staff. Men's regalia were not supposed to be touched by women; women's potential "power" should be kept separate from men's. The dance ground was referred to as a "sacred" place; some commented that people could pray with bumming sticks, which expressed the idea that people could enlist supernatural help by property sacrifice as they once had done at the Sun Dance or in sacred pipe ritual. A "pipe man" (a man who owned his own pipe) was asked to pray for good weather at the start of the powwow (Fowler 1987, 168, 171–72).

The powwow committee worked to attract as many participants in the powwow as possible. They implemented the sponsoring of several "mourners' feeds" during the year, where they provided dinner to families who had lost loved ones. These feasts both allowed the families to leave the stage of mourning and reenter society (without showing disrespect to their deceased relatives) and obligated them to help with the powwow in some way. Multiple feasts replaced the earlier mourners' feed held at Hays at Christmastime.

The committee also distributed bumming sticks throughout the community. The gift of such a stick obligated the recipient to donate to the powwow – sometimes the desired item was even written on the stick. The idea of distributing sticks as a promise for future delivery of property (usually a horse) has great historical depth on the Plains, and the introduction of the bumming stick custom by the powwow committee (as a request for a donation) was a twentieth-century interpretation of this older custom.

The giveaway component of the powwow also took on a new meaning in the modern context. The Gros Ventres had an ethos that stressed individual prominence and tribal primacy on the Northern Plains in the late eighteenth and nineteenth centuries. Primarily expressed in horse ownership in those times, after the late 1970s the cultural ideals of prominence and primacy were symbolized in individual acts of generosity and in Gros Ventre innovations and "improvements" to the powwow, which was formerly presided over by Assiniboines, the focus of Gros Ventre competition after reservation settlement. Some Gros Ventre individuals, particularly those who had lived away from the reservation and who wanted to reactivate kinship networks and inform powwow participants that they had ancestors and relatives in common, used giveaways to acknowledge such ties by distributing gifts to individuals they identified as relatives. In earlier times gifts were given to people who were not relatives (Fowler 1987, 165–68, 171–72, 278n13).

The youths who grew up in urban settings and participated in the American Indian Movement in the 1970s organized another powwow at Fort Belknap, the Chief Joseph Powwow. This powwow, started in 1974, was named for Joseph, the Nez Perce warrior and leader of a group of Nez Perce from Idaho who defied the federal government and attempted to flee to Canada. The powwow honored and memorialized Joseph and his people, who were viewed as victims of the United States' unfair policies. The Nez Perce were defeated with heavy casualties in a battle with federal troops and Assiniboine scouts near Fort Belknap in 1877. The Gros Ventres took no part in the battle. Gros Ventre youths also emphasized that this new powwow was evidence of Gros Ventre primacy and prominence.

The organizing committee officers of the Chief Joseph Powwow were chairman, secretary, treasurer, and a cultural advisor who selected a pipeman, princesses, and head dancers for the event. A delegation of Nez Perce attended the powwow and placed wreaths on markers that indicated where their ancestors fell. The Nez Perce also made a gift of an eagle staff to one of the founders of the powwow; this staff is prominent during the powwow (Fowler 1987, 172–74, 191).

The Gros Ventre and Assiniboine organizers of this powwow focused on reviving nineteenth-century religious institutions, rejecting symbols of federal dominance and Euro-American values, and encouraging intertribal political bonds. They emphasized that the ritual was introduced after an Assiniboine man had a vision experience that validated the innovation. A pipeman (from other tribes) was invited to bless the event by praying with a pipe. The American flag was not incorporated into the ritual; instead, the eagle staff made for this powwow was carried by the person selected as head of the powwow each year. Symbols of anti–United States sentiment included the absence of the American flag, the lack of contest dancing (everyone who danced received gifts), and fewer, modest giveaways.

Gros Ventre youths who supported the Indian Days powwow viewed their participation in the Chief Joseph Powwow as problematic because, in their interpretation of Gros Ventre history, Gros Ventre chiefs made a sacred pledge to ally with the federal troops. To honor Joseph would have been a rejection of Gros Ventre tradition. The Chief Joseph supporters challenged their rivals' interpretation of history and stressed the importance of intertribal opposition to federal dominance. This conflict also reflected competition among youths for leadership positions in the revitalization movement at Fort Belknap generally.

The southern divisions of the Cheyennes and Arapahos were forced out of Colorado and Kansas by the westward expansion of the United States. President Ulysses Grant established a four-million-acre reservation for them in western Oklahoma in 1869. In 1892 their reservation lands were allotted despite their objections, and the unallotted land (the majority of the acreage) was opened to settlement by non-Indians. This initiated an era of repression in which the Cheyennes and Arapahos were closely supervised by federal agents at three subagencies who used coercion to try to end large camps and gatherings, property redistribution (giveaways), extended kinship, complementary gender relations, and Native religion. The surrounding non-Indian community publicly characterized the Cheyennes and Arapahos negatively and appropriated symbols of Indianness for the economic development of local towns. These negative characterizations appeared in local newspapers and were expressed in the daily interactions between Indians and non-Indians in the small towns established throughout the former reservation area (Fowler 2002, xx, 29, 76).

In the 1890s two revitalization movements swept through Oklahoma, the Ghost Dance and peyote religion, which coexisted with the Sun Dance, an annual ceremony of prayer sacrifice that varied in form by tribe. Intertribal exchange of ritual forms in, for example, the transfer of the Omaha Society ritual (the Grass Dance of the Northern Plains) also encompassed intertribal visiting. Intertribal exchange was aided by the settlement of thirteen Plains tribes in west and north Oklahoma as well as the relaxation of travel restrictions that accompanied the opening of the reservations. Peyote ritual became more important among Cheyennes and Arapahos during the early twentieth century. Intertribal dances involved several tribal dance and song traditions, all mutually influential. Giveaways, which functioned as prayer sacrifice, took place in these contexts (Fowler 2002, 28–36).

Extended families camped together with other families on an allotment cluster, often the cluster of a band headman. Gradually allotments were sold, and fewer gathering places were available. Missionaries encouraged gatherings because they were sources of converts; townspeople used gatherings as public attractions to generate business by advertising Indian dances as exhibitions of "savagery" and primitivism. Persistence in holding gatherings was an act of resistance and part of the chiefs' responsibility when they protested Cheyenne and Arapaho treatment. Chiefs also took personal responsibility for accumulating food for a gathering (Fowler 2002, 40–48, 63–68, 74, 81, 84–88).

By 1939 about 68 percent of the Cheyenne and Arapaho lands had been sold and the remainder were tied up in fractionated heirship. The loss of land continued in the post–World War II years. The decline of the postwar economy led to many Cheyennes and Arapahos pursuing careers in the military and many others relocating to urban areas, particularly Wichita, Dallas, and Oklahoma City. Although relocation was a significant factor in Cheyenne and Arapaho life, as it was at Fort Belknap, relocation sites were close enough that individuals in urban areas could return frequently to participate in dances and other events. Dances for soldiers entering training, returning for home visits, and leaving for duty were held frequently (Fowler 2002, 93–96).

The economic and social conditions during the "Indian boom" in the 1960s and 1970s led to large numbers of Cheyennes and Arapahos returning to work or to retire in Cheyenne and Arapaho country. These returning members increased their level of involvement in the powwows that were held in the Indian communities. Many were reincorporated into the dance and gatherings tradition, often as respected elders with ceremonial knowledge. Prominent participation of veterans encouraged the use of the American flag in opening and closing ceremonies and in the Grand Entry. The return of veterans to the Cheyenne and Arapaho community also sparked new interest in military society membership and chieftainship. The community dances began to be called powwows in the late 1940s, and people from different communities began serving on organizing committees for powwows. Some powwows became identified by community, some by tribe, and some as Cheyenne-Arapaho gatherings. Although the War on Poverty and the civil rights movement caused an increase in the number of powwows and the level of participation in them, powwows were not primarily instruments of cultural revitalization, as at Fort Belknap (Fowler 2002, 95, 96, 98, 313n7).

The powwows and community dances were held on "Indian land" in counties where most of the land is owned by non-Indians. A few dance sites were on allotments that were never sold and some were on land recovered from the federal government by Cheyenne and Arapaho leaders. Powwow oratory often includes acknowledgment of the history of land loss, the federal government's duplicity, and neighboring non-Indians' fraudulent acquisition of Indian lands. The fact that gatherings still are held on "Indian land" is both an act of resistance and a way to celebrate the persistence of Cheyenne and Arapaho as distinct peoples with sovereign rights.

The components of powwow ritual, including the giveaway "special," offer opportunities to express identity at the individual, family, community, tribe, and joint-tribe levels. Families sponsor specials to honor a family member by acknowledging a birthday, first entry into the dance arena, graduation, military service, achievement in general, or death. A special may also accompany a family's support of an individual who is trying to effect a life change, to change a pattern of behavior, or to reverse emotional problems. Family members cooperate to accumulate items to be given away as gifts and, at the time of the special, inform the powwow emcee what two songs they want to use. The family dances clockwise during a War Dance song that holds symbolic meaning for them; during the dance spectators around the arena approach them to donate money and then often dance behind them. The family then dances a Gourd Dance facing the drum in the center of the arena, while spectators again contribute and dance behind them. Afterward the family has the emcee call the names of individuals who are to receive gifts from the family (blankets, shawls, and baskets of groceries). The spectators refer to their participation in a family's special as "helping out" (Fowler 2002, 252–62).

The special reinforces the Cheyenne and Arapaho view of the family as a large group of people whose kinship is based both on bilateral descent with great collateral depth and on supportive behavior. Individuals may be adopted or "taken as" kin if a close, mutually supportive relationship exists or is being established. Helping out includes the commitment to help in various ways, including providing emotional support. Males and females play necessary and distinct roles in the ceremony; women are said to be the "managers" of the special. The money collected is immediately donated to others (generally to the host group sponsoring the powwow), and the entire ceremony is meant to express generosity and sharing between family members and between families. This contrasts with the Fort Belknap emphasis on the family's giveaway as an expression of prestige and status through one-way gift giving. The generosity shown in the special is also regarded as a prayer sacrifice that brings supernatural assistance (Fowler 2002, 260–69).

Powwows also have "head staff" (for the Cheyennes and Arapahos, a mid-

1950s innovation). The committee or host organization that organizes the powwow selects head staff. These positions, which are based on age and gender and are distributed among different families in a community, include the following: emcee, arena director, head singer, head male dancer, head teenage boy dancer, head little boy dancer, head lady dancer, head teenage girl dancer, and head little girl dancer. Each member of the head staff holds a special with the help of his or her family. A blanket (and nothing else) is given to the emcee, arena director, head singer, head male dancer, and head teenage boy dancer. A shawl (and nothing else) is given to the head lady dancer and head teenage girl dancer. The little boy and little girl dancers each receive small baskets of candy and snacks. A large basket with groceries and a blanket or shawl is given to the host organization (Fowler 2002, 256–61, 274–75).

The head staff innovation was an effort by community elders to motivate people to participate in dances during a time of outmigration and increased poverty. Initially there were only a few positions. In response to the return of many relatively prosperous individuals to the local community and the tribes' new job programs in the 1960s, more positions were added. The one-gift-per-recipient standard and the prescription of the type of gift create an egalitarian balance among head staff. Although some members are financially comfortable as a result of military or other retirement pensions or full-time jobs, they are restricted from being more generous than the poorer members of the community (who can call on family members for help in accumulating the gifts for head staff). Wealth differentials may be expressed in the Sun Dance religious organization, but not in the context of head staff specials. The custom of head staff also expresses the Cheyenne and Arapaho communities' value of interfamily cooperation.

The powwow tradition also contains a critique of the treatment received by the Cheyennes and Arapahos from the federal government and the surrounding non-Indian community. In powwow ritual Cheyennes and Arapahos demonstrate that extended kinship and complementary gender relations are preferable to Euro-American notions of family; that generosity and sharing are preferable to a perceived Euro-American pattern of materialism and individualism; that egalitarian social relationships are preferable to social hierarchies promoted by Euro-Americans; and that, in contrast to Euro-American views, song and dance are ways of praying. In specials and other components of the powwow, Cheyennes and Arapahos also reflect on and critique their colonial past, sometimes in quite explicit and direct ways. As one tribal member wrote to the editor of the *Wyoming Republican*, a local newspaper published near one of the Cheyenne and Arapaho communities: "[Despite the fact that] our careers were planned out by the [federal] government . . . we mean to hold on to our identity through our religion, cultural ways, language and art" (Fowler 2002, 275).

The powwow allows for the expression of religion, "cultural ways," Native language, and art (particularly in the manufacture of dance regalia). During the powwow itself the emcee's commentary includes overt comparison of Euro-American with Cheyenne and Arapaho philosophy, customs, and values. For example, one emcee's remarks included the following: "We're not in love with that money; we're not in love with material things. That's what those old people taught us. They told us, don't ever fall in love with that money. . . . That type of character belongs to the dominant society. White people like to have lots of things. . . . They don't like to give anything away unless they're going to get something back in return. That's where we're different from them." Cheyennes and Arapahos frequently affirm the practice of not charging admission to powwows; this is a repudiation of the towns charging admission in earlier times to people attending the Indian dances sponsored by the towns. One tribal member referred subtly to the effort of federal officials and missionary organizations to suppress Native religious and ceremonial life when he told an interviewer from the *Watonga Republican*: "We pray for the same things as other churches, and we all pray to the same supreme being." The powwow ritual serves as both a critique of the dominant society and its treatment of Cheyennes and Arapahos and a reinforcement of the Cheyenne and Arapaho social institutions that hold the community together, mobilize people politically, and provide a forum for intratribal competition and challenge of the status quo (Fowler 2002, 269–75).

Throughout the year families and groups sponsor gatherings called "benefit" dances or powwows. These occasions are used to generate public support and enlist the help of individuals in particular political causes. Sometimes the sponsors challenge the tribal establishment, raising money for an effort to file a lawsuit or organize a protest. Other times rivals for a political position or opponents in some struggle organize rival dances or powwows where they can attract and demonstrate public support.

The powwow at Fort Belknap and among the Cheyennes and Arapahos is a modern ritual that, in many respects, represents a consolidation of multiple rituals that were once central to nineteenth-century life: rites-of-passage ceremonies (naming, first significant task, death); military recognition and preparation; political mobilization (including public feasting and gift giving by leaders or would-be leaders); and prayer sacrifice (through feeding elders and property sacrifice) (see also Grobsmith 1981, 46–60). Formal orations on group values and tribal history once occurred in several ritual contexts; now the powwow is probably the most common setting for such speeches. The modern powwow provides the context for all these activities, which allow for the reinterpretation of identity as well as ideas and values associated with group tradition. These reinterpretations facilitate sociocultural continuity. Expressing modern identities (age, gender, individual, family, tribe, reservation, or community) is an important part of powwow ritual, and these ideas are configured differently in different local contexts.

The powwow is probably the most important vehicle for individuals' attempts to motivate others to accept new ideas and to validate new social arrangements. At Fort Belknap the youth leaders worked to negotiate with elders; the Gros Ventres negotiated with the Assiniboines to develop new interpretations of old symbols and to create new symbols to express shared community ideas. Youths, who were initially dismissed by the older people on the reservation, eventually were able to build reputations for effective leadership, first in the context of their powwow activity and later more generally. Among the Cheyennes and Arapahos, groups and individuals tried to use powwows to change both Indian and non-Indian views about Cheyenne and Arapaho life.

For both the Fort Belknap and Cheyenne-Arapaho communities, the powwow provided a context for validating authority in innovative ways. For example, a major transformation in concepts about ritual authority has been occurring in Plains communities. The possession or use of certain regalia or other symbols of human relationships with supernatural forces once was a matter of individual achievement through an exploit or a vision experience or through a long apprenticeship. Now the powwow is one context in which some individuals publicly claim rights and statuses through inheritance from an original owner rather than through achievement or apprenticeship. Thus individuals call attention to family genealogy and history in the context of the giveaway and other activity to generate public support for innovative ideas about authority in ritual or religious realms.

The differences between the Fort Belknap and Cheyenne-Arapaho powwows show how powwow ritual is a product of local histories as well as intertribal exchange. In the 1980s the emphasis at Fort Belknap was cultural revitalization. Because ritual there had been secularized and Native religious traditions phased out, more introduction of sacred elements into the powwow occurred there than in Oklahoma, where the Sun Dance and the Native American Church have had unbroken, ongoing wide support and participation.

Different outmigration patterns also contributed to differences in powwow leadership goals. Youths at Fort Belknap, who were influenced by their off-reservation experiences, assumed responsibility for revitalizing Gros Ventre "tradition." The Cheyenne and Arapaho, on the other hand, had an unbroken history of dances and gatherings in which elders played central roles and children were encouraged to participate. In the Cheyenne and Arapaho powwows, the children's participation and mentoring of children by adults in a powwow setting has had historical continuity and is reflected in the emphasis on children's and teenagers' head staff positions.

In the Cheyenne and Arapaho powwow, speakers more directly confront their colonial experience than do the orators at the Milk River powwow. I argue that this is so because, in Oklahoma, Cheyennes and Arapahos were far less isolated from non-Indian hostility and demeaning public characterizations than were the people at Fort Belknap.

The giveaway ceremonies were a vehicle for prominence and primacy at Fort Belknap, where these values were part of the cultural revitalization process. Among Cheyennes and Arapahos, specials have been more oriented toward community unity in the face of non-Indian hostility – thus the use of the head staff tradition to minimize tension over wealth differentials.

The powwow site also had different meaning for these two communities because of their respective histories. The Milk River powwow at Fort Belknap was held on the site of an older powwow at Fort Belknap and represented revitalization to the people there. The Chief Joseph Powwow, held on the site of the battle, symbolically revisited the battle and allowed powwow participants to critique what happened there and reassert "traditional" values. Among Cheyennes and Arapahos, powwows were held on the few remaining parcels of trust land (some of which was recovered by tribal leaders from the federal government). To Cheyennes and Arapahos the powwow and powwow grounds represented resistance to federal policies of assimilation, including alienation of land and cultural repression.

REFERENCES

Fowler, Loretta. 1987. *Shared Symbols, Contested Meanings: Gros Ventre Culture and History, 1778–1984*. Ithaca NY: Cornell University Press.

———. 2002. *Tribal Sovereignty and the Historical Imagination: Cheyenne-Arapaho Politics*. Lincoln: University of Nebraska Press.

Grobsmith, Elizabeth S. 1981. *Lakota of the Rosebud: A Contemporary Ethnography*. New York: Holt, Rinehart and Winston.

Kertzer, David I. 1988. *Ritual, Politics, and Power*. New Haven CT: Yale University Press.

PART 2

Performance and Expression

R. D. THEISZ

5. Putting Things in Order
The Discourse of Tradition

In the wake of the recent "culture wars" within the academy, the concept of a single Western legitimizing *metanarrative* or *master narrative* – featuring material progress, unified humanism, rational liberalism, and the like (Lyotard 1984, xxiii–xxv) – has been replaced in some circles by the postmodern notion of a myriad of *micronarratives* or *little narratives* (Lyotard 1984, 60), which have now come to represent the complexity of our global historical situation. Applying this notion of micronarratives to American Indian nations or cultures would, in turn, allow us to refer to tribal discourses as actual metanarratives in their own right, only within their own, more limited tribal contexts. In the past, outside bureaucratic or scholarly perspectives (Clifford 1988; Said 1979) have often cavalierly assumed inappropriate, interpretive discursive authority without recognizing the validity of tribal nations' metanarratives. Examining the metanarratives active within contemporary Lakota communities can thus serve an important, and even corrective, heuristic function. I believe two metanarratives may now be said to inform contemporary Lakota culture. The first, less popular in public discourse, is the tandem of formal education and economic progress. The second seeks to celebrate and regenerate cultural integrity through heritage, the Lakota tradition, and particularly, for this inquiry, the powwow complex.

I have elsewhere made the argument that public Lakota identity formation has come to be centered on spirituality and especially on the powwow (Theisz 1987). A variety of sources support the unequivocal centrality of the powwow for self-identification, including Powers (1990), Hueneman (1992), Black Bear and Theisz (1976), Heth (1992), and West (1992). Powers, in his *War Dance: Plains Indian Musical Performance* (1990), observes that in spite of the spread of the Northern and Southern Plains style of powwow, since 1955 few scholars have devoted their attention to this subject (pp. 3, 11, 58). In contrast, he notes, American Indian scholars themselves have recently demonstrated a growing interest in the American Indian song and dance tradition. Four of these important studies, which have been published in the last two decades, are Marcia Herndon's *Native American Music* (1980), Charlotte Heth's *Traditional Music of North American Indians* (1980), Tara Browner's *Heartbeat of the People* (2002), and especially *Native American Dance: Ceremonies and Social Traditions* (1992), edited by Charlotte Heth. These four works share the conviction that Native dance is "among the most profound expressions of what it means to be Indian" (West 1992, ix) and that its value to Native American people "cannot be overestimated" (Heth 1992, 17). Out of the varied tribal dance and music traditions, the powwow, based on the evolution of Plains dance traditions, has emerged as the quintessential public American Indian cultural expression.

To gather the perspectives of actual powwow dancers and singers themselves, I have over time repeatedly sought out and recorded their responses. In one instance as part of my ongoing inquiry into American Indian verbal art – especially the oral tradition, and particularly the song and dance of the Lakota – I designed a survey in 1980 to elicit the responses of well-known, respected Lakota dancers and singers I knew regarding the role of song and dance in their lives as well as in their communities (Theisz 1987). Most of them graciously responded to my questions. In interpreting their responses to song and dance questions, I noted the repeated mention of the importance of "passing down oral traditions," of "keeping up and expressing traditions," and of "keeping the heritage going" in the responses of Fred Stands, Matt Pumpkin Seed, Cordelia Attack Him, and Severt Young Bear Sr., all Pine Ridge Oglala Lakota, and of David Clairmont, Leo Her Many Horses Jr., and Howard Bad Hand, all Rosebud Sicangu Lakota (p. 117). Another set of personal responses from Verdell Blue Arm, a Cheyenne River Lakota, and from William Horn Cloud, Severt Young Bear Sr., Marvin Ghost Bear, and Cordelia Attack Him, all Oglala, commonly stressed the joy of getting together with other participants, the significance of honoring one another, and the importance of recognizing the spiritual dimension of song and dance (p. 118).

To these brief survey comments may be added the more extensive comments of the late Ben Black Bear Sr., a Rosebud Lakota who stressed dancing as healthy exercise, as a release for stress and conflict, and as a way for being open to others and the Great Spirit instead of being restricted to oneself only (Black Bear and Theisz 1976, 27). These various fragmentary or anecdotal individual perspectives on the role of song and dance have been institutionalized in many K–12 school, tribal college, university, and community youth programs that see traditional song and dance activities as building healthy pride and self-esteem (Theisz 1987, 118–19).

The remainder of this study will selectively present and interpret the extended and collaboratively organized comments of the late Severt Young Bear Sr., a widely known and respected singer and keeper of Lakota traditions, on the role of traditional Lakota song and dance. His extended narrative observations extend and deepen the academic insights as well as the brief views of the active song and dance participants presented above. His perspectival discourse may be seen as a variant of the Lakota metanarrative that places tradition, particularly as expressed in traditional song and dance, into the pivotal role of providing a cultural coordinate in the postmodern search for meaning.

Severt Young Bear hails from the Brotherhood Community in Porcupine District on the Pine Ridge Reservation. Born in 1937 he came from a long line of singers traced back to the 1860s. I became personally acquainted with him in 1963 as he was embarking on his own career as a traditional Lakota singer, a *hoka wicasa*. When I moved permanently to the Rosebud Reservation in 1972, we began traveling together as members of the well-known Porcupine Singers, of which he was the acknowledged leader. For the next twenty years we traveled to powwows, locally but also often far and wide from South Dakota to California, from New York to Canada to Texas and many reservation communities and cities between. Over the years we recorded eight albums of songs and received many honors. In his last years Severt Young Bear's status and established authority led him to also become an announcer and lecturer. His many experiences and his insightful perspectives on the powwow phenomenon fortunately were preserved, at least in part, in our collaborative autobiography, *Standing in the Light: A Lakota Way of Seeing* (Young Bear and Theisz 1994), which took shape in our conversations between 1986 and 1994. His reflections echo in ample detail the cursory comments of various academics and Native practitioners presented above.

In *Standing in the Light: A Lakota Way of Seeing*, the late Severt Young Bear Sr. repeatedly and emphatically returned to a paradigm of four concentric circles as a way of conceptualizing the cultural spectrum of contemporary Lakota song and dance as well as Lakota culture in general. I like to think that his model also offers universal applications for other colonized societies and perhaps even for all human cultures seeking to keep things from "falling apart," in the postcolonial formulation of Nigerian novelist Chinua Achebe. Tellingly, Severt Young Bear's various and pivotal experiences as a singer of traditional Lakota songs led him to construct and advocate his four-circle conceptual model. Here is one of his more extensive summaries:

> Last spring I was visiting with an elderly man from Fort Thompson on the Crow Creek Reservation. He was saying that a long time ago there were some people who were called Standing-in-the-Dark. What he means is that when our people gather, they always sit in a circle for ceremonies or for powwows or for any public gatherings. There are always some people who are respected and honored, who are out in the center, whether as dancers, singers, announcers, or committee members. Next, outside of them, there is a circle of people around at a little distance who are supportive of the activities going on out there in the center and who might understand what they mean but are not the real leaders and doers. In outdoor gatherings these are the people who sit under the pine shade and look on and occasionally take part. Outside of them lies the third circle, mostly young people whose main interest in life is courtship and the opposite sex. Rather than sitting, these young people are always restless and on the move, circling the arena over and over, looking to do what is called "snagging," to make time, or whatever term is used. But then another fifty or a hundred or more feet away there is another ring of people way back from the center. This outermost circle includes those Lakotas who lost most of their Lakota values and family traditions and maybe even their language. They've lost their cultural center and so they wait out in the dark away from the center of activity and the center of light. (175–76)

Severt Young Bear then goes on to propose that this model can be applied to secular and ceremonial public gatherings as a means of reflecting about Lakota identity in various contemporary contexts. He reflects:

> The idea of the four circles of Lakota culture today is another way of trying to understand ourselves. . . . What is so disheartening is the amount of people in the outer ring, the circle of darkness, where people live without direction. They need to put things in order, to know their cultural and their family history, to recognize and to keep the limits in this life, to realize the time and preparation needed for the balanced, meaningful life – what we call *canku luta*, the red road. (178–79)

Severt Young Bear pursues his notion of "putting things in order" as a way of centering modern Lakota cultural identity by sharing his experiences with the traditional Lakota music and dance tradition. At a time when the ravages of deculturation are threatening the fabric of indigenous societies more insidiously than ever, he advocates the centripetal potential of understanding and committing to Lakota song and dance traditions as a way of encouraging his own people – as well as all others – to realize a meaningful identity.

Severt Young Bear pursues several characteristic strategies fleshed out by many observations, shared experiences, and anecdotes. In the fifteen years since we began our collaborative project and the seven years since Severt's death and the publication of *Standing in the Light*, a great variety of readers – both Lakota and not – have found his views insightful, informative, and humble but also provocative. In the following pages I will recapitulate selectively his most trenchant insights into the Lakota music and dance traditions, the so-called powwow complex, augmented by some thematic editing and commentary on my part.

Severt Young Bear's superstructure of diachronic reflections emanates from his personal experiences, his family experiences, and the experiences of his singing group, the Porcupine Singers. All three ground his insights and recommendations. Perhaps the most memorable experience he shares stresses the transformative potential of participating authentically in the Lakota song and dance tradition:

> The day I could sit down at the drum and throw my voice out in the pitch, tune, rhythm, and the words of the song, and I could see the people getting up to dance, some women getting their shawls and some guys tightening their belts and fixing their porcupine head roaches and then moving out to dance, it changed me. I never thought I had the gift to make even fifty people dance at a small powwow, or twelve hundred people at a big powwow. Or to have three hundred people crowd around my drum to record my song. That really changed me, my whole way of life. I came out of my shell. A lot of the guys I grew up with thought I was quiet and shy. But singing brought me out into the public with more and more confidence. I began to look at myself and cut down on the thoughtless side of my life. . . .
>
> I think that can happen to anybody. You just have to want to apply yourself and dedicate your life to something special. Whether it's running sweat lodges or Sun Dancing, there are special hardships that you'll have to put up with, but the people, after a while, will know you for that. I think first you have to earn that respect and honor. But it will have meaning and give you a positive direction. (38)

His personal transformation as a result of the song and dance experience is magnified by Severt Young Bear's conviction that although the song and dance experience has always been central to Lakota cultural life, in our day there is a pressing need to recall the proper order of things in Lakota life; he believes that a thorough knowledge base in the Lakota song and dance tradition can have salutary effects on contemporary Lakota people, particularly the young. He states elsewhere: "Singing gives you an identity. So many of our singers today are younger men and boys for that reason. It gives them pride. . . . I think the act of singing gives us a positive identity" (43).

However, pursuing an identity grounded by the song and dance tradition under contemporary circumstances faces significant challenges imposed by over a century of attacks from various institutions, including the federal government, churches, education, and mass media. Two other forces of cultural erosion may also be seen: first, in the Lakota diaspora, also referred to as Relocation, which has dispersed Lakotas to many smaller and some larger cities, such as Cleveland, Dallas, Los Angeles, Minneapolis, and Denver; and second, the influence of Pan-Indianism, which has pulled Lakotas from their tribal identification to a more generic Indian identity. Gone then is the previous experience of growing up in reservation or near reservation Lakota communities and participating in various ways in the Lakota life ways, the *Lakolwicoh'an*. Severt Young Bear recalls the inherent cultural knowledge in place in the early reservation communities:

> Before the reservation days each warrior, woman, or child identified with special songs; they knew and respected sacred songs, individual and public songs. . . . It's the *tokala* (Kit Fox Warrior Society) side of my family that I identify with the most. And all those songs had to be in order. No one before 1880 would go out in public without knowing the proper order for ceremonial songs in sequence. Ceremonial events were *wakangliotake*, the gathering of sacred things, and involved respect and order. These are all traditions we need to put back in order. (86)

Hence Severt Young Bear sees the explication of the song and dance tradition as the vehicle to counteract some of the maladies of contemporary Lakota life, as a sort of cultural damage control. He states:

> I know there's lots of books on culture and history, but what we thought about was sitting down and doing a common-sense kind of thing so our children and our grandchildren and their children can use this book and

> kind of do a positive thing and reorganize those four rings of people I mentioned. (xxi)

> This is kind of a beginning where we're trying to identify those four circles so people can read this book and identify themselves and which circle they stand in. (xxii)

His characteristic strategies are the systematic presentation of personal song and dance experiences, the pursuit of historical contextualization, the etymological implications of song and dance concepts, and ultimately the inquiry into the cultural significance of diverse song and dance issues. In this way Severt Young Bear intends to utilize traditions of song and dance to provide parameters of cultural identity.

He uses the verification of historical evidence to validate a continuity that sheds light on contemporary song and dance practices.

> Music is at the center of Lakota life in the old days and since the reservation days started. No matter what you do, whether it's a man singing to himself because he is a brave warrior, or because he is feeling bad, or is singing to himself because he wants to identify more closely with God, anything you do in your band or community requires singing. Music helped Lakota people survive a great deal of hardship and endure lots of pain because there was a song there. We've proved that in World War I, Korea, Vietnam, Wounded Knee II, and in prisons. Songs give you a lift in life: you sing a song to yourself, or somebody sings an *alowan*, a special song, and you can go on. Singing gives you a chance to feel good, to be healed from sickness. I think this is why long ago we didn't need psychiatrists to come and put us on the buffalo robe in a tipi and counsel us for many hours for ten head of horses. (43)

Thus the historical centrality of Lakota song and dance provided avenues of coping and therapy. In addition, however, the maintenance and healing function of song and dance relies on the tradition of song within a family.

> People go through the traditional steps of Lakota education from their birth. If his father is a singer, he will hold the baby against his chest or have him on his knee or have him sit by him as he sings to implant in that baby the rhythm, pitch and tune while he's young. These will be stored inside of that young boy so that later on, when he wants to be a singer, he will already have some background in singing. We call this

> family tradition. Still today it is an honored and proud tradition to be from a singing family within a tribe or *wicoti* (camp). The grandfathers or fathers would talk to their sons or their grandsons and say, "If you want to be a singer, you've got to learn this song." In the same way, if a woman is a good singer, she will encourage and pass on her gift to her daughter or granddaughter. This is why very early in the morning grandfathers would be singing a song; this is why fathers would be singing songs in the evening, take out their hand drums and start singing. Constantly there is singing in the family. (40)

Particularly after the 1880s when churches and United States Indian policy intensified their deculturation efforts to pull indigenous people – although only marginally – into mainstream American life, traditional song and dance was one of the clearly identified eradication targets of such efforts and, at the same time, remained one of the prime cultural factors of resistance to acculturation. Severt Young Bear illustrates these dynamics in the following anecdote:

> [The traditional singer] is there to satisfy the need of a family with his drum and drumstick, his facial expression and the tone of his voice with which he puts that song across. If it's a happy feeling song, he puts gladness to it. If there is sadness or mourning in the family, he'll sing it so there's sadness in it. And once you start, your throat – its muscles and nerves – and your mind have to be trained constantly by singing. I think of two of my grandfathers. I used to hear them every time they would go someplace; right away they would start tapping a chair or box or the wall and there would be a sound like a soft whistling or they'd actually be singing a song softly to themselves. Even after they got to be very old men, they were still there tapping, whistling and singing. We used to want to sit beside them at church, at Christmas, Easter, or any Sunday, because here the preacher would be preaching up there: "It's devil worship to dance and sing Indian, and you have to be a Christian in order to get to heaven, and so many Indian things are sinful, and you have to watch how you live and save yourself from the eternal fire!" He would point fingers at people and say, "Don't be sinners! Those Lakota dances and songs are for the devil!" All of a sudden Grandpa would start tapping the pew seat and be whistling a song. He used to make us kids laugh because singing was always so much a part of his life. (40–41)

Until the 1970s what would today – one would hope – be seen as a simplistic, misguided, and even vulgar application of Christian thought targeted Lakota spirituality, kinship practices, and the music and dance tradition (including the fundamental giveaway tradition, which will be examined below) as the most odious Native practices. The assimilation efforts of these outside agencies, which correctly recognized the centrality of song and dance, resulted in such strategies as the infamous *Indian Dancing* circulars of 1921 and 1923 distributed by Bureau of Indian Affairs Commissioner Charles H. Burke to area superintendents, directing them to take action to "reduce to the minimal all objectionable conditions attending Indian dances or ceremonial gatherings" (quoted in Beck 1992, 154–57).

Severt Young Bear continues his blend of the personally transformative, the historical, and the familial with his notion of the nature and importance of the singer:

> The traditional word for the singer is *hoka wicasa*. The original term for it is a little longer, *hokaka wicasa* (a man who can rattle his voice), because a man who has dedicated his life to singing has practiced and developed his throat so that he can "rattle his voice" to any kind of song. Maybe the idea of a mastersinger would be a good translation. (39)

> I've come up with a classification of the Lakota man singer. The first one is the individual singer who can get up and sing a birthday song, a memorial song, or a love song. He has a real nice tone to his voice and a pleasant pitch but he is just that individual kind of singer. You put him in a drum group and he cannot sing because he's not loud enough. Then the second kind of singer is what I call part-time singers who sing once in a while just for the fun of it, just for one powwow. They might really sing well and even make a song, but it's just for that one time, temporary. Then we have the third kind of singer, who is just a follower, doesn't sing loud or anything but sits with the group around the drum. He has a drumstick and hits the drum with the other singers, but he can't start a song and you can't hear him sing; he barely contributes. Some just want to be part of the group to share in the giveaway money donated to the group or to be seen as a part of that drum group. I call them drummers. The fourth group . . . [the] *lowan wicasa* are called singers. They follow, they can sing loud, they sing well, but they can't start songs and they don't know that much about the songs. They follow the lead singer or support the two or three main singers around the drum.

Then the fifth category is the very unique singer I referred to as *hoka wicasa* above. He's the guy that can start any song by himself; he can get up and explain a song; he knows which song belongs to which family and, often, who composed it. He knows the history and meanings of songs. He has the unique gift of knowing how exactly to sing each song in the best way to bring out its pitch, rhythm, tune, and words to catch people's responses and to motivate them. We have lots of singers but very few *hoka wicasa*.

Singers can also be classified by the special kind of singing they can do. One is a man that spends all his time just remembering and singing old-time *tokala* (Kit-Fox Society) songs, chief songs, or Brave Heart warrior society songs. That's all he sings. I call them traditional singers. They're older and all they do is sing warrior-era songs. A second one is the Sun Dance singer, a guy who sings those songs from the first Morning Star song clear to the end of the Sun Dance. He'll sing these various songs in special order over and over until he gets them down pat. That's his specialty. We have one like that – John Around Him Jr. A third kind is the ceremonial singer. A medicine man might have a singer or two with little hand drums who know the songs he needs at his ceremonies. So that's all they practice for their father's or grandfather's ceremonies. I can think of Everett Lone Hill, whose specialty was to sing for his grandfather Frank Fools Crow's ceremonies. We also have social dance singers, guys who just spend their time singing those different social-type songs where men and women dance together as partners or in a circle to the left.

Next we have powwow singers who are gifted with full and strong voices because they can throw their voices out so as many as eight hundred or a thousand dancers can dance to them. Yet this powwow singer, if you ask him to sing a ceremonial song or a Sun Dance song, often can't do that. Finally, we come again to those rare gifted unique ones, the ones who can do it all, the *hoka wicasa*, the master singers.

The mind of such a *hoka wicasa* is very unique. It is almost a big song library that he has there. He has to know the meaning of the words, what song belongs to what family or how to put it together, how to get in front of people with that drum, be able to open his mouth wide in front of many people, look people in the eye and start a song. And that's very difficult.

One of the guys that I feel is very respected in that way is Mathew Two Bulls from Oglala. No matter where you go, Montana, North Dakota, even around here, whether it's a powwow or just a small gathering of people for various occasions, people always say, "Matthew Two Bulls, come out to the center! You're a *hoka wicasa*, so we ask you to sing this song." He'll get up and start a song that will fit that place and time and situation. There are lots of good singers around but they're not gifted like him. Everybody looks up to him with respect and honor.

One of the special things about him is that his wife, Nellie, accompanies him.

She is also very gifted as a *wicaglata* (woman singer) who sings behind a man. Matt sets the rhythm and pitch of the song and Nellie comes in an octave higher to blend her voice. She herself remembers many of these songs and often sings one to Matthew to remind him. She also often sings a song by herself and has a wonderful voice that's hard to describe, so clear, high, and full of emotion. No matter where they go, it's always "Matt and Nellie." They are honored by the people and given gifts on many occasions just for being present at some doings. They are the only two around who can do that. Who's going to be the next man and wife to sing like that together? (42–43)

Severt Young Bear's categorization above exemplifies the process of his reflections in his mature years. He seeks to provide an ordered template of different aspects of traditional Lakota song and dance in order to exemplify their interrelationships. His purpose is generally not to achieve hierarchical categories, although he is not loath to establish the *hoka wicasa* as the most highly accomplished "master singer," or to praise those like Matt and Nellie Two Bulls, Ben Black Bear Sr., John Around Him Jr., or Bad Hand Singers, who along with his beloved Porcupine Singers exemplify in his mind the quintessence of the respectful and gifted singers and composers. Finally, in this regard, it should be noted that he repeatedly refers to the "gift" of given talent, rather than personal talent or achievement.

As we absorb Severt Young Bear's shared analyses of Lakota song and dance and the related cultural dynamics, his modus operandi becomes apparent. Categorization allows him to provide intellectual and affective heuristic order to the complexity of Lakota tradition. He also establishes historical and etymological coordinates; supplies his own connected, personal experience; and ultimately provides exemplary representatives of Lakota song and dance who exemplify its various components. At the same time, never in our many years of association did he express any kind of vindictive judgment or personal negative criticism of others. If he disapproved of certain attitudes or behaviors, he expressed his disapproval of the action or behavior itself, not of any individual. In fact, on one public occasion in spring 1993 on the campus of Black Hills State University, which sponsored a program of commemorating Wounded Knee through art, when he was asked as a *takini* (family of Wounded Knee survivors) his opinion of the art in question, he responded: "Who am I to criticize my brother's vision?" He then proceeded to share his family history in regard to Wounded Knee but did not engage in the kind of critical, evaluative aesthetics common in Western thinking.

Yet Severt Young Bear recognizes that criticism has become a common occurrence at contemporary *wacipis* (song and dance celebrations, commonly called powwows).

> I also know that most people sit around a dancing arena, maybe one thousand or two thousand people, to feel good as they listen or dance. But sadly, many of them also go there to criticize. It's really true! They go there to find something wrong: a dancer didn't dress right, or she didn't dance correctly but won anyway, or the committee didn't do this right, or the announcer didn't explain that song properly. But I think, in a way, if you learn to understand criticism, then you know how to deal with it. You can deal with it next time and it will have positive consequences. I'll push that song up a little higher next time I start it, sing it a little slower, pronounce the words more clearly, maybe hit the drum more softly. Sometimes I think about it because you can always learn from it. Other times, when it comes from certain families, it doesn't bother me because I know they don't understand it. There's always good in bad, but if you take it to heart negatively, you can get hurt by it. If you learn how to understand it, you grow as a person. If I didn't live the life I learned from my grandmother and my father or if I didn't hang onto my family traditions, or didn't understand criticism or myself, then at every powwow I'd be fighting somebody or I'd be drunk and make fun of other people. Maybe then I'd slide over to the dark circle. When you are a dancer or a singer, you learn to cope with problems by falling back on traditional Lakota skills. (39)

It should be clear from this particular reflection, as well as others in this summary, that for Severt Young Bear the song and dance complex acts as a nexus for living the Lakota way. This should become even more evident as we proceed.

Singing gives you an identity. So many of our singers today are younger men and even boys for that reason. It gives them pride. Even when a guy gets drunk and sings, he's singing a song to express himself. I think the act of singing gives us a positive identity. You don't need psychiatrists.

It helps to understand singers when you look at their paraphernalia and how it's used. First is a hat. A long time ago, my uncle Henry Young Bear, Irving, and other guys, when we went around singing, we always wore a western hat. Back in the 1950s and '60s, I remember uncle Henry at New Year's or Sun Dance time would buy a felt or straw hat. He'd shape it carefully, and would then put a red plume on the side. It took me a while to understand why. One time I asked him why he always wore a red plume; why not white or blue? He said: "My older sister, Young Bear blood, was killed at the Wounded Knee Massacre while she was just a baby. Since her blood was spilled there on the snow, when I go out in a crowd I put this red plume on to honor my sister and remember."

A hat played a very important part in the traditional singer's life. He wore a felt hat, or straw hat in summer, and shaped it all different ways. There were many different fashions in shaping one just right. They would put shiny pins on it or tie feathers to it. Since the middle 1970s some young guys started wearing beaded baseball caps or feed-and-seed caps, or whatever you call them. But the older traditional singers still wear hats. Even in North Dakota the older singers still wear hats. Most of the Porcupine Singers still wear hats. (43–44)

Severt Young Bear goes on to portray other ingredients of the singer's life, often historically or humorously. He points out the importance of sunglasses, of singers' clothing, of cowboy boots and the drumstick.

Lakota song and dance is, of course, unthinkable without the drum:

Still another sign of the singer is the drum and how the members of the singing group take care of the drum, whether it's a traditional hide drum or a bass drum. Lots of singers now have the name of their drum painted on their drum: Pass Creek Singers, Red Scaffold Singers, or Porcupine Singers. Again, you can tell how sincere those singers are by their drum. Some even honor their drum after a while and treat it as if it were a person. Take our Porcupine Singers, for example. We named our drum *Oyate Ho Nah'umpi* (The People Hear Its Voice) in a drum ceremony in 1974 because that drum brought honor and respect to those singers that sat around the Porcupine drum. We also set some rules: We put tobacco

> on the drum before we start singing and we pray briefly when we make that offering. We never put food or coffee on it; anyone who has been drinking must stay away from the drum; we sing a special drum song as the first song at any gathering; and we conduct ourselves in a respectable way when we set that drum in the center of our circle. Whether it's a powwow, a Sun Dance, or a dancing contest, we treat that drum with respect. (45)

Once again, Severt Young Bear traces the history, etymology, different categories and meaningful aspects of the drum.

> The drum, as far back as I know, has always played a big part in public events. We have three different drums that we use. The first is the rawhide drum, usually deerhide. It is homemade, with a round wood frame. These drums are used mostly for ceremonies today. Also, some families request that you sing at their gathering but that you bring your traditional hide drum. Since you can't control the pitch of these drums except with heat, they are today used mostly only at ceremonies and Sun Dances. Some singing groups like Howard Bad Hand's Red Leaf Takoja Singers (Red Leaf Grandsons) prefer the hide drum on a regular basis for all their singing.
>
> The second kind of drum is the commercial bass drum. Some singers have always liked using them because you can control the pitch with the turnkeys on them. The bass drum really became popular around 1960 when Cook Brothers Singers from Red Scaffold on the Cheyenne River reservation came around this area. They used long sheepskin drumsticks and a bass drum. While the rawhide drum has a sort of flat, solid rhythm with not too much bounce to it, the bass drum has a bouncy one to it. Since the Cook Brother's singing group became real popular in the early sixties, everybody hit the secondhand stores and talked to high school bands to try to buy a bass drum. The tone of your voices and the tone of the drum has to match up, and a bass drum, if you replaced the plastic hide with a deerhide, could be adjusted to do that at any time.
>
> The third type is the hand drum, which was usually used at traditional social dances and some ceremonies. A long time ago, at social dances, four or five guys with hand drums would sit against the wall and sing keeping the same rhythm on their drums. Sometimes they would ask them to stand in a single file in the center of the hall or wherever the dance was being held, and everybody could dance around them because

they didn't take up that much room. In addition, the hand drum was always important for individual singing.

One of the things my dad used to talk about was that a long time ago the Lakota people never had psychiatrists, they never had mind problems or social problems, because every tipi or home always had a hand drum in it and somebody in the family was always singing. He would always get that drum and would sing songs in the evening, or in the morning he would sing. That kept singing in the family. Happy feelings, sad feelings, or whatever feelings that family was going through would have songs that fit the mood. But if you look at that today, that's changed also. The hand drum is no longer hanging on the wall above the head of the father or grandfather or the singer in the family. (45–46)

Severt Young Bear recognizes the role of Native radio stations, such as KILI, in bringing traditional music to reservation communities at different times of the day: "The drum on the wall has been replaced by the radio on the dresser" (47). In our discussions he also acknowledged the place of tape and compact disk recordings, although he was concerned that the latter often introduced non-Lakota intertribal music to undiscerning young Lakota listeners. He emphasized that Lakota youth should ground themselves in their own traditions before embracing intertribal or non-Indian ways.

I think way back a drum was a sound *bu'uta* (hitting the drum). They would strike it to send messages throughout camp. If there was going to be a *tokala* warrior society dance, they'd hit it in a certain way. If it was another type of event, they'd hit it in a certain other way. Sometimes they'd hit it close to the ground by the ankle for a certain kind of vibration; sometimes they'd hit it up high for that sound to go out and echo. The sound of the drum would add a loud sound that accompanied your voice to give it strength and power, or for the Great Spirit to hear your songs beyond your own limits.

Old people said the drum was the heartbeat of *unci* (grandmother) earth, the sound vibrating in the earth. The word for drum is *cancega*, or wooden bucket. It was made of cottonwood and there was usually only one person in the band or tiyospaye (extended family) gifted in the making of drums. It was he who would go to mark a cottonwood tree and at a certain time of the year would cut it down and cut out a certain section for the drum rim. He would then thin it out to the right thickness. He'd then select the right part of the hide to get the same thickness throughout

> the drumhead. If the head was going to be of buffalo hide, the rim would be thick; if elk, thinner; and if deer, still thinner yet. He would put the raw hide on it and then, in his own way of tightening the hide, get the right tone from it. That was based on his dream and his gift. (47)

Once again, Severt Young Bear seeks to establish time-honored practices to provide validity or at least a deep structure of meaning for contemporary variations. It is clear from his next comments that historical precedents serve to validate modern practices.

> There used to be honored drumkeepers in a *wicoti* (camp) who would *bu'uta* (sound the drum) in different ways, so that people in that camp knew right away what kind of dance or ceremony was being announced. Also, like I said, the sound of the drum goes beyond our physical being so the Great Spirit can hear it. Still today, the drum plays an important role in our ceremonies, our Sun Dances, and even our powwows. I think young singers should learn how to treat the drums respectfully and treat their drums according to what their drum is to be used for. (48)

In his customary diachronic epistemological manner – having considered history, etymology, categorization, and meaning – Severt Young Bear proceeds to personal specificity.

> I know of one drum that has developed in a special way. Back in 1963 I bought a bass drum from George Whirlwind Soldier from Rosebud for five dollars. My uncle Dick Elk Boy then put a new deer hide on it. The singing group known as Porcupine Singers traveled with that drum for many years all over the country. That drum received many honors over the years. As I said above, back in 1974 the drum received its own name at Ring Thunder Wacipi Days Powwow. Four respected singers, Dave Clairmont, Ben Black Bear, Matthew Two Bulls, and Cecil Spotted Elk, gave it the name *Oyate Ho Nah'umpi* (The People Hear Its Voice). They hit the drum four times and then sang four different types of songs on it while out in the center of the dance shade to give it the proper breaking-in. That name made the drum a person and over the years it was given a war bonnet, a sacred pipe, and an eagle-feather staff by way of recognition. Every celebration we went to we would write that on the drum: "Mandaree Powwow June 1976," "Fort Totten Powwow July 1978," "Minneapolis AIM Powwow 1975"; you could read all over the drumhead

> where we had sung over the years. As one place and date faded away through use, we wrote in a fresh one.
>
> Old people and young people have come to touch the drum to share its energy over the years; dancers have thrown money on it in appreciation for the music it helped to make. I think that drum also took care of the singers who sat around it in a respectful way. Many years later, when our drum group started having difficulties . . . one day, for no reason at all except political jealousy, someone stole the drum and we never saw it again. Maybe it was meant to be that way. We didn't know who took it; it just disappeared from my house. Months later, one day a woman in my community drove up to the house and after some heavy sighs told me that she found out that her son had taken the drum and burned it in a fit of jealousy. She felt very sorry and didn't know how to tell us but knew she had to. We thanked her for telling us and said we had no hard feelings. We would have to go on. We got a new drum and began a slightly different tradition with it, but it wasn't quite the same; we missed *Oyate Ho Nah'umpi*. (48–49)

This summary of the history of the Porcupine Singers' drum demonstrates how, in the traditional manner of Lakota song and dance, personification – in the sense of creating personhood for "things" – can replace objectification in order to create meaningful, respectful relationships. The inference for today is, of course, to continue to avoid objectification and to carefully seek meaning through creating respectful categorizations, primarily through ritual.

A further dimension of interpolating traditional song and dance heritage to lend cultural substance to modern indeterminacy is song composition.

> Another important part of singing in our tradition is making up songs. It takes many years of singing or a long tradition of singing in the family. Sometimes you just hear a melody on the wind or in your memory, or an emotion causes you to start humming, or you're looking at clouds or some hills, and a pattern in them gives you a melody. The words, by comparison, are provided by something that's already happened or is going to happen that you're aware of in advance. In both cases you know that you won't have that many lines to say something because most of our Lakota songs are short. So you have to try first to cut the expression down to just a couple of lines, but these words still have to tell a story of some kind. Making up a song for yourself to use at a powwow or for a social dance is different from when some family comes up to you and

asks you to make a song for their son or daughter for next summer and then explains the occasion. I might ask about a couple of things related to it so I have the necessary information, and I ask what the ceremonial Indian name is that I will be using in that song. Then, I usually create a new melody or use one I've made up before and haven't used yet. If it has the right tempo, spirit, and emotion, then I begin to put in the words; sometimes words of encouragement, sometimes sad words to make family members cry but at the same time help them to wipe their tears, sometimes strong words to praise someone or give thanks to them for their courage or generosity for being a leader, sometimes romantic courtship words for a rabbit song for couples or a round dance, and sometimes even sassy or humorous words. It all depends on the occasion.

When you make a song, unless it's just a powwow song for dancing with no words in it, then you have to tell a story. You have to tell a story about the person you're dedicating it to. Maybe it's about a veteran and how he was wounded in battle or that he was killed overseas, or how he came home after hardships. You select some words that capture the heart of the story of the person you're singing about or for. (50)

It's funny that these last few years some of the younger singers are making songs with words in them that don't tell a story of any kind. Francis Menard, who passed away a couple of years ago, and some of the other older singers used to get mad and say, "Those are not songs! Those are not songs!" he used to say. Some of these songs would just say, "Mani, mani, mani" (Walk, walk, walk) or "Waci pelo" (Dance) over and over again. Now, in the real traditional songs these words might often appear, like the word *mani*, "walk," showed up in warrior songs because the warrior was walking among the enemy, or his comrades were walking with him, carrying him out of the battle, but these words were part of a longer text that told the story in shorthand form. Now they make these songs with a couple of Lakota words in them but no real meaning. They might have a good rhythm and nice melody but the meaning isn't there. Maybe today's way of honoring people is less personal, just putting some words together. (51)

Once again, rather than identifying specific individual composers or groups who are composing songs lacking narrative content, Severt Young Bear reminds us that in spite of their allusional shorthand, traditional word songs maintained the cultural discourse of Lakota songs that signified a narrative of some sort. He thus exhorts younger song makers to remain within this narrative song tradition.

> It's a unique gift that after a family asks you to make a song, you can sit down at a drum, or while you're riding along someplace or just spending the evening under the pine shade in back of your house – with a gift from the Great Spirit you have the ability to put a song together and fulfill that family's request. . . .
>
> When you honor somebody with a song, you make a song for dancers to dance to. You should then give it as a gift to those dancers so that they, too, can sing it. When someone else sings it, you should be glad and honored that they like your song enough to sing it, and not say, "Hey, that's my song and you can't sing it, because I made it and I gave it to that person or that family." I like it when a song maker hears one of his songs sung by somebody else and donates some money to them and says, "I'm happy this group sang one of my songs and want to thank them with this monetary gift." I've heard in some places that I've gone that certain singers claim certain songs and don't like to have others sing them, but I think the traditional belief is that once you make something, you give it to people – as long as it's not a personal sacred song or a restricted one because it's someone's family song. But then even you as the composer should only sing it for that family or when the proper time arrives.
>
> The Bad Hand Family, my brother-in-laws from Red Leaf Community on the Rosebud Reservation, are really gifted in putting songs together. . . . That Bad Hand family tradition of making all kinds of songs is being carried on by one of their sons, Howard Bad Hand, and some of his brothers who compose lots of good songs. (51–52)

Here again Severt Young Bear establishes the proper historical and ethical context for contemporary song composition as he honors model singers and groups.

In his exposition he then moves along to examine the current notion of the Grand Entry, as the opening pageantry of a powwow, and its place within the Lakota song and dance tradition (54). He also points out how the confluence of *Omaha wacipi* (Omaha Dance society) and Plains *peji wacipi* (Grass Dance) eventually leads to the modern powwow (55–57). At the same time he clarifies how mainstream American holidays were used by the Lakota to circumvent restrictions against traditional ceremonial and warrior society dances. A song and dance occasion, whether fostered by a ritual or a warrior society, and even a purely social dance event would be prohibited by government reservation authorities beginning in the 1880s. A New Year's or Fourth of July celebration would be so much more acceptable (55).

Wrapping up this summary of Severt Young Bear's efforts to establish a coherent diachronic infrastructure for contemporary Lakota song and dance, we must consider his emphasis on giving and feeding as the ultimate purpose for Lakota celebrations.

> Dance, song, and dress are the elements of the performing side of our Lakota powwow or celebration tradition. But the foundation beneath these performances has to be understood. The values we have tell us that once we put on a powwow, when we bring people together, two of the most important things that are supposed to happen are the feast and the giveaway.
>
> Over the years these people here in Porcupine have had some big giveaways. All kinds of material things are spread out in the arena during the honoring ceremony and then are given away: cows, horses, money, quilts, blankets, clothes, dishes, beadwork, etc. Some used to drive a live cow into the arena and have the announcer say, "Okay, the visitors from Rosebud come and kill this cow and divide the meat among you!" They might release a colt *iyuskia* (turning a horse loose) and have all the young boys try to catch it, or they would give a quarter horse to someone. They might also tie money to the mane and tail, or put quilts and blankets on it.
>
> Why do all this – give so many things away to people, sometimes hundreds of dollar's worth or even a couple of thousand? The traditional way of thinking tells us that when you have material possessions, the best thing you can do with them is to give them away, especially to those who are without or are having a hard time. A leader is not the guy who can store up and keep lots of things, but instead someone who will share them with the people. We are taught as young boys and girls that in order to honor ourselves and our relatives, we should always be ready to share. One of our Lakota songs tells us: "There isn't anything I won't give away because my parents are still alive." The ones we love are much more important than material objects. Also, we believe that when you give, you create good feelings and harmony in your community. If you keep everything, you are inviting envy and jealousy. (57–58)

It's funny, when you think of the Christian principle of charity, that once we were put on reservations, both the missionaries and the BIA opposed the sharing of material goods because it kept us from becoming modern, self-supporting American citizens.

I think that the most prized possession to be given away was a horse. It showed our respect for the person we gave it to and also our willingness to give not just little things but also things that meant a lot to us, to give all that we could. There is even a special honor song for a guy who gives a horse away called *sunkah'abiya* (giving a horse). Also they would sing a *wopila* (thanksgiving) song like this one: " . . . *taku ota luha kte, ohunkesni wicak'uwo toksa ake luha kte!*" (. . . whatever you possess, give it away to the needy. You will have it again.) These are powerful words that encourage people to give away shawls and material, wagonloads and pickup loads of goods, or a team and wagon, horses and saddles. There are always special honor songs for those kinds of people. The singers involved might actually sing three or four songs before the giveaway is finally done. And they, too, would get gifts and money as donations from the family. This is why long ago during traditional powwows, the *eyapaha* (announcer) did a lot of speaking, explaining the reason for the giveaway, explaining the person's Indian name and the song sung, praising the person being honored by the family doing the giving, and calling out people to receive gifts. Such a traditional giveaway is pretty time-consuming. But people knew that and prepared themselves to stay a long time. (57–58)

Here again Severt Young Bear extols the importance of appreciating time-honored practices – in this case providing a meal and distributing gifts – the fading of which threatens the very heart of the modern powwow.

But like everything else, the giveaway tradition is changing. We've got brand-new pickups and new cars and can easily drive a couple of hundred miles and stay for just a couple of hours after the seven o'clock Grand Entry and then head home again. The holding of giveaways is also changing for the worse. The feast and giveaway is one of the family traditions that teaches your child respect and honor.

We believe that if something good or bad happens to a family and the family honors that publicly, then that family should pay for the public time and support they receive. This could be graduating from high school, going into the service, getting an Indian name, being honored as a committee member, or because of something bad such as a death in the family or remembering a deceased veteran. You don't just celebrate or bring something sad before the public and forget your obligation to say thank you to people – with words, by feeding, and by giving away. If you do the best you can, the people will then remember that child in a good way because they'll think of that feast and that giveaway. . . .

My grandmother Emma Smoke was a real model for me in these things. She always said: "When you give away, no matter how big or little, give it away in a respectful and honorable way. When you lay things out in the arena and announce that people can come and get whatever they want, then it's like throwing a bone out there and letting the dogs fight over it." (58–59)

Thus thoughtfully preparing and personalizing the sharing of food and material goods establish a climate of reciprocal warmth and obligations and the cementing of social bonds. In addition to giving things out personally and respectfully, Severt Young Bear reminds us why the family giving away will prepare for a year or more to honor one of its own and that we should not give to members of our own family.

In this way the celebration, or powwow, is based on the notion of feeding all who come to participate or look on.

The purpose for feeding is based on similar values. The feast and giveaway go together. First you feed everyone, then the announcer and singers honor the person it's being done for, then that person's family shares what it can and wants to with all the people there. Butchering and feeding are done by the family members themselves or they have someone who is good at it do it for them. One of my grandmother Emma Smoke's ways was that if you're putting on a feed, you're going to kill a cow, you butcher from the knee up and from half the neck down. She always said only a stingy or lazy person cooks the bone and all. . . . I remember her saying, "They are hungry for meat, not for bones and grease."

My grandmother's interpretation was that by doing this in the right way, the next time you have another feast and giveaway, you will have plenty again. That's the way of the Great Spirit blessing you because you held nothing back. (60–61)

Maintaining his basic plan of "putting things in order" through the recovery of time-honored practices, Severt Young Bear concludes his comments of feeding and giving away as follows:

> So the feast and giveaway were the heart of it all and the committee made it happen and was centrally involved. I think if we are going to revive that inner circle and have our youth identify with that inner circle, we should bring back the traditional way of giving ribbons and pennies and say in a nice way: "Okay, grandson, I give you this ribbon and this penny because you have an Indian name. They gave you that name in a *hunka* (making of relatives) way, so now you are on this committee. We want people to come, so prepare yourself for a feast and giveaway so you can properly feed the people, give something to them, and help them have an enjoyable time during the next celebration." In this way, they would learn to understand that in the Lakota tradition responsibility and honor are intertwined. (62–63)

In other sections of *Standing in the Light*, Severt Young Bear shares his views on other aspects of Lakota song and dance. He presents the history of his Porcupine Singers, discusses Wounded Knee II, shares family stories, and reflects on a variety of related subjects. He is careful to avoid any undue claims of authority.

> We didn't want to do this book because I'm a holy man or Ronnie is a most educated person. I think we're trying to orient this, like I mentioned before, from two minds in one and two hearts in one to do something educational. . . . We talked about the four circles in ceremonies and dances and then discussed how this book would do more than just our talking to give some kind of identity, a good identity, for those who are searching. (xxiv)

The Lakota virtue of humility is exemplified throughout Severt Young Bear's discourse and reflects the prevalence of this same dynamic at powwows. Humility is the mark of the mature personality. In the same way patience accompanies adulthood. Once again dance can serve as a metaphor.

> When you do a rabbit dance, you take two steps forward and one step back. . . . So if we can encourage our children, our grandchildren, to do just that, two steps forward, one step back, that way in kind of a warm feeling and at a slow pace, we can encourage our children to identify themselves as Lakota. If we do this, our generation will never end, our

> lives will never end, our family values, traditions, family beliefs – that world will never end. It will be continuous. (xxiv–xxv)

Conclusion

The basic premise of our cooperative narrative *Standing in the Light* is our dialogic valorization of Severt Young Bear's personal, family, and representative Lakota perspectives on the traditional Lakota song and dance tradition. His formulations lend emic support to the scholarly efforts that have emerged since the 1994 publication of *Standing in the Light*.

Representative studies, such as Nagel and Snipp (1993), Hill (1996), Hughes-Freeland and Crain (1998), Guss (2000), and Greci Green (2001), have sought to interpret public performances, such as ceremonies and dances, as "sites for the expression of collective identity" (Greci Green 2001, 1). Uniting these studies is the inquiry into how colonized, indigenous people used public performance as events of self-expression, of resistance, of negotiation of collective identity, and of communal, integrative participation.

In a culturally reductive manner, one that lends authenticity through the vision of Severt Young Bear Sr., a practicing singer of the Lakota heritage, the interpretation of the centripetal function of the song and dance tradition provides a template for the possibility of cultural vitality and coherence. Severt Young Bear's views as a perceptive and widely recognized Lakota participant in traditional song and dance performance provide the credence of an authoritative, personal narrative voice, a voice that should be heard not so much as echoing epigonic nostalgia but rather as providing a significant strain of the Lakota metanarrative celebrating the connective affirmation of tradition, particularly as expressed in the powwow.

REFERENCES

Beck, Peggy V., Anna Lee Walters, and Nia Francisco. 1992. *The Sacred: Ways of Knowledge, Sources of Life*. Tsaile AZ: Navajo Community College Press.

Black Bear, Ben, and R. D. Theisz. 1976. *Songs and Dances of the Lakota*. Aberdeen SD: North Plains.

Browner, Tara. 2002. *Heartbeat of the People: Music and Dance of the Northern Pow-wow*. Urbana: University of Illinois Press.

Clifford, James. 1988. *The Predicament of Culture: Twentieth-Century Ethnography, Literature, and Art*. Cambridge: Harvard University Press.

Greci Green, Adriana. 2001. "Performances and Celebrations: Displaying Lakota Identity 1880–1915." PhD diss., Rutgers University.

Guss, David M. 2000. *The Festive State: Race, Ethnicity, and Nationalism as Cultural Performance*. Berkeley: University of California Press.

Herndon, Marcia. 1980. *Native American Music*. Norwood PA: Norwood Editions.

Heth, Charlotte. 1980. *Traditional Music of North American Indians*. Los Angeles: University of California.

———, ed. 1992. *Native American Dance: Ceremonies and Social Traditions*. Washington DC: Smithsonian Institution Press.

Hill, Jonathan, ed. 1996. *History, Power, and Identity: Ethnogenesis in the Americas, 1492–1992*. Iowa City: University of Iowa Press.

Hueneman, Lynn F. 1992. "Northern Plains Dance." In *Native American Dance: Ceremonies and Social Traditions*, ed. Charlotte Heth. Washington DC: Smithsonian Institution Press.

Hughes-Freeland, Felicia, and Mary M. Crain, eds. 1998. *Recasting Ritual: Performance, Media, Identity*. London: Routledge.

Lyotard, Jean-Francois. 1984. *The Postmodern Condition: A Report on Knowledge*. Minneapolis: University of Minnesota Press.

Nagel, Joane, and Matthew Snipp. 1993. "Ethnic Reorganization: American Indian Social, Economic, Political, and Cultural Strategies for Survival." *Ethnic and Racial Studies* 16 (2): 203–35.

Powers, William K. 1990. *War Dance: Plains Indian Musical Performance*. Tucson: University of Arizona Press.

Said, Edward. 1979. *Orientalism*. New York: Vintage.

Theisz, R. D. 1987. "Song Texts and Their Performers: The Centerpiece of Contemporary Lakota Identity Formulation." *Great Plains Quarterly* 7 (2): 116–124.

West, W. Richard, Jr. 1992. Foreword to *Native American Dance: Ceremonies and Social Traditions*, ed. Charlotte Heth, ix–x. Washington DC: Smithsonian Institution Press.

Young Bear, Severt, Sr., and R. D. Theisz. 1994. *Standing in the Light: A Lakota Way of Seeing*. Lincoln: University of Nebraska Press.

ROBIN RIDINGTON, DENNIS HASTINGS, & TOMMY ATTACHIE

6. The Songs of our Elders
Performance and Cultural Survival in Omaha and Dane-zaa Traditions

The Plains Indian powwow has become central to the identity of many Native people in both the United States and Canada, even in areas where its music and dance are not indigenous, yet other First Nations maintain indigenous traditions unrelated to the Plains powwow. This chapter will compare the music of two peoples whose traditions have deeply indigenous roots but have evolved in very different directions. One, the Omaha tribe of Nebraska, is a source of many elements that became the intertribal powwow. The other, the Dane-zaa of northeastern British Columbia, maintain an indigenous Dreamers' Dance tradition unrelated to the powwow.

The Omaha tribe is one of the five Degiha Siouan tribes of farmers and hunters, who are thought to have migrated to various locations from the Ohio River valley in protohistoric times (Ridington and Hastings 1997, 45–46). The Dane-zaa are subarctic Athapaskan hunters of Canada's Peace River area. Geographically and culturally the two peoples have very different histories. One is central to the powwow culture that developed on the Plains; the other is peripheral to that tradition but is the locus of an indigenous form of music and dance. Omaha musical tradition is a source of the contemporary powwow, while Dane-zaa songkeepers known as Dreamers have gathered together influences from other subarctic cultures to create a tradition that is distinctively a marker of Dane-zaa kinship and cultural identity. Omaha musical culture has radiated centrifugally to influence many other tribes. Dane-zaa music has incorporated more widespread subarctic genres centripitally to create a uniquely indigenous form. Omaha songs are known throughout the Plains, while Dane-zaa songs define the experience of a relatively small circle of related people.

The Omahas now live in the middle Missouri River area of northeastern Nebraska. Their tribal name, which means "upstream people," refers to their migration "against the current" of the Ohio River. Their traditional ceremonies, language, songs, symbols, and social organization reflect what appear to be core elements of an ancient Siouan culture that dates back to the Mississippean cultures of the thirteenth century. The Omahas today are central to the cultural diffusion that has become the contemporary powwow. They have been in direct or indirect contact with Europeans for at least four centuries.

The Dane-zaa are an egalitarian, band-level society. Unlike the Omahas, who have an elaborate tribal organization that includes clans, a priesthood, and numerous societies, the Dane-zaa organize themselves into families and small bands of related people who come together in larger groups only seasonally. Their kinship system is inclusive, so that every person knows a term of relationship for every other. Rather than a priesthood of ritual specialists whose positions are in part inherited, the Dane-zaa follow the teachings of visionary people they call Naachin, or Dreamers. Their ceremonial life centers around the Dreamers' Dance, in which people dance to songs "brought back from Heaven" by Dreamers who can be located genealogically within the Dane-zaa kinship universe. While contact with Europeans began in the late eighteenth century, the Dane-zaa remained "bush Indians" until after the U.S. Army Corps of Engineers pushed the Alaska Highway through their territory in 1942.

The comparison of the Omahas and the Dane-zaa results from collaboration between Dennis Hastings, director of the Omaha Tribal Historical Research Project; Tommy Attachie, Dane-zaa songkeeper; and Robin Ridington, an ethnographer who has worked with both the Dane-zaa and the Omaha tribes. In spring 2001 Dennis and Robin interviewed Omaha singers, elders, and tribal leaders on the Omaha reservation to document how they understand the place of Omaha songs, both in their own community and within the contemporary Plains powwow repertoire. In July 2001 Dennis spent ten days in Dane-zaa territory, where he witnessed several traditional Dreamers' Dances (known in English as Tea Dances) in which Tommy was lead singer. Tommy spoke with Dennis and Robin about the origins and meaning of Dreamers' songs. Robin recorded eight hours of Tea Dance performance and also recorded a talk by Chief Garry Oker explaining the Tea Dance tradition to younger members of his community. Here we will present the transcribed voices of Omaha and Dane-zaa singers to compare the two traditions.

Omaha He'dewachi

In recent years the Omaha tribe has identified its annual tribal powwow as a continuation of the traditional He'dewachi, or harvest ceremony, that took place in the summer, "when the plum and cherry trees were full of fruit" (Fletcher and La Flesche 1911, 251). The program for the 2000 celebration called it the "196th Annual Omaha Tribal Harvest Celebration" and "the oldest powwow in North America." That date, the program explained, is derived from the date of Meriwether Lewis and William Clark's visit to Omaha territory in 1804. Program notes go on to state:

> As originators of the He'dewachi and the warriors who danced the Hethu'shka, the Omaha people of today have a proud heritage to not only look back upon, but to pass on to our future generations. Because of the Omaha and the "Omaha Dance" as other Tribes soon started calling it, other Tribes began dancing in this manner too. Theirs they call a "powwow," which is a term the Omaha adopted for awhile. However, in light of constant research about the Tribe, the Omaha have returned to their ancestral traditions and now, among themselves, refer to this colorful dance of thanksgiving as the He'dewachi. The War Dance is the Hethu'shka. The Omaha Dance is what is now termed the Grass Dance. The term "powwow" is a federal, non-Indian word, employed by earlier interpreters for lack of a proper term to describe what they saw. (Omaha Tribe 2000, 12)

When Robin and Dennis talked to tribal chairman Elmer Blackbird about the Omaha He'dewachi, he stated:

> In just recent years, they started calling it "Harvest Celebration" in Omaha instead of calling it powwow, which I was glad to hear. Because in the early beginnings, that's what they did. At the harvest season, people gather and they share things with each other, food and material things. They gather like that and sing the religious ceremonies, giving thanks to our Creator for harvest year, coming through the summer in a good way. So that's how our annual celebration began. And eventually from one generation to another, we began to lose the significance of our religious ceremony. And now, it's become a social event. But in a war dance song, they still use a prayer song. You still hear the word *Wakon'da* in our song in the powwow as a reference to God. And that we have retained. And even

> the sacredness of that big drum, they still show respect to that. People go around it and show respect that way. (Ridington/Dane-zaa Archive, OFN01-2, May 28, 2001)

Similarly, lead singer Rufus White acknowledged the powwow as having begun as a harvest festival. He told us:

> A long time ago, when they first got started with this powwow, they called it Harvest Dance. What they did was, they brought all their vegetables that they raised, whatever they raised, they brought it into this village, and they got together and they made a circle. They shared whatever they brought. Put it out in the middle. And they talked about things up ahead, that the winter months coming, they'd stored something back home and they put some in the ground, where they could use that during the winter. That's how they got together. That's how this powwow come about. (Ridington/Dane-zaa Archive, OFN01-3, May 29, 2001)

The Hethu'shka or Grass Dance

Grass Dance songs were originally the property of the Hethu'shka (pronounced "Helushka") society of the Omaha tribe. Fletcher and La Flesche (1911) write that this was one of the largest and most important of the Omaha societies. They tell us that it dates back at least to the seventeenth century, when the Omahas and the Poncas were a single tribe. Originally, the Hethu'shka society was sponsored by the Kon'ce clan because of its special relationship to lightning, wind, and thunder. "It is said that the object in establishing the Hethu'shka society was to stimulate an heroic spirit among the people and to keep alive the memory of historic and valorous acts. Thunder was the tutelar god of the Hethu'shka" (Fletcher and La Flesche 1911, 459). Fletcher and La Flesche also report:

> During the last century or more the Hethu'shka has spread among other branches of the Siouan family; tribes differing in language and customs have adopted it, so to speak. Among these are the Pawnee, who, according to tradition, were at one time close allies of the Omaha; they still call the Hethu'shka by its Omaha name. They and other tribes, who, to this day, delight in dancing to the rhythmic cadence of its songs, have songs of their own composition; but all these songs follow the model of the original Omaha songs. (p. 640)

In an earlier publication Fletcher paraphrases a story she was told that describes a possible early instance of the Sioux acquiring Hethu'shka songs from the Omahas. "After many years of warfare," she writes, it was decided that "a party of Omahas would visit the Sioux tribe." Upon approaching the Sioux village, "the Leader stood up and said, 'We have made peace, and we have come in good faith, we will go forward, and Wa'konda shall decide the issue.' Then he struck up this song [Hethu'shka "Song of the Leader"; A Rest Song] and led the way; and, as the men and women followed, they caught the tune, and all sang it as they came near the Sioux village" (Fletcher 1900, 21–24).

Fletcher gives no indication of when this event took place, but a similar peaceful encounter is recorded from a Sioux perspective in Cloud-Shield's "Winter Count" of 1791–92 (Mallery 1893, 385). The picture shows an Omaha on the right and a Dakota on the left. The Omaha's hand is outstretched, and the Dakota has placed his palm over it. While no further documentation exists of just how this peace was made, it is certainly possible that the Hethu'shka song Fletcher mentions accompanied the event and that this picture represents an early instance of Hethu'shka songs passing from Omahas to the Sioux.

Whatever the first instance of this transfer may be, contemporary scholars agree that the Omaha Grass Dance became widely accepted by many Plains tribes during the nineteenth century. According to Powers (1990): "The concept of today's powwow is a vestige of the Grass Dance complex that spread across the Great Plains during the mid-nineteenth century" (p. 64). He reports that "Among the Lakota on the Pine Ridge and Rosebud reservations, it is called the 'Omaha Dance,' because the dance was historically learned from the Omaha tribe" (Powers 1990, 30). Eric Lassiter, himself an accomplished singer of Plains powwow songs, reports that the Kiowa O-ho-mah dance "began to grow popular on the Plains in the second half of the nineteenth century." Lassiter writes that although it was originally not unlike other Plains warrior sodalities, "it began to develop as a social rather than a warrior society's dance." The rights to perform the dance, he observes, "rested on the 'bustle' – essentially an assemblage of eagle feathers attached to the back of the waist." Kiowa singers told him that the Cheyennes "had received the rights of the bustle from the Omahas and passed it to the Kiowas in 1883" (Lassiter 1998, 95).

Fletcher and La Flesche attribute the name "Grass Dance" to "a long bunch of grass representing scalps the wearer had taken," which in time "became part of of the Hethu'shka dress or regalia" (1911, 461). Hethu'shka leaders traditionally wore a bustle called "the Crow," which symbolized "a battlefield after the conflict is over" (Fletcher and La Flesche 1911, 441). Some Omaha dancers today still wear the Crow as part of their dance regalia. When Dennis and Robin talked to sixty-six-year-old Omaha singer Rudy Clark, he offered a different explanation for the origins of the Grass Dance: "The Grass Dance, that was originated here too. But people refuse to recognize it. They say they used to dance out in the open field out here, the Grass Dance. Guess an old man was out in that field. He saw those, that wind blowing, and that grass was going like that. And he started imitating the movements of that grass. And that's how that Grass Dance got started" (Ridington/Dane-zaa Archive, OFN01-2, May 28, 2001).

Rufus White gave us yet another explanation:

> *Hethu'shka wachi* they say, "Dancers are dancing." In them days, they never had a grand entry. There was no such thing as grand entry. When the dancers came to the door, and the arena director brought them in and set them on the seats. Everybody come in and took their seats, then they start dancing from there. In later years, these other tribes started having the grand entry, they kind of copied out from them and started having grand entry here. We trying to reorganize, get that out, do it the original way, but still they couldn't get out of that. One copy off another tribe. In them days, they all dance with the feathers and the grass dancers, they made this fancy yarn, put it out over the dancing outfit. That's why they call them Grass Dancers. (Ridington/Dane-zaa Archive 2001, OFN01-3, May 29, 2001)

Dennis and Robin also talked with Ed Webster, who held the position of whipman for the 2000 He'dewachi and is also a tribal educator. He described having discussed the Omaha contribution to the Sioux powwow with Alex Lunderman, former tribal chairman of the Rosebud Sicangu Sioux:

> He talked about how he had a great respect for the Umo^{n}ho^{n} (Omaha) people. And the reason he did that, he said, "We still have that song here, and they gave us the Grass Dance." He said his grandfather told him that story. Alex, at the time, I bet he was sixty-five. It was his grandfather that told him. That put him maybe clear back to 1870, 1880. They had the song, and they sang it. . . . To paraphrase the song, what I was told by Alex was that it was honoring the Omaha for their great gift, the gift of dance. And he was told that that gift was to celebrate with the Creator.

I heard that back in 1987. (Ridington/Dane-zaa Archive, OFN01-2, May 28, 2001)

When we asked Rudy Clark whether other tribes recognize the Omaha contribution to their own powwow traditions, he said that although some non-Omahas "refuse to recognize them," there is no doubt that Hethu'shka belongs to the Omahas: "But this Omaha powwow was where Hethu'shka was originated, and then they start carrying it around to different powwows. And they sing those songs. But when I go to a powwow and hear a song, I can tell you whether it's an Omaha song or not. The Omaha people, they was the one that originated the Hethu'shka, old Hethu'shka dance. And that's where it started out. Started and went all over. The fancy dance was originated by a Ponca man in Oklahoma" (Ridington/Dane-zaa Archive, OFN01-2, May 28, 2001).

When we asked Rudy whether the Omaha powwow has changed much in his experience, he replied: "No, it hasn't changed. Oh, they got electricity and everything, but actually the songs haven't changed. Every once in a while you'll find a different tribe come up over here. They'll sing a a song and you listen and it's Omaha tune, but they changed the words in it. I recognize that all the time. Quite a few times" (Ridington/Dane-zaa Archive, OFN01-2, May 28, 2001).

Rudy Clark was confident that young people are keeping up the Omaha musical tradition:

> They're some old songs way back there that the old people sing. The Omahas, every once in a while, one of them will pop up, the tune. Then I had a tape from the Smithsonian Institute [Lee and La Vigna 1985], had the Omahas singing on there. And I could recognize the tune, but you know, I couldn't hear the words. Kind of slurred, like. Some of them will outlast me. The younger generation will be singing those same songs. They'll go on and on, because they belong to the Omahas, the Omaha people. They never change. Could be down here a hundred years from now and I bet you still hear them songs. (Ridington/Dane-zaa Archive, OFN01-2, May 28, 2001)

Elmer Blackbird also felt that although some Omaha traditions were being diluted by those of other tribes, the music is being passed on:

> I feel that we're losing some of our traditional Hethu'shka songs, because a lot of our young people are getting involved in the annual powwows of

other tribes, and they're learning other tribal songs, and they use them here, too. But I was kind of glad to see one young group sit, even compose some Omaha songs using Omaha words in their songs. It's real good that young people are learning some of them. And to kind of revive some of the songs of our old people. It's good to see it and to hear them singing Omaha songs. Saturday night, this past weekend, my family sponsored a graduation handgame, one of our traditional social activities, for my grandson that graduated. They were all young singers there, and they all sang a lot of Omaha songs. I really enjoyed listening to them sing. I really did appreciate them singing. So that's what's happening to our people right now. (Ridington/Dane-zaa Archive, OFN01-2)

Hethu'shka songs and a memory of the He'dewachi connect contemporary Omahas with their past. While ceremonies dependent on the buffalo hunt are long gone, singing and dancing to give thanks continues to unite the different clans and families into a single tribe. Some traditions antedate the Omahas' split from the Poncas, dating back at least to the seventeenth century. Omaha songs are alive and well, both within the Omaha tribe and among the many other tribes with whom they now share the tradition. As Rudy Clark said above, "They never change. Could be down here a hundred years from now and I bet you still hear them songs."

DANE-ZAA TEA DANCE

All these songs [*yine*], how many years ago.
Makenunatane *yine* [songs of "He Opens the Door"]
and Aledze [Powder],
Maketchueson [He Shows the Way],
Naachan [The Prophet].
How many years ago. Old prophet.
When you sing it now, just like new.
(Tommy Attachie, Ridington/Dane-zaa Archive, CYTommy 4-A, 1998)

In contrast to the He'dewachi, which is both indigenously Omaha and ancestral to the modern powwow, the Dane-zaa Dreamers' Dance or Tea Dance is a form of the Northern Drum Dance that has become rooted in the particulars of Dane-zaa experience, genealogy, and narrative tradition.[1] Songs in the repertoire of contemporary singers derive from the dreams of about twenty Dreamers or Prophets (Naachin), among whom are the people Tommy named above. A knowledgeable songkeeper like Tommy brings their songs and stories into the lives of people living today. As Tommy said, "When you sing it now, just like new." Both Tommy and Robin knew the last Dreamer, Charlie Yahey. With Tommy's help the Dane-zaa First Nations have produced a series of compact disks documenting recordings Robin made of Yahey's songs and oratory in the 1960s. When Dennis and Robin spoke with Tommy about the Dreamers' Dance, he began by describing how he became a singer:

My name's Tom Attachie. I'm fifty-eight year old.
When I was young, I want to drum.
I want to drum. I like to drumming with people.
And finally I grow up and I started drumming and now,
I start, I'm a song leader. I like drumming.
And Makenunatane [He Opens the Door], that's the first.
Very, for start, Prophet's name, Makenunatane.
He's the first one and, he's the first one dream to Heaven.
And another one's name, Aledze [Powder].
And another one, Maketsueson [He Shows the Way].
That's the one, big prophet, too. Just like Makenunatane.
Maketsueson. And after, Sam Aku's grandpa,
that's another prophet.
And another prophet, Prophet River, Louis Notseta's dad,
His name is Naachan [The Prophet], that one.
And another one, Aske Kwolan [Boy-Oldman] from Halfway.
He's another prophet.
And nineteen fifty, Oker, Annie Oker's dad.
Oker. That's a Dreamer, too, prophet.
And last one, Charlie Yahey.
And another one name is Atisklise [Birchbark-paper].
That's another prophet, too.
And Kayan, he's a big prophet. He's from Alberta.
All these Dreamers, not anybody become a prophet.
God choose them, certain people.
(Ridington/Dane-zaa Archive, DZ01-20, July 24, 2001

Almost all of the Dreamers Tommy mentions can be clearly identified genealogically in relation to people living today. They appear on a genealogy Robin constructed from oral interviews in 1968. They also turn up in government, church, and trading post records that a genealogical research team recently studied.[2] Many of the Dreamers have names that symbolize their ability to communicate between worlds in addition to their personal or family names. The names Makenunatane (He Opens the Door) and Maketsueson (He Shows the Way), for instance, refer to their roles as guides and messengers. Atisklise (who appears as a signatory to Treaty 8 in 1899) is called "Paper" (literally, "birchbark") because he brings messages from heaven. Powder's name derives from the capacity that gunpowder gave people to reach out over a long distance. Makenunatane, the prophet who dreamed of Swans (see Tommy's comment below) and first predicted the coming of the white men, is probably the chief named in a 1799 Northwest Company journal, "The Cigne," that is, the Swan Chief (Ridington 1988, 139–40).

Kinship encircles the Dane-zaa universe, and the Dreamers' songs bring people together with their relatives. Yagatunne, the trail to heaven, is a trail of song that relatives in heaven use to make contact with people on earth. When asked in 1966 about how Dreamers get their songs, Charlie Yahey responded:

Just like right now when we sing
it is just like we knew that song before.
Then he starts to sing.
That is how he gets it.
They just grab it up there
and they wake up with that song.
They just start to sing it right then.
They know how it turns,
how the song turns up and down.
(Ridington 1988, 104)

The Dreamer is a guide to the trail because he has been there. He has experienced it in his dreams. Charlie Yahey said that Dreamers are like Swans, in that both "can just go right through the sky to Heaven without dying" (Ridington 1988, 104). Tommy also told about how Makenunatane dreamed a song for Swans and another for daylight, to make their journeys shorter:

Even this daylight coming from East,
"This world is too far."
When Makenunatane was dreaming, sleeping,
he dream about this daylight coming.
That daylight was singing. Sing a song.
He sing a song, and he tell Makenunatane,

"Help me. I want to go fast.
I don't go too fast. Help me."
Even that daylight come, he dream about that song.
And now all kinds. And he dream about Swan, too.
Makenunatane was sleeping.
He dream about Swan in a big lake.
Big lake, two Swan.
He dream about that Swan there, you know in the lake.
Pretty soon, them Swan look at the sky. This way.
Pretty soon they start to fly.
They start to fly all the way up.
When you going to rest, you know,
just go 'round, and keep going up.
When that blue sky go through there,
go through to that Heaven there,
even that Swan can't make it.
He just go 'round and 'round.
He can't go through it.
And them Swans started singing. Praying and sing.
Sing a song. And that blue sky just went like this,
and they went through.
That's only them two things without die, get to Heaven.
That's how Creators are really strong. That's only one.
Anything got to die first. But the only thing.
Then Makenunatane dream about that, and he tell,
he sing that song and he tell everybody,
"Two Swan went to heaven without die.
Alive and they went through."
And all these things happen,
and that's why people believe that is true,
there's Heaven, person die, get to Heaven.
(Ridington/Dane-zaa Archive, DZ01-20, July 24, 2001)

The Tea Dance provides an opportunity for people to come together and listen to the Dreamers' songs. It brings them close to the spirits of their relatives in heaven. They dance together around the fire, joining individual tracks into a common trail. For nomadic hunters the metaphor of merging tracks is particularly powerful. Following in the footsteps of relatives around the fire reminds people that their trails on earth follow the paths their ancestors knew. The dance is very much a family gathering, in that, traditionally, every person within the Dane-zaa community addresses and refers to every other by an appropriate kin term. Just as the songkeepers remember the names and stories and kinship positions of the Dreamers whose songs they sing, people within the community know the life stories of the people with whom they share a trail. Dancing together literally brings a community of relatives together. Chief Garry Oker spoke to the dancers at a Tea Dance Dennis and Robin attended, for which Tommy was the lead singer:

> Ladies and gentlemen, thanks for coming to the Tea Dance tonight.
> We've been doing this for hundreds and hundreds of years.
> This is the place where Dane-zaa people have gathered,
> many, many years. Every year, we gather here to sing these songs.
> These songs come from our Prophets.
> We call it *naachine*.
> They're the Dreamers. They're the ones that dream ahead for everybody.
> And with these songs,
> Dane-zaa people are supposed to maintain their trails.
> Many of us have gone off the trails
> and walked away from Dane-zaa drums.
> At one time,
> used to be hundreds and hundreds of people here dancing.
> And now look at us.
> A handful of us coming here to listen to our drummers.
> Our lead singer Tommy Attachie here has been guiding us,
> helping us remember these songs.
> The Elders. Thanks for coming.
> It's for you guys we're doing it.
> I think it's important here,
> that those of you that are here, this is our spiritual,
> this is our Bible.
> You know, like when people talk about praying through Bibles.
> Well, this is Dane-zaa way of praying,
> so that our spirit can become light when our time is coming.
> Every time you go around the fire, your spirit become lighter.
> They say that, old Dreamers they said,
> "Every time you go around it, you are forgiven.

Your deeds or your sins you have done is forgiven."
So that's why it's important that each one of you come and dance.
We need to bring this back to the people.
Too many people are going to, [Garry speaks in Beaver].
That's what they said. As soon you take the drink,
your spirit jumps out and wanders around,
doesn't know what to do.
It's with these songs that we help bring the spirit back
so that each one of us can have a purpose, a reason to live.
In this valley, hundreds and hundreds of years,
our people gathered from all over to remember these songs.
They told us,
"Never, never forget these songs and always maintain it."
My grandpa, Oker, was a Prophet.
My step-grandpa was a music keeper [*shin hataen*].
So that's why we do this.
We need to maintain it for the next generation
so that if they go too much the white way,
they don't know who they are.
And a lot of our people on the street,
you see them, walking back and forth, back and forth.
That's not being Indian. They're lost.
And it's really sad to see that.
[Tommy says, "I was one of them, one time."]
Yeah, Tommy said, "Oh yeah," he was one of them, too.
"Number one," he said. But anyways, he found his path back to the drum,
and he's helping us out.
The point is, we need to do this. Get together here.
Because it's important to find out.
This is about who we are as Dane-zaa people.
It's through this drums that we can go on
and have a balance in our lives, so that,
Onli Nachi nin chi la je' [The giant animal won't catch you].
At least we got a drum.
Those old-timers, *hon adawachi, onli nachi naen cha ade.*
This is what they say:
"Giant animals are going to come back.
They're going to catch your shadow.

But if you dance and drum, you'll be OK."
So come on. Let's dance, everybody.
(Ridington/Dane-zaa Archive, DZ01-32, July 28, 2001)

Traditionally, members of different Dane-zaa bands converged on a single place in the late summer to sing and dance. Charlie Yahey said that coming together was like meeting your relatives in heaven. One such place was called Suu Na chii K'chi ge (The Place Where Happiness Dwells). In the 1930s the Dreamer Kayan made a song about the place. Robin recorded Charlie Yahey singing it in 1966. When the Fort St. John Band chose reserve land in 1914 under Treaty 8, they chose this land, known to the government as IR-172, or "the Montney reserve." In 1945 government agents engineered a surrender of the land. Forty-four years later, following a lengthy court battle, members of the former Fort St. John Band received compensation for the loss of mineral rights on IR-172.

In celebration of their court victory and their survival as a people, the Doig River First Nation sponsored the recording of a compact disk that brought together songs by every Dane-zaa singer Robin had recorded over the past thirty-five years as well as songs Garry Oker had recorded from his step-grandfather, Albert Askoty. We called the CD *Suu Ne chii K'chi ge*, because, as we said in the album notes: "We hope that this CD will itself become a place where happiness dwells for the Dane-zaa, young and old." The last song on the CD is Charlie Yahey's rendition of Kayan's Suu Ne chii K'chi ge song.

Song, Spirit, and Identity

Native American songs are more than entertainment; they are also points of entry into the spirit world. In both Dane-zaa and Omaha traditions, singers know and share the drum's heartbeat. They know that it creates a path enabling dancers to move around a common center, yet the drums and the songs differ in ways that suggest fundamental differences between Omaha and Dane-zaa cultures. Dane-zaa singers play individual hand drums, which are generally single sided, with snares stretched across the inside of the drumhead. The singer tensions the snare with his thumb and tunes the drum between songs by holding it over an open fire. Then he directs his voice into the drum and feels the intersecting waves of sound as drumbeat and voice and buzzing snares merge to become a spirit path, *yagatunne*. The drumbeat replicates the fall of feet along a trail, while the song's melody corresponds to the trail's turns as it negotiates a complex and storied landscape. Singers and dancers follow the turns of the Dreamers' songs to come close to their relatives in heaven.

In contrast Omaha singers gather in a circle around a large common drum, with each person's drumstick beating in time with that of every other. The big drum creates a shared heartbeat that resounds beyond the powwow arena out to the circle of families and clans gathered together. The drumbeat and voices of the singers invoke the power of Wakon'da, the creative spirit that Fletcher and La Flesche describe as "an invisible and continuous life" that "permeates all things, seen and unseen" (Fletcher and La Flesche 1911, 134). Omaha Hethu'shka songs, like others in the powwow repertoire, shift between a regular rhythm and a pattern of alternately stressed beats. Originally these songs belonged to the Hethu'shka, or warrior, society, whose members were men pledged to defend the tribe from danger. Omaha singers and dancers remember the original meaning of devotion to their own people, while people from other tribes who perform Hethu'shka songs in the intertribal context have lost that meaning. In both Omaha and Dane-zaa traditions, drummers and singers follow the lead singer's rendition of a song, while dancers coordinate their movements to its rhythm. Dancers take pride in bringing their dance to an end just as the drummers finish. In competitions they are judged on their ability to know exactly when the singers will finish a song.

Both Dane-zaa and Omaha songs have secular as well as sacred functions, but the paths of the two traditions have diverged widely. The Omaha tribe originated the Hethu'shka, or Grass Dance, tradition, which furthered the evolution of the contemporary Plains powwow. Omaha songs that originally marked the defense of the tribe have now become intertribal, while those of the Dane-zaa remain in the keeping of a few singers. For Omahas these songs continue to be indigenous and remain within the context of a changed but remembered harvest festival. Hethu'shka songs and the Grass Dance exert a powerful influence on young Omahas, and – even for a generation whose knowledge of the Omaha language is slipping away – they constitute an important link with tribal tradition and identity. Scores of Omahas and hundreds of people from other tribes know and sing songs from the Hethu'shka repertoire. The tradition is alive and well. Songs that go back to the ancient Siouan past are now integral to a range of Indian identities far beyond the Siouan tribes. The songs have moved centrifugally from a tribal center into a larger circle.

By contrast the Dane-zaa took a widespread Northern Drum Dance tradition and made it distinctively their own. Each Dreamers' Dance song comes from a particular Dreamer, beginning with Makenunatane, whose name Billy Attachie translates as "He Opens the Door." The name can be translated literally as *Ma ke* (his feet or tracks) *nun* earth, *atunne* trail, meaning that his trail goes around the earth like the sun. His name signifies that he dreamed ahead to prophesy the coming of Europeans to Dane-zaa territory. In Tommy's words: "He's the first one. He's the first one to dream to Heaven." Makenunatane took an ancient tradition of song, oratory, and prophecy and made it relevant to the new conditions brought on by the fur trade and contact with Christianity. The dance itself presents a centripetal image that concentrates the energy of people who are related to one another. By dancing on a common trail around the fire, people on earth come closer to one another and to their relatives in heaven. The trail around the fire replicates *yagatunne*, the trail to heaven. Perhaps because their dance tradition is so closely tied to kinship and narrative, and also because until recently they have remained relatively isolated from outside influences, the Dane-zaa have not taken up Plains powwow dancing as a marker of Indian identity. They continue to think of themselves as Dane-zaa, "original people," rather than as "Indians."

As the CD and recent digital recordings of vigorous Tea Dances testify, the Dane-zaa Dreamers' Dance tradition continues to be symbolically and spiritually important to the life of Dane-zaa communities. However, as Garry Oker said, where once there had been hundreds and hundreds of people dancing, now there are only "a handful of us coming here to listen to our drummers." Unlike the Omaha Hethu'shka songs, which are sung by hundreds of people, knowledge of how to "sing [the Dreamers' songs] now" and make the tradition "just like new" rests with a few precious individuals who know the songs and the stories behind them.

The Dreamers' Dance songs are strongly rooted in kinship and narrative. The story of each person's life connects with that of every other within the closely knit Dane-zaa community. The songs are like a circle of stories, brought into being as knowledgeable songkeepers re-create them within a circle of relatives. Almost singlehandedly, Tommy has continued to sing and teach what he knows. In the Doig River community Garry Oker, Sam Acko, Jack Askoty, Leo Acko, Freddy Askoty, and Robert Dominic are also knowledgeable singers. Others may be found in the Halfway River and Blueberry River communities, but at the moment Tommy is the only songkeeper. Whenever someone in any of the Dane-zaa communities passes away, it is necessary to hold a wake in which singers and dancers help to send the person's spirit along *yagatunne*. Tommy is the singer who can be counted on to take up the lead for these occasions.

Tommy is now in his sixties and is a knowledgeable elder. He strongly encourages younger people to go beyond following his lead and to take up the role of songkeeper, just as the late Albert Askoty encouraged Tommy to become a songkeeper. Robin's role has been to document Tea Dance (Dreamers' Dance) performances whenever possible and to make available, in CD format, the recordings of songs, stories, and oratory of the great Dane-zaa singers. Robin now has enough years, if not enough cultural knowledge, to join Tommy in the role of elder. With digital technology now readily available, Robin has been privileged to join Tommy and others in recording a wide range of stories about Dane-zaa history and the Dreamer's Dance tradition. We trust that these recordings will become a resource for future generations. A generous grant from the British Columbia Museums Association has made it possible to transfer recordings in the Dane-zaa archive to a secure digital medium.

Conclusion

The Plains powwow represents a widespread, rapid diffusion of cultural images and practices that is not new to Native Americans. Long before contact with Europeans, Native American peoples exchanged goods and ideas over large areas. We know from archaeological evidence that a set of symbols sometimes called "the southeastern ceremonial complex" spread rapidly through Mississippean cultures hundreds of years before European influence. There is no reason to believe that what Wallace called revitalization movements began only after first contact. The diffusion of cultural information that we see in the current spread of the powwow tradition has precedents in more ancient times. Powerful expressions like those of Wovoka's Ghost Dance, Native American Church ceremonies, and the powwow continue to energize and integrate the experiences of Native American people across tribal lines. Becoming a singer of powwow songs offers its participants both transcendence and cultural identity. Joining other singers around the big drum gives ordinary people an experience of intense beauty and fellowship in a community of singers who trace their ancestry back to the land before it was colonized by outsiders. The power of song and the drum's heartbeat connect people alive today to the heartbeat of the land.

Both Omaha and Dane-zaa musical traditions may be seen as revitalization movements as defined by Wallace. Both synthesize new identities out of old practices. Omaha songs originally realized ancient Siouan tradition in support of tribal identity. They kept the tribe together through the years of its migration from the Ohio Valley and its readaptation to life as mounted Plains buffalo hunters. More recently these songs realize the identity of Indians beyond tribal boundaries. Dane-zaa songs reinterpret the Northern Drum Dance repertoire as markers of shared kinship. In both cases songs are like stories. Singers share and remember a song's melodic turns, its rythmic structure and its symbolic associations. Dane-zaa songs realize *yagatunne*, the trail to heaven. They re-create the dream experiences of relatives who are no longer alive. They bring the living together with the spirits of those who have passed along the trail to heaven. Omaha songs bring present generations into contact with Indian history. They make that history relevant to the experience of people beyond tribal boundaries.

Unlike music from Africa that evolved into the jazz and blues of America, Native American musical traditions have not significantly crossed over into popular culture. Despite the mainstream popularity of such singers as Buffy St. Marie and Robbie Robertson, most Native American song traditions remain markers of indigenous experience and identity. Powwow singers and Dane-zaa songkeepers are similar in practicing traditions that identify them as indigenous people. The traditions are different largely in scale. Powwow songs mark a community of intertribal Indian identity, while Dane-zaa songs mark a community of identity as defined by kinship. While nonaboriginal people (among whom is Eric Lassiter, the editor of this volume) have become proficient in the Native American musical idiom, they have done so by entering into an indigenous tradition rather than by borrowing from it to augment mainstream forms.

Omahas today refer to their powwow as a way of "dancing to give thanks." The Dane-zaa understand their dancing as walking *yagatunne*, the trail to heaven. Omaha Helushka songs in the intertribal powwow tradition bring people from different tribes together to share a common experience. Dane-zaa songs re-create the experience of coming together at Suu Ne chi'i K'chi ge, The Place Where Happiness Dwells. In both traditions dancing is an integral key to maintaining indigenous culture and identity. In both traditions singers and dancers come together to celebrate community. For the Dane-zaa that community is defined by kinship; Omaha powwow songs have come to define the community of a larger Indian identity. In both cases "the songs of our elders" bring people together with the heartbeat of those who have gone before. We would like to close this comparison of Dane-zaa and Omaha traditions with a heartfelt invocation that resonates in both cultures: All My Relations.

NOTES

The authors would like to thank the Canadian Social Sciences and Humanities Research Council for making the collaboration that produced this chapter possible.

1. For descriptions of the Dene Tea Dance and other subarctic Drum Dance traditions, see Helm (1981), Asch (1988), and Goulet (1998).

2. As part of research in 2000 and 2001 related to an investigation of treaty land entitlement, Jillian Ridington and Robin Ridington collaborated with researchers from the Arctic Institute to correlate information from Robin's 1968 genealogy with available written documents and place the entire corpus on a computer database.

REFERENCES

Asch, Michael. 1988. *Kinship and the Drum Dance in a Northern Dene Community*. Edmonton: Boreal Institute for Northern Studies.

Dorsey, James Owen. *Omaha Sociology*. 1884. BAE Third Annual Report. Washington DC: Smithsonian Institution.

Fletcher, Alice C. 1900. *Indian Story and Song from North America*. Boston: Small Maynard and Company. Reprint, Lincoln: University of Nebraska Press, Bison Books, 1995.

Fletcher, Alice C., and Francis La Flesche. 1911. *The Omaha Tribe*. BAE Eleventh Annual Report. Washington DC: Smithsonian Institution.

Goulet, Jean-Guy. 1998. *Ways of Knowing: Experience, Knowledge and Power among the Dene Tha*. Lincoln: University of Nebraska Press.

Helm, June. 1981. *Subarctic*. Vol. 6 of *Handbook of North American Indians*. Washington DC: Smithsonian Institution.

Lassiter, Luke E. 1998. *The Power of Kiowa Song: A Collaborative Ethnography*. Tuscon: University of Arizona Press.

Lee, Dorothy Sara, and Maria La Vigna, eds. 1985. *Omaha Indian Music: Historical Recordings from the Fletcher/La Flesche Collection*. Washington DC: Library of Congress.

Mallery, Garrick. 1893. *Picture-Writing of the American Indians*. Tenth Annual Report of the Bureau of American Ethnology. Washington DC: Smithsonian Institution.

Oker, Garry, Robin Ridington, and Stacy Shaak. 2001. *Suu Na chii K'chi ge: The Place Where Happiness Dwells*. Vol. 1 of *Dane-zaa Dreamers' Songs*. Doig River BC: Doig River First Nation.

Omaha Tribe. 2000. *Omaha Tribal Powwow 2000 Program*. Macy NE: Omaha Tribe.

Powers, William K. 1990. *War Dance: Plains Indian Musical Performance*. Tucson: University of Arizona Press.

Ridington, Robin. 1988. *Trail to Heaven: Knowledge and Narrative in a Northern Native Community*. Iowa City: University of Iowa Press.

———. N.d. Ridington/Dane-zaa Archive. Available at http://www.fishability.biz/Doig.

Ridington, Robin, and Dennis Hastings. 1997. *Blessing for a Long Time: The Sacred Pole of the Omaha Tribe*. Lincoln: University of Nebraska Press.

Wallace, Anthony F. C. 1956. "Revitalization Movements: Some Theoretical Considerations for Their Comparative Study." *American Anthropologist* 58 (2): 264–81.

DANIEL J. GELO

7. Powwow Patter
Indian Emcee Discourse on Power and Identity

The Southern Plains Indian Powwow is a festival of dancing and dance contests, feasting, gift giving, camping, and other social activities derived from the old Plains Indian Grass Dance ceremonial complex. Modern powwows may be huge urban affairs, such as the annual Red Earth celebration held at the Myriad Convention Center in Oklahoma City, but more typical are the smaller gatherings in rural areas that are hosted by a family or men's club from within a single tribe. Whether large or small powwows attract participants from different Indian cultural groups. In all cases today the event is an amalgamation of traditions that have blended over many decades, if not centuries. *Pan-Indian* is the old term proposed by anthropologists for the resultant culture, though today it is usually called "intertribal" by powwow participants. The most accurate terminology would be processual, recognizing a dynamic among tribal, intertribal, and non-Indian influences.[1]

An ongoing dialectic exists between the tribal and intertribal spheres such that innovations in song, dance, regalia, and ancillary activities enter the intertribal sphere from distinct tribal practice while the intertribal setting stimulates the reinvention of explicitly tribal customs. This dialectic proceeds within a larger non-Indian environment. Thus it is possible to talk about a coherent contemporary powwow culture, one that bears explaining with reference to the cultures of various Indian groups as well as non-Indians. This study relies on tapes and observations made between 1982 and 1997, primarily among the Comanches in Oklahoma but also among their neighbors the Kiowas, the Kiowa-Apaches, and the Pawnees; the Alabama-Coushattas of East Texas; and mixed urban Indian populations in Oklahoma City and Dallas.[2]

Powwows are usually sponsored by one principal organization, often in conjunction with other organizations that serve as cohosts. The sponsoring organizations are civic clubs that may perform many functions throughout the year apart from staging powwows, though for some clubs the annual powwow and the monthly benefit dances are their main reason for being. Some of these civic clubs are continuations or revivals of the sodalities of buffalo days, which centered on military or ritual obligations; others are modern associations based on this model but with no direct antecedents. Examples include the Comanche Gourd Clan, (Comanche) Little Ponies, and Comanche Indian Veteran's Association as well as the Kiowa Black Leggings, Tiah Piah Society, and Ohoma Lodge. Such clubs are referred to as "nonkin organizations" because they recruit from various families and thus promote tribal cohesion, but recruitment of the new generation of members often follows lines of descent. Other clubs, such as the Comanche Chief Wildhorse Descendants and Esa Rosa (White Wolf) Descendants, are formed explicitly through the descendants of famous leaders.

Individual "families" (nuclear or extended families relying on a larger network of kin) also sponsor dances, often with the help of the civic clubs. The sponsors compose or select a powwow committee to oversee the arrangements for the dance, including the appointment of a "head staff" of song and dance leaders for the event. A sample head staff might include a head War Dance singer, head Gourd Dance singer, head Fancy dancer, head Straight dancer, head Gourd dancer, head lady dancer, and powwow princess. Except for the princess, who normally has been elected independently by the club for a one-year term, the staff is drawn specifically for the event from among noted personalities in the community or beyond. There is an arena director, who sets up the public address system and dancer's benches and brings water to the dancers with a bucket and dipper, usually with the help of assistants called water boys. An important member of the head staff is the male master of ceremonies, or emcee, who regulates the event through the use of the public address system.

The emcee is a key figure in the proceedings, at once the voice of authority who represents the wishes of the sponsors as well as an entertainer in his own right. From his position at a table (sometimes on a platform) overlooking the arena from the west side, he summons the dancers to the ring in an opening ceremony and sequences and announces the dances and dance contests in consultation with the sponsors. He coordinates the activity of the singers by calling for types and numbers of songs and thereby regulates the dancing as well. He supervises the formalized gift presentations, or giveaways, which punctuate the dance schedule, summoning forth the gift recipients from lists provided by the givers, making speeches of gratitude on behalf of the organizers and individuals who hold the giveaways, and occasionally echoing the thanks of gift recipients.

The emcee may conduct raffles for shawls, blankets, other regalia items, or groceries, which benefit the hosts or the singers. He makes announcements about general policy, parking, camping, seating, alcohol, etiquette, and rules for non-Indian observers. He issues warnings if rowdyism or a medical emergency occurs, announces lost children or items, and publicizes upcoming events. The emcee also improvises prayers at the beginning and end of the day and at mealtime. He oversees the arena director, setting him to task where needed. The emcee exhorts the participants to reverence or abandon as the hour requires, explains the history and meaning of customs, recognizes people in the dance circle and crowd, and fills time with jokes and commentary. These functions are all fundamental to the success of a powwow. Emcees are critically evaluated by powwow-goers through word of mouth, and the best ones are in continual demand.

Historical Background

The powwow emcee role is deeply grounded in Native tradition. Army sign language authority W. P. Clark was one of many to note the significance of Indian speech making: "With the Indian as with the Romans, the two professions, 'oratory and arms,' established men in the highest degree of personal consideration."[3] In Comanche belief the possession of *puha*, spiritual power, is the basis for personal abilities; one important way that *puha* is manifested is through speech. For example, an animal spirit power donor or "guardian" might be distinguished from an ordinary animal by its ability to speak.

The voice is an indication of personal power and an important means of expression and control in both ritual and secular settings. Women *katakakitteʉ* ("cry a war whoop") to assert the strength of their relatives and bestow honor on them. The characteristic ululations that both women and men make during dances are a way of announcing their own vitality as well as enthusiasm for the day. People who "lose their lulu" will suspect witchcraft, while harmful ghosts can be fended off with a forthright demeanor and some steady words: "Go 'way! Don't come around here."

In sociopolitical life personal power is demonstrated through speech. "Good talkers" (*tsaatekwaninʉʉ*) are considered best qualified to be leaders and leaders' assistants. They demonstrate personal power and can articulate in two senses of the word. In Comanche a chief was called *paraibooß* in his role as decision maker, but as an enunciator of policy and a builder of consensus he was *tekwawapi̱* – *tekwa* referring to speech and *-wapi̱* indicating a professional or specialist with honorific overtones.[4] At some point in his political career the chief usually found it efficient to appoint an assistant as *tekwawapi̱* on his behalf. The Comanche relation between a chief and his announcer was modeled by other similar ones in Numic tradition, such as the roles of medicine men with assistants and the mythic dyad wolf:coyote.[5] Selecting an announcer would have been not only an administrative convenience but a metaphor for the process by which individualistic will was forged into group motivation. Another name for the announcer is *nanikaroikʉ*, explained as "a sound coming from, like, over the hill," or the camp crier could be referred to metonymically as *waaßakitʉ*, "hollering." So prominent were these figures in Plains social life that the Spaniards of the frontier had their own term for them derived from Nahuatl: *tlataleros*.[6]

Public speakers are still seen as having strong influence and a responsibility for shaping social life correctly. The adept speaker can calm people down with his talk (*nißtsußnarʉ*, "talk-calm down"). The *tʉnikepisaß* is a spokesman who strengthens others with his talk, as in the sentence "*Taahpʉß Tsaß nʉ tʉnikepisaß*" (Our Father [God] is my strength).[7] Orations and extemporized prayers are still a primary way that people present themselves in public, and the recitation of war deeds by men, once basic to claims to social standing and supernatural power, continues in limited form during powwows. Voice, power, and authority are all closely associated, and speech indicates *puha* in its form of personal ability and harmonious social relations, the latter especially a concern of the powwow emcee.

The emcee is not only a modern camp crier but also a composite drawn from this role and other similar ones. Sodality dances of old and some of their modern derivatives employ a leader called the "whip man," whose job it is to exhort the other dancers by threatening them with a ceremonial notched wooden club with rawhide lashes. Another immediate prototype would be the announcers at the rodeos and livestock auctions that Indian people have attended and participated in since the reservation era. Rodeo announcers operate a public address system and not only preside over a schedule of exhibits and contests but lead prayers, announce the flag, and recognize visitors, just as the powwow emcee does. Rodeo is an integral part of small-town life in rural Oklahoma: Comanche youngsters sometimes ride among the whites at the small rings in towns like Cyril, and the All-Indian Rodeo sponsored by Chevrolet, Coca-Cola, and Levi Strauss comes each year to the Caddo County Fairgrounds in Anadarko. This latter event features a white emcee who travels the circuit and does most of the announcing, plus a secondary Indian emcee who is better known in the region for his powwow work.

Many powwow participants have family members who over the years have worked in Wild West shows or in dance and cultural programs aimed at white audiences. Quanah Parker was a regular co-organizer of such shows in Oklahoma and Texas in the early 1900s; these events often combined Indian dancing with rodeo contests and speechmaking by Indian and white orators.[8] Comanche elders today remember Albert Attocknie as an active recruiter for Indian programs before World War II. Members of one Comanche extended family made their living between 1964 and 1980 by working every summer at "Indian villages" in upstate New York, mostly the one at the Magic Forest amusement park in Lake George. They danced, put on archery exhibitions, and demonstrated beading and leather work over a daylong schedule. The father of the central nuclear family in this group was the announcer and was acclaimed by his relatives for his talent in this role.

Circumstantial evidence points to the barkers and carnies that have traveled through rural Oklahoma towns as influences on powwow emceeing. The accepted account of the origin of the dance called "the '49" places the innovators at the 1911 Caddo County Fair in Anadarko, listening to a barker pitch the "Girls of [18]'49" sideshow, a simulated gold-rush dance hall; the Indians were barred from the show and so decided to start their own "'49".[9] At the 1983 American Indian Exposition, held at the same fairgrounds, a tape loop blared enticement into the midway tent show ("Bigfoot . . . Bigfoot . . . See the giant snakes alive . . . Bigfoot").

Additionally, various fundamentalist preachers currently bring their crusades to local schools, churchyards, and the Anadarko fairgrounds, drawing many Indians. Their counterparts on Sunday morning radio and television programs are among the many media figures heard routinely in Indian households. Secular talkers in the form of television game show and talk show hosts – Oprah, Geraldo, Bob Barker, Letterman – are also constantly present in the Indian homes. But since the wide institution of the electrified, automotive intertribal powwow following World War II, perhaps the most influential models for the aspiring powwow emcee have been other powwow emcees.

Powwow technique "kind of goes down the road," one emcee told me. With so many Indian and non-Indian inspirations, it is no wonder that powwow culture has produced talkers who display outstanding wit and control.

Powwow Space and Time

The ideal site for a powwow is a flat field without tall grass, with shade trees and running water nearby, a place that replicates the archetypal campsite of buffalo days.[10] The site should be away from the main roads yet be reasonably accessible. Electric lines are brought in to power the floodlights and public address system, and well water is usually available. Outhouses grace some of the frequently used places; otherwise one finds an array of rented portable toilets. Most dance grounds have an "arbor" constructed from four-by-fours, a more durable counterpart to the willow brush arbor that used to provide shade at Southern Plains dances. Benches are set up for the dancers around the dance ring, either permanent seats or temporary ones fashioned from planks and concrete blocks. Spectators bring their own aluminum, folding lawn chairs, and the singers carry in auditorium-type metal or wooden folding chairs. Chairs are marked on the back with the owners' last names.

Powwows may be held on the private property of the sponsoring family or on grounds maintained by the various patriotic and descendants' organizations. The clubs also often have halls adjacent to the dance ground for winter powwows; these are metal buildings with concrete or dirt floors that can do double duty for bingo games or traditional hand games. Occasionally dances are held on school grounds; at municipal parks, ball fields, or rodeo arenas; or on the grounds or in the gymnasium at the tribal government complexes.

Except when a dance is held in an urban location, many attendees will camp at the site during the event. Campers drive in and stake out their space among the shade trees, away from the dust of the parking area. Those who arrive early may save adjoining space for their relatives. The campers prefer canvas wall tents and cots reminiscent of reservation-issue equipment over trendy backpackers' tents and sleeping bags. Tipis may be seen here and there around the camp area.

The camp area lies in the outermost of several "concentric circles of attentiveness," theoretical boundaries that mark the participants' actual involvement in the dance activity.[11] Around the tents the atmosphere is informal and relaxed. Families take their meals, dancers get their outfits ready, and singers lounge in their cots, listening to tapes of the previous night's singing.

Much visiting and gossiping – an essential part of the powwow experience – takes place in the camp area. This zone is out of earshot of the emcee's announcements.

Between the camps and the dance arena is a space that may be occupied by one or more food concession booths and traders' tables. Here soft drinks and fast foods, including fry bread and Indian tacos (fry bread topped with lettuce, chili, and cheese), are available, along with jewelry, beadwork, shawls, recordings of Indian music, and such items as "powwow power" baseball caps and bumper stickers ("Got 'um teepee, need 'um squaw"). This area between the tents and arena also serves as a circular walkway, around which people stroll when looking for friends or selecting a place to set up their chairs to view the dancing. At night teenagers roam the area in groups, smoking, eating, and flirting, trying their best to appear uninterested in the singing and dancing. Onlookers who are just stopping by for a few hours may drive into this area to watch from the hoods of their cars, and day visitors also use the area for parking when a separate lot is not available. From this distance people can often hear the emcee but do not respond continually to his announcements.

The arena itself consists of more concentric circles. The dance ring is bounded by the arbor and adjacent unshaded areas, where the spectators set up their lawn chairs, sometimes several rows deep. The more marginal dancers are seated in the lawn chair section. These include men in street clothes who may enter the ring for special dances, and women who are entitled to dance many of the dances in their street clothes as long as they wear a shawl over their shoulders while in the ring. The women fold the colorful fringed and appliquéd shawls neatly over the backs of their chairs when they sit down. Those seated in this area are encircled with sound from the loudspeakers and are expected to be attentive. They should be listening and watching. Though they are permitted to talk most of the time, they must stand in silence at solemn moments, as directed by the emcee.

The east side of the arena has an opening that serves as the general entrance to the dance ring and the path of the Grand Entry procession that starts each evening's program, though otherwise dancers may step in from all directions. The announcer's table is set up opposite the opening, within the spectators' zone. Thus the arena resembles a tipi, with its door to the east (*tabetoinakwʉ*; "sunrise direction," or *muhyʉnakwʉ*, "door direction," in Comanche) and the seat of ownership or authority to the west (*kahpinakwʉ*, "bed direction"). The emcee holds forth at the west, sitting behind the table for routine matters but stepping in front, to the edge of the dance ring, and standing there for giveaways and special invocations.

By so moving, the emcee signals the gravity of his talk at certain points, for the perimeter of the dance ring, marked by the dancers' benches, is sacred space. Movement within this circle, whether dancing or approaching the emcee's table, is generally clockwise, in harmony with the path of the sun as viewed from the northern hemisphere. Sunwise direction connotes sacredness in many ritual contexts; for example, it is the proper way to move in the peyote tipi. Except during "specials" (dances in which relatives and friends come out to join an honoree), people are not allowed in the dance area without regalia (the emcee, singers, arena director, and water boys are exempt from this requirement). Spectators are not to stroll across the dance area, even if no one is dancing. Children and pets are to be kept from wandering in, and prior to some serious dances the emcee issues a warning to this effect. He may state that any dogs entering the dance ring will be shot, an allusion to traditional warnings of the past. And he will announce that any women who are "in their moon" should please leave the area, referring inexplicitly to the belief that menstrual blood is a polluting influence that harms men's supernatural power.

Placement of the drum in the center of the dance ring marks the consecration of the area. The men singers set their chairs in a circle around the large horizontal drum, and any women singers who join them encircle the men partly or fully with another row of chairs. The circular drum raises associations with other material and metaphysical circles – the tipi floor, the old-time camp circle, the sun and moon – suggesting domestic, tribal, and cosmic harmony. The drum is personified; it receives tobacco offerings; its beat is the heartbeat of the powwow. It is an individual, for in Plains directional symbolism the center is reckoned as the position of ego. Thus powwow space is defined as a series of ever smaller circles, each one requiring more intensive involvement in the celebration, until ultimately, through metaphoric connections suggested by the drum, contemplation is directed beyond the dance ground. With his talk the emcee regulates the movement of people through these circles as well as directs their thoughts within and without.

Although the powwow is often described as "secular," much ethical and religious ideology is expressed throughout the event, and sacred and secular time periods alternate during the powwow day. The emcee demands a reverential attitude at various points by calling on the audience to stand. The American flag is brought in by veterans at the head of the processional at the emcee's order: "Gentlemen, bring in the colors." He commands, "Dancers, this is our flag. Respect it!" as the flag bearers make their way around. These exhortations likely have a direct basis in the native language directions given by the camp criers of old, delivered with imperative grammatical constructs in such Indian languages as Comanche.[12]

Emcees are adept at improvising prayers before mealtime. Unlike most of an emcee's commentary, which is in English, prayers may be delivered in Indian languages with an English synopsis. In more relaxed moments the emcee keeps ritual value in the forefront by relating a myth or extemporizing on the symbolism of some proceeding or nearby object. At one dance in 1983 the audience was treated to the origin story of the Comanche Tuhuwíhi ("Black Knives" or "Crow") Dance and the war exploits of the nineteenth-century Kiowa chief Big Bow. A replica of Big Bow's painted tipi had been set up outside the arena, and the emcee explained the pictures and colors on the lodge. In addition to infusing the audience with feelings of reverence, the announcer's alternation between a sacred and a secular focus mirrors a more general concern with structuring turn taking according to Indian rules.

The "this is our way" speech is a standard device in which the emcee addresses onlookers to explain the significance of ritual details. If an eagle feather falls off of a dancer's outfit, the dancing must stop, and a veteran is called out to recall a war deed, pray over the lost feather, and then pick it up and formally restore it to the dancer. The preservation of ritual order and respect for elders and warriors is inculcated with the tag "this is our way." Generosity and hospitality are reestablished as "our way" when the emcee explains the giveaway or the supper. The phrase "our way" is then used by onlookers to justify powwow customs. With such comments the emcee sets up a didactic chain; he reminds the Indians present of their own ideals while also teaching the non-Indian onlookers, who are then taught further by the Indians among them. Because all hearers are relearning or learning, some solidarity is engendered across the audience. At the same time a reminder is given that the event is an Indian one, with Indian rules. The emcee further sustains the moral tone by encouraging campers to invite strangers to supper and issuing warnings that alcoholic beverages are not permitted.

Other devices have a more overt purpose in promoting a feeling of togetherness, though, again, always while placing Indians in a central or superior position. Over the course of the weekend, it is common for the emcee to make frequent requests for information about who among the non-Indian visitors has traveled the farthest to attend. At the 1995 Comanche Nation

Fair a man and woman from France were so noted. "We have some friends visiting from France," the emcee told the audience. "Parle-vous Français?" he queried them with excellent pronunciation in an on-mike aside. The crowd laughed. "Je m'appel Bob," he said, this time with tenuous grade-school inflections, ridiculing himself but also drawing attention to his previous demonstration of competence. "We're more worldly than some people expect" was the metamessage. Sometimes during giveaways goods are set out around the arena by the host family, which then directs the emcee to call up anyone anonymously who wants to take a gift; the emcee will urge strangers by saying that whoever has come far should take one. With these practices the emcee not only emphasizes the core value of generosity but also underscores the reach that his event has had, perhaps even harking back to the times of exploration and frontier diplomacy, when whites were the minority visiting Indians on their turf.

The emcee also manages powwow time, or gives the illusion of doing so, in a difficult balancing act. The dance usually occurs over a three-day weekend with segments scheduled by the hour and published in a program. The emcee must see that the schedule plays out in order to execute the wishes of the sponsors. But participants come to enjoy a release from quotidian time, and their expectations must be met too. They are on "Indian time," a phrase they use to describe time unregulated by the clock, time that may be allowed to pass without activity or anxiety.[13] Even with the onus of running on schedule, the emcee appreciates and sometimes encourages this disregard for clock time. He knows that suspending time as ultimately imposed by the dominant white society is an expression of ethnic identity. He also understands that Indian time can suggest what Bergson called "duration": undivided eternity that in its inconceivability is equated with the supernatural.[14]

The emcee is often at the mercy of dancers who are slowly assembling or of hosts with an overly long giveaway list. He can hurry them if necessary or wait for them to get going and then add formal commands as if he were in control. If he allows delays he fosters reverence and perhaps dissociation, thereby giving some segments a sacred cast. Other times, when the dancers delay or a giveaway seems interminable and the seated dancers signal their impatience by gently shuffling their legging bells, the emcee must rescue the onlookers from timelessness with his offhand commentary.

The Emcee's Commentary

"Beautiful music for beautiful people," the emcee warbles as the music soars and the arena pulses with color.[15] This stock phrase is elaborated time and again as he encourages the participants.

> Ah, ladies and gentlemen, got some beautiful songs out here; Round Dance, everybody, all of you come out and Round Dance.[16]

> Once again I'm inviting you to come out . . . those of you sitting around the arena. Maybe your hearts are heavy tonight, but if you come out and dance a little while it will be lifted. Put your troubles aside and come on out and join in and war dance.[17]

Later the beauty of the women's dance contestants is noted.

> All these ladies are beautiful, every one of them. This is some of the finest. . . . All of these ladies have competed throughout their lives, all of them are winners. Sad to say, only three will win this contest. I would not want to have the job of a judge. However, I know one judge – I'd like to have his job. All these ladies . . . look at all these smiles and smiles and smiles looking at me. No nepotism here, not at all allowed. All my sisters are getting angry. Judges are turning in their tabulations; ladies, you may be seated. Good sportsmen, congratulating each other because they know only three can win.[18]

Then, announcing the winners in the Golden Age category, the emcee said he was calling the ladies by their names because their numbers were written next to their ages and he did not want to confuse the two. Here as in many instances the emcee employs humor to make his performance more entertaining and take the edge off serious management concerns. He fills time while the judges tabulate their scores and frankly raises the issue that is always on people's minds: whether the contest judging will involve favoritism.

Most humorous statements are met by those in the audience who are paying attention with a standard interjection: "aayyyyyy," with rising intonation, fading into laughter.[19] It is a sound reminiscent of Indian song vocables, many of which serve cueing functions for the singers and dancers.[20] It is a sound that says, "That was an Indian joke, and I got it." The emcee also uses this device as a cue, often following his wisecrack or punch line immediately with "aayyyyyy" so that his reaction and that of the crowd occur together, giving the exchange a unified conclusion and again promoting solidarity. As a signal of frame shift, "aayyyyyy" comes late in the utterance; this surprise timing adds humor, for the emcee often maintains the same serious vocal tone for his jest and utters no setup remark to indicate the frame shift at the beginning of the joke. The following joke even incorporates this device in its punch line: "What's the difference between a white dog and an Indian dog? A white dog goes 'ruf, ruf, ruf,' and the Indian dog goes 'ruf, ruf, ruf, aayyyyyy.' "

Constant joking is also a means of broaching Indian identity: first, it is axiomatic among powwow-goers that Indians have a distinct and well-developed sense of humor; second, the remarks and canned jokes often refer explicitly or implicitly to issues of Indian identity. Some jokes reflect on Indian ways. To this end the emcee turns his wit on himself and those around him. After introducing dignitaries from distant places, he adds, "I'm all the way from Cyril [two towns away]." Bid by the sponsoring family to take a giveaway gift himself, the emcee announces that the next recipient is a "wonderful person." To divide up the dance contestants, the arena director counts them into two groups by walking the ring and pointing: "one, two, one, two." "He can't count past two," the emcee quips, and "Our arena director used to be a Fancy dancer but he had to stop. His braids kept whipping his face." As a well-known champion War dancer ambles by, the emcee improvises a salutation: "Jonathan Windy Boy . . . lookin' for a windy girl." He makes a brief serious announcement: "Would the parents of Myron White Elk please come to the speaker's stand and get your child; he's lost." But this is closely followed with, "Parents, if you can't hold on to your kids, don't have any more, please!" Other public service announcements name a real person but have a fake purpose: "Kenneth lost his muffler. If you see it, please pick it up." This last joke raises the image of the stereotypical dilapidated Indian car, called "one-eyed Ford" in old '49 song lyrics.

Comments frequently play with the idea of endemic Indian poverty: "We Indians are poor. We shop at [K]row Mart in Billings and [K]ree Mart in Regina. Is there a Kiowa Mart? Actually, I shop at Target – [I] call it 'Targét' [pseudo-French pronunciation]." "He's a Crow," the Comanche woman I was sitting next to laughingly explained. "He's a dirty bird." A few minutes later the Crow emcee shifted to the common subject of Indian incompetence:

> "These Indians were flying home after a powwow. They got drunk the last night after the dance. Some of 'em repented next morning – those were the Christian Indians. They got on the plane finally, and as it taxies

down the runway [jet sound over microphone] they lurch to a stop. They hear over the loudspeaker, [slurred Indian dialect] 'Hey, I don't know how to drive this thing.' "

For listeners this story corresponded to a familiar pattern. When the oil boom of the late 1970s brought unusual cash flow into the Indian communities of southwest Oklahoma, many people purchased new vehicles. Often buyers opted for the fancy vans that were fashionable at the time, with poor gas mileage but paneled interiors, swiveling seats, and beds. In 1982 a story was circulating about a Comanche man who was traveling down the H. E. Bailey Turnpike in his new van and decided to try the cruise control: "So he set the button and went back to take a nap." Barnard collected a Comanche story in 1940 in which a young man donned a pair of newfangled dark glasses as he put on his regalia. Then he decided to nap until dark to refresh himself. He slept through till daybreak, but when he awoke he thought it was nighttime with a full moon: " 'Ah, what a night for romance,' he said as he crept toward the girl's tent. The girl's family was eating breakfast as he rounded the corner of the tent."[21]

The women in one Comanche family like to tell how everyone was watching television one day when the opening for the soap opera *Days of Our Lives* came on: the image of an hourglass and the announcer's ponderous observation, "Like sands through the hourglass, so are the days of our lives." One of the men asked, "What is that thing?" His wife told him that when white people die they cremate them and put the ashes in one of those things, and they just run back and forth from one end to the other. He believed this for a while, they giggle.

Indian food ways are another topic for jokes. Meals sponsored by the hosts are a significant part of the powwow, and the emcee announces when these are ready, often summoning guests to queue up for the food in some particular order (elders first, guests first) and marking the beginning of the mealtime by improvising a prayer. It would not be appropriate for an emcee to joke about the food actually being served, but emcees do sometimes joke about Indian food ways in general at other times during the powwow. "You know it's Indian soup if after you eat some you whistle backwards and your lips turn blue" and other references to the fat content are heard, as much a commentary on the self-conscious heart healthiness of the idealized non-Indian diet as a satire on Indian food ways. Similar comments and jokes about the standard fare then erupt as powwow-goers gather with their plates under the shade by their tents, in the outermost circle of involvement.

Tripe is occasionally served as traditional food, for in the old days organ meats were relished immediately after a buffalo was killed. Unlike the Scottish Burns's Night haggis, which is transformed by mincing and mixing with oatmeal and is often served in an antiseptic-looking paper cup, Indian tripe is ladled out in obvious pieces and retains a strong flavor. In Comanche "stomach" is called *sapʉ*, and in the language of the neighboring Kiowa it is called *bote*. These words sound enough like the English words *soap* and *boat* that their mere mention in the presence of white visitors can provoke chuckles and knowing glances as well as stories about confusion. The emcee may pick up on this motif: "This Indian atc too much bote [this word delivered with a belching sound]. He was driving home and got stopped by a cop. 'Let's see your license.' Then he made him walk the line. 'Okay, let's smell your breath – oohhh!' Aayyyyyy!"

Like some of the previous jokes, this one takes a turn against non-Indians, in this case remarking on the highway patrol officers called "Holsteins" (CB radio slang referring to black and white patrol cars), who are said to hassle late-night Indian drivers, be they powwow-goers or teenagers out for fun and minor delinquencies. Another cop joke uses a framework that is often applied to other supposed unfortunates, such as Texas aggies:

> These two Indians were driving along, and they see a loose pig. They look around, you know, then they grab that pig and put it between them in the front seat and put a hat and some sunglasses on it. Pretty soon they get stopped by the highway patrol. "Have you seen a loose pig?" "No." "Okay, go ahead." As the pickup drives off, one cop says to the other, "What do you suppose that pretty white woman was doing with those two ugly Indians?"

A localized variant was told to me some weeks later while driving through the Wichita Mountains Wildlife Refuge:

> My two friends were driving through the wildlife [refuge] here, and they hit a deer. They decided to keep it, but they were afraid of being caught because the animals are protected there. So they put it in the back seat and wrap it all up in shawls and put a bandanna [on] to cover those antlers. Pretty soon they stop at the store for some gas and some pop.

> The attendant looks in the back seat and says, "And would your mother like some ice cream?"

The last line here was delivered in a tone satirizing the whites' eagerness to please that Indian people often find superficial and cloying.[22] Paradigmatically, the equation is made between the policeman and the white man. Another white man joke epitomizes the nativistic vision of a landscape free from non-Indians:

> A white man sees an Indian jumping up and down on a manhole cover, saying "27, 27, 27 . . ." The white man is curious, so he goes over and says, "What are you doin'?" The Indian just smiles, pulls the cover off and points down into the manhole. The white man bends over to look, and the Indian boots him in and puts back the cover . . . starts jumping again: "28, 28, 28 . . ."

A favorite Anglo historical construct and name-brand fetishism are assaulted simultaneously with the stock epigram, often delivered in stereotypical "heap-big Injun" dialect, of "Custer wear arrow shirt." Columbus vies with Custer as the archetypal bungling white man in powwow jokes.

It is the postmodern condition that Indian people can comment on their commentators, and emcees do so with postmodern irony. On the first night of the 1994 Pawnee Homecoming powwow, someone turned in a lost tribal identification card. The emcee announced that they had found the man's ID card; he said that the government had spent a lot of money making them into Indians, so would he please come and get the card. Time passed and the emcee called again for the man to pick up his tribal ID card, "'cause you can't be an Indian without one."[23] On the last day of the same powwow, three anthropologists introduced themselves to the emcee, and he introduced them to the audience. Then he added that he himself was an anthropologist with a "PhD from OU" but was currently working in Nebraska, studying non-Indians.[24] In addition to the bureaucrats and social scientists, well-meaning white tourists also feel the lash of the emcee's tongue, as at the 1993 American Indian Exposition:

> I am a tour guide out on the Sonora Desert. I take rich white folks from the East Coast out into the desert and show the visitors the saguaro cactus which grows only in the Sonora Desert and at various Indian sites. I sing three songs, one of which is the Eagle Song. One day after I had finished singing the Eagle Song, I noticed a white lady. She was misty-eyed. I

> asked what was wrong. She said, "While you were singing the Eagle Song three eagles came and were circling you." I did not have the heart to tell her those were buzzards. I let her believe she had had a mystic experience.[25]

This capacity to effect ironic reversals is a hallmark of good emceeing, whether the barb is aimed outward or inward. At a small Comanche powwow one June Sunday the emcee noted: "Today is Father's Day. They ought to have brother-in-law's day. A day you can just beat him up." Instantly he subverted the non-Indian observance to address the area of supreme tension in Comanche kinship, the relationship between brothers-in-law, itself defused by a traditional joking relationship (the Comanche word for tarantula, *pʉhʉ reʃʃhtsi*, literally means "hairy brother-in-law"). Parodying his counterpart on television, an emcee at a 1983 Kiowa dance mimicked Richard Dawson, host of the then-current *Family Feud* game show: "One hundred Indians surveyed; favorite TV show: 'Love Bote.' One hundred Indians surveyed; favorite car: 'One-Eyed Ford.' One hundred Indians surveyed; favorite song: 'I'm Dreaming of a White Woman.' "

Some emcee remarks thus touch on the low-key sexual energy that is allowed to emerge at times during the weekend. The Lakota saying that "children are born nine months after the Sun Dance" reminds us of the erotic potential of Plains gatherings and that some of the assemblies that preceded the modern powwow featured institutionalized sexual license. On the Southern Plains this interest is pursued in song lyrics, particularly those accompanying the Round Dance, one of the few dances in which men and women are equated choreographically, and the similar '49 Dance, which is usually held late at night away from the main powwow grounds to isolate the less wholesome activities that are alleged to occur. Around the powwow campfires men tease one another about their "snags" (trysts). Miscegenation, which is a concern of Indians as well as non-Indians, is a subtopic in sexual songs and jokes.[26]

Aspects of Verbal Art

Powwow emcee activity clearly exemplifies "the nexus of tradition, practice, and emergence in verbal art."[27] Through this conjunction the emcee as performer builds for himself and his sponsors prestige, control of the event, and influence in shaping general ideology and social structure.

Besides the traditional foundations previously mentioned, it is noteworthy that Plains cultures typically rely on respect and joking relationships for social control and status delineation.[28] The emcee therefore carries into the public domain features of everyday conversation as it occurs in traditionalist households. Parallels also exist between powwow discourse and the trickster tales that are still told in many powwow families. In the emcee's jokes and stories, Indians often assume the trickster role, an identification that is also achieved in, for example, the Comanche narrative corpus, either by implication in the ambiguous human-coyote trickster character Kaawosa̲ or directly through the substitution of "Indian" for "Coyote" and "white man" or "soldier" for the trickster's animal dupe in tale variants.[29] Both the emcee's Indian subject and the Coyote betray their inadequacies through false pride; both also display mastery of situations, all in the name of establishing social standards.[30] The emcee himself assumes the role of "every Indian" – and thus trickster – by ridiculing himself, playing jokes on others, and broaching topics that, if not strictly taboo, are normally inappropriate in polite or ethnically mixed company.

As a matter of practice emcees exploit the paradoxical relation between power and solidarity.[31] Their formal commands promote structural order and thus produce ritual cohesion, but they also bring to the foreground social power distinctions of rank, ethnicity, and race. Their joking signals solidarity but is at the same time aggressive. The little aggressions that counteract the structural equality of joke sharers are of three kinds.[32] First, there is a mild attack on the subjects of the jokes. Second, the jokes are understanding tests imposed on the audience; they ultimately enhance common understanding, but initially they are a challenge. Third, whatever else their function, the jokes are told to control the timing and spatial arrangement of the event, so their performance is always coercive and sometimes even disruptive of regular discussion.

The power-authority paradox in powwow discourse replicates other salient paradoxes in Indian society, namely, the tension between communal and individualistic tendencies or the contrast between egalitarianism and rank. Such contrasts are acute among the Plains groups, whose hunter-gatherer egalitarian mores were tenuously balanced against individual initiative and nascent stratification stimulated by warfare, horse wealth, trade, and eventually incorporation into the state cash economy. The powwow mediates these contrasts through a variety of expressive means, including the giveaway and the alternation of communal and competitive dances. The emcee manages the expressions while at the same time his announcing embodies the desired mediation.

The emergent quality of the emcee's performance is evident not only in his improvisations but in the degree of longer-term influence that he establishes. To appreciate this influence it helps to recognize how he engages listeners in a set of common themes and stimulates responsive commentary around the powwow camps during the event and, later, in Indian homes. Viewed over time the emcee's performance appears to be dialogical. A few examples of this phenomenon follow.

In camp one evening during a 1983 Kiowa dance, some of the emcee's bote jokes were repeated and the conversation fell to old-time Indian food. Then a blond white woman who was married to a Comanche told about the time years ago when she was sitting in the bleachers at their son's Little League game. As the boy rounded the bases, a white man next to her yelled, "Come on, get that little gut-eater out." The woman told how she turned to him, righteously saying, "That little gut-eater is mine."

In a second example, a 1989 Comanche powwow in Cache, Oklahoma, was plagued by mosquitoes. Late into the night the emcee remarked that he was being eaten alive, that the dancers needed to dance to forget the mosquitoes, that they were dancing faster because of them, and so on. He directed the singers, "Let's have a *mutsikwàß aaß* [mosquito] song." To the audience he said, "Don't swat the mosquitoes. We've been raisin' them all year." Later, alluding to the hopelessness of bureaucratic responses, he remarked, "If you get bit tonight, just put your name on a slip of paper and pass it up." The next morning a man who had been to the powwow came by the household I was staying in. His first words were (in Comanche), "That boy is a real Comanche now." Everyone laughed immediately, recognizing his suggestion that I (a non-Indian) had undergone a blood transfusion. Blood is the operant metaphor for racial and ethnic identity, and people qualify for membership in a state- or federally recognized tribe on the basis of "blood quantum," the percentage of tribal ancestry they can demonstrate.

The powwow emcee deserves standing among the distinctive "American talkers" who have prompted interest in the folk artistry of verbal performance.[33] Their role and the powwow generally are secure fixtures in the Southern Plains cultural landscape. Appropriately, the staying power of the powwow is asserted in an emcee's joke: "This man who was a real good dancer died. His best friend, who was a good singer, mourned and mourned. Then one day, the dead man visits his friend. 'I've got good news. Heaven is wonderful. Every week they have a big powwow.' His friend says, 'That is wonderful! A powwow every week!' The ghost says, 'Yeah, but the bad news is, you're the head singer next week.' "

ACKNOWLEDGMENTS

This chapter originally appeared as an article in the *Journal of American Folklore* 112, no. 443 (1999): 40–57; an earlier version was presented at the 1997 annual meeting of the American Folklore Society. Commentators at the meeting and an anonymous reader for the *Journal* made helpful suggestions toward its refinement. For the Pawnee and 1993 American Indian Exposition examples, I am indebted to Maria Corral, who kindly shared her unpublished notes. All other field material was collected by me. Jessica West deserves thanks for her editorial assistance. Research support from the Wenner-Gren Foundation for Anthropological Research, the Institute of Texan Cultures, and the University of Texas at San Antonio College of Social and Behavioral Sciences and Division of Behavioral and Cultural Sciences is gratefully acknowledged. Above all my thanks go to the many members of the tribal communities in Oklahoma and Texas who have shared their knowledge and hospitality.

NOTES

1. Howard, "Pan-Indian Culture of Oklahoma," and Powers, *War Dance*, 61–112, together constitute a review of sources arguing for different cultural dynamic frameworks and terminologies that explain the powwow. My own processual framework is original as far as I know but owes its inspiration to Powers's critique of acculturation theory and his alternative "preservationist perspective."

2. The Alabamas and Coushattas, having entered Polk County, Texas, after about 1790 from Alabama via Louisiana, are normally assigned to the southeastern culture area. Since the 1930s, however, their Muskogean songs and dances have largely given way to ones borrowed directly from, or modeled on, Southern Plains traditions under repeated and now continual contact with the Comanches, Kiowas, and others.

3. Clark, *The Indian Sign Language*, 107.

4. Shimkin, "Comanche-Shoshone Words of Acculturation," 235; Wistrand Robinson and Armagost, *Comanche Dictionary*, 277.

5. See Hultkrantz, *Belief and Worship*, 156; Liljeblad, "Oral Tradition," 645.

6. Berlandier, *The Indians of Texas in 1830*, 134; John, "Inside the Comanchería," 38.

7. Wistrand Robinson and Armagost, *Comanche Dictionary*, 134.

8. Hagan, *Quanah Parker*, 102–5.

9. Feder, "Origin of the Oklahoma Forty-Nine Dance."

10. The description of space and time is derived from Gelo, "Comanche Belief and Ritual," 197–211.

11. Young, "Powwow Power," 81–315; see also Gilbert, "Urban Powwows," and Schweitzer, "The War Mothers," 158–59.

12. See Wistrand Robinson and Armagost, *Comanche Dictionary*, 261–67.

13. Ortiz, "American Indian Philosophy," 14; Young, "Powwow Power," 345.

14. Bergson, *Time and Free Will*.

15. See Hill, "The Flower World of Old Uto-Aztecan," for some exposition of Indian symbolic linkages among beauty, chromaticism, song, and spirituality.

16. Corral, "Report," 6.

17. Corral, "Report," 30.

18. Corral, "Report," 21.

19. Occasionally heard with an initial aspirate, this interjection is widespread. Alternatives that are apparently tribal specific include "aawww" with dropping intonation (Comanche) and "booo" with a long "o" sound and dropping intonation (Pawnee).

20. See Gelo, "Comanche Songs, English Lyrics, and Cultural Continuity."

21. Barnard, "The Comanche and His Literature," 253–54.

22. See Basso, *Portraits of "The Whiteman."*

23. Corral, "Report," 38.

24. Corral, "Report," 38.

25. Corral, "Pawnee Fieldnotes," 35.

26. See Gelo, "Comanche Songs with English Lyrics."

27. Bauman, *Verbal Art as Performance*, 48.

28. See Lowie, *Indians of the Plains*, 81–83, 115; Wallace and Hoebel, *The Comanches*, 140, 148.

29. See Buller, "Comanche and Coyote"; Gelo, "Comanche Belief and Ritual," 113–15; Schoen and Armagost, "Coyote as Cheat."

30. Barnard noted among the Comanches: "Several narrators have told me . . . that the animal that 'gets the better of someone else' in a story is a symbol of the Indian who can 'outsmart' his neighbor. When he is 'outdone' by another, he still can enjoy a laugh" ("The Comanche and His Literature," 220). Deloria (*Custer Died for Your Sins*, 148–68) views teasing as an important Indian means of social control and the ability to laugh at oneself as a mechanism for maintaining group harmony and coping with acculturative stress.

31. Tannen, *That's Not What I Meant*, 102.

32. See Norrick, *Conversational Joking*, 104–27, 134.

33. See Dargan and Zeitlin, "American Talkers."

REFERENCES

Barnard, Herwanna Becker. "The Comanche and His Literature." Master's thesis, University of Oklahoma, 1941.

Basso, Keith. *Portraits of "The Whiteman": Linguistic Play and Cultural Symbols among the Western Apache.* New York: Cambridge University Press, 1979.

Bauman, Richard. *Verbal Art as Performance.* Rowley MA: Newbury House, 1977.

Bergson, Henri. *Time and Free Will.* New York: Macmillan, 1910.

Berlandier, Jean Louis. *The Indians of Texas in 1830.* Washington DC: Smithsonian Institution Press, 1969.

Buller, Galen. "Comanche and Coyote, the Culture Maker." In *Smoothing the Ground: Essays on Native American Oral Literature,* ed. Brian Swann. Berkeley: University of California Press, 1983.

Clark, William P. *The Indian Sign Language.* 1885. Reprint, Lincoln: University of Nebraska Press, 1982.

Corral, Maria. "Pawnee Fieldnotes." Unpublished manuscript, 1993.

———. "Report on the 47th Annual Pawnee Homecoming Powwow." Unpublished manuscript, 1993.

Dargan, Amanda, and Steven Zeitlin. "American Talkers: Expressive Styles and Occupational Choice." *Journal of American Folklore* 96, no. 379 (1983): 3–33.

Deloria, Vine, Jr. *Custer Died for Your Sins: An Indian Manifesto.* New York: Avon, 1969.

Feder, Norman. "Origin of the Oklahoma Forty-Nine Dance." *Ethnomusicology* 8, no. 3 (1964): 290–94.

Gelo, Daniel J. "Comanche Belief and Ritual." PhD diss., Rutgers University, 1986.

———. "Comanche Songs, English Lyrics, and Cultural Continuity." *European Review of Native American Studies* 2, no. 2 (1988): 3–7.

———. "Comanche Songs with English Lyrics: Context, Imagery, and Continuity." *Storia Nordamericana* 5, no. 1 (1988): 137–46.

Gilbert, Tamara B. "Urban Powwows: Form and Meaning." *UCLA Journal of Dance Ethnology* 15 (1991): 78–90.

Hagan, William T. *Quanah Parker, Comanche Chief.* Norman: University of Oklahoma Press, 1993.

Hill, Jane H. "The Flower World of Old Uto-Aztecan." *Journal of Anthropological Research* 48, no. 2 (1992): 117–44.

Howard, James. "Pan-Indian Culture of Oklahoma." *Scientific Monthly* 81, no. 5 (1955): 215–20.

Hultkrantz, Åke. *Belief and Worship in Native North America.* Syracuse NY: Syracuse University Press, 1981.

John, Elizabeth A. H. "Inside the Comanchería, 1785: The Diary of Pedro Vial and Francisco Xavier Chaves." Translated by Adán Benavides. *Southwestern Historical Quarterly* 98, no. 1 (1994): 27–56.

Liljeblad, Sven. "Oral Tradition: Content and Style of Verbal Arts." In *Handbook of North American Indians*, vol. 11, ed. Warren L. D'Azevedo. Washington DC: Smithsonian Institution, 1986.

Lowie, Robert H. *Indians of the Plains*. 1954. Reprint, Lincoln: University of Nebraska Press, 1982.

Norrick, Neal R. *Conversational Joking: Humor in Everyday Talk*. Bloomington: Indiana University Press, 1993.

Ortiz, Alfonso. "American Indian Philosophy." In Convocation of American Indian Scholars, *Indian Voices*. San Francisco: Indian Historian Press, 1970.

Powers, William K. *War Dance: Plains Indian Musical Performance*. Tucson: University of Arizona Press, 1990.

Schoen, Lawrence M., and James L. Armagost. "Coyote as Cheat in Comanche Folktales." *Western Folklore* 51, no. 2 (1992): 202–7.

Schweitzer, Marjorie. "The War Mothers: Reflections of Time and Space." (University of Oklahoma) *Papers in Anthropology* 24, no. 2 (1983): 157–71.

Shimkin, Demitri. "Comanche-Shoshone Words of Acculturation." *Journal of the Steward Anthropological Society* 11, no. 2 (1980): 195–247.

Tannen, Deborah. *That's Not What I Meant*. New York: Ballantine Books, 1986.

Wallace, Ernest, and E. Adamson Hoebel. *The Comanches: Lords of the South Plains*. Norman: University of Oklahoma Press, 1952.

Wistrand Robinson, Lila, and James Armagost. *Comanche Dictionary and Grammar*. Dallas: Summer Institute of Linguistics and the University of Texas at Arlington, 1990.

Young, Gloria Alese. "Powwow Power: Perspectives on Historic and Contemporary Intertribalism." PhD diss., Indiana University, 1981.

KATHLEEN GLENISTER ROBERTS

8. Beauty Is Youth
The Powwow "Princess"

In his book *The Rez Road Follies*, Anishinaabe Jim Northrup reflects on the multifaceted quality of contemporary Native American powwows and comments on the powwow princess as a dubious "new tradition." He writes: "First, why a Princess? Isn't that a concept borrowed from the Europeans, the royalty ranking system that came from their world? . . . Are we so hard up for traditions that we have to use one of these discarded ideas? Who started the Princess contests anyway? It looks like a dead-end job being a Princess. I never hear of anyone going on to become a Queen."[1]

The wry humor of Northrup's statement is undeniable, yet if we delve more deeply into the symbolic value of the powwow princess, we may come to a different conclusion. This chapter examines the yearlong "life cycle" of a powwow princess, beginning with a contest and ending with a giveaway for a princess at the conclusion of her reign. Both events suggest that the powwow princess is unique. First, the contest discourse – present in the words of both the emcee and the contestants – distinguishes young Indian women as icons of their community, less arbitrary than the sign qualities of beauty queens in mainstream America. Second, the ritual aspect of the giveaway for the outgoing princess lends insight into the power of tradition in powwows as it crosses the boundaries of womanhood and gender. I begin with a discussion of the differences between Native and non-Native "beauty pageants."

In our small world of Coca-Cola and congeniality contests, it is true that the once-"Western" phenomenon of the beauty pageant has been replicated and assimilated to fit cultures in every corner of the globe, large and small, national and local. In their book *Beauty Queens on the Global Stage: Gender, Contests and Power*, Colleen Ballerino Cohen, Richard Wilk, and Beverly Stoeltje illustrate that beauty pageants not only exist everywhere but are also powerful instruments of cultural contestation in and of themselves.[2] Even when community values do not come into conflict, it is clear that they lie at the heart of all beauty contests and that the young woman chosen as the winner is the ultimate "sign" of these beliefs and practices, because she somehow embodies them in her appearance.

For most beauty contests, especially in the mainstream United States, the physicality of the young women seems to far outweigh other aspects of their personhood. This tendency extends an inexplicable yet undeniable trope in Western culture of the woman as allegory.[3] The evidence for this is as obvious as the Statue of Liberty standing in New York Harbor or the scales of justice traditionally present in American courtrooms. The validity of the female form – in particular, the white female form – in representing liberty, justice, or any other mainstream value is unquestioned, reinforced through a socialized notion of aesthetics that privileges the female body (as an object of gaze) over that of the male.

Whatever the reason for human preferences in attractiveness and the aesthetics of the body, historically wide variation has existed between cultures and time in the standards of beauty. But the change is subtle, often imperceptible, and more and more there are clues that other cultures are subscribing to a Western ideal of beauty.[4] These global leanings toward Western norms of physical attractiveness only seem to underscore the female body's culturally sanctioned usefulness as allegory. The signification of women in beauty contests is taken equally for granted, enacted through a "show" of community identity and aesthetic norms. In her discussion of small-town American pageants, Beverly Stoeltje argues that because a young woman must find a community sponsor in entering a beauty contest, she begins the process of learning to represent something larger than herself.[5]

The "Snake Charmer Queen" contest in Sweetwater, Texas, is a classic example. In Sweetwater the dominance of physicality and "beauty" is particularly blatant: the contestants simply parade around the stage twice while the master of ceremonies describes their physical attributes and their likes and dislikes. Stoeltje writes: "Reminiscent of an auction block in which livestock or antiques or farm equipment are placed on display, described and auctioned off to the highest bidder, the young women are presented to the public, stripped of their privacy; knowledge of them is offered to the audience for their consumption. As the contestants are judged on their poise and beauty on stage, it is not possible to know just how significant any of this information is to the judges."[6]

I use Stoeltje's example here because of its stark contrast to Indian "beauty contests." If we are to take the lessons of signification taught by the Snake Charmer Queen as somewhat typical of mainstream American contests—and in fact the beauty queen literature would bear that assumption out – then we should be struck by the differences between Native and non-Native competitions. It is true that the powwow princess is another in a long worldwide list of queen variations that have emerged from the replication of the classic Western beauty contest in cultures very different from that of its origin. But, unlike queens in other cultures, the winners of Native beauty contests do not necessarily approximate a Western ideal. More to the point the Native contests seem to have very little to do with physical attractiveness at all, and everything to do with community identity, ritual efficacy, achievement, and representation.[7]

Powwow princesses do stand for something larger than themselves; they do become a sign. But the way they arrive at that status is active rather than passive and is more complex in terms of the "community" they represent. This happens in several ways during Indian events. First, the audience shows unusually strong support for all of the women involved; second, the participation patterns in the performances embody personal relationships; third, the event discourses work to forge links between identities; and finally, many objects and materials used in Indian princess contests symbolize the meaning of powwow and draw the winner into their realm of signs, thus allowing one to consider the deeper relationship between the "princess" and the powwow. To illustrate these points I offer next a narrative of the nation's "biggest" princess contest, Miss Indian World, held in conjunction with the Gathering of Nations powwow in Albuquerque, New Mexico, each April.

Powwow Princesses: Staging Community

The Miss Indian World contest demarcates the differences between Native and non-Native contests both implicitly and explicitly. It is open to unmarried women between ages eighteen and twenty-five who have no children and who have verifiable membership in a Native group. They must bring a female chaperone with them, usually an aunt or another older woman in their family. The contestants are judged in four categories: public speaking, personal interview, traditional talent, and dance. The women also vote for their favorite fellow contestant in the Miss Congeniality Contest.[8] Of the four categories the traditional talent competition is perhaps the most popular with the powwow crowd. It is staged in a venue separate from the rest of the competition, and the audience must purchase tickets for the privilege of watching the contestants perform and explain some action pertaining to the traditional way of life in their Native community. Hopi potter Ron Martinez has joked about "those Navajo girls . . . they take forever grinding corn."[9] But in reality each contestant has only three minutes to complete her performance. The traditional talent is judged on several criteria: organization, clarity, depth of presentation, authenticity, and overall talent.

I am using the term *performance* rather loosely for although nearly a thousand souls pay for their tickets to the traditional talent contest, the actions of the women on stage seem more like a communal sharing of knowledge. Only a handful of Anglos come to this event. The spectators are clearly supportive of the contestants in general, minimizing the sense of "competition" at the event.

This support was particularly evident when contestants – from a Western beauty contest standpoint – faltered somehow in their demonstration or slipped out of their performance frame. For example, one woman from the Northern Plains planned to narrate a myth from her tribe. She came out onto the stage smoothly and spoke clearly into the microphone – for one sentence. The second sentence of the story began: "The people . . ." – but she had no idea how to finish it. "The people," she said again, "the people . . . ," her voice trailing off. She stood, microphone in hand, contemplating what words were supposed to come next. The time seemed to pass swiftly, for after moments of silence, the warning lights blinked on stage to indicate that she had only thirty seconds left to complete her talent. Certainly, even if she could remember the memorized story, no time remained to tell it. So she raised her eyes from the floor, grinned at the audience, announced, "I forgot," and concluded her performance. Again, from a Western competitive standpoint, such a "failure" may have drawn at best pity and at worst denigration from the audience. At the Miss Indian World competition, in contrast, this woman received some of the most thunderous applause of the evening and warm, supportive smiles. She grinned some more, crowed "Thank you!" into the microphone, waved, and marched off the stage just as confidently as she had come onto it.

This is not to say that the Miss Indian World competition is somehow not taken "seriously" or that the quality of performance does not matter. Indeed, the sheer popularity of the event for Indian spectators clearly indicates its significance to the Gathering of Nations powwow and to the powwow Indian community as a whole. But the incident above exemplifies the disparate norms of "competition" between the powwow world and the larger American culture.

I stated earlier that the contestants in Miss Indian World are afforded the ability to represent themselves and their tribe through words as well as actions.

They are not muted like many contestants in mainstream American pageants, which are controlled by masters of ceremonies. But this does not mean that the Miss Indian World candidates go unsupported; on the contrary the structure of their traditional talent presentations allows for an unusual amount of creativity and for the symbolic representation of personal relationships.

The first startling difference between Miss Indian World and many non-Native contests is that the master of ceremonies is a woman. In 1998 it was Beulah Sunrise, a young Navajo-Pueblo woman who hosts a popular Native American music program at an Albuquerque radio station. Beulah stated each contestant's name, entry number, and tribal affiliations, then welcomed her onto the stage. Beulah exited the performance space each time, not to be heard from again until the contestant's time allotment had expired. The contestant was thus left alone to do as she wished – even to bring more people onto the stage if she chose. Many contestants performed their talent alone: tying tobacco leaves, explaining pottery, or recounting tribal narratives. Most contestants were supported in some way, however, be it overt or covert – for example, the women who danced usually did so to live music, with their singers either onstage or offstage. A few brought other dancers onto the stage with them. For example, Sunny Rose Yellow Mule danced the Crow Hop with her father, a fellow powwow dancer.

The incorporation of noncontestants into the traditional talent presentation resembles the overall discourse of Miss Indian World in its efforts to forge links among Native identities. The warmth of the joke, in particular, crosses tribal boundaries and adds to the esoteric dynamic of the contest performances. The talent presentations were peppered with "inside jokes" specific to one reservation but gleaned laughter from the entire audience. Sha Brady, a Navajo contestant, explained how to make pottery: "Then you take your 5-pound Bluebird Flour sack . . . ," she said at one point, and everyone chuckled. Another Navajo potter, Celinda McKelvey, began her talent presentation as follows: "You need to get some clay. You'll find this on any reservation, ayyy." For the paint, she continued, "I just go and get some flowers near the highway."

The reality of reservation life, especially in the Southwest, is thus gently teased out of the contestants' talents and into explicit discourse that can be enjoyed by the audience at Miss Indian World. The experience is simultaneously shared and unique: Bluebird Flour is the brand most available on the Navajo reservation, and while it would be unknown to Indians from places further afield, virtually all reservation dwellers must deal with limited choices in their grocery shopping.[10] Similarly, the references to clay and the highway – where one must go to find flowers – implicitly critiques the quality of land on reservations. At the same time these words situate the women and their traditional talents in very modern circumstances. Evie Sunnyboy, from Bethel, Alaska, recited a poem about freedom for her talent: "I want to be free / to eat fry bread," one line stated, a "universal" symbol distinctive in her stanzas of other fine imagery specific to her tribal land.

Evoking powwow-specific symbols also bounds the ritual of Miss Indian World, and other references in the speeches of the contestants help to establish a common identity within that frame. For example, the eventual winner in 1998, April Whittemore, from Fayetteville, North Carolina, drew raucous cheers from the women in the audience when she described her tribe – the Lumbees – as "matriarchal: the women were in charge." This last aspect seems essential to an Indian queen pageant such as Miss Indian World. Because the women speak for themselves, have complete freedom regarding their appearance, and situate themselves in a tribe or tribes that value their talents and knowledge, the contrast between Native and non-Native contests becomes evident. It was nonetheless a powerful moment when Beulah Sunrise took a few moments to "joke" about the differences between them:

But there is a big difference between Native
And non-Native contests.
In Native contests,
You find out *about* these girls.

In non-Native contests,
You see a girl and
You find out

How much hairspray she can use,
How much lipstick,
How much tape she can put on her –
You-know-what!
Her *butt*!
In a non-Native contest
She shakes it
And sees if she can make it!

You know I used to be in those contests.
I did the Native ones

But I also did the non-Native.
My grandmother told me
to quit it
Before I made somebody go blind!
I think our kind
Is much better.
Don't you?[11]

Beulah, like so many powwow emcees, excels in the art of self-deprecation. But beyond her narrative of participation in non-Native contests, it is apparent from her allegorical use of "girl/girls" – intentional or no – that she is critiquing non-Native events. While the women in Miss Indian World are referred to as "these girls" and are understood to typify contestants in any Native pageant, Beulah invents an imaginary, single woman when discussing non-Native beauty contests: "You see a girl. . . . She shakes it and sees if she can make it." In a sense this hypothetical woman is an allegory for non-Native contests, just as the winner of these contests becomes an allegory for whatever values are dear to their producers and supporters. Just like the allegorical woman, her appearance is supposed to "speak" for her – in a not-so-complimentary manner, it seems, here in Beulah's oratory. Beulah clearly differentiates between observing the appearance of a woman and "finding out *about*" her. The old proverb "beauty is only skin deep" may be trite, but it underpins all Native contests. There is no competition designed to show the body; women in Miss Indian World's traditional talent competition wear anything from black pantsuits to crushed velvet skirts and tunics to buckskin dresses adorned with elk's teeth. And, of course, many wear powwow regalia.

The presence of powwow dress in Miss Indian World clearly marks the salience of the princess as a sign. Although the women competing in this major contest hail from all over the continent and thus represent disparate tribal groups, their common identity is that of the powwow. They are "powwow people," familiar with emcees, jokes about reservations, frustrating shopping trips, and relying on family and friends. Thus, while the discourse discussed above plays with tribal identities, it also solidifies the common ground on which everyone – contestants and audience alike – finds himself or herself through the choice to participate in powwows.

This common ground is also reflected in the materials used by candidates in Native "beauty" contests. First, as I mentioned, the contestants in Miss Indian World choose their own outfits for the traditional talent competition. In this beauty pageant, juxtaposed as it is with the wide range of dress, powwow regalia emphasizes the "powwow identity" that permeates the contest. Using the word *traditional* to also describe a dance style thus has a double meaning both for the dress outfits and for the contest itself: Mr. Yellow Mule's purple-sequined tunic and Evie Sunnyboy's poem about fry bread are as traditional here as buckskin dresses and the gathering of pine nuts. When the contestants place their Pendleton blankets down on the stage before beginning their presentations, they are demarcating their space as a "powwow space," reflecting the common practice at powwows of placing blankets on chairs or benches to reserve seats and situate a family's position in the crowd.

One of the most valued results of Miss Indian World is that different tribes have the chance to learn about one another.[12] The specific tribal identities displayed in the contest, then, are extremely significant. However, evoking and explicitly displaying signs of "powwow identity," such as fry bread and blankets and "traditional dress," are also a way to saturate the event and situate it in a highly contemporary context. Miss Indian World is thus a representative – and a representation – of a very complex set of values and identities.

Powwow Princesses

To say that a powwow princess becomes a sign of "powwow identity" seems absurdly obvious and yet also intriguing. Like the Pendleton blankets and "traditional" outfits that have become so commonplace and familiar, the Indian princess is taken for granted as a fixture of most Plains contests. It should be clear that the structure of the contests does call for a winner in a very different manner than do non-Native beauty pageants. Physical beauty is not a factor except insofar as the body must convey skill as a powwow dancer. The body itself is not judged by any aesthetic standard; the title of Miss Indian World, for example, has in past years been held by women of all "shapes and sizes." Again, the body is important because it carries traditional dress, because it moves well to the drums of powwow, because it performs traditional skills. These are the things that make it "beautiful."

Another obvious difference between the contests, explained so eloquently by Beulah Sunrise, is that the women in Native contests have a chance to speak for themselves. Indian princesses, above all, must be excellent public speakers. Their major duty as a princess is to travel to other powwows and represent their tribe there. During the grand entry of a powwow, all of the princesses, referred to as "royalty," enter the arena behind the flag bearers and lead all the dancers. As part of the opening ceremonies of a powwow, they are introduced to the crowd by the emcee and then each make a short speech.

A powwow princess will usually travel to one powwow per weekend from Memorial Day until Labor Day, and perhaps also during the colder months. Since she will greet crowds containing many of the same spectators week after week, she varies what she says. She is particularly respected if she begins her speech in her tribal language. She will then state her name, her title, where she is from, and her hopes and wishes for everyone involved with that particular powwow. Though brief, the speech is always enjoyed by the crowd. The princess may evoke festive imagery to reach out to the spectators; for example, "I hope you have a great time and eat lots of fry bread," as Leslie Morton told the crowd at Arlee, Montana, in 1999.

Aside from a rapport-building reference such as Morton's, however, the princess will not joke with the audience in the same way that she did in her contest or that the powwow emcee does. An interesting dyadic relationship exists between the powwow emcee and the princess during the event. While the powwow emcee breaks his discussion of serious matters with jokes and helps run the action of the powwow, the princess – in her more formal public speaking – lends a kind of "dignity" to the event, a certain "royal" presence.[13] It is her responsibility to know the concerns of the community hosting the powwow, whether she is a visitor or a member of it herself, and to reference them in her speech. Most of the princesses introduced at Arlee in 1999, for example, congratulated the organizers and the Flathead Nation on their 101st annual Fourth of July powwow. The young feminine princess, in contrast to the middle-aged male emcee, is established as a "pure" sign: she represents the "good feelings" of a powwow and its innocence.

The innocence of the princess as a sign is interesting. Indeed, teenage girls who choose to dance in powwows – let alone enter the princess contests – often make significant sacrifices in terms of their social lives. April Quiver, a Shoshone woman from Wind River, Wyoming, returned to powwow dancing at age twenty-five. "I quit when I was fourteen," April says, "because I wanted to snag."[14] "Snagging," put simply, is pursuing potential romantic partners at a powwow. This activity is very playful but can also have long-lasting consequences; most people who met their spouses at powwows refer to the beginning of their relationship as "snagging." The teenage snagging is happening all the time; outside the dance arena, beyond the spectators and usually next to the vendors, is a ring of continuous flirtation and even literal "chasing" between teenaged boys and girls. It is this part of the powwow that many teenagers would rather enjoy instead of being obliged to dance at specific times during the event.

The princess, by prioritizing dancing over snagging, thus remains discreet in her relationships and also is regarded as highly mature and responsible for her age group. Above all she proves that she is committed to the powwow as an extension of her Indian identity. She "believes in" the powwow and is one of the powwow people. She thus becomes a pure sign for the powwow itself in that it has value for her and for those who entrust her with the responsibilities of "royalty." This is the essential function of any winner in a beauty contest, Native or non-Native: the princess embodies the very values of the community. This role became blatantly obvious during the queen contest at Eastern Shoshone Indian Days, in Fort Washakie, Wyoming. One of the three contestants danced extremely well, was older and more experienced than the others, and spoke comfortably and clearly. To an outside observer it seemed that she should have won. But while her manner of speaking was very good, her *words* themselves did not reassure the judges. In response to the question "How will you represent the Wind River Reservation as queen?" she concluded her reply: "I hope to represent them in a non-powwow way."

"I don't know why she said that," April Quiver shrugged later. "It doesn't really make sense. I don't think the judges even knew what a non-powwow way could be. I mean, the queen doesn't really go any place as queen except to powwows. I can't even think what she meant." Obviously, the judges did not understand either; they named a different, younger contestant as queen. The contestant who sought to represent the tribe in a "non-powwow way" no doubt had good intentions, and probably it would have been quite refreshing and innovative to have the queen assume new duties beyond the powwow circuit. But for the purpose of the queen contest ritual, the idea of a "non-powwow way" seemed puzzling and gratuitous. The princess as a sign is, perhaps, taken for granted, but her role is to legitimate the contest itself, to solidify the world of the powwow.

This particular contestant's defeat underscores the definitive quality of the ritual, going to the heart of a common debate among scholars studying beauty contests in general: what exactly is happening during a beauty contest? Stoeltje has characterized the beauty contest as a ritual in which the winner undergoes a rite of passage into something akin to womanhood and is introduced to the semiotic value of her role as a woman.[15] If the values of the community are to be reflected in the winner of the beauty contest, then the beauty contest does what all rituals do: it reinforces that which the community considers important, it renews society's sense of order, and it soothes any disturbances associated with the changing roles of individuals.[16] Above all it legitimates the community's identity and perpetuates its social order. To quote Jean La-Fontaine: "The rite can thus be read not merely as a change of status for those who are initiated [who win the contest], but as a demonstration of concepts in which the participants are both actors and audience."[17] The beauty pageant is not hinged on the individual and how she chooses to regard her role; rather it is predicated on the communal identity that has been mapped onto her and that she is now expressing for others, as a sign. She has undergone a ritual, and so has her community.

So it is with the queens and princesses of powwows, who are signs of the powwow and also signs of the ritual that crowned them. The contest that happens every year is a marker for an event everyone anticipates with excitement; seeing the princess from one's "home" powwow is like seeing that powwow and the memory of it take form and flesh. The powwow circuit depends on the success of a cycle of powwows hosted on different reservations and in different towns; the princess is a sign of the life force of the reservation and the success of their powwow. Not only is she a young person committed to tradition – to keeping the culture "alive" – but she is also a shining reminder of festive celebration. She undergoes the ritual, becomes queen, and is a sign of the people as well as a sign of the ritual itself.

Because the powwow is always undergoing invention and re-invention, every crowning of a new princess is a renewed "show" of what is important to the powwow community. Princesses are committed to their dancing in lieu of other pursuits, take part fully in the ritual heart of powwow rather than the festival fringes of it, and establish themselves as ceremonial, dignified speakers in a dyad with the amusing emcee. Through these actions they become pure signs, legitimating the invented community and "reigning" over the social order of powwow. Like so many aspects of the powwow, the queen cycle is perpetuated annually, through the naming of a new winner. One way this happens is through the outgoing princess's giveaway.

A powwow giveaway is another ritual event in which the values and aspirations of the community are enacted through a "show" of relationships. Indeed, in many ways the community itself is formed in a powwow giveaway, granting it significance on equal footing with princess contests. Imagine for a moment, then, the saturation of meaning present in a giveaway centered around the princess herself. The following discussion considers is intended to reveal the very essence of the powwow princess by examining closely her words and actions at a giveaway.

A Giveaway Fit for a Princess

It is an indicator of the excellent planning in powwow that the queen and her attendants hold giveaways at the end of their reigning period; this gives the family a chance to store up goods and money and to carefully consider who should be included in the ritual exchange. Most importantly it also reinforces the status of the outgoing princess as a symbol; she has "represented" the tribe well, and this is her greatest moment of honor as a reward for performing her duties. She is thus a redoubled sign in her giveaway: first honored as the ideal powwow participant and now honored again for fulfilling that role for a whole year. This should have been the case in Naraya Washakie's giveaway, held at a recent celebration of Eastern Shoshone Indian Days at Wind River, Wyoming.[18] Naraya was the outgoing princess for Shoshone Indian Days, and the giveaway was an occasion to officially honor her for many accomplishments. As the master of ceremonies Wes Martel stated:

> We all take great pride
> In our children
> And this here this afternoon
> Is being held in example
> Of the pride they hold
> For their child.

Naraya's ritual giveaway was affected, however, by an event that struck her family just six weeks before Shoshone Indian Days. The passing of Naraya's godmother and maternal aunt, Maria, plunged the family into deep grief just before the summer powwow season was to begin.[19] Particularly at the Wind River Reservation, it is traditionally difficult to keep participating in powwows after having recently lost a loved one. Usually powwow dancers who are in mourning for someone will hold an "Into the Circle" giveaway before they begin celebrating at powwows again. "Into the Circle" implies that someone has left the circle, that is, that she has stopped dancing for one reason or another. Maria had told Naraya's mother, Lucy, that she wanted them to keep dancing. Making this public, Wes Martel told the audience at Naraya's giveaway:

And before she passed on
She told her sisters that
She didn't want them to
Really give up
This way of life that they hold.
They always have powwows . . .
And she wanted them to continue.

But the tradition at Wind River is such that any type of memorial giveaway – or any giveaway in which a loss is mentioned – is prone to taking on the characteristics of an Into the Circle ceremony, designed to restore the lives of the bereaved "back to normal" – normal, in this case, meaning being able to participate fully in powwows. The lines between honoring Naraya and overcoming grief through an Into the Circle ceremony became necessarily blurred.

Such a "hybrid" event, though not intended to be such, strains under the weight of ritual efficacy. This is particularly evident in an analysis of the ritual speech lent to the event by Wes Martel, the emcee for Naraya and her family. For instance, because Wes was an older man in the powwow community (and the emcee chosen by Naraya's family), his descriptions and assessments of Naraya throughout his talk were completely appropriate, and even necessary. As noted she was "royalty" at this powwow because she was a young person who had become a sign of the ideal behavior and deportment of young people in this powwow community. So Wes commended her for "always smiling / and greeting people." He talked about her representation of the Shoshone tribe, "doing the best she can," for about thirty lines. However, he also discussed her mother's feelings over the loss of Maria for nearly as long. Moreover, though the audience was meant to focus on an image of Naraya "always smiling" through Wes's facilitation of her giveaway, instead Naraya was very sad at this event and in fact cried silently through much of it.

In terms of materiality Naraya was also an ambiguous symbol. The audience learned from Wes that she was wearing a dress made for her by Maria, "who passed away a month and a half ago." Naraya's appearance itself was thus a virtual icon of grief. When the gifts began to be distributed, Wes became aware of the subdued nature of the giveaway and tuned his talk to that level, simply calling people forward. By stepping back slightly from his role, he allowed the donees to commiserate with Naraya and her family and also allowed the giveaway to retain privacy.

But while this event did emerge as unique by queen giveaway standards, it ultimately reinforced Naraya's role as royalty in this powwow system. This happened in several ways. First, we have already seen some of the discourse in Wes's speech as it pertained to Naraya and to queens in general. He continued with these words:

Naraya enjoyed being Princess
Enjoyed dancing
Crafts
Taking part in the traditional ways.

More significantly, among the many people Wes called forward to receive a gift from Naraya, he privileged the then-current queen of Shoshone Indian Days by referring to her title first:

Okay the family is calling for
This year's queen
Of the Shoshone Indian Days.
[five-second pause]
Family is calling for Brenda James.

During the pause in these lines, Wes turned from the microphone to consult Naraya as to the name of the 1999 queen, who had just been named the night before during the queen contest. The fact that the queen – no matter who she was – was deserving of a gift from the family indicated that it was the role of the queen, her symbolic value, that was emphasized.

A second way that this ambiguous giveaway underscored Naraya's status as royalty is that its form mirrored the dyad between emcee and princess. It is unusual for a central donor to speak publicly during his or her own giveaway. During Naraya's giveaway, though, Wes introduced her and said that she would like to say a few words. Naraya's speech was very short compared with the talking Wes had done:

Well first of all I'd like to thank you for all coming
I hope you had a safe trip.
That's all thank you singers and dancers for your part
For last year's attendant.
I hope you all have a safe
Trip going back.
Thank you.

Naraya was choked up during this speech; her words came out thickly, a bit tremulously, as she tried her best not to cry. After it was over she wiped away more tears and was comforted by her mother. This event truly was emotionally charged, and very moving for the audience. Naraya's speech here was in many ways like one she would make for a powwow crowd after a grand entry and her introduction by the master of ceremonies. "I'd like to thank you all for coming / I hope you had a safe trip" is typical of a princess greeting, and in fact Naraya tried to stop there, saying, "That's all." But her ritual called for some mention of the moment at hand, so she remembered to thank everyone who had supported her while she was princess. Interestingly, she referred to herself in the third person, minimizing her agency in this giveaway, and deemphasized it even more when she returned to the fixed-phrase formula of the "safe trip" in her final lines.

As Richard Bauman notes, a formula can have four functions: serving as a marker for a genre, serving to name the genre, producing a referential function for the item itself (as in "once upon a time"), or emphasizing the communicative relationship between the performer and the audience.[20] No one could doubt Naraya's sincerity in hoping for the security and health of people at the powwow, but as princess, this was something she had become accustomed to saying with a microphone. Her use of the fixed phrase "safe trip" underscored her role as the princess and as the performer in that moment, binding her to the audience.

And the formula's significance did not stop there. Naraya's sorrow throughout the giveaway, and especially during this speech, contrasted starkly with Wes's ebullience when she was finished speaking. Receiving the microphone back from her, Wes cried cheerily, "All right, how about that?" In this odd keying, Naraya and Wes seemed to be speaking at cross purposes. Wes cut off their interchange by falling back into the formula of the princess introduction following grand entry. Because very few people ever speak during their own giveaways, this was a difficult frame for Wes to maintain and he in fact abandoned it; this ritual had been rather solemn, imbued with loss and gift giving, but he was as jovial with Naraya here as he would have been after a grand entry. Clearly what had slipped was the *genre* of performance in this moment: as Bauman has shown, fixed-phrase formulae mark genres, and here we had two formulae – one from Naraya wishing everyone a "safe trip," and one typical response of "How about that?" from the emcee to switch to the familiar princess greeting. Naraya's wish to speak during her own giveaway introduced a new register to the performance of the giveaway, but in the end she embedded a totally different genre into the ritual. Her role as princess allowed her to speak but also limited her ability to break from that role when the emcee responded as if she were working in the familiar genre of princess greeting. Because of the tensions inherent in the giveaway, it was clear that her participation in the queen contest the previous year endowed her with semiotic obligations and had transformed her status.

These transformations that occur in beauty contests – which turn young women into signs – emerge from deep-seated beliefs about gender and festival. As Stoeltje points out, the woman's sign is a double one: a woman represents the community as synecdoche, but she also represents overall concepts of "female."[21] I would take powwow princesses in particular into a third semiotic realm: they represent the community, they represent their gender, and they also represent the ritual that named them and is to be performed annually as part of the overall attempt to hold the kinship of powwow together.

Powwow princesses are quite different from non-Native participants in and winners of beauty contests, as I have taken steps to illustrate. Like the cowgirls in Stoeltje's article, they have become – through contests like Miss Indian World – self-representations in addition to representing the community. They have power over the way they choose to signify in that they are able to speak for themselves, they communicate materially through clothing and props, and they act out both private and public relationships in their performances. The criteria of their selection is clear, perhaps because the idea of a "powwow community" or identity is finite and proscribed. I have been using the word *sign* rather generally here, but if we are to pin down the concept in a strict Peircean sense, we are reminded of the discrete terms behind the terms *symbol* and *icon*. Symbols, after all, are arbitrary: the grouping of the letters "q-u-e-e-n" forms a recognizable sign with a particular meaning understood by English speakers. Icons, on the other hand, have a particular meaning understood in a particular culture because of their association through resemblance. Icons are less arbitrary; they are linked to the meanings they represent in a logical or emotional way. In this sense powwow princesses are icons of their powwows. Non-Native beauty contestants seem to almost arbitrarily represent their community – for example, why is it that a pretty face, poise, and a slim body are meant to represent the hard workers of a farming community in Illinois?

The real dilemma of the princess, be she Native or non-Native, is extricating herself from the potential sign. And this, according to Elizabeth Cowie, cannot be done: women are always judged, always assessed, always embodying values.[22] Women differ from men in this quality. Deborah Tannen also argues that women are constantly and consistently marked. Their appearance can never be neutral, it always communicates.[23] When people become signs, "they are arbitrary, but they demand to be treated as essential and binding."[24] That is why Naraya's giveaway, as difficult as it is for everyone involved, must be accomplished and must mirror her identity as princess despite her attempts to deemphasize her agency and status. She is a symbol of innocence and excellence in the powwow world, choosing to dance rather than pursue other activities at powwows. She is closely bound to her family within and outside of the ritual. She is royalty in that she symbolizes the leadership of ritual in powwows, but she is not an arbitrary sign. Her individuality is important in the competitive powwow world, but her role as *icon* is equally important for the community.

The idea that powwow princesses have become icons rather than symbols – and thus are different from non-Native beauty contest participants – lends an interesting twist to the notion of woman as sign. It is indeed troubling that virtually every nation in the world today ascribes at least part of its identity, at least in a carnivalesque way, onto its women through beauty contests. But the powwow is more complex: it may be the youth of the princesses, rather than their gender, that demands semiotic status.

For example, at the same powwow in which Naraya held her giveaway, a ten-year-old boy named Kyle underwent his own ritual. A champion Fancy dancer and the pride of his family, Kyle was presented with an eagle feather for his regalia in an elaborate ceremony during the powwow competitive dancing. Kyle's father leads a drum at Wind River, and his aunt led the ritual speech, describing for the audience what was being accomplished. The eagle feather was tied to his hair, and he was given two cuffs beaded with red roses to wear on his wrists. The roses, meant to represent the Shoshone Nation, were given to him by his grandfather. His grandfather took Kyle's hands and rubbed his wrists together so that the two roses would meet. This shows a delightful link between words, actions and objects: the gifts Kyle has been given are fully his, are symbols of "the pride we all hold in our children," to use Wes Martel's words in opening Naraya's giveaway.

At the Shoshone Indian Days, Naraya's and Kyle's ceremonies end cap the competitive action by emphasizing the circular, perpetual notion of powwow. In their youth Kyle and Naraya are "representations" in more ways than one. Their familial clothing is testimony to the honor they deserve, and they are examples to other young people in the powwow world. In a culture that honors its elders as knowledge keepers, Naraya and Kyle are inverted signs in more than just a carnivalesque way: they are proof positive that the powwow identity is thriving, that the queen ritual as well as initiation rituals like Kyle's will continue in a system of many such transformations. "[Their] purpose is action to achieve transformed individuals but [their] effect is to demonstrate the power of traditional knowledge and legitimize a continuing social order."[25] Thus the circular tradition of the powwow, passing knowledge to its youth, produces beauty that transcends gender and questions the quotidian notion of the princess.

ACKNOWLEDGMENTS

Fieldwork and research for this article were supported through grants from the Folklore Institute at Indiana University, Bloomington, and through the President's Initiative for Undergraduate Research at Indiana University, Bloomington. Thanks to my undergraduate research assistants Alex Burgess, Roberta Carnaccini, Will Davis, and Brooke Roberts; to my IU professors Beverly Stoeltje, Richard Bauman, Ray Demallie, and Carol Greenhouse; to my colleagues at Duquesne University and especially to my research assistant Eric Grabowsky; to Clyde Ellis and Eric Lassiter for the editing; and to the men and women on the powwow trail who patiently gave of their time, knowledge, and talents.

NOTES

1. Jim Northrup, *The Rez Road Follies* (New York: Kodansha International, 1997), 82. A clarifying point to be made in conjunction with Northrup's statement here is that princesses are not at all "new"; men's warrior societies on the Plains, for example, for centuries have passed on titles to preteenaged females. There is thus some precedence for the idea of a princess in Indian societies, although these titles are usually inherited and not earned through competition. Nonetheless, the perception of powwow princesses as somehow "new" is widespread and is useful for the discussion of tradition and community in this chapter.

2. Colleen Ballerino Cohen, Richard Wilk, and Beverly Stoeltje, eds., *Beauty Queens on the Global Stage: Gender, Contests and Power* (New York: Routledge, 1996). See also Katherine Borland, "Performing Identities: The Politics of Culture in a Nicaraguan Community" (PhD diss., Indiana University, Bloomington, 1994); and Richard Wilk, "Beauty and the Feast: Official and Visceral Nationalism in Belize" *Ethnos* 53 (1993): 1–25.

3. Marina Warner, *Monuments and Maidens: The Allegory of the Female Form* (New York: Atheneum, 1985).

4. This seems particularly problematic in the South Pacific, where standards of attractiveness traditionally tend toward a fuller figure. This was communicated to

me personally by Julie Sword, former Miss South Pacific, in 1995; see also Jehanne Teilhet-Fisk, "The Miss Heilala Pageant: Where Beauty Is More than Skin Deep," in Cohen, Wilk, and Stoeltje, eds., *Beauty Queens on the Global Stage*.

5. Stoeltje, "The Snake Charmer Queen," in Cohen, Wilk, and Stoeltje, eds., *Beauty Queens on the Global Stage*, 23.

6. Stoeltje, "The Snake Charmer Queen," 24.

7. This is not to say that Indian contests are all without conflict. The struggle for community identity and values is often played out in non-Native and Native contests alike. For example, considerable controversy ensued in 1997 when a young woman who was half Navajo and half African American was chosen as queen in the Miss Navajo contest.

8. Complete rules for the contest are explained in the official program of the Gathering of Nations powwow and on the official Web site, http://www.gatheringofnations.com.

9. Personal communication, April 21, 1998.

10. Thanks to Meg Brady, University of Utah, for discussing this with me, April 22, 1998.

11. Emphasis is Beulah Sunrise's.

12. Beulah Sunrise, public oratory at the Miss Indian World Pageant, Albuquerque, New Mexico, 1998.

13. See chapter 7 of this volume, "Powwow Patter: Indian Emcee Discourse on Power and Identity."

14. Personal communication, June 27, 1999.

15. Beverly Stoeltje, "Gender Representations in Performance: The Cowgirl and the Hostess," *Journal of Folklore Research* 25, no. 3 (1988): 219–41; Beverly Stoeltje, "Power and the Ritual Genres: American Rodeo," *Western Folklore* 52 (1993): 135–56; Stoeltje, "The Snake Charmer Queen."

16. Arnold van Gennep, *The Rites of Passage* (Chicago: University of Chicago Press, 1909).

17. Jean LaFontaine, *Initiation: Ritual Drama and Secret Knowledge across the World* (New York: Viking Penguin, 1985), 125.

18. Names of the princess and her relatives have been changed. Although the powwow committee gave me permission to record giveaways and to use names, this giveaway has a private quality to it. I do not believe the princess's grief should be made public. Names of speakers have not changed.

19. Wes Martel, public oratory at Eastern Shoshone Indian Days, Fort Washakie, Wyoming, 1999.

20. Richard Bauman, *Verbal Art as Performance* (Prospect Heights IL: Waveland, 1977), 21.

21. Stoeltje, "Gender Representations in Performance," 221.

22. Elizabeth Cowie, "Woman as Sign," in *The Woman in Question: m/f*, ed. Parveen Adams and Elizabeth Cowie (Cambridge: MIT Press, 1990).

23. Deborah Tannen, "There Is No Unmarked Woman," in *Signs of Life in the USA*, ed. Sonia Maasik and Jack Solomon (Boston: Bedford Books, 1997).

24. Dean McCannell and Juliet Flower McCannell, *The Time of the Sign: A Semiotic Interpretation of Modern Culture* (Bloomington: Indiana University Press, 1982), 156.

25. LaFontaine, *Initiation*, 79.

JASON BAIRD JACKSON

9. East Meets West
On Stomp Dance and Powwow Worlds in Oklahoma

In the minds of many Americans, at least in those of many Oklahomans, powwow dancing has become synonymous with Indian dancing. Living for a decade among both Native and non-Native peoples in the state that describes itself ambiguously as "Native America," I have found this perception constantly driven home to me in the comments of non-Indian acquaintances. In learning of my regular attendance at Indian dances, they inevitably proceed to regale me with a tale of their experience attending this or that powwow. They always look genuinely puzzled when I explain that it is a Stomp Dance that is next weekend's destination, rather than one of the large public powwows that provide their own entry point to Indian country.

More diverse and interesting are the views of powwow held by my friends and acquaintances among the Woodland Indian peoples of central and eastern Oklahoma. While some members of these communities embrace the powwow as a rich expression of Native culture, others see it as a foreign and invasive institution that encourages, or at least symbolizes, the disruption of local tribal and regional traditions. Like the powwow, the Woodland tradition of dance and song embodied in the Stomp Dance represents an old and complex social institution that links local communities into larger social networks in which local differences in culture articulate with partially shared regional values, beliefs, and customs. Beyond this surface similarity hides a deeper realm of differences that distinguish the Stomp Dance world from that of the powwow, with which it now coexists.

In the context of this volume's exploration of the varied contexts and meanings that attach to the powwow, this essay focuses on the ways in which the modern intertribal War Dance, specifically in its Oklahoma form, variously articulates with the Stomp Dance world of Woodland Oklahoma.[1] While my frame of reference is Oklahoma, where the research on which it is based has been conducted, a similar exploration could be staged from other parts of eastern North America. Developments among the Iroquois, Eastern Cherokees, Mississippi Choctaws, Florida Seminoles, Micmacs, and other eastern groups may not necessarily match those that seem characteristic of eastern Oklahoma. Goertzen (2001) has already described the articulation of Woodland and powwow musical genres in the Carolina Piedmont and coastal plain. The patterns he discovered, different but not unrelated to those described here, reflect the distinct historical and contemporary circumstances of the Occaneechis, Saponis, and other groups residing at the eastern edge of the contemporary Woodland Indian world. There, (almost) lost Woodland music and dance genres are being revitalized for performance within powwow events. In Oklahoma the two types of music sometimes occur during the same event but in rather different ways. Such relationships are the focus of this chapter.

The goal of this research is to introduce the multitribal social world of the Stomp Dance to audiences, particularly powwow scholars and enthusiasts, who are largely unfamiliar with it. With this regional purpose in mind, a great deal of ground is covered without giving adequate attention to the nuances of local detail. More importantly and regrettably, this attempt at survey limits my ability to represent the richness and diversity of Native American opinions and knowledge on the subject of Woodland Indian music and dance in eastern Oklahoma. Interested readers will possibly find such perspectives adequately reflected in my other writings on contemporary Indian life in eastern Oklahoma. More revealing still are a growing number of published works by Native authors and musicians possessing firsthand knowledge of the area's traditions.[2]

Woodland Indian Music and Dance in Oklahoma: An Introduction

This chapter considers a tradition of music and dance found (in a broad sense) among the following peoples in Oklahoma: the Caddos, Cherokees, Chickasaws, Choctaws, Creeks, Delawares, Miamis, Natchez, Ottawas, Peorias, Quapaws, Seminoles, Seneca-Cayugas, Shawnees, Wyandottes, and Yuchis. These people share a common heritage rooted in homelands in the southeastern or northeastern Woodland region. Their song and dance traditions are referred to here as "Woodland Indian music." The heritage music of some other Oklahoma groups of eastern background, particularly the Citizen Pottawatomies, Kickapoos, Sac and Fox, and Iowas, share many characteristics with these groups and should also rightfully be characterized as Woodland music. However, these four groups are not discussed here solely because they do not – at present (and did not in the recent past) – participate in the Stomp Dance world described here. Even within this qualification exist various exceptions, such as the Kickapoos assisting the Absentee Shawnees in their annual War Dance ceremonial (not to be confused with the War Dance of the powwow). Similarly the Wichitas share some songs and dances, such as the Turkey Dance, in common with the Caddos.

In Oklahoma the world of Stomp Dance music and dance is organized at either a tribal or a community level. Among the Cherokees, Creeks, Seminoles, Yuchis, Absentee and Loyal Shawnees, and Seneca-Cayugas, "ceremonial grounds" host Stomp Dances. One way of thinking about a ceremonial ground is to recognize its identity as a town or village. Ceremonial grounds possess a town square (or a longhouse among the Seneca-Cayugas) and household residences (today, permanent "camps") that correspond architecturally and socially to structures characteristic of Woodland villages of the seventeenth, eighteenth, and nineteenth centuries. The "members" of such a ceremonial ground are the residents of a local community, many or most of whom trace their ancestry back to earlier generations of community members. For instance the members of the Arbika Ceremonial Ground are identified closely with the Creek "tribal town" of Arbika, live in the region near their "square ground," and trace their history back to a settlement of the same name in Alabama.

Another way of thinking about ceremonial grounds is to view them as congregations. A ceremonial ground is a group of people sharing a common cultural background that assembles at a fixed location in order to undertake a regular calendar of religious rituals or ceremonies. Ceremonial grounds possess chiefs, orators, and other ritual officers, and they have a corporate identity as a group of people associated with a particular place (their ceremonial ground) but are also capable of acting as a social unit outside the precincts of this place. Ceremonial grounds, as congregations, are also associated with particular cultural traditions (Yuchi, Shawnee, and so forth) even when their memberships are culturally diverse. A "Delaware" man can be a member of a "Shawnee" ceremonial ground with or without possession of Shawnee ancestry. Such memberships, fostered by intermarriage, friendship, or other factors, do not diminish the Shawnee identity of a Shawnee ground. In this sense ceremonial grounds are superorganic phenomena – places and groups viewed as having corporate cultural identities. This corporate aspect is crucial to understanding how ceremonial ground life does and does not intersect with the more individualistic world of powwow.

Although they possess tribal dance grounds where Stomp Dance and social dance music is performed, some Woodland peoples lack ceremonial grounds in the congregational and town/village senses. The most obvious reason for this distinction is that these groups no longer practice the daytime ceremonials they once possessed. These groups, including the Eastern Shawnees, Ottawas, Peorias, Miamis, Delawares, and Quapaws, host Stomp Dances as tribes, either through event committees or directly as tribal governments.[3] More closely comparable to a powwow committee, the officers and personnel organizing such events tend to be ad hoc rather than permanent. In addition the dances organized as such tend to be viewed in more secular and less religious terms than those hosted by ceremonial grounds. The significance attached to local customs varies tremendously, both at local community levels and in the views of individual participants. The organizational basis for Woodland dances is important because it provides the framework for understanding who is involved in this tradition and how dance events reflect the distinctive cultural circumstances of Native peoples in eastern Oklahoma.

Woodland music and dance is striking for how it differs from Plains-derived traditions. In addition to the organizational differences just noted, some cultural and musical differences are briefly introduced here.

The name *Stomp Dance* holds two meanings. At a larger level the term refers to a nighttime dance event. This broader meaning derives from a narrower one, as the most common dance genre occurring within such an event is also known in English as "Stomp Dance." Along with the Stomp Dance (also known as "leading dance" and by a host of Native language terms), Stomp Dance events can feature a number of other specifically named dances, a category widely known in English as "social dances." Some social dances are imitative and have animal names, for instance the Duck Dance and the Alligator Dance. Others take their names from a distinctive aspect of choreography, including the Go Get 'Em Dance and the Stirrup Dance. The Quapaw Dance and Seneca Dance are examples of social dances named for the tribal groups believed to have originated them. The Stomp Dance, together with such named social dances, constitutes a nighttime dance repertoire familiar (with tribal and local variations) throughout eastern Oklahoma.[4]

These nighttime dances are contrasted with daytime "ceremonial dances." Understanding such distinctions requires a return to the corporate organization of ceremonial grounds. One factor distinguishing a ceremonial ground from a tribal dance ground is the performance of daytime ceremonial dances or rituals. Such events include the Turkey Dance of the Caddos, the Soup Dance Feast of the Yuchis, the War Dance of the Absentee Shawnees, and the Sun Dance of the Seneca-Cayugas, together with the widespread Green Corn ceremonies held in specific ways by many groups. Generally, such activities are seasonal undertakings important to a local community of traditional tribal people.

What links such events into the larger network of Woodland Indian communities is the universal custom of incorporating a nighttime Stomp Dance into such tribal ceremonies. The daytime activities are undertaken by the members of the ceremonial grounds alone, but such rituals are to be concluded with an all-night Stomp Dance to which visiting delegations from other communities are invited to attend and participate. Such visitation establishes reciprocal relationships of support in which groups benefiting from the participation of visiting communities in turn attend the dances of their former and future guests. Through such "visiting," groups come to know their neighbors, to appreciate patterns of cultural similarity and variation, and to perceive and acknowledge one another in corporate rather than strictly individual terms. The salience of groups rather than individuals extends directly into the performance of Woodland Indian music as well.

Except among contemporary Caddo singers (who constitute a special case worth considering), Woodland musical performance lacks the "big drum" that symbolizes the powwow. In the Stomp Dance world, comparably representative symbols are "shells" and "cans," the instruments women use to provide the rhythmic foundation to Oklahoma Stomp Dance performance. Both shells and cans are a type of paired leg rattle. The older form of instrument is known as a "set" of shells, which is a pair of rattles each comprised of five to fifteen tortoise shells that have been emptied, perforated with holes, filled with small stones, closed, and strung together with leather lacing around a leather backing. Cans are leg rattles constructed similarly but out of emptied tin cans (those used for condensed milk and tomato sauce predominate). Rather than being laced together, sets of cans are built by linking individual cans together with steel wire. Women wear such rattles – whether made of cans or shells – around their calves beneath a loose-fitting cotton skirt or dress. They are tied on with laces after being positioned on top of a cloth or foam pad. With a few local exceptions, women do not sing Woodland dance music but instead provide accompaniment through skillful manipulation of their cans or shells while dancing.[5]

The vocal component of Woodland music is the work of men. In the Stomp Dance specifically, a different man is chosen (or volunteers, depending on local procedure) to "lead" each dance episode. The singing is done in an antiphonal, or call-and-response, style. All Woodland Indian dances in Oklahoma can be thought of as group dances, in which the participants coordinate and synchronize their movements. In the Stomp Dance itself the dance is conducted in a spiral with the "leader" first walking and then "stomping" at the head of a line that circles counterclockwise around a fire. Behind him is a woman who "shakes shells for him." Behind this woman follows a long line of alternating men and women. The women follow the rhythm established by the lead woman, and the men "answer" the songs performed by the leader. Depending on the skill and inclination of the man leading, an episode of Stomp Dance can last only a few minutes or as long as fifteen or twenty minutes. While a Stomp Dance event may consist of nothing but performances of the Stomp Dance, dances from the social dance category are often interspersed throughout the night. Each social dance has its own distinctive choreography and music, but they all share the same characteristics of men singing, women shaking shells, and coordinated movement.[6]

Modern powwow dance genres have become closely associated with elaborate and emblematic clothing styles, such that of the Men's Traditional Dance, Jingle Dress Dance, Fancy Woman's Shawl Dance, and so forth. This focus on the visual aspects of dance has led in turn to particular material elaboration of the performance context, such as the use of grandstands and bright lights. Such visual differences most obviously separate the Stomp Dance and powwow worlds. Because all attendees at a Stomp Dance are expected to participate, there is essentially no audience. This also means that street clothes are normal Stomp Dance dress, although some items of attire, such as a loose skirt for women and a western hat for men, signal full and regular participation. Beyond these basics, Stomp Dance clothing in its most elaborate form (reserved for the most important ceremonial occasions) remains simple and optional (Jackson 1998). (Powwow dance clothing, and its association with particular dance styles, is widely discussed in the literature. One recent source is Young and Gooding 2001.)

Stomp Dances take place in almost full darkness. Most ceremonial grounds lack electric lighting, and even at those tribal dance grounds that do have lighting (as among those groups that host both powwows and Stomp Dances at the same site), this lighting is reduced or eliminated during Stomp Dances. The lighting for a Stomp Dance comes from a (commonly sacred) wood fire around which the dances take place. Between dances visiting groups sit as delegations in folding lawn chairs outside the dance area, while local community members sit on benches permanently constructed as part of the ceremonial ground. At tribal dance grounds (as opposed to ceremonial grounds) everyone sits in lawn chairs, but the pattern of sitting in community groups is retained less formally. To state the distinction clearly, powwows are typically characterized by bright lights and individual, separate seating for dancers and spectators, whereas Stomp Dances are held in darkness, encircle a fire, and organize their seating by communities, the members of which are all participants.

The Stomp Dance is performed today in three settings. The oldest of these is the ceremonial ground context, where stomp and social dances are often the nighttime component of daytime tribal ceremonies. Second, over about the last one hundred years, the Woodland stomp and social dance music has been gradually incorporated into the powwow as practiced by the Quapaws and their neighbors in northeastern Oklahoma. The third, and newest, form of Stomp Dance is held indoors throughout eastern Oklahoma during winter. The following sections will examine each of these types as they relate to the better-known Oklahoma powwow tradition.

Traditional Ways: Stomp Dances and Woodland Ceremonialism

Not long ago a very talented Creek Stomp Dance singer was speaking conversationally with a Yuchi ceremonial leader prior to the start of a Yuchi Stomp Dance. The Yuchi man and I know each other very well, and the Creek singer and I have been acquainted for several years. Because they are both much older than I am, I listened rather than participated fully in the discussion. The Creek singer introduced the topic of powwows, explaining that he had participated recently in a trip to Alabama in which Creek ceremonial ground people had been invited "back" (to their old homeland) to demonstrate southeastern Indian music and dance. The demonstration took place within the context of a larger powwow event. Never having attended a powwow, the singer dutifully went to watch the dance, placing his chair outside the circle with other spectators. The humor (and point) of his anecdote came when he reported being asleep in his chair within the first twenty-minutes of the dance session. My Yuchi friend seconded his views, using an expression I have heard countless times: "I am like you; I sure can't get excited about those powwows."[7]

It should come as no surprise that such complete disinterest in powwow is most common among "ceremonial ground people." For the members of active ceremonial grounds, the responsibilities of full participation effectively preclude involvement in the powwow or one of the other Indian "circuits" found in Native Oklahoma (including Indian golf tournaments, Indian softball, and the Native American Church). Just as there is a powwow circuit, with an endless cycle of dances to attend, Stomp Dance people can go to a dance on almost any Saturday of the year. Their first responsibility is to attend the ceremonies of their home community but, because their ground receives support or "help" from visiting communities, they are also expected to participate when their community goes to attend and assist in the dances of these allies or "friends."

Such patterns, which both endure and shift through time, produce what Roark-Calnek has called "performance circuits." As she has characterized them, performance circuits are social "interconnections between performance occasions" (Roark-Calnek 1977, 525). Such patterns of reciprocity also characterize the powwow world, but decision making on the powwow circuit operates at an individual or family, rather than group, level. Because a ceremonial ground chief, together with his councilors, makes such choices and because participants are expected to attend with "their group," ceremonial ground visiting is much more of a collective affair (Jackson 2003; Roark-Calnek 1977, 525). Thus, for Woodland music and dance, performance circuits are also reciprocal relationships among communities that mutually support one another.

Ceremonial ground attitudes about the powwow are not simply a reflex of time management or community alliances; they are also, more importantly, an expression of cultural values. Jackson and Levine (2002) argue that Pan-Indianism is a poor model for understanding Woodland music and dance because it misconstrues the nature of strictly tribal ritual and expressive culture, treating it as too bounded, while also misrepresenting phenomena (such as Stomp Dance) that have an "inter-tribal" character. The world of Woodland ceremonial ground visiting is not a new phenomena that originated within a unique Oklahoma context. It represents a continuation of ways Woodland Indian communities have long interacted with one another. In committing themselves both to the continuation of their own tribal ceremonies and to participation in the larger Woodland Indian social world indexed by the Stomp Dance, Native people in eastern Oklahoma keep faith with the ancestors who handed this world and its customs down to them. This is a theme regularly explored in ceremonial ground oratory, condolence ceremonies, and everyday conversation. Stomp Dance is part of the fabric of both a regional cultural tradition ("us eastern Indians") and specific tribal cultures ("he sure sings the old-time Shawnee way"). (The relationship between this study and the nature of Pan-Indianism is reexamined in the final section of this chapter.)

(North) East Meets West: Stomp Dance at the Powwow

Beginning in the late nineteenth and early twentieth centuries, a small number of communities in eastern Oklahoma began combining Woodland Stomp Dance musical performance with elements from the Southern Plains powwow. The motivations underlying this phenomenon varied greatly from community to community, and the history of the process in any particular place is local and not well known. Following is a description of some of these variations based on my participation in such events in the company of Yuchi ceremonialists.

Among some of the tribes of the Quapaw Agency near Miami, Oklahoma, Stomp Dances are held within the context of an annual summer powwow or celebration. Promotional information for the Fourth Annual Peoria Pow-Wow (June 15–16, 2001) nicely summarizes the ways such events are structured in the Miami area:

> Activities will get underway with a gourd dance at 7 p.m. Friday, June 15. Social dances and stomp dancing is scheduled to begin at 9 p.m. Once again, James Squirrel and John Daugherty of the Shawnee tribe will sing the evening's social dances, which will include "Go Get 'Em," "Bean Dance" and other dances that are not done at most powwows. More gourd dancing will be held Saturday afternoon, starting at 3 p.m., immediately following the General Council Meeting, until supper break at 6 p.m. Supper will be "on your own" this year, since the concession stand will be operating to help defray the cost of putting on the pow wow. Anyone who would like to volunteer to work in the concession stand, or help sell raffle tickets will be appreciated. At 7:30 there will be more gourd dancing. The war dance will get started around 8:30 and last until 11 p.m. A stomp dance will follow. (Peoria Tribe 2001)

Combination Stomp Dance/Gourd Dance/War Dance/tribal meetings are held each summer by the Ottawas (at their dance ground southeast of Miami), the Peorias (at their powwow grounds east of Miami), the Eastern Shawnees (at their powwow grounds near Seneca, Missouri), the Miamis (at the Ottawa County Fairgrounds in Miami), and the Wyandottes (at their powwow grounds north of Wyandotte).

Some of these annual tribal dances began only in the last couple of years, but one model used in developing them is the famous Quapaw Powwow (132 years and counting), which is held south of the town of Quapaw. The Quapaw people have long possessed cultural traditions found both in the Woodlands and on the Plains, so their role in establishing the pattern for this combination is easily understood (Young and Hoffman 2001). Held each year during the week surrounding July 4, the Quapaw Powwow has long combined the features of a Southern Plains contest powwow with nightly Stomp dancing. Also featured during the event is a game of "Indian football," a ritual contest that is also played, by men against women, during the ceremonials of the Shawnees, the Yuchis, the Delawares, and other Woodland groups. The eight tribes of the Quapaw Agency, together with the Eastern Delawares, the Loyal Shawnees, and those Quapaw who settled on the Osage Reservation (who now organize the annual Ki-hekah-steh Powwow), constitute a clear example of a performance circuit. This is the only network in which powwows and Stomp Dances co-occur today (Hamill 2000, Jackson 2000, Quapaw Pow Wow Committee 1992, Roark-Calnek 1977).

"Leading" and "shell-shaking" contests are another innovation to the Stomp Dance tradition that has emerged in the powwow context of northeastern Oklahoma. These contests are conducted on the model of War Dance contests with judges evaluating the performances of the men taking the role of leaders and of the women shaking shells behind such leaders. Awards for best shell shaker and best leader are typically given, sometimes with prizes.

Many Creek and Cherokee people do not know that such events occur because during the summer they are busy with ceremonial ground activities closer to home. The patterns at work here are significant. During this time of year, it is not considered worth the effort to travel two or more hours to the northeast for a Stomp Dance held at the conclusion of a powwow. Recall that ceremonial ground people attend the summer dances of those communities with whom they are allied. Hence, during the busy summer ceremonial season, performance circuits become geographically constricted. One example is the case of the Yuchi ceremonial grounds. There are three Yuchi ceremonial grounds, each of which holds six ceremonial dances. Thus, to support one another, these communities are committed on eighteen weekends. Add to this the additional reciprocal visiting with non-Yuchi communities with whom they have longstanding relationships (such as the Absentee Shawnees), and it is clear that no single community can be well acquainted with the entire Stomp Dance world.

During the winter, when calendars are less filled and the indoor dances discussed in the following section are held, the lack of serious "ceremonial" dances means that dancers have fewer obligations to their summer partners and can venture further afield. Yuchi people, for instance, tend to visit the Miami area during the winter and to also see dancers from this area at their own winter dances.

Stomp Dance contests occur in northeastern Oklahoma during the summer and are a part of that area's local tradition. Returning to how this practice is perceived, dancers outside the northeastern part of the state who are aware that such contests happen are generally skeptical about the idea. Their views relate to the coordinated, collective character of Stomp Dance performance and to some basic cultural values that will be discussed below. One hears such comments as "How could a good singer do well without good helpers? Wouldn't he, in turn, be competing with these same helpers?" and "These dances are supposed to bring us together. They aren't for competition." While they obviously do not feel this strongly about Stomp Dance contests, people in the Miami area are clearly not wedded to the idea of them either, as the dances form an occasional rather than a regular feature of their dance events. Judging from event flyers and general discussion, the number of such contests held each year seems to be diminishing while the number of Stomp Dances held in Oklahoma seems to be increasing.

If this last observation is true, then it may relate to a countervailing force at work in the powwow–Stomp Dance relationship. In the 1960s anthropologist James Howard began a shift in his research interests away from a focus on Plains Indian cultures toward those of Woodland peoples in Oklahoma. Among his earliest writings on such topics is a little-known paper, "The Compleat Stomp Dancer," (1965), which provided an introduction to the Stomp Dance world during a time when almost no one outside eastern Oklahoma had noticed it. While it reflects Howard's knowledge at a point before he became well acquainted with Woodland Indian people, it is particularly interesting for its description of the Stomp Dance within a powwow context. In addition to noting Stomp Dances at the Quapaw Powwow, Howard reports that "many Prairie and Plains tribes have also taken up the Stomp" (1965, 1). He describes witnessing Stomp Dances at Sauk, Kickapoo, Pawnee, Ponca, Omaha, Winnebago, and Southern Arapaho powwows, often as specialty dances inserted into the War Dance program (Howard 1965, 1).

In the era described by Howard, the dance was "generally performed after the ceremonial dances at a Busk or Greencorn ceremony by Eastern tribes, or after the costumed War and Round dancing at a Prairie or Plains pow-wow" (1965, 17). Howard's descriptions (along with those of Powers 1990) suggest several things about the powwow–Stomp Dance relationship between about 1955 and 1975. First, the Stomp Dance could then be found in a remarkably wide area on the Plains as a specialty dance within the powwow. No corroborating evidence on this topic for that time period is available, but the Stomp Dance is no longer used in this way among groups such as the Sauks or Pawnees. Its other use within the powwow, as a late night dance to be held after a War Dance session, is continued in the dances of the northeastern Oklahoma area tribes (i.e., those in the Miami area and at the annual Eastern Delaware Powwow (near Copan) and the Ki-hekah-steh Powwow (held near Skiatook with heavy Quapaw involvement), but such use does not extend to any Prairie or Plains groups.

This is another place where Howard's predictions about the trajectory of Pan-Indianism have turned in unexpected directions. In the 1965 paper he wrote: "Increasingly the Stomp dance, like the War and Round dances, is coming to be regarded as the property of all Indians, and is performed by many groups whose ancestors never knew the dance" (1965, 17). In contradiction of Howard's finding, however, there are no groups today for whom this can be said. Despite the occasional Pawnee singer or Navajo shell shaker (usually of part-Woodland heritage or a close friend of eastern people), no community today hosts Stomp Dances without a deep ancestral claim to the dance. The Stomp Dance today is far from a symbol of generic Indianness, even when it occurs with an "intertribal" War Dance.

In contrast to the changes predicted by Howard, the increasing number of Stomp Dances hosted among the Woodland tribes of the Quapaw agency (along with their Eastern Delaware neighbors) can be instead interpreted as a desire by these groups to intensify their engagement with their own traditional cultures. Such motivations also clearly underlie their current work in many other domains, from language revitalization to oral history research (see comments by Rementer and others in Lee 1995, 74).

A final observation on the incorporation of Stomp Dance with the War Dances held in northeastern Oklahoma can be made. Despite the existence of some more complex historical antecedents, such as the moribund Bird Creek Ceremonial Ground (Loyal Shawnee), where powwow and tribal ceremonialism co-occurred, the pattern today is clear. The War Dance and the Stomp Dance have been joined together in those northeastern Indian communities that lost or gave up their tribal ceremonials. Structurally and functionally the

War Dance has taken the place of these daytime ceremonial dances, despite the powwow's rather different history. This becomes obvious when ceremonial ground people go to the northeast to attend a Stomp Dance. Just as they would when visiting a ceremonial dance, they arrive in the late afternoon or evening as the "daytime" dancing is concluding. They hope to be (and almost always are) fed dinner and then they sit and socialize while waiting for the nighttime Stomp Dance to begin. For ceremonial ground visitor and "homefolks" alike, the pattern is the same even when the dances came from "out west."

(South) East Meets West: The Special Case of the Caddo and Their Neighbors

In the previous section northeast Oklahoma was isolated as a special region in which the powwow and Stomp Dance worlds come together. Before moving on to consider indoor Stomp Dances, the different case of the Caddo requires mention. The Caddo reside around the town of Binger, north of Anadarko. Along with the Western Delaware and Wichita, with whom they once shared a reservation territory (and the Wichita Agency), they present a cultural contrast to their Southern Plains neighbors. In terms of music and dance the Caddo and their congeners represent an older mode of cultural integration.

While I was working as a curator at Tulsa's Gilcrease Museum, I had the good fortune to meet two very knowledgeable Caddo elders who visited the museum as part of a Native American Graves Protection and Repatriation Act consultation. They were the first Caddo whom I had met, and we had a great time together exchanging stories about music, dance, and "traditional" Indian cultures. Discussing Woodland music they made a point of explaining that, despite being surrounded by Plains Indian neighbors in southwestern Oklahoma, they – the Caddo – were different. The first gentleman (now deceased) noted: "We're not fighters, we're . . ." While the speaker finished his sentences with "farmers," his joking buddy of many years, inserted "lovers." We laughed, and they then described for me their own tradition of music and dance, which includes the full repertoire of social and Stomp Dance music, as found to their east, and a rich array of genres, such as the Ghost Dance and Round Dance, that derive from the Plains traditions of southwestern Oklahoma.

At the Caddo dance ground at the "Binger Y" and elsewhere in Caddo country, one finds the westernmost outpost of the eastern stomp and social dances. While not powwows in the traditional sense, Caddo social dances can also include performances of Flag Songs, the Round Dance, the Ghost Dance, and a host of other genres familiar to the Southern Plains. Also in powwow style an emcee is used, as is a "big drum." In keeping with the Caddos' Woodland orientation though, a daytime ceremonial dance – the Turkey Dance – is combined with a remarkably large repertoire of eastern nighttime social dances. At Caddo social dances the Caddos' neighbors the Wichita and the Western Delaware are regular participants. Thus the Caddo, Wichita, and Western Delaware tribes form another special performance circuit within which the Stomp Dance and powwow connect in a distinctive way. Full consideration of the rich music and dance traditions (both eastern and western) among the Caddo, Wichita, and Western Delaware awaits additional study in collaboration with the remarkably talented singers found in this community.[8]

Just for Fun: Stomp Dance Secularized

In the 1970s and 1980s another transformation of the Stomp Dance occurred. This one did not combine it with powwow music and dance but instead borrowed organizational and formatting features. Held indoors in school gymnasiums, community halls, and other public buildings, these secular Stomp Dances take place during the winter months, when most ceremonial grounds are inactive. Primarily social in function, the dances are held as fund-raisers in support of a ceremonial ground, a local Indian education program, or some other worthwhile cause. They derive from an older tradition of fund-raising events in eastern Oklahoma's Indian country. Indoor Stomp Dances thus incorporate many features also found in community cakewalks, box suppers, and "grocery bingos."

Some of these elements are also found in community powwows – for instance, the sale of raffle tickets and the presence of concession stands run by the sponsoring organization. Also incorporated into indoor Stomp Dances but absent from the region's powwows are cakewalks. Cakewalks at Stomp Dances take two forms. The walk itself is reserved for children. Before the dancing begins, paper plates are numbered consecutively and arrayed in a circle in the dance area. Children pay a small fee, usually a quarter, to participate. They stand outside the circle of plates and, once all are lined up, a recording of Stomp Dance music is played on a tape player. The children walk counterclockwise (as in dancing); when the music stops (after the fashion of musical chairs) each child stops and stands on the plate in front of him or her. A number corresponding to one of the plates is drawn at random, and the child standing on the matching number wins a cake of her or his choice, selected from those donated by adult participants. After the game ends the second form of cake walk begins. The plates are sold to the adults and used as raffle cards. Throughout the rest of the Stomp Dance additional numbers are drawn and the holder of the "winning plate" selects a cake. In a study similar to this one, Krouse has described social dance events among the urban Iroquois in Rochester, New York. Among the activities that compose their social dance gatherings are cakewalks similar to those held in Oklahoma (Krouse 2001, 402).

Ceremonial ground people in Creek and Cherokee country have little familiarity with the mixture of powwow and Stomp Dance I have described above. Instead, these people participate regularly in the indoor Stomp Dance, which they identify as an innovation that has incorporated such modern or powwow elements as the use of a public address system and a named master of ceremonies. At ceremonial ground events, public speaking is typically divided between a traditional town speaker or orator, who delivers long ritual speeches, and a "stickman," who selects Stomp Dance leaders and announces them in the local Native language. The emcees of indoor dances speak English and remain seated on a speaker's stand. They entertain the crowd throughout the event, telling jokes and stories and announcing upcoming events. These are all features alien to ceremonial ground dances but common to the powwow emcee (Gelo 1999). A similar borrowing from the powwow world is the creation and circulation of handbills. Such flyers are used to spread the word about upcoming indoor dances, but they are never used to publicize outdoor ceremonial dances.

Another innovation associated with indoor Stomp Dances is aimed at preserving their traditional aesthetics. Because an actual fire cannot be built indoors, a novel substitution has developed. Indoor dances are oriented around an imitation fire composed of actual firewood arranged around a flashlight that has been covered in red cellophane, cloth or tissue paper. Even if fires could be built indoors, as they once were in ancestral long houses and council houses, they would not be desired for modern secular indoor Stomp Dances because such actual fires require (in the view of ceremonial ground people) special care and ritual tending. They are powerful, sacred things associated with a host of "rules" and linked directly to the power of a community's "medicine." For this reason an actual fire would not be appropriate in the informal context of a contemporary indoor dance.

For similar reasons some ceremonial ground participants will not participate in indoor dances, seeing them as an inappropriate use of music and dance that is sacred and should not be "taken outside" of its ceremonial ground context. Such perspectives today represent a healthy minority opinion among Stomp dancers. Those who favored the initiation of indoor dances have argued that they could serve some vital functions, bringing together communities that would otherwise be inactive during cold winter months, raising funds for worthwhile causes, and giving people who might not be active in a ceremonial ground, particularly children and teenagers, exposure to traditional music and dance. In this latter goal it is hoped that those casual participants who come to an indoor dance and then take an interest in dancing will then have an opportunity to join a ceremonial ground and experience the tradition in its fuller, more spiritual dimensions. Even if indoor dances fail in this intent, they do provide drug- and alcohol-free, community-focused events accessible to and popular with children and teenagers.

The following announcement for the annual indoor dance of the Miami Tribe illustrates the format for such indoor stomp dance events.

> JANUARY 26–27, 2001 – Annual Indian Art Market & Winter Gourd & Stomp Dance. Art Market begins on Friday, Jan. 26th at 11:00 a.m., closes at 8:00 p.m. The Market will be held in the Tribal Dining Hall at 202 S. Eight Tribes Trail, in Miami, OK. The Gourd Dance & Stomp will be held on Saturday night, Jan. 27th, at the Ottawa-Peoria Cultural Center in Miami, OK. (Miami Nation 2001)

Such dances may feature a potluck meal or may rely solely on a concession stand for food service. They typically begin with preliminary activities around six in the evening with dancing beginning between seven and eight. They typically conclude between midnight and 1:00 a.m. As is the case with the Miami dance just cited and the annual "Euchee Heritage Days," they can also be linked to larger community cultural events. At their smallest such dances will include about fifty participants, evenly divided between men and women. At their largest these indoor dances can attract many hundreds of dancers, as for the Annual Spring Stomp Dance hosted by the American Indian Student Association at the University of Oklahoma.

Cultural Correlates of the Powwow and the Stomp Dance

In contrast to powwows, Stomp Dances attract only participants. Attending a Stomp Dance as a visitor typically involves leaving home around three or four in the afternoon and then traveling for as little as forty-five minutes or as long as three hours. Arriving at a dance ground somewhere in rural Oklahoma sometime around six or seven in the evening, visitors may watch the conclusion of the daytime dances or ceremonies performed by the local community. Afterward such visiting groups are invited to eat dinner in one or more family camps. After dinner visitors and hosts may sit and socialize until 10:00 or 11:00 p.m., when the dance begins. Once the dance starts it will most often continue until sunrise, around 7:00 a.m. Although visitors may depart early, they are encouraged to stay until the dance ends, at which time they will likely be served breakfast. After staying through breakfast and then departing sleepily for home, a visitor who carries passengers needing to be dropped off might not arrive home until eleven in the morning.

All of this time will have been spent outdoors at a beautiful but rustic ceremonial ground site that probably offers nothing more than old-fashioned outhouses as facilities. Doing this weekend after weekend is immensely rewarding for those committed to a "traditional" way of life, but it is a rather daunting commitment of effort for casual spectators. Compounding the challenge is that this world functions through only word-of-mouth communication. White land owners living less than a mile from a ceremonial ground typically do not even know that it is there and that, while they sleep, hundreds of Indian people can be gathered in celebration on the other side of the pasture. It should not be surprising that non-Native people in eastern Oklahoma today know little or nothing about traditional Indian life or their Native American neighbors. Keeping a low profile is a strategy that has long served the interests of traditional Woodland Indian peoples (Thomas 1953, 1961, 1962).

In addition to the public-private distinction, a comparison between powwow and Stomp Dance reveals differing values associated with the individual vis-á-vis the group. With the exception of the contests discussed already, nothing approaching the competitive individualism of powwow dance contests is found in the Stomp Dance tradition. In a ceremonial ground context, expressions of competition are not only out of place but are viewed as dangerous.

Among the Creeks, Yuchis, and Seminoles, the Ribbon Dance is an episode of the annual Green Corn ceremonial. I was once present when a young man, proud of his own community, observed among a group of his fellow townspeople that their Ribbon Dance was the largest (meaning it had the most women participating) and best among all the ceremonial grounds. With looks of concern and the shaking of heads, this man was quietly but firmly warned by an elder that speaking in such a prideful manner endangered the community, both socially and spiritually. This is a world governed by real or feigned modesty and the active avoidance of situations of contention, conflict, or controversy. A high premium is placed on cooperation, deference to others, hospitable treatment of guests, and studied avoidance of those groups or individuals with which one disagrees or is in conflict. Social relationships have a spiritual and cosmological aspect, embodied in the health of a community's "medicine." Poor social relationships harm this collective power and, in turn, risk the health and well-being of a community. Such values, a recurring theme in the ethnography of the region, are probably best known through the "Cherokee harmony ethic" described by Thomas (1961, 1962; see also Bell 1984 and Jackson 2003).

At the level of performance a successful Stomp Dance episode is one in which the leader is a strong singer capable of joining all the dancers into a coordinated unit. In this, he is greatly assisted by a shell shaker who knows his songs and his style and can thus provide appropriate accompaniment and set the pace for those who follow. At this level attendance by groups reappears as a crucial theme. When a man is selected to lead, those who follow him first in line to the fire are friends and townspeople (or fellow tribesmen and tribeswomen) who know him and his songs best. They are also those who want most to make a good showing, not only for him but also for their community or ground. The larger and more unified this group is, the better the performance is likely to be and the more likely it is others present will recognize a large and socially integrated community of performers. Not only are such groups fun to dance behind, but they are also accorded respect, establishing for them a positive reputation that has both commonplace and cosmological ramifications.[9]

Woodland Indian people in Oklahoma are well aware of the powwow, even those who have never attended one. They hear fantastic stories about fees paid to Oklahoma singers willing to go sing "someplace back east." Some ceremonial ground people (as well as some anthropologists) view powwow as the dance for those who have lost the dances they should have held onto in the first place. When their own tribe's people fall into "that powwow rut," these ceremonial ground people see it as lamentable, a sign of weakness ("They're done dancing and are in bed before we've even gotten started properly.") and community disengagement ("It's too bad, because they already have a place to dance. Their grandparents were here."). They feel that, on principle, the powwow is a respectable "Indian way," but they know that it is not their "way." Coming from someplace else, it thus has something of the hegemonic quality seen more readily in the products of the dominant American culture.

For some northeastern Oklahoma people, Stomp Dance is a way to let their hair down when the War Dance has wound down for the evening. At the same time it maintains a connection with tribal and regional cultures augmented but not superseded by the powwow. While the music itself is one expression of this tie, perhaps more important is that by – "keeping up with our stomp dancing" – northeastern peoples maintain collective social ties with other Woodland communities. From time immemorial Woodland peoples have shared more than similar ways of life; they have also shared a world of social relationship. Then as now the Stomp Dance is part of the glue that maintains such community bonds.

American Indian people throughout the continent live in a world defined largely by European American institutions, yet it is worth remembering that this was not always so. Similarly, for Woodland Indian peoples and those of other areas into which the powwow has spread, there were (and thankfully often still are) ways of singing and dancing that existed before the powwow came. My research has benefited from spending time with those who love to powwow, those who love to Stomp Dance, and those who don't mind a little of both, sometimes even on the same day. While studies of the powwow dominate current scholarship on Native American music and dance, I hope this study calls attention to the alternative cultural worlds with which the powwow coexists.

Afterword

Commenting on an earlier version of this chapter, an attentive reader urged that the patterns described above be formally linked to the arguments made in Jackson and Levine (2002) and elsewhere about the broader problem of replacing the theory of Pan-Indianism with a perspective that is more historically nuanced and sociologically sophisticated. This is an important undertaking, one to which many different scholarly projects can contribute. Since I had already explored this issue in several works, I was initially hesitant to take up this issue again directly (see Jackson and Levine 2002; see also Jackson 2000, 55–57). In addition, the scholars most closely associated with the development of the Pan-Indianism model are also those whose extensive fieldwork has contributed most productively to my own work and that of my collaborators. Thus it seemed unfair to rely mightily on the published and unpublished work of James Howard, Gertrude Kurath, Karl Schmitt, and others of their generation while rehashing a now-established critique of their theoretical model. Despite this hesitation it may be useful to briefly situate this essay vis-á-vis the Pan-Indian problem.

Revisiting Pan-Indianism requires distinguishing between two issues covered by the same label. Coined in a theoretical context, the term was offered as a variety of acculturation theory aimed at *explaining* a set of phenomena that may themselves also be (and often are) *described* as being Pan-Indian in nature. Thus the powwow, in certain forms, can be described as a Pan-Indian social gathering, containing Pan-Indian cultural forms, and expressing aspects of a Pan-Indian identity or ideology. At such a descriptive level, the term has entered everyday discourse among Native and non-Native peoples in North America. Many people use the term descriptively in such a manner without subscribing to the theoretical position from which the term emerged. In such a descriptive context, Pan-Indianism is a phenomenon to be explained as much as it is a means of explanation. The distinctions between different uses of the term *Pan-Indian* have been examined recently by Scales (2002). The problems associated with Pan-Indianism *as a theory* are now well documented (see Powers 1990, 86–110). (Among the key sources articulating Pan-Indian theory are Howard 1955, Kurath 1957, and Newcomb 1955).

As developed in American anthropology and ethnomusicology in the mid-twentieth century, Pan-Indianism was a theory intended to explain the emergence of new American Indian cultural forms and social patterns in the years following World War II. As an explanatory framework the theory of Pan-Indianism drew on the dominant anthropological model of its time – acculturation theory – to argue that the emergence of generically Indian cultural forms, social groupings, and ethic identity was a progressive step toward full assimilation into the dominant society, one in which such Pan-Indian forms took the place of distinctly tribal cultures, societies, and identities. The emergence of Pan-Indian phenomena was a means of coping with the stresses of this acculturative process, and their emergence was made possible through social changes – such as urbanization, military service, boarding schools, and wage labor markets – that brought Indian people into sustained interaction with one another. Oklahoma was seen as the cradle of Pan-Indian phenomena because so many different and distinct tribal groups were consolidated there through the "removal" policies of the nineteenth century, by which the U.S. government pursued a form of "ethnic cleansing" east of the Mississippi. The dissolution of reservation lands that preceded Oklahoma statehood further accelerated both acculturative processes and the formation of a Pan-Indian social world.

As discussed in several recent publications (Jackson 2003; Jackson and Levine 2002; Waselkov and Jackson 2003), this is too simple a model in that it posits too much cultural uniqueness prior to the experience of intense daily contact with non-Native Americans and, in the present, too little tribal and community distinctiveness after the effects of such acculturation are felt. The social dance musical genre described in Jackson and Levine (2002), as well as the variation in musical performance context discussed above, provides evidence for a different model of American Indian culture and culture change, one predicated on mapping social networks that link groups together through time as well as on comparative examination of how long-shared practices are localized in ways that express distinctive community identities.

The varied but mutually intelligible manner in which the powwow has interacted with, and affected, the performance of Woodland Indian music and suggests that there is a social network present in eastern Oklahoma that links the Woodland Indian communities together. The existence of this social network is an obvious social fact that one can observe when attending a Stomp Dance event. Jackson (2003) formally described the form and nature of this social network. Stomp Dance performance is one of a number of (shared but localized) cultural expressions found in this social network. (Indian football is another; see Jackson 2003, 117–40.) That the powwow has influenced, in certain ways, the Stomp Dance social world suggests that, at some points at least, in this social system there are also ties connecting Woodland Indian people to those non-Woodland groups for whom the powwow has a deeper cultural history. As noted earlier in this chapter, far northeastern Oklahoma and the Wichita-Caddo-Delaware community are the two clearest cases of this wider linkage.

In certain respects and in certain contexts, the powwow is a Pan-Indian phenomenon. For many people it does express generalized Indian values and identities. It is exactly this Pan-Indian identity that many Stomp Dance people resist, in the belief that tribal and "eastern" identities (and the cultural forms on which they are based) are more historically valid and therefore preferable. Indian, "eastern," and tribal identities can coexist in any individual and may shift both contextually and through time (Roark-Calnek 1977). My arguments here and elsewhere have not touched on identity in an individual sense; rather, they consider only expressions of corporate identity manifest in public discourse and social practices. Individual views on such matters can vary widely, while collective social life can play out within a narrower range.

My interest in the Stomp Dance partially derives from the manner in which it is simultaneously a tribal and an intertribal phenomenon but not a Pan-Indian one.[10] Contact between the modern Pan-Indian powwow and the Woodland Stomp Dance community in Oklahoma is a relatively modern, historical process that can be documented. While the specifics of its nature have changed over time, the existence of a Woodland Indian social network, of which Stomp Dances are a part, is not new. Jackson and Levine (2002) sought to demonstrate this on comparative musical grounds. By providing an overview of some social and cultural patterns characteristic of this network, this chapter furthers our understanding of the links connecting Woodland Indian people. Roark-Calnek (1977) and Jackson (2003) have described the manner in which communities sustain their own tribal identities through participation in a Woodland Indian social network. Future work is needed to push the emerging model of social connection back in time to better understand the manner in which eighteenth- and nineteenth-century Woodland Indian people interacted with one another. This work would provide a valuable Native-Native complement to the dominant concern of Woodland Indian ethnohistory – the nature of Indian-European relations (Waselkov and Jackson 2003).

ACKNOWLEDGMENTS

For allowing and encouraging me to join in the events that mean so much to them, I am grateful to many friends among the Woodland Indian people of eastern Oklahoma. I am particularly thankful that the elders and leaders of the Yuchi ceremonial grounds have consistently encouraged and instructed me in matters of Yuchi and Woodland Indian custom. That an outsider like me has been allowed to become a Stomp Dance regular is a testament to the generosity of these communities. For tutoring me as a leader, I am especially grateful to Mr. Newman Littlebear, an all-around Stomp Dance man of remarkable talent. For supporting my studies among the Yuchi and their neighbors, I acknowledge the Wenner-Gren Foundation for Anthropological Research, the Gilcrease Museum, Indiana University, the University of Oklahoma, the American Philosophical Society, the Oklahoma Humanities Council, the Whatcom Museum Society, and the Parsons Fund for Ethnography of the Library of Congress. An earlier version of this essay appeared in *Plains Anthropologist*, volume 48, number 187. I appreciate the assistance provided by its editor, Mary Adair.

NOTES

1. In summary the powwow is an important contemporary American Indian dance event, usually open to any would-be participant, including non-Native publics who are often present as spectators and as customers for any retail activities associated with the gathering. Music and dance performance is embedded within a larger ceremonial and festival context that often includes vending of foods, crafts, and other merchandise; family camping; celebratory food ways; and social events, both formal and informal. Community rituals, such as giveaway ceremonies and baby namings, can occur within powwow events, as can such secular activities as beauty pageants and tribal business meetings. The powwow derives from the dance traditions and celebrations of the Plains peoples, but it has diffused widely in North America during the twentieth century, being adopted by American Indian groups throughout the United States and Canada. Published sources on the powwow are now far too numerous to catalog. Significant recent studies include Browner (2000, 2002), Ellis (1999, 2003), Gelo (1999), Goertzen (2001), Lassiter (1998), and Young and Gooding (2001).

2. Less authoritative, more dialogical approaches to ethnographic reporting of American Indian expressive traditions have been advocated by many contemporary scholar-researchers. A survey oriented toward Native American studies is provided by Lassiter (2001). For Native reflections on music and dance in eastern Oklahoma, see the contributions of White Deer (1985), Carter (1995), and Rementer and Donnell (1985) to the collection *Remaining Ourselves: Music and Tribal Memory*, edited by Lee (1995).

3. The Eastern Delawares have recently constructed a new ceremonial ground and appear to be moving toward shifting the organization of their performances of traditional Delaware (social) dance and music back to the older approach I have just described. Similarly, the Chickasaws have recently constructed a ceremonial ground and are currently revitalizing their tribal tradition of music and dance along such lines.

4. For an introduction to the social dance genre in the context of a critical reexamination of Pan-Indianism, see Jackson and Levine (2002). Pan-Indianism is also considered in the final section of this chapter.

5. Among southeastern groups, whose use of shells extends back into antiquity, such rattles are more highly esteemed than those made of cans. Among such northeastern groups as the Delawares and the Seneca-Cayugas, whose dance tradition (prior to relocation to Oklahoma) lacked the use of women's rattles, cans are preferred. Shells possess a religious connotation that cans lack. This explains the

prohibition of cans at one important Cherokee ceremonial ground and motivates the comments of northeastern women who associate shells with specifically "Creek" ceremonies. The use of cans originated in the early to middle twentieth century. Their use also occurs among the Florida Seminoles. Among the Delawares and other northeastern groups, men once wore dew claw leg rattles during Woodland dances, but this practice is moribund. For some of the social dances, male singers use hand rattles or a small water drum (or both).

6. For those seeking an acoustic introduction to Stomp Dance and social dance music from Oklahoma, several commercial recordings are available. The most extensive selection is from Indian House Records of Taos, New Mexico. A complete discography is beyond the scope of this essay.

7. While there were precursors to such demonstration dance performances in the 1950s, it was only in the 1980s that such trips to the Deep South became common. Not all ceremonial ground people approve of such "exhibitions," whether held close to home or on trips "back east." I have not treated them in this essay, but they might be viewed as a fourth type of Stomp Dance performance venue. For the attitude of conservative ceremonial ground people toward the powwow, see Howard (1984, 250).

8. For the music and dance of the Caddo, see White and Boley (1999). The music of the Western Delaware is touched on in Adams's (1991) study of Eastern Delaware music.

9. Drawing on the work of Erving Goffman, I have elsewhere looked at questions of community and individual face work as expressed in such patterns. See Jackson (2003).

10. Note that I do not share Powers's view that tribalism and intertribalism are dialectical opposites or poles between which individuals or groups might move. I have sought to demonstrate how, among Woodland singers and dancers, these positions can be communicated concurrently, as in the case of Stomp Dance events and social dance performances (Jackson 2003; Jackson and Levine 2002; Powers 1990, 109).

REFERENCES

Adams, Robert H. 1991. *Songs of Our Grandfathers: Music of the Unami Delaware Indians.* Dewey OK: Touching Leaves Indian Crafts.

Bell, Amelia. 1984. "Creek Ritual: The Path to Peace." PhD diss., University of Chicago.

Browner, Tara. 2000. "Making and Singing Pow-wow Songs: Text, Form and the Significance of Culture-based Analysis." *Ethnomusicology* 44:214–33.

———. 2002. *Heartbeat of the People: Music and Dance of the Northern Powwow.* Urbana: University of Illinois Press.

Carter, Cecile E. 1995. "Caddo Turkey Dance." In *Remaining Ourselves: Music and Tribal Memory*, ed. Dayna Bowker Lee, 31–36. Oklahoma City: State Arts Council of Oklahoma.

Ellis, Clyde. 1999. " 'We Don't Want Your Rations, We Want This Dance': The Changing Use of Song and Dance on the Southern Plains." *Western Historical Quarterly* 30:133–54.

———. 2003. *A Dancing People: Powwow Culture on the Southern Plains*. Lawrence: University Press of Kansas.

Gelo, Daniel J. 1999. "Powwow Patter: Indian Emcee Discourse on Power and Identity." *Journal of American Folklore* 112:40–57.

Goertzen, Chris. 2001. "Powwows and Identity on the Piedmont and Coastal Plains of North Carolina." *Ethnomusicology* 45:58–88.

Hamill, James. 2000. "Being Indian in Northeast Oklahoma." *Plains Anthropologist* 45:291–303.

Howard, James H. 1955. "Pan-Indian Culture of Oklahoma." *Scientific Monthly* 81:215–20.

———. 1965. "The Compleat Stomp Dancer." *Museum News, South Dakota Museum* 26 (May–June): 1–23.

——— (in collaboration with Willie Lena). 1984. *Oklahoma Seminoles: Medicines, Magic, and Religion*. Norman: University of Oklahoma Press.

Jackson, Jason Baird. 1998. "Dressing for the Dance: Yuchi Ceremonial Clothing." *American Indian Art Magazine* 23 (Summer): 32–41.

———. 2000. "Signaling the Creator: Indian Football as Ritual Performance among the Yuchi and Their Neighbors." *Southern Folklore* 57:33–64.

———. 2003. *Yuchi Ceremonial Life: Performance, Meaning and Tradition in a Contemporary Native American Community*. Lincoln: University of Nebraska Press.

Jackson, Jason Baird, and Victoria Lindsay Levine. 2002. "Singing for Garfish: Music and Community Life in Eastern Oklahoma." *Ethnomusicology* 46:284–306.

Krouse, Susan Applegate. 2001. "Traditional Iroquois Socials: Maintaining Identity in the City." *American Indian Quarterly* 25:400–408.

Kurath, Gertrude Prokosch. 1957. "Pan-Indianism in Great Lakes Tribal Festivals." *Journal of American Folklore* 70:179–82.

Lassiter, Eric. 1998. *The Power of Kiowa Song*. Tucson: University of Arizona Press.

———. 2001. "From 'Reading over the Shoulders of Natives" to "Reading alongside Natives,' Literally: Toward a Collaborative and Reciprocal Ethnography." *Journal of Anthropological Research* 57:137–49.

Lee, Dayna Boker, ed. 1995. *Remaining Ourselves: Music and Tribal Memory*. Oklahoma City: State Arts Council of Oklahoma.

Miami Nation. 2001. "Tribal Events Calendar." Retrieved August 7 from http://miami nation.com.

Newcomb, William. 1955. "A Note on Cherokee-Delaware Pan-Indianism." *American Anthropologist* 57:1041–45.

Peoria Tribe. 2001. "Fourth Annual Peoria Pow-Wow Set for June 15–16." Retrieved August 3 from *http://www.peoriatribe.com*.

Powers, William K. 1990. *War Dance: Plains Indian Musical Performance*. Tucson: University of Arizona Press.

Quapaw Pow Wow Committee. 1992. *Quapaw Pow Wow 1992 Program*. Quapaw OK: Quapaw Powwow Committee.

Rementer, Jim, and Doug Donnell. 1985. "Social Dances of the Northeastern Tribes." In *Remaining Ourselves: Music and Tribal Memory*, ed. Dayna Bowker Lee, 37–41. Oklahoma City: State Arts Council of Oklahoma.

Roark-Calnek, Sue N. 1977. "Indian Way in Oklahoma: Transactions in Honor and Legitimacy." PhD diss., Bryn Mawr College.

Scales, Christopher. 2002. "Pan Indianism Revisited." Paper presented at the Society for Ethnomusicology Meetings, Estes Park, Colorado.

Thomas, Robert K. 1953. "The Origin and Development of the Redbird Smith Movement." Master's thesis, University of Arizona, Tucson.

———. 1961. "The Redbird Smith Movement." In *Symposium on Cherokee and Iroquois Culture*, ed. William Fenton and John Gulick, 161–66. Bureau of American Ethnology Bulletin 180. Washington DC: Government Printing Office.

———. 1962. "Cherokee Values and Worldview." Manuscript in the author's possession and on file at the Library of the University of North Carolina, Chapel Hill.

Waselkov, Gregory, and Jason Baird Jackson. 2003. "Exchange and Interaction since AD 1500." In *Handbook of North American Indians*, vol. 14, ed. Raymond D. Fogelson. Washington DC: Smithsonian Institution.

White, Glenn H., and Mary Boley. 1999. Liner notes to *Songs of the Caddo: Ceremonial and Social Dance Music*. CR-6146. Phoenix: Canyon Records.

White Deer, Gary. 1985. "Pretty Shellshaker." In *Remaining Ourselves: Music and Tribal Memory*, ed. Dayna Bowker Lee, 10–12. Oklahoma City: State Arts Council of Oklahoma.

Young, Gloria A., and Erik D. Gooding. 2001. "Celebrations and Giveaways." In *Handbook of North American Indians*, vol. 13, pt. 2, ed. Raymond J. DeMallie, 1011–25. Washington DC: Smithsonian Institution.

Young, Gloria A., and Michael P. Hoffman. 2001. "Quapaw." In *Handbook of North American Indians*, vol. 13, pt. 1, ed. Raymond J. DeMallie, 497–514. Washington DC: Smithsonian Institution.

PART 3

Appropriations, Negotiations, and Contestations

SAMUEL R. COOK, JOHN L. JOHNS, AND KARENNE WOOD

10. The Monacan Nation Powwow
Symbol of Indigenous Survival and Resistance in the Tobacco Row Mountains

On Sunday afternoon, May 23, 1999, two eagle feathers dropped in the arena at the Monacan Indian Nation's Seventh Annual Powwow. This, of course, is one of the most serious occurrences at any powwow and may be dealt with in a variety of ways depending on regional, tribal, and community norms. In this case the emcee cleared the arena and an elder retrieved the feathers while the host drum sang an appropriate honor song.

Approximately an hour and a half later – around 4:30 p.m. – the emcee announced that Thomasina Jordan, then-chair of the Virginia Council on Indians (a state-funded advisory group consisting of representatives from Virginia's eight state-recognized tribes), had passed away that afternoon after a long battle with cancer.[1] Ms. Jordan's passing occurred at the same time that the eagle feathers fell in the powwow arena. Whether anyone attached any supernatural significance to this occurrence, all Virginia Indians (and anyone who knew something of the peculiar and turbulent history of Indian–white relations in the state in the mid-twentieth century) realized the symbolic shock of the coinciding events. Jordan was a vocal political activist and proponent of Indian rights in a state where, until recently, Indians did not dare express discontent with state and local policies and power structures that relegated them to second-class citizenship at best. As Jordan drew her last breath, the feathers fell on soil in a county that (as will be discussed later in this chapter) was at the vanguard of Virginia racial integrity policies aimed at removing them from the state's legal record – a county where no one would have dared to hold a powwow until the late 1990s.

Yet such a powwow did become a reality in the late 1990s, and, in addition to becoming a well-known intertribal gathering in the Southeast/mid-Atlantic corridor, it marks one of the largest annual gatherings of Monacan tribal members. This is an interesting phenomenon considering that the majority of people in the Monacan community had never attended a powwow (nor do many of them frequent other powwows) until the advent of the Monacan Nation's annual gathering. This chapter explores the meaning of the Monacan powwow to those who live in the host community. We contend that this powwow constitutes a political expression for the Monacan people, a celebration of survival as indigenous people not only in a state where Indian policy took the form of "documentary genocide" but in a county where power brokers managed to configure a local political economy in which Indians were integrated at the bottom of a virtual caste system.[2] Considered in a community context, this gathering also constitutes a space where the Monacan people can articulate on their own terms their existence as a contemporary indigenous people with a unique history. In other words this now-integral event based on Plains cultural forms must be seen not as a wholesale cultural appropriation but as a means of expressing the Monacan community's relationship with the rest of the world.[3]

From Plains to Woodlands: Powwows in the Southeast

No discussion of the powwow as an intertribal/interregional phenomenon would be complete without referencing Robert K. Thomas's provocative article "Pan-Indianism."[4] Writing in the context of post–Termination era Indian activism in the late 1960s, Thomas proposed an explanation for the rapid appropriation of Plains cultural forms by indigenous peoples across North America. On one level he saw "Pan-Indianism" (as he termed this collective appropriation) as an attempt to forge and adhere to a common "Indian" identity based on similarities in historical experiences across disparate indigenous groups. However, elaborating somewhat on James Howard's observations in Oklahoma, Thomas also suggested that in some tribes "where aboriginal traits have disappeared, these new symbols of 'Indianess' are *the* distinctive traits of the community."[5]

While Thomas is correct in explicating the inevitability of a new ethnic (and, hence, political) identity emerging from prolonged intertribal activity, one must not automatically assume that the adoption of intertribal symbols and activities, such as powwows, by indigenous groups beyond the Plains are mere acts of appropriation. Nor are they necessarily attempts to reclaim indigenous culture without historical insight. Indeed, that was not Thomas's point. However, contemporary critics have elaborated on that line of argument regarding indigenous groups in eastern North America (especially those who are not federally recognized) to suggest that these groups' prolonged contact and relations with non-Indians have diluted any semblance of "tribal" or "traditional" culture.[6] Specifically, certain writers have leveled such criticism toward southeastern indigenous groups in a manner so general as to be dangerous, arguing that appropriations of generic "Indian" culture by groups of questionable indigenous heritage are mere ploys to reap the benefits of federal recognition.[7] Such approaches fail to look critically at how such traits were situated in the context of the actual *communities* that have appropriated them.

Lerch and Bullers offer an alternative approach to understanding the intrinsic complexities involved when indigenous groups beyond the Plains, particularly in the Southeast, appropriate Plains cultural forms. They point out that "powwows and other Pan-Indian activities may exist alongside of more traditional activities or behavioral patterns that mark off *local* Indian identity and social community."[8] They make their point through an examination of the Wacamaw Sioux Powwow in North Carolina, an event that has played an important role in local community life since 1970. Through structured interviews and factor analyses, the authors convincingly illustrate that this powwow is an important "identity marker" for the Wacamaw people insofar as it is a *community* event that distinguishes them from their non-Indian neighbors and bolsters their visibility as indigenous people to a larger public.

Here we intend to supplement Lerch and Bullers's approach with a phenomenological methodology that delves even deeper into the community context by focusing on actual dialogue within the Monacan community about the annual powwow.[9] This ethnographic model is what Lassiter refers to as a collaborative approach because as it "fully embraces dialogue in both ethnographic practice *and* ethnographic writing."[10] In other words it is a "multivocal" rendering of community reality, not simply because of our extensive reliance on oral reflections from tribal members but because two of the authors are themselves Monacans who actively participate in the powwow and all endeavors necessary to make the powwow possible.[11]

Through this approach we intend to convey, if only to a limited extent, the meanings that Monacan people attach to the annual powwow. While it might be said that powwows have emerged as something distinct from any tribal or regional culture over the past thirty years, our conversations and experiences suggest that the Monacans (if not many other tribes) have incorporated the powwow into the ebb and flow of community life as a means of celebrating their existing indigenous culture and identity. Our contention is that the Monacan powwow is, indeed, an identity maker but not an identity *appropriation*. In a subtle but powerful way, the powwow is a means through which the Monacan people articulate their identity as indigenous people who survived a peculiar set of historical circumstances in which such survival seemed unlikely – in other words a political act of resistance, endurance, and celebration.

"Just Like the Dust We Come From": The Historical Context

The present-day Monacan Nation – both as an ethnic community and as a polity – evolved from a once-vast alliance of Siouan-speaking tribes that inhabited most of the Virginia and Carolina Piedmont (and the Virginia Blue Ridge Mountains) at the time of Captain John Smith's arrival on the Virginia shores in 1607.[12] From then until the inception of the American republic, the history of most of the Monacan-allied peoples was one of tribal diasporas and ever-shifting sociopolitical configurations.[13] Those who remained in the vicinity of present-day Amherst County, Virginia, were descended from Tutelos and Saponis as well as possibly from some fragment settlers from Algonquian communities from the Virginia Tidewater.[14] These Indians seem to have deliberately enclaved themselves in the remote Tobacco Row Mountains (a front range of the Blue Ridge) in order to avoid excessive contact with Euro-Americans. In particular, a core community was present around Bear Mountain by the 1750s, whose residents are the ancestors of the contemporary Monacan Nation.

However, like most indigenous groups in the East, contact with non-Indians was inevitable and, ultimately, prolonged. And as was true for most other tribes in the Southeast, such contact yielded both interracial unions and tensions. Prior to the Civil War this translated into a situation in which Indians were almost uniformly classified as "free people of color," the lowest possible tier of citizenship.[15] Yet, even though the legal status of "free colored" theoretically disappeared with the emancipation of slaves, Indians in Virginia found themselves in a precarious legal situation that ultimately denied them the right to ethnic self-identification as indigenous peoples. After the Civil War miscegenation laws (laws prohibiting interracial marriage and often defining criteria for determining the race of individuals) became much more rigidly enforced in those states where they existed. To be sure, this reflected fears of challenges to the status quo with the (theoretical) enfranchisement of people of color.[16] This trend, of course, coincided with the advent of the eugenics movement, which found one of its most stalwart proponents in Walter A. Plecker, director of the Virginia Office of Vital Statistics from 1916 to 1946.

A physician by training, Plecker was obsessed with the notion of racial purity. He single-handedly drafted the 1924 Virginia Racial Integrity Law – perhaps the most explicit articulation of miscegenation law to date – which essentially stated that there were only two "races" resident to Virginia: "White" and "Negro." This effectively made it illegal for anyone native to Virginia to claim to be "Indian," and Plecker knew it. He drafted a so-called scientific method for identifying people of color on the basis of surnames located in nineteenth-century vital records (where Indians were typically classified as "free colored"). Interestingly he seems to have developed a particular vendetta against the Monacans, who were perhaps more fervent in asserting their Indian heritage than any other tribe in the state.[17] Unfortunately, local planters, who had turned toward an orchard economy on the slopes of the Tobacco Row following the postwar depression, found in these new miscegenation policies a means of exploiting Indian labor to perpetuate the quasi-feudal political economy of the antebellum years. Monacans found themselves effectively integrated at the bottom of a local caste system. Not only were they providing cheap, if not virtually free, labor for local orchard owners and farmers, but they were not allowed to attend county schools until 1963 – not even those established for African Americans.[18]

Needless to say, these conditions had a severe effect on the collective psyche of the Monacan people. Many Indians who could find the means left Amherst County and Virginia entirely for such places as New Jersey, Maryland, and Tennessee, where they could either conceal their identity or live as Indians without fear of persecution. Many of those who remained in the county internalized racial iniquities in ways that created rifts within the Monacan community.[19] It was during this period that any vestiges of indigenous language faded away. "If you will join me," recalled the late Lucian Branham, a beloved patriarch in the Bear Mountain community for many years, "[Monacan] people didn't want to speak Indian. That's what it was. . . . They was pushed down to dirt and dust, just like the dust we come from."[20] Another woman expressed the pain of being an Indian in Amherst County during the mid-twentieth century in very sobering terms: "I can definitely sit here and say there were times when I was going through school [after public school integration], and things was happening to me, and [non-Indian] people was treating us like they was. . . . There were times I didn't want to hear the word *Indian.*"[21]

The early to mid-twentieth century was undoubtedly a devastating time for the Monacan people. However, while many Monacans took no pride in who they were, there was certainly a core group of people who consistently asserted their Indian identity. In 1908, when the Episcopal diocese of Southwest Virginia opened St. Paul's Mission at Bear Mountain (the only place Indians could attain any semblance of an education in the county until 1963), the founding missionary noted that the people in the community who gathered around the mission referred to themselves as "Indian" in a very stalwart manner. He noted in particular that they made a point of distinguishing themselves from other people of color in the county.[22] During World War II, when Virginia Indians were placed in African American regiments at Walter Plecker's insistence, a group of Monacan men initially responded by resisting the draft and finally filing suit in the U.S. district court for western Virginia, where they won the right to self-identification as "Indians" for the purposes of military service.[23]

Yet for many the mere act of remaining in Amherst County without conceding to be anything other than "Indian" constituted the ultimate act of resistance. Reflecting on those who fled the area, Lucian Branham recalled: "A lot of them got up and left [Virginia]. They kept after me, said, 'Well, why don't you pull up and leave,' see? 'We ain't got a chance to make nothing for ourselves.' And I said, no, probably not. But I was born here, and I'm gonna still fight and stay here until I'm gone. . . . If I was ten years old, I still wouldn't leave."[24]

Today the Monacan Nation's Annual Powwow is a fundamental symbol of that spirit of resistance and survival.

The Monacan Powwow: Beginnings

During our conversations with Monacan people, we asked whether anyone thought that the Monacan powwow could have taken place in Amherst County thirty years ago. The unanimous answer was no. For one thing the sociopolitical climate in Amherst County at that time was still not favorable for Indians. "I don't think the outsiders would probably have come," said Dovie Ramsey. "Because it's still a stigma, you know. Not as much. Not everybody, but they [non-Indians] make jokes. They think some of the customs of the Indians . . . is really funny, and far out, and irreligious."[25] Although racism in Amherst County has retreated into latency, it undeniably still exists and was considerably more blatant thirty years ago. Certainly few local farmers or landowners wanted to have any association with the Monacans that did not place Indians in a position of subservience. As will be discussed, the first four Monacan powwows were held in neighboring Bedford County because the tribe found it difficult to find support for the event in Amherst County.

However, most Monacans believed that the internal barriers to putting on such an event in the past were equally as formidable. Kenneth Branham, who has served as chief of the Monacan Nation for six years and has lived around Bear Mountain since he was born in the mid-1950s, stated: "Even if we had our own land to do it, the know-how to do it would not have been there. And the connection with other Indians."[26] Diana Laws, who grew up in East Tennessee, where her grandparents (along with many other Monacan families) fled to escape the wrath of Virginia racial integrity policies in the early twentieth century, placed a great emphasis on how many Indians internalized the pain associated with even claiming to be "Indian": "I think it took a time out for our people to be able to come to accept things. It took time for it to become acceptable to them [to embrace their Monacan heritage], for them to understand, for them to be able to receive it and then express it."[27] One of the most profound statements came from Buddy Johns, who as a youth in the early 1970s was active in indigenous political movements. He also attended the mission school for as long as he could and experienced firsthand the hardship of public school integration in Amherst County (described below). As he sat back and watched Saturday evening events at the 2001 powwow, he pondered the past:

> Thirty years ago this wouldn't have been possible. The atmosphere here wasn't right. I know some people in the tribe wouldn't have liked it. They would have been scared to try it thirty years ago. The pressures and the prejudices wouldn't have allowed it. I'm just trying to think thirty years ago who owned this land. They would have never allowed anyone on this land to do it. Now, I'd like to consider myself one of those who was, maybe, more to the forefront of pushing for our rights, and tribal status and things. And thirty years ago, no, I wasn't even ready for it.[28]

In fact thirty years ago the Monacan people were facing profound changes in the social, political, and economic climate – locally, regionally, and nationally – that would allow them to challenge the bonds of racial oppression that had damaged their collective self-image and to assert their autonomy and survival as an indigenous community. By 1963 every county in Virginia had integrated people of color into its public schools – with the exception of Amherst, where a $30,000 bond was pending to build a separate school just for Indians. However, the county abandoned this plan after much pressure from the Episcopal Church, and Monacans were finally accepted into the county's schools. Their experience there was far from pleasant in the beginning, as evidenced by the fact that the first Monacan did not graduate from public high school in the county until 1971.[29]

With time public school education did benefit Amherst County Indians, and their matriculation coincided with the decline of the local orchard economy, the rise of a more diversified service sector, and the abolition of miscegenation and racial integrity laws. All of this transpired during the civil rights movement, which tended to instill in many ethnic groups a renewed sense of pride in their heritage. These changes motivated the Monacans to become more assertive – if not organized – as an ethnic entity, a change recognized symbolically in 1989 when the Monacans received official recognition as an Indian tribe from the State of Virginia.[30]

Encouraged by these profound changes within and beyond the Monacan community, scores of Monacans who had left the area during the Plecker years or who were the progeny of such migrants began to move back to Amherst County. Some of these people had developed a long association with other indigenous groups in a Pan-Indian context. One such individual was George Branham Whitewolf, born in Glen Bernie, Maryland, where his parents moved (as did many Monacans) in the mid-twentieth century. During the 1970s Whitewolf became active in the American Indian Movement and concomitantly became deeply involved in powwow circuits across the United States. Eventually he began sponsoring his own circuit on the East Coast. In the early 1990s the charismatic Whitewolf moved to Amherst County and became an active leader on the tribal council. He was determined to see the Monacan people sponsor their own powwow, and with his guidance (the Monacan powwow was officially part of his circuit for the first four years of its existence), the First Annual Monacan Indian Powwow became a reality in 1993.

However, recalling the climate of dwindling but latent racism in Amherst County, the path to making the powwow was not easy. Not only was Whitewolf the only person in the Monacan community at the time with a solid knowledge of how to plan and sustain a powwow, but the tribe simply had no place to hold it. At that time the Monacans had no substantive official land base, and non-Indian landowners and civic organizations in the county typically found convenient ways to sidestep Monacan requests for a venue. Tribal historian Diane Johns Shields recounted: "I know that we approached Amherst County to have our powwow here, and they, of course, could not seem to find a place that they would let us have it. And we approached Sweet Briar College [a private women's college near the town of Amherst], and of course, they couldn't.

And then once we had it in Bedford and they found out how much money Bedford County made, then they wanted us to bring it back to Amherst."[31] Indeed, from 1993 to 1996, the powwow was held at a community center in neighboring Bedford County. Each year the crowds grew, as did the revenues, until 1997, when an Amherst County farmer in Elon, Virginia, volunteered his land for the event. Despite pouring rain most of the weekend, that powwow drew its largest crowd of participants and spectators yet. It also marked the pinnacle of tribal participation in putting on the powwow.

That the powwow drew such support from within the community in a relatively short period of time is impressive. After all, most Monacans had never attended a powwow until their own tribe became sponsors, and those who were returning to Amherst County had to work to bolster respect in the community. Diane Johns Shields recounted her own return in 1994: "You know, when I first came, I had the feeling that they [Monacans who lived their entire lives in Amherst County] were afraid. They were afraid of things that were changing. Because they had come out of a dormant time, where everything just kind of stayed the same. And then all of a sudden, everything's starting to change." If those returning home had to endure the gauntlet of community scrutiny as "outsiders" before being accepted as vital members of the collective, one must wonder what the allure of a seemingly foreign institution such as the powwow might have been for the people. From Diane's perspective it was because "things were beginning to change, and they were either going to change with them or just kind of be pushed aside. And people are beginning to change now, and accept who they are and be proud of who they are. Because for so many years they were put down, and they didn't want to just accept that."[32]

Community Institution or Pan-Indian Event?

Perhaps there was a temporal symbolism in the fact that the first Monacan powwow took place at a community center in neighboring Bedford County, twenty-some miles from Bear Mountain. Not only were Amherst County officials and landowners reluctant or unwilling to endorse such an event, but many Monacans were still coming to grips with the negative ramifications of even claiming publicly to be "Indian" in Virginia. Some even feared possible backlash from local non-Indians for such a bold display of ethnic pride. However, for other Monacans it was time to catch the current of changing circumstances and to make sure that the times continued to change for the better.

The first powwow, which took place in July 1993, was modest but successful. Perhaps its most significant outcome was that it convinced many wary Monacans that such an open celebration of indigenous culture could proceed in the area without negative repercussions. As mentioned earlier, by 1997 the Monacans were able to move the powwow back to Amherst County to the community of Elon, where many Monacan families live. By then it had become the largest regular Monacan community event in terms of both the turnout from the Monacan community and the amount of effort tribal members put forth to prepare for and operate the powwow.

The Monacan powwow is one of two major tribal events that take place each year. The second is the annual homecoming bazaar, which takes place in October. While the homecoming is an impressive affair in itself, it is safe to say that it does not draw as many Monacans at one time (especially from those who live in and near Amherst County) as the powwow does. Even though the homecoming is not as much a "public" event as the powwow is, one reason it does not attract certain Monacans is because it has often been perceived as a "church" event. The homecoming actually began as a gathering for those who attended the Episcopal church at St. Paul's Mission, all of whom were Monacans. However, past missionaries tended to exhibit favoritism toward certain Indian families over others, arguably on the basis of skin color. This exacerbated tribal rifts that were either created or worsened by the racial integrity laws in Virginia in the late nineteenth and early twentieth centuries. While people in the Monacan community are coming to grips with these factional tensions and the homecoming is slowly becoming more of a tribal (as opposed to congregational) event, from its inception the powwow seems to have offered an alternative collective space for *all* Monacans to express their historical identities as local indigenous peoples.

It should be noted that some Monacans, especially those who live out of state, regard the powwow and the homecoming as events serving similar purposes. As Kenneth Branham pointed out: "You know a lot of our people travel from out-of-state. Some from Illinois, and even from Texas come to these two functions. When someone will travel that far just to socialize, that makes a difference."[33] For many Monacans-at-large, then, both events serve as a means of reconnecting to the community and reinforcing familial ties that might otherwise be severed by distance. For some, such as Diana Laws (whose grandparents moved to East Tennessee during the Plecker years), both events help to narrow the distance between generations as well:

> Well, I know for one thing that it [coming to the powwow and homecoming] is important to my grandfather because he gets to come up here and he gets to talk to people, you know, maybe once or twice a year that he doesn't see very often. And I know that it brings peace to his heart. And it's good for me to see that in him, and it's good for me to listen to the stories he tells when we're seeing these things. Because when we see these things it provokes him and reminds him of things to tell me that he may not remember otherwise.[34]

However, for many Monacans there is a marked difference between the homecoming and the powwow. Buddy Johns put it succinctly: "I guess basically 'homecoming' is a good word because there's more fellowshipping going on among the people. They're not busy trying to run booths and maintain ticket lines. Some of the guys, of course, are parking vehicles and all, but not nearly as much. I think it gives our people more time to fellowship with each other."[35] Indeed, the homecoming is not nearly as labor intensive as the powwow, and it allows for more flexibility and open socializing among tribal members. This, however, evokes an important point. Many Monacans will turn out for the powwow and work all weekend – and even days before and after, setting up and cleaning up – who may not appear at any other tribal events for the rest of the year. A regular crew of Monacan men spends three days parking cars in the fields adjacent to the pasture where the arena and vendors are set up; other men haul water and trash nonstop after having set up temporary fences and electrical circuits. Women tend the tribal concession stands and set up the tables for the Saturday night feast with food they have prepared in their own homes. As previously noted, most of these people do not regularly attend other powwows, and few dance at the Monacan powwow except during specified honoring songs. What accounts for their dedication to this event?

It is tempting to attribute their efforts to the fact that the Monacan powwow is the tribe's primary source of annual revenue. With money raised from the first two powwows, the tribe was able to purchase 120 acres of land on Bear Mountain, which included a symbolically important settlement and a Monacan cemetery. By 1999 the land was paid for in full, almost entirely from powwow revenues. However, many of those who pour their efforts into the powwow are not on hand the rest of the year to reap such material benefits of powwow revenues.

Dovie Ramsey, who grew up in neighboring Rockbridge County in the mid-twentieth century, spoke for many who have found the powwow to be particularly appealing: "To be in the circle, you know, with the Indian people, the Native Americans, that's a time of renewal. And when you come to the homecoming, that's coming home to gather. I say it's a spiritual difference in it."[36] These words may sound like common utterances in a Pan-Indian context, but they must be understood in a local and *personal* context. Dovie came from one of a number of families in neighboring counties who, in spite of their proximity to Bear Mountain and surrounding areas, were increasingly isolated from social and political life in that community as the twentieth century progressed.

While the situation in Rockbridge and other counties was no better for people whose surnames fell on Plecker's so-called hit list of people to be classified as "colored," they were not subjected to the layer of chastisement as a *community* of racial "others" that salient groups such as the Amherst County Indians were. At the same time they had to contend with being victims of racial integrity policies without the same semblance of an empathetic community as Indians in historically visible communities had. Thus Dovie was part of a generation of Monacans who knew they were "Indian" but who were discouraged (if not forbidden) by parents and policy makers to voice or pursue a tribal affiliation per se (ironically, Dovie is now regarded as an authority on certain aspects of traditional Monacan culture, as her knowledge of local flora and its uses is impressive). Her use of the term *renewal* is understandable and telling in this context, and many Monacans concur for varying reasons.

Phyllis Hicks is one of the most respected individuals in the Monacan community. Even though she has always attended and worked closely with St. Paul's Church, she is held in high regard by those who have felt alienated by missionaries in the past and by those who have never cared to attend the church. She grew up in the Bear Mountain community during the mid-twentieth century and was among the first Monacan children integrated into public schools (she attended the mission school through the third grade). Phyllis also spearheaded the Monacans' effort to gain state recognition as an Indian tribe in the 1980s. Now she devotes most of her time to the Monacan Ancestral Museum, which she helped found.

For Phyllis the powwow and related activities generate a message of pride in Indian heritage that she believes will motivate tribal members – especially children – to grasp and preserve their heritage as Monacans. She expresses a strong desire for "our young people to dance, and for them to learn how to sing the Indian songs. Things that I didn't get to do. I'm hoping all our young people will stay in it and try to learn it so they can pass it on to their children." However, even though some dance styles and songs are adopted from Plains tradition, she regards this learning of "Indian" songs not as an act of cultural appropriation but as a means of escalating pride in tribal and community heritage:

> Most importantly, as my great-grandmother would say all the time, just remember who you are – you're Indian. And that's the reason the museum means so much to me, is that I want *our* history to be put in there so that when our children say they're Indian they got history to back it up. They can say, 'Hey, I got it, I know where it's at, and I'm proud of who I am, and my history's all together. And I don't have to worry about trying to prove something, or trying to tell someone who I am and they not understanding who I am.[37]

Phyllis's words speak of both fear and lethargy as barriers to preserving and reclaiming Monacan history. Indeed, the politics of race coupled with the colonial political economy that plagued the Monacans (and other Virginia tribes) for over three centuries resulted in intensive cultural loss and placed a strain on tribal, communal, and familial ties that held many indigenous communities together. Yet these ties were not severed completely, and paired with the immense sociocultural fluidity of most North American indigenous groups, they have allowed the Monacans and others to survive as distinct indigenous communities.[38] For Kenneth Branham the powwow is a celebration of the Monacans' capacity to survive through adaptation to changing cultural and political circumstances, even when the odds seemed stacked against them: "I think [the powwow] shows that although we are Indian, and we're different in some ways, but yet we're so much alike, the community here in Amherst County and the state of Virginia, that that's why a lot of people don't feel like there are Indians here. Because we do blend in. But if it hadn't been for that capability of blending into our surroundings we *would not* be here today. And that's very important that we were able to do that."[39]

The recurring themes of survival, renewed pride, and change ring strong as Monacans ponder what the powwow means to them. Dovie Ramsey's eyes grew misty as she related her thoughts on what the powwow means to her and what it should mean to all Monacans: "There comes a time in all of our lives when we need to stop a while – if they would do it, and while they're going in the circle – just think, 'What a heritage we've got!' And how things had been once, and now we can really have a powwow, where before they couldn't even have a decent life."[40] Indeed, there does come a time during the powwow when all Monacans are beckoned into the arena, when they all leave their booths, gates, and sundry duties, to make a round in the circle for an honor song. Whether all share her sentiments while making the round is difficult to ascertain. However, it is perhaps clear to everyone in the circle at that time more than any other that the powwow is an overtly *public* event.

In their study of the North Carolina Wacamaw Sioux Powwow as a tribal "identity marker," Lerch and Bullers point out that the particular powwow in question, from its inception in 1970, was important to the community as a means of "communicating the presence of the Wacamaw to a much larger audience than ever before possible."[41] Indeed, this is true of many tribally sponsored powwows in the eastern United States, particularly when the host is a non-federally recognized tribe. As Lerch and Bullers point out, the importance of "being known as Indian" is both personal and political.[42] While many Wacamaws have come to perceive their powwow as a "traditional" community activity (perhaps because it has been in existence for over thirty years), tribes such as the Monacan Nation can certainly admit to the same personal and political interest in their powwow. The Monacan powwow marks the nexus of and blurring of lines among three worlds for the Monacans – the Monacan community, the Pan-Indian or intertribal sphere of activity, and the larger public of which Indians and non-Indians are a part. It is this interaction with the non-Monacan world that makes the powwow meaningful in the community context. On the final morning of the Monacan Ninth Annual Powwow, Chief Branham contemplated the importance of the interactions taking place at this event:

> I think it's one of our major learning tools that we have. Ten years ago most of our kids, none of our grownups, knew how to do any type of dancing. And you know, we were just like the normal public, even though we were Indian people. Since then we've realized that there are a lot of different Indian people across this country and on this continent. And a lot of them went through the very same thing that we went through, especially the ones on the East Coast. And we can also explain to people

> [who ask], "Hey, you know, why don't you look like the Indians we see on TV?" The powwow has enabled us to get into our culture. I think it has brought a lot of respect to our young people and to our elders.[43]

Buddy Johns concurred:

> [The Powwow] is very important to us. It demonstrates the community, our pride in who we are. It gives us a chance to show ourselves off in a good light to the county and surrounding areas. It also brings in other tribes and cultures, and we can share with them, and learn from them. They can learn from us. We get to see people from other nations, see how they react to things and what pride they take in their tribal status, or whatever. And I think that's very enlightening to our people.[44]

Implicit in both of the above statements is a notion of encouraging *political* solidarity with other Indians. Given the Monacans' unique and turbulent history in their dealings with non-Indians, they can certainly find collective comfort in relating to other indigenous groups with similar historical experiences. Such recognition from other indigenous groups also helps to bolster the Monacans' political image as Indians at a time when the tribe (along with Virginia's seven other state-recognized tribes) is seeking federal recognition. Nonetheless it is dangerous to assume that acquiring federal recognition is a prominent motive behind the powwow for any Monacans. In fact many Monacans, although they support efforts to pursue federal recognition, do not care whether they ultimately gain such acknowledgement. Instead, bolstering their political image as "Indians" is simply part of reclaiming their history as a community and as Monacans.

How might the powwow, which is a fundamentally intertribal activity, aid the process of historical and cultural reclamation (and in some cases, revitalization) within the Monacan community? Quite simply it provides inspiration to pursue hidden elements of the Monacan past and to revitalize dormant traditions, however subtle. This occurs in a variety of ways. For instance, one finds that while relatively few Monacans own ceremonial regalia, many of those who do are trying their best to emulate traditional Eastern Siouan clothing. While the use of Plains-style regalia dominates many powwows, movement is growing in the eastern United States toward the use of Eastern Woodland styles that are tribally specific when possible. While historical information on such clothing among the Monacans and their affiliates at the time of European contact is scant, efforts have been made to reconstruct the material past through subsequent anthropological data and through comparative research on other Eastern Woodland cultures.[45]

When Kenneth Branham was first elected as chief of the Monacan Nation, he was presented with a Plains-style headdress and buckskin shirt and leggings for ceremonial occasions, including the powwow. While he took pride in wearing this regalia, primarily because he remembered a time when it would have been dangerous to do so, he explained his own transition toward more accurate regalia: "You know, we've lost so much here on the East Coast. Again, we get into the stereotype stuff. But I think we need to show them [the general public] that yes, we're Indian, but we're also different. And I think we need to teach everybody that not all Indians killed buffalo and lived in tipis. So I think it's very important [to wear regionally accurate regalia]. And the reason I've been slow is because I've been trying to find what type of headwear that the chiefs wore."[46] Kenneth now wears an Eastern Woodland contact-era outfit that is made mostly of trade cloth. Fittingly enough, he is also employed as a cultural and historical interpreter at a contact-era model Monacan village at Natural Bridge Park, thirty miles west of Bear Mountain.

Dovie Ramsey, on the other hand, has never worn Plains-style regalia. She considers it important to dance with Eastern Woodland regalia (which for her includes a calico trade cloth dress) out of respect for her ancestors. Dovie said: "That was our grandmothers that wore the long dresses, you know. And after the settlers started coming over and they got material, they made dresses like this I got on. And I think it reflects your respect for them."[47]

By trying to wear (to the best of their knowledge) distinctly Monacan – or at least Eastern Siouan – regalia, Monacans seek to distinguish themselves from other Indians. The powwow presents the ideal occasion for such a moment of distinction. However, as the above statements indicate, it is also a time for the Monacans to realize what they hold in common, historically and politically, with other indigenous peoples. These statements also allude to the importance of the powwow, both as an intertribal and as a community gathering, in conveying a message to the non-Indian public. While it is a positive experience for Monacans to have Indians from other nations attend their gathering and thereby embrace them as indigenous peoples, it is also critically important that non-Indians respect the Monacans' open assertion of tribal identity.

Given the deplorable record of Indian and non-Indian relations in Amherst County, one can understand how sensitive many Monacans might be, especially because it took four years before the Monacans could actually move their powwow to Amherst County. Yet the move seems to have paid off in many ways. Despite rainy weather the 1997 powwow drew a record crowd, most of whom were non-Indians, and grossed over $35,000 at the gate. Moreover, if the entire endeavor is too young for the Monacans to consider it a "tradition," it seems that it is not far from becoming one for many non-Indians in the community. As Buddy Johns observed: "I was talking to a friend of mine who's Caucasian, and he was talking about how there's a group [of non-Indians] there that's talking about how they enjoy coming to the powwow. That they see people here that they don't see but maybe every powwow, and how it's really become a thing that's galvanizing the community. A lot of these people I see here every year. Seems like it's something that draws them all together."[48]

The Monacan powwow has had a galvanizing effect on the larger community of Amherst County and surrounding areas. County schools send busloads of elementary school children for Students' Day at the powwow (the Friday before the grand entry – the same buses that once had refused to pick up Monacan children who were legally entitled to attend public school. County law enforcement officials gladly provide assistance in traffic control and security (which has never really been an issue), when forty years ago their primary interaction with Indians entailed keeping them out of local restaurants. Most importantly, scores of local non-Indians *willingly* attend the powwow on a regular basis.

Words can barely convey what this means to many Monacan people, especially those who had to endure the peculiar politics of race that left no space for Indians in Virginia during much of the twentieth century. In the 1980s a core group of Monacans started the movement to reclaim their history (and community pride therein), a movement that was given a significant boost in 1984 when local historian Peter W. Houck penned a highly speculative but sensitive book on the Monacans entitled *Indian Island in Amherst County*.[49] However, the book was not uniformly celebrated by all in the Monacan community, and the process of gaining community support for the movement to reclaim Monacan history has not been easy.

Yet the powwow has made a difference, as Buddy Johns described as he relaxed after the Saturday evening meal during the 2001 powwow: "I just passed a lady there a couple of minutes ago that, well, I can remember when Dr. Houck wrote the book, *Indian Island*. I know a number of years went by she wouldn't even pick the book up. She didn't want to even mention the word 'Indian,' you know. She'd been beaten so badly with the prejudice over the years she didn't want to do anything or get involved at all. And I passed her there and she's one of the most active members now. It definitely makes a difference."[50]

The question remains: Is the Monacan powwow an identity maker? Perhaps not in the strict sense that Fredrik Barth crafted the term to explain how many ethnic groups use their most salient and distinct cultural elements (language, specific art forms, and so forth) to distinguish themselves as unique from all other groups with a single symbol.[51] However, it is an identity marker in the more flexible sense that Lerch and Bullers use the term – not as a traditional activity but as a community event that occurs alongside (and often accentuates) Local cultural forms and dynamics. As stated earlier, it is the only powwow that many (if not most) Monacans attend (and many do not wear regalia), thereby obscuring the argument that it is a simple appropriation of Pan-Indian cultural forms.

Nor is it a distinctly (or exclusive) community event, as is the case with the Monacan homecoming, which adds a layer of regional distinctiveness. For example, many Virginia tribes – notably the Chickahominies – incorporate their annual powwow into their homecoming festivities. Yet many Monacans attend the powwow who do not attend the homecoming within the community. For them the powwow provides a somewhat neutral space to reconsider their place in the community, while for all Monacans the powwow provides a space to reconsider and rearticulate their status as indigenous people in Amherst County. Thus the Monacan powwow constitutes a fluid identity marker that not only distinguishes the Monacans as a people but offers a point from which to negotiate their cultural and political identity in relation to non-Indians locally and to other Indians nationally – and, just as significantly, to one another.

"That's What a Powwow's About"

On Saturday, May 19, 2001, sometime around 3:00 p.m., emcee Marvin Burnette called all dancers into the arena at the Ninth Annual Monacan Nation Powwow and announced a dance contest to begin immediately. Within seconds Bob Seger's song "Old Time Rock and Roll" blasted through the public address system, taking everyone by surprise. A few seconds passed before the shock and confusion wore off and almost everyone present burst into laughter as dancers ad-libbed the lyrics.

However, not everyone laughed. As Kenneth Branham stood on the outskirts of the arena trying to contain himself, a non-Indian woman with her children stood next to him with a half-scowl and thought out loud, "Well, this is not what I expected." As chief of the Monacan Nation, Kenneth recognized a situation calling for tact and diplomacy when he saw one. He explained to the disappointed spectator, "Ma'am, we're just like everybody else. We're having a little fun. That's what a powwow's about."[52]

Such is the ongoing predicament of being Indian in Virginia in the twenty-first century. Like most indigenous groups in the East, Virginia's Indians have endured contact with non-Indians for almost four hundred years. Ironically, the larger non-Indian public expects them to behave as if such contact has been extremely limited or to resign any claims to Indian heritage entirely. However, the Monacans know as well as anyone that culture is not static. This understanding has allowed them to survive. It also lies at the heart of the powwow. While most tribal members work until they are thoroughly exhausted to produce it – so hard that it would be difficult to imagine them enjoying themselves by any means – they understand it as something that they present on their own terms. It is a space where they negotiate – or, more appropriately, articulate – their identity as *contemporary* Monacans and as people of integrity with other indigenous peoples and with non-Indians. They have the powwow because they *can*.

NOTES

1. The eight state-recognized tribes in Virginia are the Chickahominy, Eastern Chickahominy, Mattaponi, Upper Mattaponi, Monacan, Nansemond, Pamunkey, and Rappahannock tribes. None of these tribes is federally recognized as yet. In addition to including one representative from each Virginia tribe, the Virginia Council on Indians (VCI) includes "at large" members who reside in the state but belong to other Indian nations. The VCI also includes certain state legislators who have demonstrated an interest in Indian affairs.

2. J. David Smith, "Dr. Plecker's Assault on the Monacan Indians: Legal Racism and Documentary Genocide," *Lynch's Ferry: A Journal of Local History* 5, no. 1 (1992): 22–25.

3. For information on the most recent Monacan powwow, see http://www.monacannation.com/powwow.shtml (accessed April 28, 2005).

4. Robert K. Thomas, "Pan-Indianism," in *The American Indian Today*, ed. Stuart Levine and Nancy O. Lurie (Baltimore: Penguin, 1968), 77–85.

5. James H. Howard, "Pan-Indian Culture of Oklahoma," *Scientific Monthly* 80 (1955): 215–20; Thomas, "Pan-Indianism," 81.

6. James Clifford provides an innovative, multivocal discussion of such criticism

and its negative impact on a New England indigenous group in his essay on the Mashpee Wampanoags in James Clifford, *The Predicament of Culture: Twentieth Century Ethnography, Literature, and Art* (Cambridge: Harvard University Press, 1988), 277–346.

7. William W. Quinn Jr., "The Southeast Syndrome: Notes on Indian Descendant Recruitment Organizations and Their Perceptions of Native American Culture," *American Indian Quarterly* 14, no. 2 (1990): 147–54.

8. Patricia Barker Lerch and Susan Bullers, "Pow Wows as Identity Markers: Traditional or Pan-Indian?" *Human Organization* 55, no. 4 (1996): 391 (emphasis added).

9. We use this less structured approach as a means of placing emphasis on *local* meaning. Such an emphasis on community dialogue guides Lassiter's work on the Kiowa Gourd Dance song, the meaning of which, he argues, can be understood only through such discourses (as opposed to standard interpretations such as musical notation). See Luke E. Lassiter, " 'Charlie Brown': Not Just Another Essay on the Gourd Dance," *American Indian Culture and Research Journal* 24, no. 4 (1997): 75–103; Luke E. Lassiter, *The Power of Kiowa Song* (Tucson: University of Arizona Press, 1998), 154–67.

10. Lassiter, *The Power of Kiowa Song*, 10. For earlier discussions of the concept of collaborative or dialogical ethnography, see, for example, Elaine J. Lawless, " 'I Was Afraid Someone like You . . . an Outsider . . . Would Misunderstand': Negotiating Interpretive Differences between Ethnographers and Subjects," *Journal of American Folklore* 105 (1992): 301–14; and Dennis Tedlock, *The Spoken Word and the Work of Interpretation* (Philadelphia: University of Pennsylvania Press, 1983).

11. Dennis Tedlock, "Interpretation, Participation, and the Role of Narrative in Dialogical Anthropology," in *The Dialogic Emergence of Culture*, ed. Dennis Tedlock and Bruce Mannhelm (Chicago: University of Illinois Press, 1995), 253–87.

12. For a basic description of precontact Monacan society and territory (ca. 900–1600 AD), see Jeffrey Hantman, "Between Powhatan and Quirank: Reconstructing Monacan Culture and History in the Context of Jamestown," *American Anthropologist* 92, no. 3 (1990): 676–90. Some of the better-known indigenous entities in the alliance were the so-called Monacans proper (settled near the falls of the James River at the time of European contact in 1608), Tutelos, Saponis, Occaneechis, and Manahoacs. While some scholars, including Hantman, often refer to the indigenous groups in this vast territory as comprising a "confederacy," we prefer the term *alliance*, as it more accurately reflects the sociopolitical fluidity of the region.

13. Horatio Hale, "The Tutelo Tribe and Language," *Proceedings of the American Philosophical Society* 21, no. 114 (1883): 1–3. Many of the Tutelos and Saponeys migrated into the Iroquois Confederacy in the mid-eighteenth century and were adopted into the Cayuga Nation. Vestiges of their ceremonies and language survive on the Six Nations Reserve, Ontario, Canada.

14. Samuel R. Cook, *Monacans and Miners: Native American and Coal Mining Communities in Appalachia* (Lincoln: University of Nebraska Press, 2000), 51–53. Peter Houck's suggestion that the settlers from the east were predominantly white traders (who brought with them English surnames, such as Johns and Branham, which became common among Monacans) has been commonly accepted until recently. However, the authors and others have recently found documents linking the lineal ancestors of certain Monacan families to Tidewater Indians in the early eighteenth century. For Houck's account see his book *Indian Island in Amherst County* (Lynchburg VA: Lynchburg Historical Research Company, 1984).

15. Cook, *Monacans and Miners*, 56–60; Sherry S. McLeRoy and William R. McLeRoy, *Strangers in Their Midst: The Free Black Population of Amherst County, Virginia* (Bowie MD: Heritage Books, 1993).

16. For a good discussion on how miscegenation law was elaborated on and interpreted to maintain white privilege in the postbellum South, see Eva Saks, "Representing Miscegenation Law," *Raritan* 8 (1988): 39–69.

17. Cook, *Monacans and Miners*, 85–108. For an excellent discussion of the eugenics movement in Virginia, including Plecker's role in the international movement and his obsession with Amherst County, see J. David Smith, *The Eugenic Assault on America: Scenes in Red, White, and Black* (Fairfax VA: George Mason University Press, 1993). In fact the Monacans were the focus of a major eugenic study during Plecker's tenure that characterized the people in the community around Bear Mountain as chronically retarded, mixed-race degenerates. This widely circulated book, entitled *Mongrel Virginians*, is etched in the collective memory of the Monacan People as a dark moment in their history. It has also created a historical wariness of scholars seeking to do research in the community. See Arthur H. Estabrook and Ivan McDougal, *Mongrel Virginians* (Baltimore MD: Williams and Wilkins, 1926).

18. Cook, *Monacans and Miners*, 65–77.

19. Cook, *Monacans and Miners*, 108–14. There is another Indian community in Amherst County known as the Buffalo Ridge Cherokees, many of whom share lineal descendants with people in the Bear Mountain community. The contemporary existence of these two (relatively) mutually exclusive indigenous groups can be attributed largely to historical factionalism among local Indian families that was aggravated by racial integrity policies. See, for example, Horace R. Rice, *The Buffalo Ridge Cherokee: The Color and Culture of a Virginia Indian Community* (Madison Heights VA: BRC Books, 1991).

20. Lucian Branham, recorded conversation with Samuel R. Cook, July 1, 1996, Bear Mountain, Virginia.

21. Anonymous collaborator, recorded conversation with Samuel R. Cook, June 20, 1996, Bear Mountain, Virginia. Some collaborators opted to remain anonymous due to the sensitive nature of some of the information they provided.

22. Arthur Gray, "A Virginia Tribe of Indians," *Southern Churchman* (January 4, 1908): 1. Gray was specifically commenting on the Monacans' opposition to being called "Issues." Derived from the pre–Civil War term *free issue*, in reference to slaves who had been *issued* papers for freedom, by the turn of the twentieth century it had evolved into a derogatory term in Amherst County, roughly the equivalent of calling someone a mixed-race degenerate.

23. For a comment on the lawsuit, see Karenne Wood, "The Monacan Indians of Virginia," http://www.monacannation.com/history.shtml (accessed April 28, 2005).

24. L. Branham, July 1, 1996.

25. Dovie Ramsey, recorded conversation with authors, May 20, 2001, Elon, Virginia.

26. Kenneth Branham, recorded conversation with authors, May 20, 2001, Bear Mountain, Virginia.

27. Diana Laws, recorded conversation with authors, May 19, 2001, Elon, Virginia.

28. Lloyd "Buddy" Johns, recorded conversation with authors, May 19, 2001, Elon, Virginia.

29. Cook, *Monacans and Miners*, 114–16; Houck, *Indian Island*, 104–8.

30. Cook, *Monacans and Miners*, 116–24. The process through which tribes become state recognized in Virginia is quite rigorous. While the state legislature is responsible for codifying the act of recognition, the actual decision is in the hands of the Virginia Council on Indians, which examines evidence of a tribe's historical existence and community continuity.

31. Diane Johns Shields, recorded conversation with Samuel R. Cook, June 27, 1996, Amherst, Virginia.

32. D. Johns Shields, June 27, 1996.

33. K. Branham, May 20, 2001.

34. D. Laws, May 19, 2001.

35. L. Johns, May 19, 2001.

36. D. Ramsey, 20 May 2001.

37. Phyllis Hicks, recorded conversation with Samuel R. Cook, June 20, 1996, Bear Mountain, Virginia.

38. Cook, *Monacans and Miners*, 60–65, 97–103. For a discussion of the endurance of indigenous (ethnic) groups in the context of intense culture change and nation-state development, see Edward H. Spicer, "The Nations of a State," in *American Indian Persistence and Resurgence*, ed. Karl Kroeber (Durham NC: Duke University Press, 1994), 27–49.

39. K. Branham, May 20, 2001.

40. D. Ramsey, May 20, 2001.

41. Lerch and Bullers, "Pow Wows as Identity Markers," 392.

42. Lerch and Bullers, "Pow Wows as Identity Markers," 392.

43. K. Branham, May 20, 2001.

44. L. Johns, May 19, 2001.

45. Anthropological data on Tutelo-Saponi ceremonies that were incorporated into the Cayuga ceremonial complex after the latter were adopted into the Iroquois Confederacy have yielded some clues regarding Monacan ceremonial regalia. See, for example, Frank G. Speck, *The Tutelo Adoption Ceremony: Reclothing the Living in the Name of the Dead* (Harrisburg: Pennsylvania Historical Commission, 1942); and Gertrude P. Kurath, *Tutelo Rituals on Six Nations Reserve, Ontario* (Ann Arbor: Society for Ethnomusicology, 1981).

46. K. Branham, May 20, 2001.

47. D. Ramsey, May 20, 2001.

48. L. Johns, May 19, 2001.

49. Houck, *Indian Island.*

50. L. Johns, May 19, 2001.

51. Fredrik Barth, *Ethnic Groups and Boundaries: The Social Organization of Cultural Difference* (Boston: Little, Brown, 1969).

52. K. Branham, May 20, 2001.

BRIAN JOSEPH GILLEY

11. Two-Spirit Powwows and the Search for Social Acceptance in Indian Country

Ben, a Two-Spirit Chickasaw, nervously paced the floor in his yellow southern cloth dress as he and Jim eagerly awaited the drum and singers. The previous year's drum had shown up late and acted in ways that were taken to be overtly homophobic. Jim reassured Ben that his drum would arrive shortly and "blow the doors off" the small Park Service mess hall–turned–powwow arena. Ben, along with the other Two-Spirit men dressed in various styles of powwow regalia, were participating in the fourth annual Green Country Two-Spirit Society retreat powwow, held every July.[1] Over the last four years the powwow had grown from a smallish affair with few people dressing in regalia and a couple at the drum into an event with an amazing number of people "dressed" and a large group of non–Two Spirit friends and family. A chorus of "lulus" rang out as Jim's friends brought in the blanket-covered drum and began to set up. Shortly after the singers seated themselves at the drum, Gerald the emcee began the powwow with "I want to welcome all you ladies, gentlemen, and transgenders."

Ben and Jim are part of a movement among gay Native men seeking access to traditional social practices while desiring the freedom to express their sex and gender identity.[2] Two-Spirit identity draws on the belief that they are of "two spirits" or essences – part male and part female. Individuals may lean more toward femininity or masculinity in their social, sexual, and cultural practices. Although gays and lesbians in America are gaining more acceptance, many gay Indian men feel alienated from their Native communities. As a result they also feel estranged from participating in the traditional cultural practices of their tribe, ceremonial communities, and mainstream Native cultural events. While many Two-Spirit men do participate in community events, they feel they must hide their orientation and attempt to "pass" as "straight."

In an effort to bring together their Native, sex, and gender identities in social practices, Two-Spirit men organize cultural events geared toward their specific needs. In this way the powwow – as a portable, universal symbol of Indian identity and cultural involvement – becomes a traditional means of expressing Two-Spirit identity. Just as mainstream Native society uses the powwow as a means of emphasizing "Indianness," the Two-Spirit powwow emphasizes both Indianness and the sex and gender diversity of "Two-Spiritedness." By dressing in regalia, dancing, and simply being present, the men at the Two-Spirit powwow reaffirm the "traditional" nature of their identity. In this way Two-Spirit powwows allow individuals to incorporate their sex and gender identity into Native social practices as well as access the cultural practices that generate "traditional" Native identity. Because Two-Spirit powwows are "secret" affairs not advertised to the general public, the men feel free to express their gender identity and sexual orientation in a Native cultural context. It is this use of traditional Native contexts that demonstrates the importance of Two-Spirit powwows in affirming identity.

The powwow as a form of "traditional" cultural participation fits nicely into the structure of the Two-Spirit men's community, which is based on what Sanchez calls "intertribal negotiation" (2001, 51). While Two-Spirit men may not come from the same tribal ceremonial traditions, most have been to powwows and are aware of regalia categories and powwow etiquette. Powwows do not require large amounts of specialized knowledge; therefore Two-Spirit men with various levels of involvement in traditionalism can participate. This is important for many of the younger Two-Spirit men, who may have little experience with the traditions of their specific tribe. Powwows are not tied to the specific practices of one particular tribal tradition and thus are easily modified to reflect regional influence and social agendas (such as sobriety) and can be various sizes. The flexibility of the powwow allows Two-Spirit men to modify the focus to reflect their specific needs, such as community ideas about sex and gender and what it means to be an Indian man in public cultural contexts.

This chapter examines the ways the Two-Spirit men of the Green Country Two-Spirit Society use the powwow to not only satisfy their longing for cultural participation but also make their identity intelligible to other Natives, particularly their nongay relatives and friends. In making the powwow "Two-Spirit," the men strategically use powwow regalia and tradition to express identity. The Two-Spirit powwow comes to reflect their desire to make "Two-Spiritedness" a recognized aspect of "Indianness."

Two-Spirit Identity, Societies, Gatherings, and Powwows

The Two-Spirit powwow is a natural development from within the history of Two-Spirit identity, community, and gatherings. Use of the term *Two-Spirit* as a way to identify oneself as gay or lesbian, and Native, gained popularity in the 1990s as an outgrowth of academic interest in historical Native gender diversity combined with increased political and social activism by Native gays and lesbians (Lang 1998, Thomas and Jacobs 1999, Roscoe 1998). More recently "Two-Spirit" has moved beyond a term used to identify oneself as gay and indigenous toward the development of a specific identity with distinct social organization and practices. Support for a Two-Spirit identity is found in small, regional social groupings known as Two-Spirit societies, which have led the social and political push for gay and lesbian indigenous issues.

Two-Spirit societies are multitribal organizations usually found in urban and semiurban areas of the United States. The first Two-Spirit society, Gay American Indians (GAI), began in the late 1970s in San Francisco (Lang 1998, Roscoe 1998, Williams 1986). Over the past twenty-five years GAI has inspired the development of many other societies across America, from cities as large as New York to towns as small as Fort Smith, Arkansas. Two-Spirit societies consist of Native gays and lesbians who organize meetings, ceremonies, and other events with the goal of bringing together gay Native people from a particular area for social participation and support. The activities, size, and makeup of societies differ according to region. Most societies have regular meetings where they socialize, make crafts, learn traditional practices, and conduct ceremonies. Some societies are geared toward men or women only, while others make attempts to incorporate both.

Two-Spirit societies function to provide a social outlet away from the popular gay scene, which is seen as dominated by non-Indians ("Whites") and which promotes negative behaviors considered specifically detrimental to Indians, such as using alcohol. In addition, societies allow Two-Spirit people to come in contact with Native peoples and traditions without fears of homophobia and alienation. Being a member of a Two-Spirit society is a source of healthy living, social participation, and a path to self-acceptance for many Two-Spirit people. In recent years a national network of societies has emerged, largely because of an increased use of the Internet to post events and make contacts.

As an extension of one's society, the Two-Spirit gathering is a crucial aspect in maintaining Two-Spirit identity. In addition to the weekly or monthly meetings held by most Two-Spirit societies, annual multisociety gatherings provide a space where Two-Spirit people from across North America can come together to share their experiences and make acquaintances. Such national gatherings also allow Two-Spirit people to participate in cultural practices that they may not feel are available to them among their tribal or local Native communities. Two-Spirit gatherings are fairly large social events in which one society hosts other Two-Spirits at a campground, urban community center, or reservation, usually over a weekend, to participate in cultural activities specific to their needs.

A crucial aspect of Two-Spirit gatherings is the access they provide to cultural practices in an atmosphere in which people feel comfortable expressing their sexual and gender identity. While some gatherings emphasize the "traditional" ceremonial aspects of Two-Spirit identity, other gatherings are more social and combine gay community–influenced activities, such as drag shows, with Native ceremonial and social practices. Many Two-Spirit people describe social gatherings as places where they "can be Two-Spirit" – that is, social gatherings are places where Two-Spirit people are comfortable being both gay and Indian. The comfort level of gatherings, as places where sex and gender identity meet cultural practice, provides the ideal atmosphere for Two-Spirit powwows.

Most of what we know about the origin of Two-Spirit powwows comes from an oral history about the first gatherings. Many Two-Spirit people now in their forties remember some of the first Two-Spirit gatherings in San Francisco, Minneapolis, and Winnipeg. Their memories of these early gatherings include some aspect of the powwow, whether it was the use of regalia or singing powwow songs around a drum. The success and size of powwows at Two-Spirit events are explicitly linked to the increased participation in Two-Sprit communities by gay Natives who participate in traditional practices. As the number of people involved in the larger Two-Spirit community increased, so did the number of people who had the knowledge to organize and participate in gathering powwows. As a result powwows at gatherings have become more common. To date no powwow has been organized for Two-Spirit people independently from a gathering. However, many Two-Spirit people strongly desire to sponsor a powwow where they can take on public roles in mainstream communities and where gender regulations are relaxed.

Putting together a successful Two-Spirit powwow can be more difficult than running a mainstream powwow. The greatest obstacle is having access to people from the mainstream powwow community who know the proper way to run a powwow and are also "gay friendly." For example, the Green Country Two-Spirit Society spent several months trying to locate a drum to sing at their powwow. Several groups committed but then canceled because of homophobia or community pressure. At the last minute Ben was able to find a drum, but while they were singing at the powwow, they were visibly snickering and behaving disrespectfully. More recently the Green Country powwow hired drums with Two-Spirit men in them or used singers from close friends and family.

A second problem is having enough people within the Two-Spirit community who know how to "put on" a powwow and also have the regalia needed to participate. The problem of waning participation in tribal and mainstream Indian cultural practices seems doubly so with Two-Spirit people. Some Two-Spirit people share the same lack of contact with traditional practices as do many other Native peoples; however, their situation is complicated out of fears of homophobia. That is, many Two-Spirit men as they were growing up attempted to avoid contact with cultural practices because they viewed their Native communities as potentially hostile. Many Two-Spirit men are making efforts to "get their regalia together" so that they can participate in the Two-Spirit powwow. The hope is that as they become more comfortable with participating they will begin to dance at mainstream powwows. Giving men an opportunity to come in contact with the proper way of assembling one's regalia, the proper ways of dancing, and the customs of the powwow makes the Green Country Two-Spirit powwow an important proving ground for cultural participation.

The annual Green Country gathering powwow begins with a call to line up for Grand Entry from the emcee down to the cabins where people are getting dressed. Inevitably one person "holds up the show" while eager participants stand outside the dining hall door. People who are not dancing, as well as visiting friends and family, are seated in a large circle around the drum, transforming the dining hall into a powwow arena. As the drum warms up, a Two-Spirit veteran is asked to carry the American flag and someone else is honored with carrying the eagle staff in Grand Entry. As with any powwow in Indian country, people line up according to dance categories behind the powwow princess. The Green Country powwow princess is a man dressed in women's regalia, with a sash and beaded crown. After everyone enters the circle, the usual Prayer, Flag, and Round Dance songs are sung. Because of the small numbers of people dancing in regalia, usually around fifteen or twenty, almost all of the dances throughout the night are intertribal. Two-

Spirit men also use the powwow as an opportunity to honor one another or visiting friends with giveaways. Except for the freedom with which the men are holding hands with their partners, dressing in female regalia, and giving away to "families" of same-sex couples, the atmosphere and tone of the event are no different from any other powwow one might see in Indian country.

Making the Powwow Two-Spirit

Most people who know Ben as a Straight dancer at powwows around Oklahoma and Kansas would be shocked to see him in his Southern cloth dress. Although most people who know Ben believe that he is probably gay, they are unaware of his "calling" to participate in the powwow in female regalia. Ben traces his desire to dance in female regalia to an old black and white photograph of himself as a child wearing a dress and carrying a flag. Ben commented that this photo reminds him of being a child who was always more comfortable with feminine clothes and objects than with those of boys. However, as with the families of most Two-Spirit men, Ben's family vehemently discouraged his expression of female tendencies throughout his childhood and adolescence. Ben's family consistently encouraged him to participate in "boy's" activities and reminded him of the social, public, and religious obligations of Indian men.

Because Ben grew up in a strict household in rural Oklahoma, he felt a need to hide his sexual orientation until he was old enough to move out of his parents' house. As an openly gay young adult, Ben also felt alienated from Native community events out of fear of homophobia. Now, as Ben approaches middle age, he has taken the opportunity to express his gender difference within Native cultural practice at the gathering powwows. Ben pointed out: "As far as having a powwow for Two-Spirit people . . . we do it because there are not any powwows yet that honor or allow the Two-Spirit people. So we have our own to create a safe environment for our people, so we can dress any way we want without being shamed."

Most Two-Spirit men operate under the assumption that the tightly knit world of powwow would not support outward displays of their sexual orientation, such as men holding hands or exhibiting transgressions of gender identity. Two-Spirit men fully recognize mainstream powwow as something explicitly heterosexual in its social focus, from the community-sanctioned public interactions to the kinds of dancing. Although powwow communities may not be explicitly homophobic, it is assumed that any public behavior construed as gay or not in keeping with notions of Indian masculinity runs the potential of "shaming" one's family and would be strongly opposed. Therefore many Two-Spirit men either participate in mainstream community powwows by "passing" as straight or avoid them altogether. For those men who do Straight, Traditional or Fancy powwow dance, they assume that any knowledge of their sexual orientation would prevent them from winning prizes in their category or result in their being alienated. At the same time Two-Spirit men desperately want to participate in cultural practices. As Eric pointed out: "I didn't grow up traditional and I want to Straight dance, but I'm afraid they won't accept me, especially if they were to find out that I'm gay." In this way Two-Spirit men presume a lack of compatibility between their sexual orientation or gender and powwow as mainstream Native communities represent it.

Two-Spirit powwows are both a response to the alienation their participants feel elsewhere and an expression of Two-Spirit identity. Two-Spirit people use the powwow in the same way mainstream Native communities use it – to promote solidarity and the transmission of values and to serve as a source of cultural identity. Using the powwow as a source of common ground and identity, Two-Spirit people take its fundamental components and adjust them to fit their specific needs, such as flexibility in gender roles. Through the powwow Two-Spirit identity and mainstream Indian cultural practice are brought together under a single cultural framework through the use of, for example, traditional forms of regalia, the powwow princess, and traditional forms of honoring. The powwow is made "Two-Spirit" by opening up the gender regulations on the roles that people can take and expanding the available meanings for cultural practices to include alternative interpretations.

Being Two-Spirit and Dancing

Although not many Two-Spirit men dress in women's regalia, those who do approach crossing with the same respect that they would any form of Native practice. As Sheila, a Lakota man living as a woman, stated, "Dressing in female regalia is not some form of drag." Rather, Two-Spirit men are resolute about the serious nature of using women's regalia. Because they are using symbols of respect recognized communitywide, they are careful about the ways they represent themselves when wearing women's dance clothes. Accordingly they put a lot of time and energy into acquiring their dance outfits and learning the dances.

Ben and Will both spent almost a year consulting female dancers and family, praying, and accumulating the components of their female regalia. Ben eventually put together a yellow broad cloth dress, matching moccasins, and a shawl. He also adapted his Straight Dance belt and a few other items from his male regalia to create an impressive transformation. Will put together dance regalia that more closely reflected his family's Mvskoke cultural roots. Both Will and Ben meticulously followed the requirements for their regalia forms to ensure that they reflected the tradition properly. In the arena Will, Ben, and the others in female regalia dance and behave the same ways that women do at any powwow; they enter behind the men during Grand Entry, dance behind the men in the Round Dance, and pay close attention to swinging their fringe with the drumbeats.

One of the most obvious ways Two-Spirit conceptions of gender are incorporated into the powwow is through reconfiguring gender lines in regalia. As Ben explained: "We dance in women's regalia to get in touch with and honor our female energies." At the Two-Spirit powwow regalia is one medium through which Two-Spirit people express their masculinity or femininity in ways that also reflect their Native identity. It is assumed that men who dance in female regalia are more comfortable with the feminine aspect of their "spirit." Buckskin, southern cloth, and jingle dresses represent the ideal of Indian womanhood and emphasize cultural ideas about femininity in mainstream powwows. In similar ways Two-Spirit men use the association between women's regalia and Indian femininity to express their gender as well as their cultural identities. Some Two-Spirit men participate in the powwow by dancing in the male styles of straight, fancy, or traditional. These men are equally as Two-Spirit as those who gender cross, but their "spirits" tend to gravitate more toward masculine ideals. Expressions of gender associations with regalia carried over from the mainstream powwow to the Two-Spirit powwow thus remain relatively intact; however, they also become forums to challenge alienation, to honor, and to "heal."

Dancing at the powwow not only is about expressing gender identity but also becomes a setting for Two-Spirit men to express their feelings about being Two-Spirit. As Ben explained, Two-Spirit men use female regalia to connect with the historic tradition of gender mixing in Native communities. The mixing of gender characteristics in both cultural practices and dress was a prominent feature of precontact and early historic gender diversity in most tribes in North America (Lang 1998; Roscoe 1991, 1998; Williams 1986). Two-

Spirit men see themselves as upholding this tradition by switching or "mixing up" the gendered aspects of powwow dance.

Ben also sees dancing in female regalia as a way to honor "the Old Two Spirits that have passed over and the ones who cannot be present." He is referring not only to Two-Spirit people who cannot be present at the powwow because they are "no longer with us" for a variety of reasons, including HIV/AIDS and hate crimes, but also to those people who feel "too much shame about their sexual orientation" to participate. During his giveaway at the most recent Green Country powwow, Ben said, "We dance for everyone, and we dance so that our people will be accepted someday, and it is coming soon." Ben sees his dancing in female regalia as an act of "healing" as well as an expression of his gender identity. He went on to explain: "We dance to heal the small female child in us that was suppressed when we were children." Ben, like most Two-Spirit people, perceives his alienation as a "wound" or a missing link in the medicine hoop that needs repair. Therefore, he and the other Two-Spirit people dance at the powwow as a way to heal themselves and to repair the larger Indian community.

Although Two-Spirit people rely on mainstream ideas about the relationship between regalia styles and gender to express their identity – such as wearing southern cloth dresses to express femaleness – they also challenge mainstream ideals by altering gendered associations with anatomical sex, sexual orientation, and regalia in the powwow context. Simply wearing Straight Dance regalia at a Two-Spirit powwow challenges the ways Two-Spirit men feel they are alienated from their communities by homophobia – that is, they feel that any knowledge of their sexual orientation would result in their alienation from dancing at community events. Although these dancers do not alter their regalia for the Two-Spirit context, just knowing that they can participate in Native cultural activities without "worrying about being outed" is crucial.

Removing the heterosexual focus of powwow participation also provides an opening in the kinds of behaviors that are "acceptable" at powwows. For example, it is not uncommon for two men dressed in Straight Dance regalia to Indian two-step with each other. The Indian two-step is a social or courtship dance in which male-female couples dance holding hands and snake around the arena being led by the head man and lady dancers. At Two-Spirit powwows the head man and lady dancers do lead the two-step, but the couples that follow are made up of men dancing with men as well as women dancing with women. Other gender alterations are also made, including women sitting at the drum, women carrying the eagle staff or American flag in Grand Entry, and a man dressed in women's regalia addressing powwow participants without going through the emcee or "male" member of the family. These gender transgressions are intended to create a space in which multiple interpretations of Indian and Two-Spirit identity are acceptable.

Bringing Gay and Native Together in the Powwow Princesses

Will seemed the most unlikely person to be competing in the Green Country gathering princess competition. He is usually a very soft spoken, shy person who does not look people straight in the eye. However, during the pageant, Will was gliding around the dining hall miming lyrics to a Celine Dion song with the exaggerated poise and skill of any professional drag queen. Will's performance was so well practiced and convincing that it was no surprise when he was named the winner of the pageant. The next evening at the Green Country gathering powwow, Will was the princess at Grand Entry. With the same attention to detail given to his drag outfit, Will's Mvskoke dress was "flawless," to quote another Two-Spirit man. Will, with his Miss Green Country sash and beaded crown, slowly stepped to the Grand Entry song with the grace of any Indian woman. Later that evening he held a "special," in which he honored the people who had helped him with both his drag outfit and his Indian dress.[3] For Will, performing in drag and being the powwow princess were a way to bring together two aspects of his life, gay and Indian, that were seemingly opposed until he became involved in the Two-Spirit community.

The explicit reconciliation of gay and Native culture is also closely seen in the role of the powwow princess at the Green Country Gathering powwow. Although the powwow princess is to some extent a parody on Indian princesses in general, the role continues to do the work of cultural compromise. The Two-Spirit powwow princess brings together the tradition of drag queen titles (modeled after beauty pageants) in the gay community with the Indian princess pageant. Drag queen titles are given in pageant-style competitions usually sponsored by gay bars or gay social organizations. Individuals are judged on their commitment to gay community causes, their singing or other talents, and the degree to which they successfully parody women. A recognizable part of gay society, drag queen titles carry significant cultural capital in the gay community.

Powwow princess titles are similar in that they are a form of community-recognized status, they are bestowed by organizations (such as veteran's societies), and they are the result of judged competitions. Just as drag queen titles are unconventional, powwow princesses in mainstream Native society are selected for reasons different from conventional "beauty" titles in non-Indian pageants, such as commitment to cultural survivability, living a "good life," helping their Native people, and the potential to represent Natives to non-Indian society (for further discussion on the powwow princess, see chapter 8, "Beauty Is Youth"). Most Two-Spirit individuals recognize and respect both types of titles. As a result, the Two-Spirit powwow princess is part drag queen title and part Indian princess title. At the same time, the cultural construction and obligations of the Two-Spirit Indian princess are mostly Indian. In the same ways as mainstream Indian princesses, Miss Green Country is obligated to participate in the Grand Entry at the powwow, have a giveaway, and be present the following year to transfer the title. In more recent years the powwow princess has also represented the Green Country group in gay pride parades and events as well.

Broadening "Community" at the Two-Spirit Powwow

The sight of Sheila in her fully beaded buckskin dress Indian two-stepping with Zach in his Straight Dance regalia might not seem unusual to most powwow-goers. However, Sheila is a man who has been living as a woman for the past fifteen years. She has many more anecdotes about "being found out" at mainstream powwows, and being disqualified or looked over for competitions, than she does about the "truly traditional people" who have accepted her. Unlike most of the other Two-Spirit men who dance in women's regalia, Sheila lives a woman's life daily. She often publicly confronts homophobia and intolerance at mainstream powwows by dancing in women's categories and vehemently challenging negative reactions. What is crucial about Sheila's performances and about Two-Spirit men's fear is that they both reflect an awareness of powwows as forums for public identity.

Two-Spirit people have created a public space to express their identity in the powwow as well as a space that emphasizes the diversity of Native society and cultural practice. They recognize the powwow as a place where identities can be presented, negotiated, alienated, and possibly incorporated. As Mattern points out: "[The powwow] plays a unifying role in Indian life while providing a public arena for negotiation of differences and disagreements" (1996, 183). Just as mainstream powwows are forums for individuals to negotiate their cultural differences within a multitribal context, Two-Spirit powwows are places where individuals can negotiate their sex and gender differences within dominant cultural conceptions of Indianness. Two-Spirit men use the powwow as a way to move their differences from a secretive or "closeted" context, as some put it, into the realm of public recognition. The men of the Green Country society see their annual gathering powwow as a way to publicly demonstrate that the cultural practices of Two-Spirit people are adhering to what is recognized as traditionally Native.

In publicly affirming their identity, Two-Spirit men are expressing that they are not simply "gay Indians;" rather, they are "Two-Spirit," which they consider a legitimate traditional Native identity. Also, by incorporating Two-Spirit social practices and ideals into the powwow, Two-Spirit men are making their identity intelligible to other Natives as well as creating a powerful association between Two-Spirit and the traditional. For example, the use of female regalia, discussed above, is a way to communicate Two-Spirit identity through signs and symbols recognized as "Indian" by dominant Native society. The public association between Indian cultural practices and Two-Spirit identity affirms the Two-Spirit community through the practice of honoring, by being recognized by family and friends, and by receiving the approval of elders and other recognized members of Native communities. The hope is that being Two-Spirit in a public context will eventually produce greater acceptance by mainstream Native communities.

Ways of Honoring

Honoring is a common ideological principle among Native social practices that is also a crucial aspect of the powwow. Honoring at powwows takes many forms, including the honoring of veterans with a song, special dances, and giveaways. Honoring establishes and confirms social relationships, recognizes an individual's achievement and commitment to a community, and legitimizes the honoree's place in a particular Indian community. Two-Spirit powwows also incorporate many of these aspects of honoring. Much like any mainstream powwow, the Green Country Society holds a giveaway to honor the head man and lady dancers, the drum, and various people who worked on the powwow. Individuals, including the head man and lady dancers, also ask for time during the powwow to honor other people and the powwow committee and to hold specials to honor the drum.

One distinct aspect of honoring at the Two-Spirit powwow is that individuals may choose either to speak for themselves or to follow the tradition of speaking through another person. Speaking for oneself is extremely important for a group of people who feel that they do not have a voice in mainstream Native communities. Although not all participants speak for themselves, it is not uncommon for a man dressed in women's regalia to break with the tradition of having a woman speak through a male relative or the emcee.[4] In allowing people to speak for themselves, Two-Spirit powwows are negotiating with dominant conceptions about who has the right to public space at Native community events. They are also drawing on the precontact tradition of gender diversity in Native societies in which Two-Spirits were not necessarily bound to specific gender roles or regulations. As Lang points out: "Gender role change . . . obviously did not follow rigidly circumscribed rules; the individual had latitude, differentially determined culturally, in crossing beyond his gender role and also in the componential organization of an ambivalent woman-man status" (1998, 90). Two-Spirit people fully exploit this tradition of ambiguity in gender roles and of alternative forms of honoring in public ways.

A major component of powwows is the practice of honoring individuals and families. In the Two-Spirit context the notion of family is expanded to include same-sex couples. People who are honoring another "family" during a giveaway will call on the family of "Jim and Chuck," for example. This expansion of the notion of family is in keeping with the diverse ways the gay community recognizes nonblood kin and same-sex relationships as family. It also legitimizes same-sex relationships in a Native context. Most Native communities, as in mainstream American society, do not recognize same-sex couples as a legitimate form of marital commitment or "family." The lack of recognition of same-sex couples by one's Native community further alienates individuals from publicly being Two-Spirit and from incorporating their entire family into cultural practices, such as ceremonies and the powwow. Taylor, a Two-Spirit Otoe who is active in powwowing, spoke of how he wanted his partner to help him get dressed in his Straight Dance regalia at powwows by doing things that women might do for a husband, such as straightening scarves, putting on bells and belts, and fixing his hair. He also spoke wistfully of the two of them having a "family camp" where they could host friends and relatives during powwows.

The kinds of social practices Taylor yearns for are entrenched in the heterosocial nature of Native communities and the powwow. Therefore, honoring couples at Two-Spirit powwows, as well as having Two-Spirit couples cook the powwow feed, help one another "dress," and hold positions on the powwow committee, goes far in allowing the men to incorporate their partners in ways that the mainstream Native community takes for granted. Honoring at the Two-Spirit powwow not only is a way to expand the notion of family to include Two-Spirit conceptions but also provides a context for Two-Spirit people to publicly affirm their relationships with blood kin and friends.

Family, Friends, and the Community "Showing Support"

After Sean finished his giveaway, his mother stood in the middle of the arena by the drum and addressed onlookers. Sean's mother and his aunt were at the powwow in their regalia as a sign of "support" for Sean and his partner, Karl. Sean's mother spoke of the difficulty she had when first learning that Sean was gay. She went on to say that she had come to accept Sean's sexual orientation and was glad that he was living a "good life" with Karl. While Sean's mother's speech was meaningful for him, it also had a significant impact on the Two-Spirit people present at the powwow. The fact that a member and elder of the Native community spoke up in support of Two-Spirit people provided the kind of affirmation they are continually seeking.

The "support" of family, friends, and other social relationships is a well-known, crucial aspect of mainstream powwows. Such support makes dancing and fulfilling social obligations easier while also reaffirming that a person is being in a "good way." The non–Two Spirit friends and family members who attend the Green Country powwow are usually impressed with the ways Two-Spirit people conduct themselves and their social events. Ben, reflecting on stereotypes about gay people, commented: "Most of our people think of being gay as something negative and unhealthy, like what we see on TV. When people come here they see that Two-Spirit people are doing things in the right way; that we are traditional."

The Two-Spirit powwow, therefore, becomes a forum to challenge the dominant notion of gayness as hypersexed, over-the-top flamboyant, and lacking in social and personal responsibility. With this in mind the Green Country Society encourages Two-Spirit men to invite their friends and family to the powwow as a way to show others that the Two-Spirit lifestyle is a way of "going in a good way." The "good way" is a common expression among Native peoples that encompasses Indian notions of honor, respect for oneself and community, and adherence to the principles of Indian philosophy and spirituality. Demonstrating that being Two-Spirit is one of the many ways to "walk in a good way" is crucial to most Two-Spirit men. Accordingly the powwow allows Two-Spirit men to show that their identity is more about their spirituality, traditionalism, and commitment to Indian peoples than it is about sexual orientation.

Despite the importance of having family at the powwow, very few relatives actually attend. In some cases, family members simply live too far away to make the trip. Also, many Two-Spirit men are not "out" to their families, and most of the men who are out have families that "misunderstand" or are hostile to their sexual orientation for various reasons, including religion, shame, and the idea that their son has a "problem." Most Two-Spirit men would want their family's support but know that it is not available. As a Two-Spirit Cherokee said: "I would like my family to see what we do here, and that we are being traditional. But I'm afraid they still wouldn't accept who we are."

However, not all Two-Spirit men's families are hostile to their lifestyle. Every year a few Two-Spirit men have at least their mothers come to the powwow; other female relatives also attend occasionally. Most friends who attend the powwow are nongay Natives or non-Indian gays. Many friends come to the powwow every year and dance in regalia to support the Two-Spirit men. In many ways these visitors' support of their friends and family is a necessary aspect of the powwow, because it provides representation for the mainstream Indian community as well as the mainstream gay community. As Ben frequently points out: "When they come here they see that we are being true to our traditions. They will go back to their communities and talk about what they have seen."

Having people from the community come to the powwow has produced mixed results. As mentioned earlier a group of singers from the local Indian community came to sing at one of the first Green Country powwows. They demonstrated their homophobia by staying for only forty-five minutes, despite having been paid for four hours. The singers were clearly making jokes among themselves and were visibly uncomfortable with the men dressed in women's regalia. For the most part, however, people from the community who are not friends or family of Two-Spirit participants have shown respect for the event. At the most recent powwow, the Green Country Society had a well-known elder emcee the powwow. He gave a powerful speech during Grand Entry praising the Two-Spirit community for their commitment to their culture and survivability. Also present was a well-known elder and singer who led prayers and the powwow drum of Two-Spirit people. After the powwow ended he commented to Jim that he was glad to see so many good outfits and traditional

Indians and said, "You all should 'come out' to the powwow and not be ashamed." Not recognizing the double entendre of "coming out," he was puzzled by the laughter.

Conclusion

In the same way that Two-Spirit identity alleviates the tension between mainstream Native male and gay identities, the Two-Spirit powwow alleviates the tension the men feel concerning cultural participation. The Two-Spirit powwow attempts to reconcile the two seemingly different worlds of gay and Indian through the performance of "traditional" Native practices within the conception of Two-Spirit. By holding their own powwow Two-Spirit people are revising notions of tradition to include the gender diversity that was historically prevalent in Native North America. As Todd made clear: "We are not making this stuff up. We are holding a traditional powwow and doing things in the right way."

At a fundamental level a man dressing in female regalia disrupts the association between anatomical sex and dance categories. In challenging this association Two-Spirit people emphasize one's felt gender rather than one's socially prescribed one. The use of the powwow emphasizes Two-Spirit men's solidarity with Native communities while at the same time providing a way for them to express their distinctiveness within Indian traditional ideology. Practices such as Two-Spirit men dancing in female regalia demonstrate their intimate knowledge of the construction of contemporary Indian identity. A man wearing female regalia distinguishes Two-Spirit as a particular interpretation of Indianness while it also stresses the commonalities with mainstream Native identity.

Such commonality with the Native community is key for Two-Spirit men, and for this reason Two-Spirit men closely adhere to the fundamental components of the powwow and regalia. Components of the Two-Spirit powwow, such as the Green Country princess, do the work of reconciliation between Two-Spirit identity and dominant conceptions of Indianness by manipulating mainstream ideology in Native cultural practices. Honoring same-sex couples, as well as having family, friends and community members attend the powwow, helps to solidify the fundamental ways Two-Spirit is an interpretation of Indian identity that deserves a publicly recognized legitimacy. Two-Spirit people are well aware of the ways Native communities once accepted sex and gender diversity and see their powwow as a move toward finding that acceptance again. As the elder emceeing the Green Country Two-Spirit powwow said: "Indians shouldn't waste people."

NOTES

1. I have disguised the real names of the individuals mentioned in this chapter. At the request of the participants and organizers, I also have disguised the names of the Two-Spirit societies mentioned here as well as the locations of the annual Two-Spirit events.
2. While this chapter focuses on Two-Spirit men, I use the phrase "Two-Spirit people" to include gay men, lesbian women, and transgender Native people who identify as "Two-Spirit."
3. A special is a dance and giveaway used to honor certain people at a powwow.
4. Custom about publicly addressing powwow participants varies according to region. However, in most instances, women speak through a male relative or the emcee. Emcees will also speak for other men on occasion.

REFERENCES

Lang, Sabine. 1998. *Men as Women, Women as Men*. Austin: University of Texas Press.

Mattern, Mark. 1996. "The Powwow as a Public Arena for Negotiating Unity and Diversity in American Indian Life." *American Indian Culture and Research Journal* 20 (4): 183–201.

Roscoe, Will. 1998. *Changing Ones: Third and Fourth Genders in Native North America*. New York: St. Martin's.

———. 1991. *The Zuni Man-woman*. Albuquerque: University of New Mexico Press.

Sanchez, Victoria E. 2001. "Intertribal Dance and Cross Cultural Communication: Traditional Powwows in Ohio." *Communication Studies* 52 (1): 51–72.

Thomas, Wesley, and Sue-Ellen Jacobs. 1999. "' . . . And We Are Still Here': From Berdache to Two-Spirit People." *American Indian Culture and Research Journal* 23 (2): 91–107.

Williams, Walter. 1986. *The Spirit and the Flesh*. Boston: Beacon.

RENAE WATCHMAN

12. Powwow Overseas
The German Experience

My anticipation of going to a powwow transcends borders. Here at Stanford I eagerly await the annual Mother's Day powwow; I also travel across the San Francisco Bay to the Oakland Friendship Center for Thursday night dance practice. I love to attend the Gathering of Nations in Albuquerque, and I frequently find myself back east at Schemitzun in Connecticut, which is always fulfilling. During the summer months I absolutely must travel home to the Dinè reservation and attend the traditional powwows and ceremonies before heading north to Canada for their traditional and contest powwows.

Visualize the bustle of pre-powwow jingles and bells, a master of ceremonies (MC) calling for warmup songs by the various drum groups, the activity of vendors selling their wares, and the anticipation of Grand Entry. Now imagine the pre-powwow mixture of noises – conversations, the sounds of dancers and drums – in German!

I attended contest powwows in Germany, organized by Germans with attendees who are German. At the first powwow the MC imitated typical powwow discourse verbatim – "*Testing, testing, eins, zwei, drei.*" And "*Grand Entry in 20 Minuten!*" He even cracked jokes: "*Ja, Ich bin Indianer . . . Meine Urgroßmutter war eine Cherokee Prinzessin, Aye!*"[1] That Germans can adopt and use "Aye!" correctly is astonishing and reveals their attention to detail. Needing to recompose myself I returned to the parking lot, crowded with vehicles marked by elongated, white, rectangular German license plates and sporting bumper stickers in English that read, "This car stops at all Powwows," and "I like Indian Powwows."

Contest powwows continue to grow in popularity in Germany, and today there are approximately 120 powwow dancers and fourteen drum groups in the country. Powwows are still relatively unknown in other parts of Europe, though some dancers can be found in Poland and the Czech Republic. The cultural transfer of powwows to European soil thousands of miles away is contributing to the transcendence and globalization of an event whose origins are rooted in Indian country.[2] Since the opening of its borders, the former East

Germany has had greater access to media and to North America itself, allowing interested Germans from all parts of the nation to observe powwows directly in Indian country. Ease of travel also enables Native peoples from the United States and Canada to perform in powwows in Germany.

Indian entertainment had come to Europe during the late nineteenth century in the form of Wild West shows. Today those romanticized performances have been replaced by contemporary powwow dancers from Indian country, invited by Germans to travel and share their stories for educational rather than entertainment purposes. Through these contracted educational performances, Native people have reformed and encouraged Indianthusiasts (people who appropriate Indian culture in various ways) by modeling powwow as a diverse, vibrant celebration of song and dance rather than as a kitschy, romanticized Plains display. Such empowered Natives act effectively as mentors, passing down knowledge and exposing and converting Germans to powwow culture. A few hundred Indians currently live in Germany, most in the American military; some belong to the Native American Association of Germany (NAAoG). These Indian people organize powwows, but such Indian-sponsored events are rare and participation in them is often restricted to only the Native community.[3]

The foreign location of a powwow is not the pressing concern here. Powwow's place is neither fixed nor absolute; the powwow circuit is a telling example of the fluidity of its location.[4] If I vacationed outside of North America and came upon a powwow with participants from Indian country, I would probably feel "at home." What is at stake at German powwows is the replication and appropriation of an event by people who choose on some levels to divorce themselves from their own culture and embrace aspects of another, equally rich way of life.[5] As Indian people we need to ask ourselves whether playing Indian overseas – and our own role in encouraging that transfer – threatens an integral component of Native North American identity and culture.

Germans and Indians

Indianthusiasm has been part of German's history for a long time.[6] I employ the concept of appropriation in the same sense as Deborah Root: "When an outsider decides which aspects of a cultural and aesthetic tradition to take up and emphasize and which to ignore, these decisions may have nothing to do with the internal meanings of the dances, art forms, and ceremonies within the culture in which they were created."[7]

The oldest form of appropriation is traditional hobbyism, which has been practiced since the early 1920s and has a membership exceeding forty thousand Europeans.[8] Other types of Indianthusiasm include practices by spiritualists, political activists, and researchers.[9] Many hobbyists grew up reading the novels of Karl May (1842–1912), whose protagonist was an imaginary, buckskin-clad Apache Indian known as Winnetou. Fascinated with characters like Winnetou, drawn to a romanticized notion of North American Indians, and believing that contemporary Native people are no longer "real Indians," hobbyists attempt to re-create prereservation culture in summer camps. The Indian practices they re-create include living in tipis, beading, hunting, playing "Indian games," and dancing.

At these summer camps the dances are specifically but erroneously referred to as "powwows."[10] Such "powwows" have been examined in the documentary films *Seeking the Spirit: Plains Indians in Russia* (1999), by Bea Medicine, and *If Only I Were an Indian* (1995), by John Paskievich. Hobbyist powwows are fueled by caricatured displays of Indian people – the Plains warrior whoops and hollers while "sedated maidens" drag their moccasins around the dance arena.[11] Their bizarre, offbeat dancing is complemented by the sounds of Boy Scout–like singing from people sitting on the ground around a handmade drum. Although clearly a good attempt at singing in a language not their own, their version of powwow singing tends to be offbeat and thus could not be danced to at a contemporary powwow.

One of my memorable encounters with German hobbyists occurred in 1998 while I was waiting outside a theater in Hamburg. A child in line was dressed in a Pocahontas costume. I was perplexed because it was the middle of July, far from Fasching season (the German version of Carnival or Mardi Gras), and no one else was dressed in such a manner. I approached the mother, garbed in civilian clothes like me, and politely asked, in German, why her daughter was dressed like Pocahontas. The mother, obviously embarrassed, admitted that her daughter just wanted "to be an Indian for the day." Introducing myself and my family to the child, I told her that we were "real Indians" from the United States and that we never dress like Pocahontas.

However, not all Germans interested in Indians view Native America through the nostalgic lens of hobbyism. As Karl May's readership aged and matured, some no longer took his work seriously. Many of the German powwow dancers and attendees I spoke with recall that their interest in *modern* North American Native peoples escalated in the 1970s as a result of international attention to such political happenings as the siege at Wounded Knee in

1973. During that time North American powwows grew markedly in popularity, along with the Red Power movement, and became increasingly politicized while concomitantly maintaining their role as a traditional gathering in reservation communities and urban centers. After the fall of the Berlin Wall in 1989, powwows began appearing in Germany that were strikingly similar to those currently practiced in Native North America, featuring contest dancing, live singing, and vibrant outfits. The oldest such German powwow took place in 1990 in Hohenneuendorf, in former East Germany. Competition powwows in the country began in 2000, the same year that I was invited by the Lord Mayor of Radebeul to bring powwow dancers to the "Powwow am Hohenstein."[12] Held during the annual Karl May festival, this educational event showcases powwow categories but is not an actual powwow. In some cases Natives have actively promoted powwow culture or have mentored former German hobbyists and guided them from hobbyism to powwow life.

German hobbyists and German powwow dancers make clear to me their differences from, if not their antagonism toward, each other. One powwow dancer, when explaining his handmade Grass Dance outfit, scoffed at German hobbyist attire, labeling it as "ugly brown clothes from two hundred years ago."[13] A hobbyist counters, "We try to dress as the Natives did before the reservation period. . . . Traditional means that there are no swim shorts under the outfit. If things get too modern, then the old culture will fade away."[14]

During the summer of 2002, after fourteen years of travel to and from Germany, I finally did attend a German competition powwow. I went not to dance but to hear the stories of the German participants, seeking to discover the meaning(s) of the powwow for them and what drove them to identify as Indians, whether as an "Indian for a day" or as avid German powwow dancers. In addition to the interviews, I corresponded by e-mail with other German powwow participants. Their opinions and experiences, combined with my own observations, provide a springboard for considering more general questions about appropriation and the place of powwow beyond the borders of Native America.

A German Powwow

The Third Annual Asbach Competition Powwow 2002 was similar to a typical competition powwow in Indian country because it entailed a classic schedule of events, distinct competition dance categories (including team dancing and live singing), an entertaining MC, an appropriately dressed arena director

(AD), a head judge, donation requests in the form of blanket dances, and a dry after-hours "49."[15] Furthermore, the organizers of the event published a program that included a schedule of events, powwow rules and etiquette, and a list of the previous year's winners. Also included were sponsorship ads and a flyer stressing the protocol "Kein Alkohol und keine Drogen!" ("No alcohol! No drugs!"). This admonition is not surprising at North American powwows, but I found it unexpected at the Asbach powwow, given the German reputation for consuming beer.

What follows is a chronological framing of the Asbach powwow. As Grand Entry nears, dancers, singers, and spectators pack the gymnasium. Each of the drum groups sings a warmup song preceding the Grand Entry. Two eagle staff carriers lead the procession – both are Northern Traditional dancers, one a German from Kiel and the other a Lakota elder from Rosebud, South Dakota. The customary Northern and Southern Plains categories are represented in each of the usual, gendered age groups, from Tiny Tots to Golden Age. At Asbach "Indian Time" does not play a significant role in the organization of the powwow, because the German dancers are completely dressed and ready to dance at Grand Entry time. In contrast some dancers in Indian country are notorious for filing into the Grand Entry late, incompletely dressed, or with partially braided hair to get their points; they resort to getting dressed during the most "traditional" part of every powwow (the Flag Song, Victory Song, and Opening Prayer).

Honoring veterans with a Flag Song, followed by a Victory Song, a Sneak-Up, and perhaps a Crow Hop or Round Dance is typical of a powwow schedule and was reenacted in Asbach. After the Grand Entry the MC exclaims in German: "Danke Skunk Cap Singers! Der nächste Punkt des offiziellen Teils berücksichtigt die Veteranen. Deswegen werden wir einen Titel zu Ehren der Veteranen, ein Veteranlied, spielen. Und das kommt von den White Lake Singers aus Berlin, White Lake."[16] Then, switching to English, he continues: "White Lake, take it away!"

At North American powwows such protocol is completely appropriate; it is considered respectful to honor veterans, despite the tumultuous history of government-Indian relations. This custom could be controversial at German powwows, however, due to a general lack of acknowledgment of the country's World War II veterans. As one German told me, the purposeful distancing from the war discourages Germans from honoring those who served Hitler in the military.[17] It is not surprising then that the particular identities of the veterans mentioned by the MC at the Asbach powwow were not made clear.

Adhering to powwow practice, an Opening Prayer is given, in this case by the lead singer of the host drum. He begins by explaining to the crowd in German: "Please bear with me while I pray in my mother tongue. I come from Poland and have lived in Germany for twelve years and I am the lead singer of the Dark Cloud singers. Pray along in your own way, while I pray in my mother tongue."[18] With cameras forbidden during this moment, he prays in Polish. Afterward introductions of head staff are made, followed by a round of intertribal dances.

Competition dancing then begins with each style of dance competing to two songs. The prize money is relatively meager compared to some North American powwow purses. Hobbyist dancers do attend Asbach, but they participate only in the Grand Entries and intertribals and do not participate in the competition, presumably because they consider competition a violation of "traditional" practice. Only five dancers from North America participate, compared to the seventy-five dancers of European descent. Seven Native faces appear in the crowd of about three hundred spectators.

German drum groups, or "Bands," are a novelty to the German powwow scene. At the Asbach powwow there are seven drums present, two of which are composed only of women. Five sing Northern style and two sing Southern style. One of the two Southern drums boasts backup chorus girls. Though noticeably inexperienced, the singers are able to hold a continuous song with only occasional gaffes. A lot of drum hopping, similar to that prominent in Indian country, occurs. German drum groups turn to Northern Cree, Black Stone, Yellowhammer, Rosehill, and a plethora of others to learn songs. To avoid conflict with Native singers, some singers claim to compose their own powwow songs ("49" Songs are now being composed in the German language, providing more evidence of their attention to powwow detail).

Native oral traditions stress that if the drum is respected and taken care of, the singers too will be respected. Several examples here of a breach of drum etiquette suggest that the drum is regarded as just a prop by the powwow participants at Asbach. For example, one group bangs their drum on the doorframe as they enter, drums are left alone during the pre-powwow moments, one drum is accidentally knocked over, and another is used as a table. The host drum designates one singer to throw his body over the drum at the end of the song to prevent over-beating; thus he is nearly lying on the drum from the waist up at song's end.

At the Asbach powwow, as in Indian country, politics plays a role in the formation of – and, at times, the deterioration of – the event. Powwow politics at Asbach include the ignoring of offerings to stop a song, or a fan being waved over the drum, or a whistle being blown to continue it. A Lakota elder blows his whistle on a drum, as a means of honoring, and the singers appear confused. They are, however, merely abiding by the rules, which clearly state that the AD must approve of all whistles ahead of time.[19]

As with North American powwows, supper break is part of the program at Asbach. Fry bread the size of doughnuts is given gratis to participants.[20] The program begins anew with the second session starting punctually at 6:00 p.m.

After the contest dancing ends and while the tabulator works efficiently to determine the winners in each of the categories, social dancing fills the gym. The dancers enthusiastically participate in a Snake Dance, Round Dances, and a Two-Step. The Third Annual Asbach powwow, a two-day event, ends successfully. I have made new friends and have found a relative.[21] I accept that I leave this powwow feeling as I do when I leave all powwows – sad that the weekend has to end yet satisfied in "a good way."

The Interviews

During the two-day Asbach powwow I recorded interviews with thirty German powwowers, four spectators, and two Native dancers from the United States. Though I arranged to interview two German drum groups, they did not appear for the interview. One men's Northern Traditional dancer, who was also the lead singer of a drum group that did not set up in Asbach, spoke to me at length about his introduction to singing. During the competition I conducted my interviews outside in the food court and vendor area, where the commoditization of Indian wares was evident in the offerings of European vendors. To protect the privacy of interviewees, I have given them Non-Descriptive Nomenclatural, or "NDN," labels – for example, Dancer X, Singer Y, and Spectator Z.

Because the history of German powwows is relatively short, the narration of the powwow scene in Germany is limited to first-generation powwowers. Their children dance in the Tiny Tot, Junior, or teen categories, comprising the second generation.

Spectators A, B, and C, ranging between five and eight years of age, had not seen a "real Indian" until the day their mother brought them to the powwow. Her goal was to dispel stereotypes and educate her daughters, so she volunteered her children to be interviewed. I conducted the interview in German, dressed in street clothes. The children did not recognize that most of the dancers participating at the powwow were of European lineage. When I asked them whether they thought I was an Indian, they unanimously responded, "*Nein!* [No!]" When I asked them why they did not consider me a "real Indian," they replied that it was because I was not dressed in powwow regalia. Furthermore, other "real Indians" in attendance who were not dressed up were also mistaken as not being Indian.[22]

I first asked the adults, "What is a powwow?" The common response by German powwowers is that powwows are a "living culture," a "get-together, having fun, meeting friends, and having a good time."[23] Similarly, dancers in the United States and Canada recognize powwows as a time to celebrate and to have fun. Furthermore, they live to dance – and dance to live. For Europeans who have adopted powwow culture, living to dance and dancing to live is a relatively new concept.

Learning Powwow

As the behavior of some singers and dancers suggests, the Asbach powwow differed from powwows in Indian country primarily because of a limited understanding of traditional teachings. The stories of the participants reveal that German powwows, though exceptionally careful about rules and schedules, are not framed by the implicit teachings available only from a lifetime of experience. In North America, powwow traditions – such as obtaining and creating dance outfits, performing dance styles, and knowing origin stories and songs – are passed on orally and through experience. As a Fancy Shawl dancer since the Tiny Tots category, I learned powwow protocol from the teachings of elders, specifically family members. Nez Perce elder Steven Reuben reflects that he likes "to dance for [his] people to the songs [he] remember[s his] grandfather singing."[24] Contemporary European powwow dancers, having no familial connections to pass on powwow knowledge, rely instead on a memorized embracing of a distant, abstract form of life.[25]

At Asbach most dancers had never met an Indian and did not have a powwow informant. Instead, they rely on personal excursions abroad to observe dancers and singers at powwows. If unable to travel, the German dancers use the Internet to purchase videos, music, and books, which serve as their primary sources of learning. Dancers and singers in Indian country also learn from tapes and videos but are encouraged to understand the origin stories of a particular dance category or, in the case of singing, to learn the origin of songs, the composer, and (if applicable) whose family the song belongs to. Some songs were composed for specific purposes, and those intentions cannot be transmitted and understood through tape or video, and certainly not through Amazon.com.

When asked about their introduction to the powwow circle, five Germans explained that they were either initiated into the arena by a dancer visiting from Indian country or had their own "coming out" ceremonies on German soil, replete with a giveaway, honor song, and feast.

Powwow training from Native coaches is increasing in Germany. Two teenaged brothers, a Grass dancer and a Northern Traditional dancer, have been to U.S. powwows; both took the third place prizes at the Crow Fair in Montana. They bead, sew, and do featherwork. Their exposure to powwow occurred ten years ago through a Choctaw-Cherokee elder who resides in Germany with his German wife. He is highly influential in the proliferation of interest in powwow culture in Germany, and many German powwowers stated that they had received dance instruction from him.

One dancer began dancing reluctantly three years ago when encouraged by a persistent Native couple from the United States who dance Southern style and were touring Germany with a powwow dance troupe. Despite the language barrier they persuaded her to dance. When asked about her dance style, (Fancy Shawl) Dancer C informed me: "It is very fast and lively and for me, it is like life energy. When I danced I felt rejuvenated. I myself was very sick and through dancing the illness went away. I had cancer of the uterus."[26]

For this dancer as for other dancers I interviewed, dancing is healing.[27] Dancer C informed me that she had never wanted to dance; however, the Native couple noted above supplied her with material, sewing instructions, videotapes, friendship, and encouragement. Dancer C moved in time with the drum, graceful and energetic. The issue I had with her was not the aesthetics of her outfit nor the grace of her steps but, rather, the style of her hair. Her shoulder-length, jet black hair was parted down the middle, with braided Pippi Longstocking pigtails at each side of her head. Accepting my constructive criticism she willingly adopted a "correct" hairstyle – her Native informants had not taught her how to fix her hair once her outfit was complete. After changing her hairstyle, she emulated the fancy shawl dancers of Indian country rather well.

Other dancers said they began dancing when their dance attire was complete. Just as in Indian country, the outfits ranged from fully beaded and meticulously embroidered to hastily made. German dancers often spend years designing, beading, and sewing their regalia. One dancer's use of symbol was significant, whereas the designs of others' outfits were not. Two of the dancers inherited either all or a part of their outfits from Native powwow guests.

Does such "indigenous knowledge" automatically authenticate the German powwow participants' actions? The singers and dancers at Asbach clearly had a firm grasp of replicating songs and steps, but important nuances are not as easily mimicked, and in-depth understanding of origins and meanings not so easily achieved. A CD does not clarify drum protocol; nor does it pass down oral tradition. Their "knowing," or ability to imitate powwow singing and dancing learned through mass media, is not the same as learning the origins and contexts of powwow from elders and family members steeped in the cultural lessons of powwow ways. It is, of course, impossible for today's German powwowers to tap into the deep, multigenerational sense of identity and rootedness found in Native America. Powwow practices have only recently been learned by one generation and, as seen below, a number of Germans feel a disconnection with the actions of previous generations.

Identification

A key question put to the interviewees spoke to the depth and extent of their connection to Native America: "Do you identify on a personal level as an Indian? If so, what nation or tribe do you identify with?"

Only one of the powwow dancers felt that he was Indian in his heart; the others did not claim to be Indian, nor did they feel Indian in their hearts. Dancer B stated: "I see myself as part of the culture, not of the people."[28] Another person described it this way: "I don't consider myself Indian, nor German for that matter. I am a human being who by chance was born and grew up in Germany and who is fascinated by Native American cultures."[29] For all of their hard work, for their long hours spent watching videos, memorizing songs, beading, sewing powwow regalia, and competing in powwows, most German powwowers in my experience do not overtly claim to be biologically or culturally Indian. This could be a form of denial; perhaps some of those interviewed did not want to admit they were Indian to an Indian interviewer.

What compensatory ideal then is being fulfilled by Germans who embrace the songs and dances of another culture in such passionate detail? Many dancers in Indian country will attest that powwow was their introduction, their doorway, to seeking deeper knowledge about their specific Native nations – their cultural identity – which in turn leads to a revival of their own tribal ways harmonized with that of powwow. For some Germans, however, their national identity is eclipsed by an overwhelming collective guilt from World War II. For those people, powwow culture can distance them from a discredited national past, from their own culturally problematic identity. Through the trope of the powwow, the collective history and oppressed status of North American Native people can be appropriated internationally. It is especially sexy for Germans to go Native, to identify closely with the oppressed, because it reverses the roles of domination and oppression in their recent past. As Dancer A, a woman, remarked: "I don't know if I am Indian, but the way history is conveyed is more comfortable to me than, for example, German history. And in this respect, I don't claim to be Indian, but I am closer to this culture, closer than to that of German culture."[30]

Dancer A feels "more comfortable" with "the way history is conveyed" about Native peoples than the history of her own country. She actively embraces powwows as an alternative to German culture and history. Her rejection of German history – presumably World War II and the Holocaust – tellingly points to a distancing of Germans from their recent past. Additionally, her use of the passive voice in explaining her position could be understood as an attempt at downplaying or concealing agency in that history.[31] Dancer A's substitution of Native history for her own is also ironic, given the long tradition in the United States of not presenting Native history truthfully.

Appropriation

Whatever their reasons, do Germans have the right to participate in powwows? The fact that a Native North American enterprise is finding itself today in international circles throws into relief crucial questions about cultural propriety and appropriation.

Do powwows belong only to Natives, and should they be confined only to Indian country?

Women's Jingle: Formerly a citizen of the oe East Germany, this dancer feels that American Indian cultures are better than German culture. She designed and made the dress, while her husband beaded her belt, leggings, and moccasins.

When a Native person learns that powwows exist abroad outside Indian country, a first reaction is frequently disbelief and disgust at the apparent appropriation of yet another aspect of Native life. A Straight dancer from Indian country says he is putting his outfit away temporarily because non-Indians dancing "is a mockery of sorts. It's disappointing that you spend your whole life learning and struggling to gain respect in the powwow community, then all of a sudden they show up."[32]

German Dancer A responds to such common criticism as follows: "I think that many participants in the USA, especially the North American Indians, think that we are copying their culture and that we are deliberately forging something, and I hope that your study will show that this is not the way it is. . . . We really try to respect [the culture] and this is why we [try] to do it correctly."[33] All of the dancers echoed her heartfelt response, emphasizing they did not intend to offend or disrespect Native people, that their actions were essentially a harmless veneration and rejuvenation of Native culture overseas. Dancer D went further, arguing that German participation in powwows is legitimate because of the cross-cultural universality of adherence to ceremonial rules: "Today Powwows in Germany are carried out after the models from the USA and Canada. It is a celebration with concrete rules and traditions and as long as these traditions remain allowed, I think every person should be able to participate."[34]

Good intentions aside, the issue of appropriation becomes more complicated and – perhaps for some – unsettling when we consider, as mentioned earlier, the active involvement of a number of Native mentors, acquaintances, and paid participants in transferring powwow overseas. When German powwow people are instructed in person by Natives, sometimes at the urging of a Native mentor or friend who may encourage even further commitment to this "alternative lifestyle," then we must ask: is those Germans' participation in powwow an act of appropriation per se?

The Future

Powwow, an amalgamation of diverse Native practices, is easily replicable on the surface and thus is rapidly swelling beyond Native North America. Powwows in the future will no longer simply be a means to maintain and express Indian identity. Most Germans who participate in powwows do not claim to be Indian, nor should they. But the boundaries of who is an Indian and what constitutes Indianness are blurred increasingly because of the globalization of an event once solely Native North American. The international cloning of powwows could lead to yet another absorption or "vanishing" of Native culture.

We need to recognize that this is happening. It is evident that the growth of Indianthusiasm, and now "Powwowthusiasm," is increasing. To stop or forbid the appropriation of powwows in Germany is unrealistic. Native powwow missionaries themselves have helped convert some summer-camp hobbyists to the status of powwowers, and this has led to a superficially accurate mimicry of contest powwows. However, the hermeneutics of powwow – that is, the implicit understanding of them – are not fully recognized in these imitations of powwows. A mechanistic replication of powwow is possible in international circles, but what of the teachings of the dance styles, the passing down of songs, the importance of giveaways and of "coming outs," and the constant reminder that Native MCs give by reminding their audiences, "We are still here!"?

The German converts must continue to refer to their Native mentors in order to not be accused of appropriation. If in fact they are adopting powwow culture respectfully, then they should continue to get their information from a legitimate, direct source. Just as in academia, sources are necessary and citations are obligatory. A prohibition on powwow dance, song, and celebration is unrealistic and irrational. Traditional teachings and "Indian philosophy" broadly interpreted say that Indian people honor and recall the stories of those that came before us. The way we honor is through song, dance, prayer, and giving. These marks of respect are most apparent in powwow culture, and all are welcome to partake in it. I dare to add, however: they are welcome to partake as long as the traditions are passed down and continue to be passed down so as never to forget the toil our grandparents and their grandparents went through to enable us to be who we are today.

Given the dynamic, ever-changing, and increasingly multiethnic character of powwows, where do we see them in the years to come? In the past twenty years casino powwows in North America have evolved into large, corporate enterprises, eclipsing small, traditional or competition powwows. As a means of income, selective dancers usually attend the powwow with the biggest purse. Dancing for the pure "love" of dancing is being replaced by competition, diminishing the traditional aspect of powwows. In fifty years will powwow be a homogenous, global competitive dance, at home and abroad? Are we really prepared for a true "World Championship of Song and Dance"?

NOTES

1. "Yes, I am Indian. My great-grandmother was a Cherokee Princess, AYE!" All translations are mine, unless otherwise noted. Due to the nature of interviews, the frequency of colloquialisms and ellipses in spoken German is unavoidable. The quotes are verbatim, despite some nonstandard grammatical forms.

2. The phrase "Indian country" refers to the general area in which Native people converge for powwows, cultural events, and tribal and political events. Reservations can also be categorized as Indian country. In this context there are no specific borders or locations.

3. On powwows in Germany, see http://www.powwow-freunde.de/, and the calendar of events at http://www.powwow-kalender.de/. On the Native American Association of German, see their website at http://www.naaog.d.

4. For a detailed, philosophical analysis of place, consult Edward S. Casey, *The Fate of Place* and *Getting Back into Place.*

5. Deborah Root writes that the term *cultural appropriation* "signifies not only the taking up of something and making it one's own but also the ability to do so. People have always shared ideas and borrowed from one another, but appropriation is entirely different from borrowing or sharing because it involves the taking up and commodification of aesthetic, cultural, and more recently, spiritual forms of a society. Culture is neatly packaged for the consumer's convenience" (*Cannibal Culture,* 70).

6. Calloway et al., *Germans and Indians,* 167. The term *Indianthusiasm* was coined by Hartmut Lutz, University of Greifswald, Germany.

7. Root, *Cannibal Culture,* 78.

8. Hobbyism can be distinguished between progressive hobbyists (those who dare to explore beyond "prereservation" culture) and the traditional hobbyists (those who emulate "prereservation" culture). The two groups divided in 1997.

9. The scope of this chapter does not include a detailed analysis of Indianthusiasm. For hobbyist documents, refer to Birgit Turski, *Indianistikgruppen der* DDR, which talks about the former East German hobbyist movement and powwows, not equivalent to the powwows of interest in the present volume.

10. See Turski, *Indianistikgruppen der* DDR.

11. Quote is from Medicine and Baskauskas, *Seeking the Spirit.*

12. Dr. Anette Brauer, e-mail correspondence, February 2003. She is a powwow dancer who began as a hobbyist: "At least in East Germany . . . , I am 100% sure, there was no official Powwow before 1990 (the year of the reunification of both parts of Germany). I remember because our Greifswald hobbyist group and members of a similar group in Hohenneuendorf near Potsdam were the ones to come up with the idea of starting a powwow (tradition) in the east and our two groups were also the first to organize the powwows."

13. Dancer B, Gunzenhausen, July 2002.

14. Dancer T, Gunzenhausen, July 2002.

15. The head judge was for the dance competition; there was no drum competition.

16. MC, Asbach powwow, 2003. This translates into English as follows: "Thank

you, Skunk Cap Singers! The next official part of the powwow concerns the veterans. This is why we are going to honor the veterans by singing a Veterans' Song. And this will come from the White Lake Singers from Berlin."

17. "Ich finde diese Veteranensache überaus merkwürdig für mich als Deutsche. Wenn wir von Veteranen reden, dann niemals ohne Krieg . . . Kriegsveteranen eben. Dazu kommt, wir ehren unsere Kriegsveteranen nicht . . . dazu ist der letzte Krieg zu unrühmlich in unserer Erinnerung . . . ich weiß, das ist nicht gerade fair, den Männern gegenüber, die Jahre ihres Lebens im Krieg gelassen haben, aber das ist nunmal so." In English: "As a German, I think it's strange to talk about veterans (and veterans' issues). When we talk about veterans, then it's never without [the implication] of war . . . war veterans. With that would mean we do not honor our war veterans . . . because the last war stirs unsettling memories. . . . I know that this is not fair, since men lost their lives, but that's just how it is." Interview with Berlin Resident 1, February 2003.

18. Lead Singer H, Asbach powwow, 2003.

19. Rule number 3: "Whistle-Carrier müssen dies beim AD bekannt geben. Wer vorhat, eine Trommel anzuwhistlen, muß dies beim AD melden," which translates as "Whistle carriers need to make themselves known to the AD. Whoever plans to whistle a drum needs to report to the AD." ("Whistle" in German is Pfeifen, which is interesting because linguistically they're adopting powwow terminology.)

20. Doughnut-sized fry bread is somewhat small compared to that served at North American powwows.

21. A Dinè Jingle Dress dancer who resides in Cologne with her German husband. She is originally from my hometown, Shiprock, New Mexico.

22. A few of the Native people who, for many reasons, reside in Germany attended the Asbach powwow.

23. Comments from various dancers at the Asbach powwow.

24. Marra, *Powwow*, 47.

25. Dinè language, culture, customs, and ceremonies are still strongly adhered to and are not to be confused with intertribal powwow culture. I am from the DinÈ Nation, yet I grew up in powwow culture, which is not a distant, abstract form of life for me, as I am claiming it to be for Europeans who adopt powwow.

26. Dancer C, Gunzenhausen, 2002.

27. One Jingle Dress dancer told me that she has participated with four other Jingle Dress dancers in a traditional, healing dance. They are aware that one origin story of the jingle dress is that of a medicine dance, and thus they attempt to replicate the healing aspect of the dance, as it was intended in North America.

28. Interview conducted summer 2002, Asbach, Germany.

29. Dr. Anette Bauer, e-mail correspondence, February 2003.

30. Jingle Dress Dancer A, Asbach powwow, 2002.

31. I would like to extend my gratitude to Beth Hege Piatote for stressing the importance of the dancer's usage of the passive voice and its relevance to German attitudes about neglecting their culture for another.

32. Dancer R, e-mail correspondence, January 2003.

33. Jingle Dress Dancer A, Asbach powwow, 2002.

34. Jackie Fisher, German Jingle Dress dancer, e-mail correspondence, January 2003.

REFERENCES

Bartelt, Guillermo. "A Cognitive Semantic Framework for Syncretism: The Case of the Southern California Powwow." *Ethnos* 1/2 (1991): 52–66.

Calloway, C. G. *New Worlds for All: Indians, Europeans, and the Remaking of Early America.* Baltimore MD: Johns Hopkins University Press, 1997.

Calloway, Colin G., Gerd Gemünden, and Susanne Zantop. *Germans and Indians: Fantasies, Encounters, Projections.* Lincoln: University of Nebraska Press, 2002.

Casey, Edward S. *Getting Back into Place: Toward a Renewed Understanding of the Place-World.* Bloomington: Indian University Press, 1993.

———. *The Fate of Place: A Philosophical History.* Berkeley: University of California Press, 1997.

Churchill, W. *Marxism and Native Americans.* Boston: South End, 1982.

Dyck, Noel. "Powwow and the Expression of Community in Western Canada." *Ethnos* 1/2 (1979): 41–44.

Dziebel, G. V. "The Ideology of the Noble Savage and the Practices of Indianism: European Appropriations of Native American Cultures in the Late 20th Century." PhD diss., Stanford University, 2003.

Feest, Christian. *Indians and Europe: An Interdisciplinary Collection of Essays.* Aachen, Germany: Alano Verlag, 1989.

Forbes, J. D., U. Zagratzki, et al. *Columbus and andere Kannibalen: die indianische Sicht der Dinge.* Wuppertal, Germany: P. Hammer, 1992.

Friedrichsmeyer, S., S. Lennox, et al. *The Imperialist Imagination: German Colonialism and Its Legacy.* Ann Arbor: University of Michigan Press, 1998.

Herle, Anita. "Dancing Community: Powwow and Pan-Indianism in North America." *Cambridge Anthropology* 17, no. 2 (1994): 57–83.

Hertzberg, Hazel W. *The Search for an American Indian Identity: Modern Pan-Indian Movements.* Syracuse NY: Syracuse University Press, 1981.

Hoffer, P. C. *Indians and Europeans: Selected Articles on Indian-White Relations in Colonial North America.* New York: Garland, 1988.

Lassieur, A. *Before the Storm: American Indians before the Europeans.* New York: Facts on File, 1998.

Liebersohn, H. *Aristocratic Encounters: European Travelers and North American Indians.* Cambridge: Cambridge University Press, 1998.

Lutz, H. "Indianer" und "Native Americans": *Zur sozialund literarhistorischen Vermittlung eines Stereotyps*. Hildesheim, Germany: Olms, 1985.

Marra, Ben. *Powwow: Images along the Red Road*. New York: Harry N. Abrams, 1996.

Medicine, Beatrice, and Liucija Baskauskas. *Seeking the Spirit: Plains Indians in Russia*. Watertown MA: Documentary Educational Resources, Warrior Women Inc, 1999. Documentary film.

Moses, L. G. *Wild West Shows and the Images of American Indians, 1883–1933*. Albuquerque: University of New Mexico Press, 1996.

Paskievich, John. *If Only I Were an Indian*. Winnipeg: National Film Board of Canada, 1995. Documentary film.

Preiswerk, R., World Council of Churches, Programme to Combat Racism, et al. *The Slant of the Pen: Racism in Children's Books*. Geneva: World Council of Churches, 1980.

Root, Deborah. *Cannibal Culture: Art, Appropriation, and the Commodification of Difference*. Boulder CO: Westview, 1996.

Turski, Birgit. *Indianistikgruppen der DDR: Entwicklung – Probleme – Aussichten*. Idstein/Taunus, Germany: Baum, 1994.

———. "The Indianist Groups in the G.D.R.: Development – Problems – Prospects." *European Review of Native American Studies* 7, no. 1 (1993): 43–48.

Weber, Max. *The Protestant Ethic and the Spirit of Capitalism*. London: Routledge, 1930.

Zantop, S. *Colonial Fantasies: Conquest, Family, and Nation in Precolonial Germany, 1770–1870*. Durham NC: Duke University Press, 1997.

Zimmerman, L. J., and B. Molyneaux. *Native North America*. Boston: Little Brown, 1996.

LISA ALDRED

13. Dancing with Indians and Wolves
New Agers Tripping through Powwows

> The man announcing from the stage said that the next song/dance was a national anthem or flag song and then they began. A couple of women with a baby carriage pulled up into some empty space nearby me and the one to my right said, "Is this a prayer song?" and I replied with what I could remember of what the gentleman onstage had said. So she says, "Oh, so it's a prayer song. You know, she (indicating her friend) collects wolves and Indians." – as though it was their explanation for why they were at a powwow. I wanted to say "So where does your friend KEEP these Indians she's COLLECTING?" but it was too hot outside already.[1]

This anecdote related by Priscilla Naungigiak Hensley, a Kikitagruk Inupiaq, epitomizes the New Age attitude toward powwows, not to mention toward Indian peoples and their spiritual ceremonies.[2] Exactly what kind of Indians does the woman at the powwow collect? Are they Indian figurines like that in *Indian in the Cupboard*, exoticized fetishes to be played with at whim? Or are they imagined stereotypes of Indian peoples she amuses herself with in a mental curiosity cabinet? The woman at the powwow, like many Euro-Americans who romanticize Indian peoples, are filled with imperialist nostalgia, defined by anthropologist Renato Rosaldo as a romanticized longing on the part of colonizers for the culture they have destroyed. I consider it a tragic irony – a fetishization of a "noble savage" in mainstream popular culture after a massive genocide of indigenous peoples that is not recognized consciously by these "collectors of Indians." Evidently that sublimated consciousness of history and politics is necessary for imperialist nostalgia. According to Rosaldo: "Imperialist nostalgia uses a pose of innocent yearning . . . to conceal its complicity with often brutal oppression."[3]

Rick W. Powelson, a Commanche, aptly characterizes this imperialist nostalgia in his satire of the anachronistic romanticized Indians New Agers often seek at powwows:

> What really drives me crazy about this New Age thing is that the majority

> of these people see us Indians as they think we were 200 years ago. Even if some of our people did do some of those things back then, now hear me clearly, WE DON'T DO IT TODAY! What do you people think you're going to see when you go to a powwow – People walking around with little bags of rocks around their necks chanting boogie-woogie until the dance is over, contemplating Mother Earth, following critters around to learn their secrets, an all day smoke-a-thon of sage or cedar, folks being all mystical talking in a halting manner spouting wise sayings all day, looking around for albino calves, wondering what chief they were in a past life while staring at dream catchers, turning into animals so we can talk to trees while looking for visions as flute music with full synthesized background noise of rushing brooks plays so we can be all "Spirtchul"?
>
> C'mon! You know what you'll see? You'll see people having fun, laughing, teasing one another, people dancing in the contest and inter-tribals, just plain enjoying themselves.[4]

Powelson's sentiments are echoed by other Indians. Tabitha Whitefoot, a member of the Yakima Nation, observed that the "New Agers perpetuate some of the myths and anachronistic views of Indian people."[5] There is a tragic irony in this imperialist nostalgia. Throughout most of its history, Euro-American domination brutally tried to wipe out every aspect of Indian traditional cultures. Now their descendants carry their own kind of oppression, a sense of entitlement to define Indian identity according to their imagined stereotypes of Indian peoples in the past.

The fact that the woman mentioned above collects Indians along with wolves is also revealing. Natural history museums have long housed stuffed wild animals, such as wolves, along with waxed mannequins of Indian people. The implication is that Native Americans are not part of civilization but, rather, fall within "nature" in the forced dichotomy Western thinking draws between "nature" and "culture." Those entities attributed to the "nature" category are not seen as fully dimensional subjects with cultures worthy of equal respect. Rather, indigenous peoples and their life ways are voyeuristic spectacles to be displayed as an object of entertainment in an enclosed glass case. One wonders whether the woman's interest in collecting Indians and wolves was influenced by the film *Dances with Wolves*. This equation of Indian peoples and wolves not only relegates Indian people to the "nature" category but also perpetuates the "vanishing Indian" myth. Like wolves, Indians are seen as dwindling, an endangered species. Again, this equation contains an eerie abhorrent wave of imperialist nostalgia. Both Indians and wolves were targeted in massive campaigns to wipe out their very existence. Now their images are collectible items.

This woman is but one example of New Agers who attend powwows to "collect" Indians as well as their culture and ceremonies. This chapter will explore both the disruptive effect of New Agers at powwows and the offensive nature of powwows run by New Agers. It will then analyze these phenomena in terms of the continued colonist mind-set of New Agers, despite their claims of generating an alternative lifestyle and subculture. In particular I will focus on the tendency of New Agers, like many Euro-Americans, to see themselves as subjects while viewing Indian people as mere objects of their romantic imagination. Furthermore, New Agers, like a number of Euro-Americans, are so used to privilege that they feel entitled to appropriate other people and their cultures for their own ends and gratification.

Wannabee Invasions and Appropriations of Powwow Culture

At almost every powwow I have attended over the last ten years, at least a handful of New Agers have been present. They are easily recognized by their clothing and dancing style. As Commanche Rick Powelson points out: "We can tell newagers by the way they talk . . . [and] dress. To look at the most spiritual people I know . . . you would never now that they are holy men just to look at them. They don't wear all the newage trappings, don't walk around being all mystical and spacey-eyed, they talk and dress like normal people. They aren't going around all day spewing forth wisdom and all the other STEREOTYPICAL crap that some of you people think that REAL Indian holy people or Indians in general are supposed do."[6]

New Agers' "trappings" usually consist of a few articles of clothing that fit their stereotyped image of Indians – a headband, a fringed vest, or dream catcher earrings, for example. They often mix and match clothing from very different tribes, meshed with clothing typical of New Age subculture, such as batik skirts, Birkenstocks, and Wiccan pendants.[7] Tabitha Whitefoot, member of the Yakima Nation, commented on the problems underlying New Agers' self-styling of Native American dress: "It is my belief that when one picks and chooses their components of 'nativeness,' there is an issue of misuse, misinterpretation, alteration and adulteration."[8] I would add that such assembled outfits represent a sense of entitlement – the result of a colonizing, dominant mind-set – to define and construct another culture's identity. American Indians have long had to shoulder the burden of Euro-Americans trying to control Indian identity through their own stereotyped criteria.

New Agers can also be spotted by their dance styles at powwows, which usually take one of two patterns. Some dance free form, in the fashion of fans at a Grateful Dead concert. They pay little attention to other dancers on the floor or to what particular style of dancing is taking place at the time. Rather, they appear to be in their own worlds, emoting and improvising steps as they dance to the beat of their own imagined drum. Those who fall into the second pattern try too hard to replicate Indian peoples' dances. In their quest for "authenticity," they exaggerate the movements involved and their expressions are so deadly serious that they are quite humorous. Powelson sharply characterized these New Age expressions as "mystical and spacey-eyed."[9]

Dr. Ann Waters, a Seminole scholar and lawyer also pointed out the bizarre dance styles of New Agers at powwows: "I have been to a few small powwows in the northeast that embarrassed me so badly I wished I had not gone. The white folks were mimicking the Indian dancers and were so disrespectful, I could not tell if they were totally making fun of the Indian dances, or just trying to imitate them. I felt badly for the Indians there and also for the children."[10] Although it is certainly plausible that the mimicking she witnessed was intentionally disrespectful, my own interviews and observations of New Agers lead me to believe that their preposterous miming is not intended to make fun of Indian people. I suspect they think that they are performing the Indian dances correctly. Their self-absorption keeps them from realizing that their gestures appear as mimicking, and their sense of entitlement keeps them from recognizing how Indian people are reacting to their antics.

The Seminole woman's embarrassment is matched by other Indian peoples' anger at the New Agers' sense of entitlement. As one Haudenosaunee-Cherokee woman and powwow dancer observed: "It is their arrogance that makes them disrespectful. They feel they have the right to intrude on anyone's home(culture). Also the lack of their own tribal identity leaves them longing for their roots . . . but they use our traditions with their own twists and they think it is flattering!?!?!?!?!"[11]

The New Agers hardly seemed phased when Indian people confront their behavior. They rationalize their entitlement with New Age "logic" claiming that they were "Indian in a former life." For them this belief authenticates their Native identity to the same level as those born Indian. They then rationalize that they can speak and act with authority regarding powwow protocol. They do not see their actions as appropriating Indian culture; rather, they feel entitled to it. Some New Agers employ other defenses, such as claiming they have a First Amendment constitutional freedom to participate in Indian spirituality and ceremonies, including powwows. Obviously ignorant of tribal sovereignty issues, they incorrectly interpret and invoke the U.S. Constitution, a document that was forced on Indian people in the process of colonization.

Another New Age response strategy is an attempt to disempower Indian protests by relegating them to the category of "whining." One man posted a particularly insulting example of this strategy on the powwow.com site: "Looks like your doing your share of crying. . . . Whaaahh, I'm surrounded by wannabe's. [*sic*] Whaaah, the white man, he dun went and stole my rightful identity as a full blooded ndn. The biggest falicy [*sic*] on this board is ndn's talking about how "white's ain't got no culture, and are spiritually lacking so they are invading our culture and way of life."[12] He then proceeds to state what opportunities Indian people have been given by this society and how many important technologies they have received from white technology. He brags that he came from nothing but has advanced through his hard work, not because of white privilege. He slams insult after insult against Indian people in his self-righteous tirade.[13] Given his disdain for many Indian peoples, one wonders why he wants to attend powwows in the first place. I am reminded of the title of a painting by Gros Ventre artist Sean Chandler, "Beautiful Culture, Ugly Peoples." Chandler explained that the title refers to non-Indians' romanticization of certain aspects of Indian culture, usually from the past, while looking at contemporary Indian peoples with contempt. I see this as a kind of cultural capital exploitation of Indian people, an oppressive extrication of cultural resources from Indian peoples for consumption against their will.

And yet many Indian people are willing to share their powwows, as well as other aspects of their culture, with non-Indians. All they ask for are respect and a willingness to follow their cultural protocols while participating in their cultural events. Tabitha Whitefoot expressed this willingness in the following statement:

> I think people are welcome to come and "observe/participate" as invited, however, I think I would not be welcomed at a "family reunion/celebration" without adhering to the social norms of the group. Sometimes, it would be considered an intrusion, and non-tribal individuals should be made aware of their roles, and possible limitations, OR be sensitive to their "guest" status. Innately, many traditional Indian people are generous and inclusive, we invited the Europeans so completely into

> our parlors in previous centuries that we were eventually, no longer the masters of our homelands. And so, consequently, I am skeptical of those who reject their home/parent culture to "find/discover" their spirit through another's (ours.) If they can absorb without usurping, I guess I do not want to "exclude" anyone from the beauty of my grandmother's culture.[14]

Cherokee Tamara Walkingstick echoed this sentiment in her statement that "if they [New Agers] approach a teaching with honor, true respect, and understanding of that particular tribe's belief, they should also be able to learn."[15]

Dee Sweet, a White Earth Anishinabe and a Jingle dancer, expressed ambivalence concerning New Agers' attendance at powwows. She acknowledges that many respected Indian spiritual leaders have stated that "the drum, the pipe, Sundance don't just belong to us. The Anglos must learn to ask for help but when they do, we must step aside. They deserve happiness as much as we do."[16] Despite this advice, however, Sweet still has qualms about New Age: "I get cranky when I hear about pedophiles doing rites of passage ceremonies for young people, or when the latest tribal messiah charges for vision quests ($350 and all you can eat), but what can you do?"[17] Sweet also alluded to a summit of elders who came from across the country to discuss the influx of New Agers through the venue of powwows and what the ramifications of this theft of intellectual property have been. Ultimately she found this summit unsatisfying, noting that she "was disgusted by the level to which the people in attendance did not want to disclose the names of perpetrators."[18] Sweet indicated that she had wrestled with these issues since 1985.

It appears that many Indian people are willing to share powwows with New Agers, if only the New Agers would act with respect. This willingness fits with the general hospitality of the various tribes. However, the commercial exploitation and disrespect many New Agers display at powwows offend Indian people.

Powwows Held by New Agers

A number of powwows seem to be springing up that are run by New Agers. Unsuspecting Indian powwow dancers often attend, only to be shocked by what is going on. One such powwow was held in summer 2002 in Austin Village, Ohio. Organized by a couple, John Spiritwolf Kountz and Cindy Shewolf Kountz, the powwow was advertised as the first powwow for the Lenape village. However, neither of the Kountzes appears to be officially enrolled members of the Lenape tribe. A local newspaper covering the event interviewed John Kountz and reported that his own Indian heritage included "Cherokee blood" but that he claimed to have been adopted into the Lenape tribe.[19]

Ritchie Plass (a Menominee) attended this powwow not knowing anything about the organizers. He later related his troubling experiences on *powwow.com*, a legitimate Web site providing information for powwow circuit dancers. He was shocked at the powwow's disorganization and failure to follow any recognized protocol for Grand Entry.[20] One of the three drums there consisted of eight white women, one of whom shook a rattle while drumming with one hand, a practice he had never seen before. They called themselves "Mother Earth Beat." Plass later found out that one of their members was Cindy Shewolf Kountz. Plass was most offended by a white vendor who was selling sacred pipes. He explained to the arena director that the pipes were sacred and should not be sold. According to Plass the following conversation ensued:

> I extended my hand and said, "Hi there. My name is Richie. I am a Menominee Indian from Wisconsin and I need to tell you that by the way I have been taught, the gentleman over there selling pipes should not be allowed to do that."
>
> Even before I could say anything else, he spoke up. . . . "There is NOTHING wrong with what he is doing. This is an inter-tribal pow wow with many different culture here. You need to show him respect just as you should be shown respect."
>
> I said, "I think you're missing my point . . . those pipes are sacred items! Those are not to be sold, ever!"
>
> He then got loud and told me, "Listen, those pipes are NOT sacred. A pipe only becomes sacred once they are used. Plus, how do you know he is not selling them as just 'personal' pipes? Anyone can buy a pipe . . . it is a personal thing and does NOT become sacred until it is used."
>
> I told him, "No, I need to disagree with you. . . . ALL pipes are sacred! Plus, as I have been taught, you EARN a pipe. No matter . . . if you are not going to tell that gentleman anything, then I'm going to have to undress and leave. Out of respect to my elders and teachers, I cannot continue dancing. . . ."
>
> He then told me, "Well, I'm very sorry for that, but like I said, this powwow is for ALL cultures and you've made your decision."[21]

Plass went out to his van to begin changing when his brother-in-law, Denny, walked up and reported that he had just been kicked out of the powwow. After Plass had left the powwow, Denny had also gone to Kountz to voice his concern that the vendor should not be selling sacred pipes. According to Denny, the arena director told him "You're out of here! I'm telling you to leave right now." Kountz then called Denny a troublemaker and threatened to have him arrested if he didn't leave the powwow immediately. The arena director walked out to their van to inform them they would both be arrested if they tried to return. As Plass and his family pulled out of the parking lot, he saw his friend Donnie and told him they had been kicked out of the powwow. As Plass related: "Donnie said, 'For what?' I started to laugh and told him, 'I guess for being an Indian!' I then told him briefly what had happened. . . . I bid Donnie a fond farewell and he told me as I was leaving, 'Maybe I'll see you again . . . at a REAL pow-wow!'"[22]

Plass's experience is not an isolated one. As mentioned earlier, the number of New Age–run powwows is increasing. In response to Plass's post, other powwow dancers responded with similar stories. As one man related: "I went to a pow-wow this spring and saw some different behavior by a very pale AD. He had some kind of little ceremony after everyone was in the arena. Waved his hands in the air then waved them around at the ground. I've never seen anything like that before. There were some wagon train women and they would hold their arms in the air and turn in a circle before they would go dance. It was a first for me. Some powwows are getting stranger all the time."[23] Another person noted: "I have heard stories like this inkling around the pow-wow trail. These people must have read a book on pow-wow's and right away figured they knew it all"[24]

The Southern California Chapter of the American Indian Movement (AIM) has issued directives regarding these New Age–run powwows, urging non-Indians as well as Indians to stay away from them:

> The sponsors of these powwows are interested only in a profit and are very disrespectful of Indian culture. You can spot these non-Indian pow wows because they have a carnival atmosphere. You will see commercial food trucks, commercial products sold out of trailers, mountain men shows, palm reading, guns, arcades, an entrance fee, a parking fee, and the availability of alcohol. Sacred herbs, such as sage, tobacco, and sweetgrass, and pipes and ceremonial items are displayed for open sale.
>
> This atmosphere is NOT Indian. Please stay away. . . . Do not buy

> sacred items. Do not buy sage, tobacco, or sweetgrass. Do not buy pipes, or any ceremonial items.[25]

AIM has recognized the increased trend toward powwow markets that sell sacred items, such as the sacred pipe vendor Ritchie Plass found offensive. They have clearly delineated why such sales are highly offensive as well as condemned the sale of New Age literature by powwow vendors:

> For twenty five years there has been an increasing and disturbing trend of exploitation in powwow market places that includes the buying and selling of sacred items and artifacts. With this has come the introduction of New Age ideas and merchandise passed off as "Indian Wisdom" or "Indian Thought". Exploitation is a serious matter with serious consequences for the Indian community, and demands our immediate attention in order to preserve the cherished culture of our people. . . . Included in many markets are ceremonial pipes (particularly those made of pipe stone), sage, cedar, sweetgrass, rattles, tobacco ties and some drums. . . . The sacred must not be sold. . . . Finally, there is the bogus merchandise and New Age thought disguised as Indian wisdom, spirituality, or mysticism, which is chronicled in glossy, high-priced books written mostly by non-Indians, wannabees, and even the occasional Indian. These frauds, profiteering from sacred ideas and fake merchandise, remain a dangerous threat to our traditional way of life.[26]

The AIM document goes on to recognize that many powwow committees have issued firm guidelines for vendors, including a stipulation that they show proof of tribal affiliation under the Federal Indian Arts and Crafts Law. Part of their stated rationale is that non-Indian vendors take sales away from Indian people who do not have the same economic opportunities outside Indian cultural venues. The other reason is that "these simple but firm guidelines . . . can be instrumental in stopping the wholesale exploitation and theft of the Indian art world by wannabees and other greedy exploiters of our culture."[27]

New Age Commercial Exploitation of the Powwow Concept

Perhaps one of the most pricey and bizarre of the New Age powwows is the "floating powwow." These powwow cruises are organized by David L. Underwood, a silver-haired, white-bearded entrepreneur associated with Dream Cruises. He advertises East Coast, West Coast, and Alaskan powwow cruises on his Web site *www.powwowcruise.com*. Evidently those who come for the powwow cruise are on the same cruise ship as those on a regular cruise.[28] The powwow is held on only one day and just for a few hours. However, nationally known Native American musicians, such as Joanne Shenandoah and Bill Miller, are booked as "entertainment."

Underwood acknowledges that some Indians have pointed out to him that powwows should always be held on land as Mother Earth. He responds: "Many Natives from the Pacific Northwest and even islands off our mainland, have told us that they would never have survived without the bounty of the oceans, which cover the majority of this earth in which we all live. . . . It is unique when all things are considered, being held on an open deck of a cruise ship while at sea."[29]

Underwood also acknowledges that the question as to what can be expected of the powwow is "by far the most difficult question for us to answer and often the most controversial."[30] After expounding on the difference in powwow protocols among varying tribes, he makes the following claim: "Therefore, we are always conscious in our efforts to respect everyone's feelings as best we can. Unfortunately, due to the many tribal traditions, we do occasionally find someone who does not agree with the way things are done. We respect everyone's feelings and traditions and do our best to please all. For this reason you will always find that our powwows onboard the ship are social, intertribal, with a host drum, head man and head woman dancers."[31]

In this same statement Underwood assures: "We never allow alcohol near our arena and demand proper conduct from all in attendance."[32] Nonetheless one of the photos of past cruises shows delivery of champagne and chocolate strawberries to guests' rooms. Even if the organizers manage to keep alcohol away from the powwow arena, it is difficult to imagine how they can police other cruisers who have been drinking from observing the powwow. There is no mention of any spiritual aspect to the powwow. Rather, Underwood characterizes it as entertainment advertising: "Our powwow is for the enjoyment of those in attendance and we always ask everyone to bring their regalia and have fun dancing at "at sea". This is your powwow, it's only as good as you make [it] . . . so bring your regalia and have fun!"[33]

Richard Clark Eckert, a member of the Red River Band of Lake Superior Ojibwe and a scholar, posted the following satirical response to the "floating powwow":

Perhaps I would book a room on the cruise if I could get a National

> Science Foundation grant to bring along a bunch of Native PhD's in anthropology, sociology, psychology, and history to observe and study the non-native reactions to Indian celebrities. Of course they would have to be allowed to be just as intrusive as non-Indians are at some powwows. It would be an absolute must that we be allowed to take videos of their putting on their regalia, knocking on their tents, offer them a mere Pepsi to find out all about their families and their lives. We'd also have to be permitted to use them as a universal reference point and say "I once had a non-Indian friend who said, ". . . . . . ." We'd also have to be able to send someone a survey by their door and ask all about their employment status, occupation, and whatever else interests you. We'd have to be able to look at their diet – maybe study the room service slips to get an idea about what non-Indians like. We might have some one count the number of times the toilets flush and see if there is some correlation between what is what the non-Indian eats and how often they do it. So I think going on the cruise would offer a wonderful opportunity that can be used to the Indian advantage. Afterall, we might be able to discover a way to statistically determine which of the non-Indians are full of it and which are not. Of course the psychologists get first shot at those suffering from the wannabe be syndrome![34]

In another strange New Age entrepreneurial twist, powwows and Indian culture have been appropriated in cyberspace in a new software entitled "PowWow," developed by John McAfee, founder of the highly profitable McAfee Associates. Drawing from his New Age philosophy, McAfee started the practice of giving away the company's best brand of software, McAfee anti-virus software, to build up market share and then selling everything else, such as updates, services, Internet servers, and advertising, to generate revenue. McAfee grossed margins of nearly 95 percent, more than any other software company. Their business strategy is now used by many software companies. After a minor heart attack John McAfee sold his stake in the company and took off in a Winnebago to travel through the western United States for a year, visiting various Indian tribes. He now lives near Colorado Springs and operates Tribal Voice, which freely distributes PowWow software. It is available for download at *www.tribal.com*. McAfee now believes that software is a living tree and that the Internet is a physical manifestation of "the golden thread" he claims that Indian shamans believe in.[35]

PowWow software allows a user to connect with six other users in real time with only Microsoft Windows and a connection to the Internet. It is not a chatroom on the Web; rather, the connections are node to node, meaning that they do not go through a central location. John McAfee also offers a software called Tribe, which allows even larger groups to congregate in cyberspace. One tribal member serves as the leader and as the Web server for the others. "We let people set up whatever tribe they want. We have, for example, a gay Hispanic tribe," McAfee says. "Our biggest tribe, believe it or not, is an Icelandic tribe. We also have an enthusiastic user community in Rio de Janeiro." According to the company's statement of purpose: "Tribal Voice was created to facilitate the propagation of cybertribes within the realm of cyberspace. PowWow is the tool that provides the means of communication and shared experiences that are necessary for the formation of tribes, the first social structures to emerge on the path to cybercivilization."[36]

Z. Bauman's concept of "neo-tribes" elucidates this cybertribe phenomenon. Bauman defines a neo-tribe as a collection of individuals who may never have formally met one another. Yet, through purchase of a certain concept, or style – in this case PowWow software – they become members of a collective group. Individuals define their identity in part by membership in this neo-tribe. These neo-tribes, or cybertribes in this instance, are imagined collective group identities defined through consumerism. Individuals construct their identities based on their individual choice (or, perhaps more accurately, purchase) of lifestyle.[37]

Wannabe Stealaways

New Agers have infiltrated and co-opted powwows on many different levels. For many New Age people, like the woman who collects Indians and wolves, the powwow is an exotic spectacle to be consumed for their own pleasure. These people make little or no effort to discern what powwows mean to their Indian participants and communities. Others go further by dressing in their own stereotyped, and often inappropriate, versions of powwow dress and interrupting and insulting Indian peoples with bizarre or mimicking dance styles. The increase in New Age–run powwows has attracted unwary powwow circuit participants. The New Agers heading up these powwows not only offend by their ignorance of proper protocol but also profit by usurping a traditional event that is very important to Indian people. The floating powwow cruise is one of the most outrageous examples of this powwow-for-profit phenomenon. Even the very concept of the powwow is being misappropriated for commercial gain in such products as John McAfee's PowWow software. Underlying all of these New Age intrusions of the powwow are a lack of respect and a seeming sense of entitlement to an important tradition revered by many Indian peoples. There is no honor in a stealaway.

NOTES

1. E-mail message from Priscilla Naungigiak Hensley, received August 7, 2002, in response to a query I posted on *nn-academics@nativenet.uthsca.edu* and *nn-powwow@nativenet.uthscsa.edu* on July 29, 2002, under the subject "Problems with New Agers at Powwows" and sender *LisaAldred@aol.com*. The query was worded as follows: "I am writing a chapter for a book about New Agers at powwows. I am looking for Indian peoples' opinions, as well as experiences, with this issue. Please let me know if you mind being quoted. If not, would you like me to use your name/tribal affiliation or do you prefer to remain anonymous?"

2. The New Age is generally considered a movement that emerged in the 1980s. The term *New Age* probably was coined to reflect some adherents' vision that the world would enter a literal "New Age" of harmony, health, and spirituality through personal transformation. New Agers have tended to appropriate and hybridize spiritual beliefs and practices from various cultures they have exoticized. The New Age movement also has a huge commercial side, in which entrepreneurs have profited from selling books and paraphernalia associated with various spiritual traditions. Native Americans and their spiritual practices have been a favorite with the New Agers.

3. Renato Rosaldo, *Culture and Truth: The Remaking of Social Analysis* (Boston: Beacon, 1989), 69.

4. Rick W. Powelson, "Re: New Age or Old Prophecy," NATCHAT mailing list, originally posted on June 14, 1996. Can now be located on native.net archives at http://nativenet.uthscsa.edu/archive/nc/9605/0287.html.

5. E-mail message from Tabitha Whitefoot, received August 5, 2002, in response to my query under the subject "Problems with New Agers at Powwows."

6. Powelson, "Re: New Age or Old Prophecy."

7. E-mail message from William F. Sahme, received August 15, 2002, in response to my query under the subject "Problems with New Agers at Powwows." Sahme, who is of Nez Perce, Hopi, and Warm Springs descent, related his shock at the outfit a New Ager had dressed a child in at the Sea Fair Powwow at Seattle in the summer of 2002. As he related the incident:

> I was at the SeaFair PowWow in Seattle last summer. Usually at urban PowWows, you are guaranteed to see all the . . . wanna-be's out in fine form. Well,

I seen this little white girl and her mother. An intertribal was just starting and the little white girl proceeded onto the dance floor. It wasn't so much that seeing a white girl dancing at a PowWow that shocked me. . . . Being that this was a city PowWow, it was to be expected. . . . What shocked me was what she was wearing. Her outfit consisted of a bikini top and bottom. Something out of a Fredericks of Hollywood catalog. Definitely something straight out of there "native" line. It was a funky leather/buckskin sort of fabric with beads dangling from all over. . . . I've danced at PowWows all my life and have seen white people dress up their kids in some crazy a$$ outfits, but this definitely took the frybread."

8. E-mail message from Tabitha Whitefoot, received August 5, 2002.

9. Powelson, "Re: New Age or Old Prophecy."

10. E-mail message from Ann Waters, received on August 5, 2002, in response to my query under the subject "Problems with New Agers at Powwows." Ann Waters, a Seminole, holds both a JD and PhD and is a research associate at the State University of New York as well as president of the American Indian Philosophy Association.

11. Jazzy95, "Re: Kicked Out of a Pow Wow for Being an Indian?", posted at PowWows.com > Gathering > News > PowWow Talk on July 9, 2002.

12. Red Jacket, "Re: Kicked Out of a Pow Wow for Being an Indian?", posted at PowWows.com > Gathering > News > PowWow Talk on August 9, 2002.

13. Red Jacket, "Re: Kicked Out" (misspellings have been left intact, and my comments appear in brackets). He states:

You can go back and have your culture, straight up. . . . All I ask in return is you return a few things you borrowed from white culture. Let's see, we can start with: White man's bible, cars and trucks, bicycles, shoes and clothing that aren't buckskin (but hell, you can go ahead and use tradecloth, that'd be mighty white of me), any medicine not given to you by a tribal medicine man, white man's language, and anything else that may be benefiting you as we speak right now. [Does he really think Indian people asked for the "White man's bible"? Clearly he is ignorant of Indian history and the BIA-supported Christian missions on reservations.]

I'm not on your Rez harassing you. If you don't like white people . . . on the land allotted to you, fine . . . keep 'em out. Your land, your laws . . . your rules. And don't be hipicritical and open up your INDIAN TRADING POSTS to whitey either. Their money shouldn't be any good there.

There's people out there that have worked and died to give you opportunities that have never been afforded anyone before. Do you hear Mexicans, Peruvians, Chinese, Pakistani's, etc . . . moaning about opprtunity? People 10,000 miles away who have less than Rez boys and girls who come all the way accross the ocean . . . with NOTHING, and make it big. You aren't being held back by whitey because youre Apache or Nez Perce or Ponca or Cherokee. Hell, to whitey, American Indians are just Mexicans. (por favore?) Afganastais are bombing the hell out of us, coming to American and opening up Gyro stands and driving BMW's. [Let's insult every minority while telling Indian people how others have sacrificed to give them "opportunities" they never had before. I cannot fathom how disease, slaughter, loss of enormous amounts of land base, reduction to poverty, and the other results of oppression Indian people have faced can possibly be construed as "opportunes".]

I know full blooded indians that are engineers, scientists, marketers, business owners. . . . They still go back to the rez every year . . . and I don't hear all this smack from them. They know the score. . . . Yeah, I got me a cause, I'm oppressed. Puleez . . . I come from nothing . . . NOTHING! I'm so priveliged. It's drive and desire and determination. That's what got me out of the coal fields, not being white. I in no way directed this to all the hard working Indians bros and sis's that are trying to better their communities, their culture and themselves. It was directed toward ingraciating jerks. [So, Indian people are oppressed and poor because they have not worked hard enough. Since they have not worked hard enough to become engineers, lawyers and white collar workers, they have no right to address the misappropriation of their culture.]

14. E-mail message from Tabitha Whitefoot, received August 5, 2002.

15. E-mail message from Tamara Walkingstick, received August 5, 2002, in response to my query under the subject "Problems with New Agers at Powwows."

16. E-mail message from Dee Sweet, received August 5, 2002, in response to my query under the subject "Problems with New Agers at Powwows."

17. E-mail message from Dee Sweet, received August 5, 2002.

18. E-mail message from Dee Sweet, received August 5, 2002.

19. John Booth, "Powwow Is First for Area Village," (Warren OH) *Tribune-Chronicle*, 2002.

20. In an e-mail message written by Richie Plass to jazzy95, who posted it with permission under the topic "Kicked Out of a Pow Wow for being Indian?" at Pow-Wows.com > Gathering > News > PowWow Talk on July 9, 2002, Plass related the following:

The drum began. All of the flag bearers began to enter the arena when all of a sudden, [a] group of about five ladies walked in front of Donnie (powwow dancer) and me. As we got to the entrance to the arena, they stopped! Donnie told them, "Excuse me, please." A lady standing in front of us and said, "No, you can't go in until they are finished." Donnie looked me then told her, "Excuse me, but this is Grand Entry . . . we need to enter." She then said, "No, the flags go in first. Then, when the song is done they'll post the flags. Next there will be a flag song. When the flag song is done, there will be a veterans song. Once the veterans make circle around the arena, then all of the rest of us will be able to join them." I looked at her and said, "So another words, you DON'T have a Grand Entry." She looked at me and said, "THIS is how WE do it HERE!" I looked at Donnie in true amazement. He shrugged his shoulders and said, "Wow . . . that's how THEY do it HERE! I guess I've been doing it wrong all my life!"

21. E-mail message from Richie Plass to jazzy95, posted July 9, 2002.

22. E-mail message from Richie Plass to jazzy95, posted July 9, 2002.

23. BEZHIG IKWE, "Re: Kicked Out of a Pow Wow for Being an Indian?", posted at PowWows.com > Gathering > News > PowWow Talk on July 10, 2002.

24. n8tv_singer 4_life,"Re: Kicked Out of a Pow Wow for Being an Indian?" posted at PowWows.com > Gathering > News > PowWow Talk on July 10, 2002.

25. "Stronger Guidelines Needed for Pow Wow and Indian Market Committees," issued by the Southern California Chapter of the American Indian Movement, posted at *http://home.earthlink.net/ rosebud9/powwo.htm.*

26. "Stronger Guidelines Needed for Pow Wow and Indian Market Committees."

27. "Stronger Guidelines Needed for Pow Wow and Indian Market Committees."

28. "Most Frequently Asked Questions" section of http://www.powwowcruise.com. The following question and answer appear in this section:

> Who can go on the Pow Wow Cruise and who will be on the ship with us? Answer: ANYONE can go on the PWC! We have a goal, that being to fill an entire ship with Natives from all over North America. We know it can be done and we will do it! For now, the PWC is a well kept secret, but the word is spreading fast . . . all because of people who have been on the PWC and know what a fabulous time we all have. Until we can fill a ship, we will share it with regular passengers enjoying the cruise. This is good too, as many have been pleasantly surprised to see someone like Robert Tree Cody (6'10") walking around the ship in his buckskin regalia before the powwow! Very impressive sight."

29. "Who Can Go on the Powwow Cruise?" question and answer, "Most Frequently Asked Questions" section, http://www.powwowcruise.com.

30. "Who Can Go on the Powwow Cruise?" question and answer, http://www.powwowcruise.com.

31. "Who Can Go on the Powwow Cruise?" question and answer, http://www.powwowcruise.com.

32. "Who Can Go on the Powwow Cruise?" question and answer, http://www.powwowcruise.com.

33. "Who Can Go on the Powwow Cruise?" question and answer, http://www.powwowcruise.com.

34. Richard Clark Eckert, "Re: Floating Powwow," originally posted on NATCHAT

mailing list on July 10, 1996. Can now be located on native.net archives at http://native net.uthscsa.edu/archive/nc/9607/0078.html.

35. Red Herring Web site, *http://www.redherring.com/mag/issue38/bulb.html.*

36. Red Herring Web site, *http://www.redherring.com/mag/issue38/bulb.html.*

37. Zygmunt Bauman, "Survival as a Social Construct," *Theory, Culture and Society* 9 (1992): 1–36, quote at 25.

CHRIS GOERTZEN

14. Purposes of North Carolina Powwows

The powwow arrived in North Carolina as a mature package, and North Carolina powwows continue to match the national model in broad outline. However, these powwows are typically smaller, many details are unique, and the powwows naturally mean something rather different to Indians whose collective history contrasts greatly with that of Plains populations. Recent politics matters too. Piedmont and Coastal Indian communities adopted the powwow as part of public reemergence in the last few decades of the twentieth century. Considerable controversy – indeed, acrimony – concerning which groups ought to be legally recognized divides one tribe from another, even as the powwow system unites them.

I focus here on the community living nearest to my former home in Carrboro, North Carolina – the Occaneechi-Saponis, a very small group who recently energetically sought, and finally achieved, state recognition – as well as on the larger Haliwa-Saponis, who have been recognized for decades. These groups contrast instructively and were the North Carolina Indians I first got to know. In 1991, when I first taught a world music class, I sought opportunities for students to do fieldwork, wondering which events would be sufficiently large, resilient, and friendly that a horde of kids with clipboards, questions – and uneven sensitivities – could be gracefully accommodated. One student pointed out that her former high school, Durham's North Carolina School of Science and Mathematics, hosted a large annual powwow. For years I conveyed groups of students there, to college powwows featuring intertribal drums, and to the nearby Occaneechi-Saponi powwows.

After hundreds of hours at powwows and in conversation with North Carolina Indians, I formally researched the intersection of local powwow culture with the controversial process through which communities could seek state recognition as tribes.[1] I welcomed the invitation to revise my first essay on the topic for this anthology, both for the opportunity to rethink a situation whose openness and informality overlie complexity and pain, and for the chance to again seek the counsel of Occaneechi elder and craftsman John Jeffries; his wise and compassionate wife, Lynette; energetic Occaneechi lawyer and storyteller Lawrence Dunmore III; Haliwa-Saponi drummer and medical student Linwood Watson; Haliwa-Saponi craftsmen and leaders Dalton and Senora Lynch; and adopted Lumbee artist and teacher Joe Liles.

North Carolina's Native population of more than 80,000 is the largest east of the Mississippi.[2] The best known of many thriving communities, the Eastern Band of Cherokees, reside at the western end of the state, high in the Smoky Mountains. However, the Lumbees, whose some 45,000 members live in the southeastern corner of North Carolina and in cities, far outnumber the approximately 9,000 Cherokees and the other groups on the Piedmont and coast, while the rest of the smaller tribes (the Haliwa-Saponis number about 3,500, and the Occaneechi-Saponis only around 450) add up to many thousands. The Cherokees, the only North Carolina tribe to have a reservation or to be federally recognized, have their own history, one oriented more toward the West. They interact little with the North Carolina Piedmont and Coastal groups, who, however, find ready partners in the Native communities of neighboring portions of Virginia and South Carolina. When the Indians discussed in this essay speak of "local" events, they refer to this mid-Atlantic Piedmont and Coastal complex.

The most active of the groups that founded the North Carolina Commission of Indian Affairs in 1971 put on the first North Carolina powwows at about the same time. The Haliwa-Saponis were first: Chief W. R. Richardson attended powwows during travel to New England and arranged North Carolina's first in 1966 in order to honor the state's official recognition of the tribe the previous year. The Haliwa-Saponis have long resided northeast of Raleigh in Halifax and Warren counties: hence "Haliwa," which was adopted as the tribal name in 1953 as a result of disagreement on which ancestral strand dominated – Saponi, Nansemond, Tuscarora, Occaneechi, Tutelo, or Gingaskin; "Saponis" was appended in 1979 as the conversation continued.[3]

Powwows accumulated in the mid-Atlantic states slowly at first, then more rapidly. Other groups on the original state commission – the Waccamaw-Sioux, the Coharies, and the Lumbees – had their first powwows in 1969 or 1970. (The Eastern Band of Cherokees, who look down on and rarely participate in the commission, put on their first powwow soon after the Haliwa-Saponis; the Indians of Person County, who are on the commission, do not yet hold a powwow as of this writing.) Urban intertribal organizations on the commission – all Lumbee-dominated – initiated powwows fairly soon after each organization was chartered: the Guilford Native American Association

(Greensboro) in 1976 (charter 1975), the Cumberland County Association for Indian People (Fayetteville) in 1980 (charter 1973), and the Metrolina Native American Association (Charlotte) in 1983 (charter 1976). Many smaller communities then chimed in similarly – for example, the Occaneechi-Saponis in 1984, following their own political mobilization in 1983. Powwows continued to enter the calendar, with the youngest intertribal organizations – college groups – taking the last available winter weekends for indoor events (their arranging powwows fosters a sense of community among Indian students, making their success in school far more likely).[4] Of some fifty annual powwows in the Carolinas and Virginia, five came into being before 1980, fourteen in 1980–89, and more than thirty in the 1990s. (In this census as well as this chapter, I am neglecting the dozens of powwows put on by two Indian-run culture businesses, though these resemble tiny traditional powwows to the outsider audience.)

Mid-Atlantic Indian populations adopted the powwow to replace cultural institutions that had been recently weakened. Their societal infrastructure had consisted of their own churches and schools. As Lawrence Dunmore explained to me:

> basically, the only way we could formally function as a community was through our churches. The deacons [including his grandfather] were usually the headmen of the families, and they represented each of the different [Occaneechi-Saponi] communities, Western Orange County, Pleasant Grove, and then Mebane Oaks. All the people, no matter where they lived, maintained a membership. Even today, my mother and other people who live in D. C. still have membership in Martin's Chapel or Jeffries Cross [Church]. And they've been gone 30 to 40 years. But it still holds that cohesiveness.

Similarly, most Haliwa-Saponis had attended Indian churches since their first local one was founded in the 1860s.[5] Some Haliwa-Saponi churches and other Native churches remain largely Indian, but others, especially some of those of smaller groups, such as the Occaneechi-Saponis, have seen their Indian character diluted or lost. But churches proved easier to keep Indian than schools: churches are attended by choice and by more family members than would enroll in a given school, and churches can remain viable even if membership dips well below one hundred members. The Haliwa-Saponi Indian school, on the other hand, built in 1957, was closed as a result of desegregation in 1968. Dalton Lynch remembered: "It made me mad when they closed our school down." Students had come from nearby in both Halifax and Warren counties – now, those from one county were bused about thirty miles in one direction, while their friends and relatives were sent the opposite direction. In their new schools they were "picked on and mistreated." They lost "a total loving atmosphere, where everyone's the same. . . . There's still some hostility there."[6] Indeed, many Indian schools were closed in 1965–69.[7] Integration affected Indian schools in proportion to population. Despite repeated entreaties, small groups, such as the Occaneechi-Saponis, did not have separate Indian schools at this time, though their children might have been concentrated in a given school.

On the other end of the spectrum, the much more numerous Lumbee remained in the majority at some of their schools, though integration was aggressive, controversial, and resisted both on the spot and in court.[8] Although the long-term benefits of the civil rights movement have been critical in slowly creating a climate of tolerance, desegregation was initially a crude instrument, absolutely devastating to North Carolina Indian communities.

The powwow answered this crisis by sliding smoothly into an existing – but waning – social and ritual niche. Lawrence Dunmore pointed out that the powwow "follows the traditions of our Associations we used to have. You go back to the '30s. . . . They used to have these big Associations . . . an arbor with people selling – vendors – plus there was a preacher from one of the Indian churches, preaching fire and brimstone. And people would have religious experiences, very spiritual. They'd do the old singing there. The powwows are a take-off on that."[9] Occaneechi-Saponi chairperson John Jeffries remembered these associations vividly:

> The association was very, very similar to your fall festivals. They happened in the hot time of the year, but it was harvest time. That was when they had all of the foods and things that they'd grown through the year . . . I remember a lot of, for instance, dried peach pieces. They had all kinds of vegetables there. Watermelons were in season at that time, and all kinds of poultry, wild meats, and just whatever the families could get together: that's what they had to eat.
>
> And they had what they call a brush arbor there. Usually it was around the church somewhere; it was centered around the church. And the minister would be preaching. . . . On Sundays, Fridays, and Saturdays, they would have sort of like a revival, and people would be singing, and dancing, and praying, and whatever they do at a revival.

And the main drag of the midway – I call it the midway – was on each side of the road. It was usually – when I can remember – it was a dusty or dirt road somewhere in the country. And the dust would be knee-deep out there. People would be walking, and singing, and happy and buying all kinds of little pinwheels. Yeah, they had cotton candy at that time, popcorn, soda pops, ices, anything you wanted. It looked to me like it was – no, it *was* nothing but a powwow. As far as I'm concerned, that's what it was.

And all the neighborhood people would come in; people from out of town would come in. Only thing different [from today's powwow] was that they weren't dressed in regalia, and they weren't doing Native dances. There was story-telling going on. People had tobacco there. I remember, this one man was sitting there tying tobacco. He might have been living in that area, but was tying tobacco in the tobacco barn. If there was a pond close by, people'd be swimming.

It was long about September – last of September, first of October – is when they'd have them. I know it was still warm. And it was a *gathering* of people. People camped out there. I remember my grandmother, when I was young, would go out, and my granddaddy'd go out and set up an arbor, a tent or something, and they would be cooking under those things. People would come, just like they do to a powwow. And that reminded me more of a powwow than anything, since I've been going to powwows. As far as I'm concerned that's what it was. It was a gathering of people, and that's what a powwow is, nothing more than a gathering.[10]

With the powwow traveled a one-sentence description of its prehistory that I heard repeatedly: "Indians have always danced in a circle around the drum." A compact explanation of the various standard dances is regularly repeated for neophytes in conversation, in the dialogue of powwow emcees, and in lengthy printed programs. Typical phrasing celebrates cultural richness, noting recent historical detail while also insisting on an aura of antiquity. For example, the men's "Traditional Dance may be the original dance of the Indians of the Northern Plains," and "Formerly the exclusive dance of princesses and ladies in leadership roles, the Ladies' Traditional Buckskin Dance is now open to all ladies," and "Shawl Dancing . . . is a comparatively new style, having been around only a couple of decades," and "Originating among the tribes of Canada, the Jingle Dress Dance [while] relatively new to the Southern Plains . . . is an example of a very old dance which held a very spiritual meaning."[11] While some North Carolina Indians know that the powwow as a ceremonial complex coalesced only in the 1940s, most consider the powwow traditional, both set in form and socially sanctioned for an unknown but presumably considerable length of time.

What would the arriving powwow mean in the mid-Atlantic states? Plains song, dance, and apparel traveled with *some* values attached. Barre Toelken, drawing on his experience in the Plains and Southwest, lists these: "circularity, time as an outgrowth of event (rather than vice versa) . . . reciprocation, competition within culturally acceptable and meaningful contexts [and] the importance of the family unit . . . [with events taking] place surrounded by the whole family and the tribe."[12] Each of these values resonates to some degree with mid-Atlantic Indians, but the correspondence is far from exact. When I asked Lawrence Dunmore what the powwow first meant to him, he summarized that "it was a place where we could be with other Indian people. It was a chance to meet cousins and family . . . friends you hadn't seen all year; to celebrate our heritage together, to listen to the music, to enjoy the food and the crafts. It's really a big family reunion." He also remarked on its political importance: "[When] we started to do more with the tribe, the powwow was really the focus."[13]

Simply put, the values that Indians in the tristate area have long held most dear – and which have found new and vivid expression in the powwow – are overlapping ones: community (Toelken's "family" and "tribe") and sharing (Toelken's "reciprocation"). These communities exist as linked to geographic location and the natural world, nurture each generation in the extended family, and consist both of the "tribe" (at home and in diaspora) and of the broader Indian world (both through mutual support within this network of populations and as facing out toward the non-Indian world). And these Indians share work, sustenance, and property as well as share through valor. The following intertwined examinations of how these values endure in these mid-Atlantic Indian populations and how they infuse local powwow culture illustrate how natural the powwow's transfer to this region has been.

The largest community celebrated at North Carolina powwows is that of all Indians. In the mid-Atlantic states Indian heritage was until recently best disavowed. Early on, during the period that culminated in the Trail of Tears (1830s–1850s, broadly understood), to advertise Indian identity was to court inclusion in that disastrous process of systematic expropriation and removal. After that danger had passed, prejudice and systematic mistreatment remained.

Many North Carolina Indians now in their fifties or older were told as children to keep their Indian identity secret. Lynette Jeffries told me that her husband John's "grandmamma would whisper to him: 'You're a little Indian boy, but don't tell anybody."' And according to John, "*she* wasn't sure of what tribe, but she knew she was Indian. And she would tell me different things that my grandfather's people and her brothers and sisters had passed on. Things that they had done [were] very similar, actually, to what I'm doing now: making stuff, going out into the woods and making do with what you could find. Of course you have to realize, back in the '40s, that's what they had to do to live." Lawrence Dunmore surmised that "people knew that they were Indian and in a community, and that was what mattered . . . despite tremendous pressures to make us 'colored' by [state] law and by federal policy . . . since no Indians were supposed to be there."[14]

There were plenty of alternative ways to explain skin tint. The Indians of Person County used to be routinely called "Cuban." Wanda Whitmore-Penner, an Occaneechi-Saponi, has been called "Samoan, Black, Hawaiian and Mexican."[15] A neighbor of mine in North Carolina who had worked with John Jeffries once had vaguely thought that Jeffries was "Lebanese or something." And Lawrence Dunmore told me that when, earlier in the twentieth century, the Occaneechis were concentrated in an area nicknamed "Little Texas," white neighbors called these Indians "Texas Negroes."[16] At the same time that the larger North Carolina Indian communities were collaborating to form the State Commission of Indian Affairs and first arranging powwows, smaller, more vulnerable communities, such as the Occaneechi-Saponis remained "hidden in plain sight," as many Indians phrase it. Their eventual public reemergence as Indians came with their first powwows.

Powwows reinforce respect and affection for place, both for nature and for the human history of locations. When North Carolina Indian men over age thirty or so speak of their youths, fishing, hunting, and exploring specific wild areas dominate the narrative. John Jeffries reminisced:

> Kids don't know what they're missing now. They don't know what they're missing. We got out there – we knew every snake, every plant; we knew every bug. . . . We had water coming out of the banks down here. They did a ceremony at the springs that's coming right down at the bottom of the hill. That's a natural spring, and somebody put a pipe up . . . and my grandfather used it when he was a boy. . . . A lot of things we take for granted. I told [a visiting Navajo boy]: "This is my childhood, right

here. Before all these houses were [built], there were heavy woods, and we knew every corner and turn of these woods."[17]

Jeffries's rural upbringing was far from unusual. It was easy to fish and hunt within walking distance of home just a generation ago, since North Carolina Indian communities occupied land marginal for agriculture, neighboring or hidden within thickets and creeks on the Piedmont or swamps on the Coastal Plains.[18] Today it is difficult to make a living running these same small farms, and most contiguous wild areas have been developed. But a continued spiritual and nostalgic intimacy with nature comes out in the powwow in the emcee's remarks, in the furs and feathers so important in the regalia, and in many dances that imitate animals or hunting.

At the same time the precise locations of powwows often honor community history. At the 1997 Haliwa-Saponi powwow, emcee Arnold Richardson began with these words: "It's good to be back for the oldest powwow in the history of North Carolina, our 32nd annual. We are strong in our history, our culture; we have been in this area ever since the first Indian Wars of 1712. Behind you is the old former Haliwa Indian school, now the tribal headquarters."

The Occaneechi-Saponis gained an unusually detailed knowledge of their own history while seeking state recognition. Of their three (!) annual powwows, one is in the Virginia state park containing the reservoir that drowned the island that had been home to the Occaneechis in the 1650s (until their decimation in Bacon's Rebellion in 1676). A second one powwow marks their next home, an Occaneechi village (located in modern-day Hillsborough, North Carolina) that was visited by surveyor John Lawson in 1701 and recently exhumed by University of North Carolina archaeologists and reconstructed by the Occaneechi people as an open-air museum).[19] In his remarks as emcee of this powwow in 1997, John Jeffries explained to the powwow attendees: "The indigenous people of this land, this country, in the language of our people are the Yesah. . . . We greeted the first white man to set foot on this land and we have never left it. I was born within walking distance to this river. My father was born within thirteen miles of this river. My grandparents was born on this river. This land was my home, my play area as a child. You are on the land of the Occaneechi-Saponi people."[20]

The people who lived in this village at the beginning of the eighteenth century were absorbed by the Saponi confederation and then experienced a series of alliances, migrations, and dispersals. In the 1780s the group now known as the Occaneechi-Saponis settled near Hillsborough in Pleasant Grove, which became home to their two churches and a school their children attended – their third annual powwow is held at that school. Powwows do help level the playing field between large and small Indian communities. Since many participants come from neighboring Indian groups, a small community like that of the Occaneechi-Saponis needs just a handful of deeply committed organizers to put on a powwow as convincing as that of a larger, state-recognized tribe like the Haliwa-Saponis.

Powwows celebrate the "close-knit-ness" of Indian family life, as Linwood Watson put it.[21] Each age group in the community is served. Powwow emcees single out the oldest and youngest present for praise and regularly mention the debt owed the elders for their wisdom. (Ubiquitous formulas, such as "the Native people have always respected their elders," implicitly criticize general American culture, just as does the equally common "Indians never shunned their veterans.") Toddlers have their own moment to dance. These "Tiny Tots" may or may not move their feet much out in the arena, but their regalia are lovingly crafted, they receive ardent and prolonged applause, and they hear emcees describe them weekend after weekend as "our future leaders." As these children grow older the powwow helps them craft good self-images through group reinforcement and provides a wholesome, safe environment for playing, socializing, and eventually courting.

Pitfalls facing youths who are beginning to make their own decisions are dealt with openly. Flyers for events and admonishments by emcees proscribe drugs and alcohol. As Cherokee elder Driver Pheasant Jr. asserted: "[Powwows] help boys with family or alcohol problems."[22] My Piedmont or Coastal consultants didn't raise these issues, but when I discussed this with John Jeffries, he told me that a "powwow high" made liquor superfluous for him.[23] Alcohol does seem less of a problem in rural Piedmont and Coastal Indian communities than among either reservation Indians (including the Eastern Band of Cherokees) or in urban Indian communities. Thomas Beltrame and David McQueen found that Lumbee men at home in Robeson County drink less than do the many Lumbees working in Baltimore, far from family and church.[24] And a youth choir that performs briefly at many North Carolina powwows bears its message in its name, "Love Can Wait."

Powwows provide adults a focus for self-esteem and intellectual engagement that may be lacking during the workweek (low educational levels and a reluctance to relocate often result in humdrum jobs). And the spirituality of powwows reinforces rather than replaces the staunch Protestant faith that most of these Indians have. Early during each session of a powwow, a pastor of

Indian heritage intones a blessing consonant with both Christian and Indian beliefs, just as regional churches here with substantially Indian congregations seek out that common ground. (Although overall more explicitly Christian than powwow blessings, such services are beginning to incorporate specifically Indian elements too, according to Tuscarora Derek Lowry.)[25]

The powwow system helps North Carolina Indians cope with the modern forces that work to disperse rural communities throughout the country. The shrinking of never-generous economic opportunities at home presents many Indians with a stark choice between staying home and making a decent living. Local powwows, by representing traditional Indian and rural values and through celebrating the history of given communities, assert the primacy of spiritual health and community life over material improvement. While some rural Indians attend only their own community's powwow(s), others refocus their lives away from the workweek to fulfilling weekends by charting their own powwow circuits from among the dozens of events within a few hours' drive.

Nevertheless, many Indians have had to relocate since World War II, and more and more now go away to college. Powwows help these emigrants preserve a sense of community in two ways. First, powwows reinforce (or replace) the longstanding custom of holding onto home church membership with one of routinely returning home for the community powwow.[26] Some homecomers will dance, but many more visit with relatives and friends in the audience, giving and receiving news updates and gossip until their throats are raw. Linwood Watson, who participated in the intertribal drum Southern Sun while living away at school, said that the Haliwa-Saponi powwow became like a homecoming "because a lot of the tribe had moved to Maryland for jobs." Watson's mother added that, at the powwow, "you see people then that you haven't seen in a whole year. It's like a get-together." I then asked what Linwood mostly did at powwows. He and his mother simultaneously answered, "Talk." He added that their powwow was a specifically local event primarily because of this homecoming aspect.[27] Community events, such as a blood drive, are also planned around a powwow. An honor song might be saved for that powwow; relatively informal tribal dances on Friday evening precede the powwow proper. Dalton Lynch said: "I only missed one [Haliwa-Saponi tribal] powwow in my life, and it broke my heart. I was overseas in Korea" [in the military].[28]

Powwows also help new urban communities made up of these rural emigrants to mark and buttress Indian identity and values by putting on their own powwows. Of about fifty annual powwows in the mid-Atlantic system, urban and intertribal ones (most for laborers, but a growing number for students) slightly outnumber the rural and tribal ones.

Powwows are the main tool North Carolina Indians have for defining their collective identity to outsiders, many of whom arrive at these events knowing precious little about contemporary Native America. Powwows intrigue outsiders by displaying the most positive and colorful aspects of modern Indian life. Audience members are invited to take the measure of Indian communities flourishing among them and to empathize with Indian values, but not to become Indians. They are allowed to videotape most but not the most sacred segments of the event, and they will be warmly invited to join specific dances. They can purchase furs, jewelry, and ornaments from the Indian vendors but should not return with these stitched into regalia, expecting to join the dance circle. While North Carolina Indians I consulted warmly welcomed non-Indians who were careful to show respect and to defer to Indians' own interpretations of Native culture, less acute or attentive "wannabees" were roundly criticized. In short these Indians use powwows to encourage the surrounding world to respect both the nature and the boundaries of their communities.

Even before the dancing begins, the range of apparel bridges the gap between fantasy and home. First, dance outfits of Plains derivation are spectacular and familiar. Yes – as outsider audience members are shown – living Indians can be visually akin to those seen on television, which illustrate a romantic and generalized past to neophytes.[29] Second, in the past decade, a number of North Carolina Indians have opted for regional historic garb, involving relatively few feathers, and often with cloth replacing leather. Thus not all Indians share the same history. (The growing use of locally derived regalia reflects not a devaluing of Plains regalia but, rather, an array of choices to add to those available within the conventions of Plains outfits.) Third, the young men at the drums wear casual clothes, often including shirts and caps bearing sports logos, showing neophytes that these Indians share general American enthusiasms. Last, mothers sitting in the dance circle in street clothes as they dress their kids in regalia obviously shop at the same local stores that many in the audience patronize, demonstrating that these Indians are their neighbors.

The powwow arrived as a shared cultural complex, shared among individuals, among Indian communities, and between participants and their mixed audiences. While Carolina Indians know and employ the term *Pan-Indian*, they often cite it as an outsider's word for powwow culture, a rubric with some but limited utility. "Pan" denotates "in common, overarching," but neglects "process," that is, giving and accepting. Insiders prefer to describe powwows as "intertribal" and as "shared." Dalton Lynch said: "I kind of hate the word [*Pan*], but it *kind of* explains it good. 'Pan' means a mixture of different cultures, and we turn around, and we share things, and people share things with us. And if Indian people are sharing with Indian people, number one, they're sharing with you because they want to create a tight bond."[30]

And while the powwow is by definition not tribe specific – that is, it is intertribal in both origin and purpose – it must *remain* a shared event in the mid-Atlantic Piedmont and Coastal Plains, since few communities produce enough active dancers and musicians to support a festive powwow. The larger rural communities and urban organizations – apart from the Lumbees, this means groups with one thousand to three thousand members – must attract dancers and musicians from elsewhere to create events that are big and full of energy. The Haliwa-Saponis would have only two drums at their powwow rather than half a dozen if they employed only their own. The much smaller Occaneechi-Saponis can send a few wonderful dancers and a flutist and storyteller to others' events, and tribal chairperson John Jeffries both demonstrates primitive weapons at many powwows and emcees about two dozen every year, but there is no Occaneechi-Saponi drum as of this writing. Without the routine sharing of participants, the smaller Indian communities in the tristate area – that is, most of them – could not mount powwows. "We partied at your powwow last week – you're going to party at our powwow this week," remarked Jeffries while emceeing an Occaneechi-Saponi powwow in 1997.[31]

Much more is shared at powwows than their arrangement. Dalton Lynch mentioned that "around here, we helped each other out as far as getting our crops in. . . . When we got Grandma's in, we'd get my Dad's, then we'd go get my Uncle's."[32] While both this traditional pooling of labor at harvest time and the shared meals punctuating this long process have become casualties of the modernization of farming, such feasts and those of the fundamentalist "associations" resonate in feasts that powwow organizers mount for participants. The food served illustrates this continuity. It is southern rural fare, often with a regional focus, such as a roast pig in the Piedmont or seafood stews nearer the coast. In contrast, the vendors serving the audience supplement hotdogs and fries with such Pan-Indian fare as buffalo burgers, "Indian tacos" (ground beef and salad on fry bread), and the occasional venison stew or bear "steak-um." They market pan-festival and Pan-Indian food while the Indian dancers and musicians share a big church supper with local or regional overtones.

The honoring of veterans at powwows has to do as much with sharing as with valor. Yes, serving in the military echoes old warrior societies (certainly applicable on the Plains, less so here), and the military environment, though highly structured in some ways, is refreshingly egalitarian in others, notably in minimizing segregation and displays of racial prejudice. It also allows Indian soldiers to travel and have new experiences without feeling disloyal to their homes or families. Many southeastern Indians enlist, as is true of Indians nationwide, but few aspire to careers in the military. The experience is primarily a rite of passage, a pilgrimage during which participants offer to share the ultimate, to give up their lives for the country that includes their community. Honoring these veterans for the rest of their lives at powwows neither endorses nor criticizes American wars, and whether a given individual endured combat is not central. The magnificence of the personal offer to share that each soldier made simply by enlisting is what matters. "Any time you go away and do your duty, and you do it well, that's going to go a long ways," said Linwood Watson.[33]

Last, these powwows explicitly involve the sharing of property. Pooling resources of all kinds has been important in these economically marginal communities for centuries, and extended families who once farmed together often mitigate having been forced off the land by reassembling at the same factory.[34] They share money and goods through both necessity and preference. One reason that the components of some dance outfits may not seem fully coordinated in terms of color or texture is that their value accrues less from appearance than from personal relationships: they were gifts. And many events feature "giveaways," during which, for instance, a paid head dancer may ritually honor individuals by awarding them items ranging from blankets to apples, gifts together costing far more than the dancer was paid. As Jim Chavis explained while emceeing part of a 1997 Occaneechi powwow: "A great big part of the Native American heritage is to share with others. That goes back in our heritage many, many, many generations. Sometime during the day, you will hear us talking about having a giveaway. That's where we simply share gifts with other friends of ours."[35] (This can take awhile and is one of few times that acts expressing values important to the participants can leave audiences restless.) Youngsters heading off to school or crucial but unpaid performers (for instance, a drum that has traveled a long distance) may benefit from a "blanket dance," during which money is collected on a blanket in the arena. Just as in daily life in both ancient and recent times, achievement is measured by how much and how well one has helped others, surpluses are distributed rather than accumulated, and to have is to share.

The most energetic insiders, the Indians most committed to experiencing and communicating expressive culture, and also the most dedicated outsiders, the visitors whose avid interest in powwows brings them back over and over, constitute groups too small to sustain such events year after year by themselves. To succeed mid-Atlantic powwows must be fun, they must make cultural diplomacy entertaining to both presenters and visitors, and the cultural materials chosen for presentation must be appropriate for the festival setting.

In North Carolina, audiences (that is, the constituencies apart from resident and returning Indians) are mixed in several ways. They are racially inclusive, more so than audiences at any other festivals based on ethnicity or race. Also, as Blaine Brownell argues, what "small farmers, recent rural immigrants to the city, and a large number of urban intellectuals" have in common is that they are the "psychologically least secure in the rapidly changing world of 20th-century America" and therefore have "persisted in their preference for a non-urban environment."[36] Many visitors to powwows fit this description in that they expect powwows to anchor sensory offerings in an exotic, timeless solace – that is, the non-Indian local citizens who dominate many audiences are acting as cultural tourists without leaving home. Indians present a nonthreatening and, these days, glamorous ethnicity. Most interestingly many visitors combine the typically southern affection for "everything historical – we go to Civil War reenactments too" with a common working-class and southern way of linking interests in history and in family through pursuing genealogy. After consulting family Bibles and doing research at local historical societies, countless North Carolina audience members – both white and black – proudly cite an ancestor or two said to have been Cherokee or simply "Indian" (the name of the group often had been forgotten; in any case, the life span of the ancestor in question would have antedated most contemporary names of tribes).

For North Carolina Indians, when the novelty that powwows initially offer evaporates, it yields to a progressively more nuanced enjoyment of the considerable – and growing – variation in powwow format, in regalia, and in music and dance. Holding the performers' attention really matters – while audience members usually stay for a few hours at most, most participants commit for entire weekends. I will review in turn the richness of the basic powwow complex of music and dance, the current dynamics of change in that basic system, and the expansion of the array of powwow attractions to incorporate local elements and local syntheses in mid-Atlantic powwows.

Even the most schematic view of powwow music and dance reveals rich variety. For both men and women the dance whose regalia and steps are called "traditional" remains the most common in North Carolina. The next most frequent is the Fancy Dance (men) and Fancy Shawl Dance (women), both of which are physically taxing even for the fit teenagers and young adults who dominate these categories. Fancy dancers will drive farther than others in order to focus on contest powwows; their winnings help finance the extra travel. In the third position are the Grass Dance (men) and the Jingle Dress Dance (women), which require an intermediate level of energy and feature very distinctive regalia. In all of these dances convention governs both regalia and dance steps but leaves lots of room for individual expression: dancers perform simultaneously rather than in ensemble. Here the main solo display dance imported from the Plains, the spectacular Hoop Dance, joins honor dances, blanket dances, and social dances as relief from the basic dance categories.

In Plains Indian music, in both Northern and Southern Plains styles, the standard song form of incomplete repetition still allows variety in phrase length and rhythmic relationships. The associated terraced, descending melodic contours differ from song to song, though these sources of variety may escape audiences. But the energy and attractiveness of the music come less from form or melody than from rhythm and timbre. The steady, slowly accelerating drumbeat sets the tempo, but the sung notes rarely start with or in the exact middle of a drumbeat. This is not to say that the melody floats freely; the tie with the drumbeat is absolutely firm, however well hidden the knots may be. Rather than discrete moments of syncopation, we hear an incessant tug of war between drum and song, a vibrant rhythmic fabric. At the same time, the deep power of the drum and raw vocal timbres impart incredible energy. In a mild paradox, rhythm and timbre strike mid-Atlantic auditors as exotic, though it is precisely these elements that make powwow music accessible to many American listeners to a degree that, for instance, traditional Japanese music is not. Powwow music is just striking enough for North Carolina listeners.

As of 2001 there were at least as many Northern as Southern (Plains) drums in North Carolina. The spectacular high-pitched sound of Northern singing impresses beginners and echoes the pop culture picture of Indian music initiated in Wild West shows at the turn of the century and still passed along to all Americans through the media. Indeed, Northern sound has itself been intensified in recent generations.[37] Local powwow arrangers often try to supplement Northern sound by seeking out a Southern drum; for example, founders of the young intertribal drum Southern Sun (formed in 1994) chose Southern style partly because they suspected (correctly) that this might inspire invitations to powwows. Preferring the bold effect of the Northern sound illustrates intensification through selection, while adding the Southern sound to a powwow heightens the musical complexity of the total event.

Further buttressing this general trend toward intensification, yet undermining the historic distinctiveness of Northern style, Indian composers in both styles now write more songs that trace increasingly involved contours. Also, more drums in both styles are performing "word songs," in which the main vocal burden of vocables yields to a phrase or two of words in the repetition part of incomplete repetition form. Although these songs are harder to learn, and thus to share between drums or to be performed by pickup groups, the added difficulty presents a challenge welcomed by many singers and impressive to judges at contest powwows.

When North Carolina Indians join in the national trend to compose more word songs, they want to mark tribal identity by using their own languages. This practice is not yet common – the Piedmont and Coastal communities that are in a position to recover their historic languages are in the earlier stages of doing so – but the composers who can employ these languages consider the effort worthwhile. In the excellent Northern-style drum Stoney Creek (most of the members of which are Haliwa-Saponi), Marty Richardson writes lyrics in Tutelo, the Saponi language, while a Lumbee member writes in Cheraw, considered a historic Lumbee language. Such songs travel well, since the musical style remains that shared from the Plains.

It is expected that each tribe will have a Flag Song, and that this will be a word song. Members of the intertribal drum Southern Sun composed a Tuscarora Flag Song for powwow use. Since this drum is based in the Chapel Hill–Durham axis, just a dozen miles from Hillsborough, it contributes to many Occaneechi-Saponi events. Tuscarora Derek Lowry wrote the text, which literally means "This is our flag: it is good." As in most such lyrics, the words are few but the meaning resonates deeply. To recover their language, North Carolina Tuscaroras are learning from a handful of New York Tuscarora elders. They had no traditional word for "flag," but these elders had seen flags draped across the caskets of soldiers killed in Vietnam, a powerful image that suggested expanding the meaning of their word for "blanket," *oriquaya*, to include "flag." Lowry told me that he wrote the contour of the opening phrase to remind him of long house (thus Eastern Woodlands) tunes.[38] Since the total musical form fits Plains conventions, both tune and text have the virtue of being at once local and general.

The other main way to incorporate local music and dance into North Carolina powwow music is to perform songs associated with a specific community or with the Woodlands region. Perhaps a half-dozen of the about fifty annual mid-Atlantic powwows have done this for years, and the number is growing. For instance, a women's dance called the Skanye, said to be an old Saponi dance, has been reimported from northern Saponi diasporic communities and is beginning to be danced at several Piedmont powwows. The Haliwa-Saponis have put their own stamp on the Plains two-step, and their powwows have long been among the richest in non-Plains music and dance.

Indeed, the first few powwows put on by the Haliwa-Saponis drew quite heavily on local or regional dances because these were the genres they already knew. Then, as it became easier to attract Plains-type drums (and eventually to nurture these), Plains powwow music and dance came to dominate this and all other North Carolina powwows. At the very successful Haliwa-Saponi powwow, the contest format now leaves no room on Saturday or Sunday for local music, but Friday night still features a handful of local dances, particularly a half-dozen of the animal dances that historically had been so important here.

The many ways that modern performances of such tunes contrast with Plains music makes these Eastern Woodlands songs relatively easy on both insiders' and outsiders' ears. Voices are much more relaxed than in Plains singing (particularly than in the favored northern Plains style), and the accompanying rattle (or, in some dances, sticks or hand drum) has a timbre less imposing than that of the large Plains-type drum. Melodies often trace arches, more familiar to visitors than the descending terraced contours of Plains songs. While typical arrays of pitches match that found in the Plains-sounding Tuscarora Flag Song, the popular Haliwa-Saponi Robin Dance opens by outlining a major chord, then continues to sound less truly pentatonic than major, albeit not getting around to employing the fourth or seventh degrees of the major scale. And the rhythms are quite accessible. The Plains tension between drumbeat and vocal line yields here to simple support of the vocal line, with both melody and accompaniment in triplets. And the overall feel is a bit more metric, although shifting between loose groups of three and four beats and despite being frequently interrupted by pauses during which the dance changes direction or the dancers squat or rise.

Dalton Lynch, who knows this local repertoire well and often serves as head judge at the community powwow, sang the Robin Dance for me. He often paused to insert dance instructions. While this was an elicited performance, the dance is taught anew at each annual powwow. After a few times through the sequence of steps, the narration stops but the pauses remain, filled with a rattle tremolo and humorous suspense ("When are we going to get to stand up?"). Each sequence is faster, and dancers get tired, err, and laugh. The atmosphere recalls that of the social dances that punctuate most powwows, particularly that of the ubiquitous Snake Dance, a follow-the-leader number in which dancers constitute the snake by holding hands, with the head dancer leading the group into sinuous contours whose increasing entanglement can lead to hilarity. The Robin Dance does mark local identity through its steps and even in the vocables that make up the "text," since those are not Plains vocables. However, it, like the Pan-Indian snake dance, functions primarily as a solemnity-relieving novelty. Indeed, at a handful of powwows, Woodlands dances like this one are not relegated to Friday night but instead enter the general powwow as "specials" in the same broad change-of-pace niche as the Snake Dance, the Two-Step, and the "49."

While most dances at the powwow balance spirituality and conviviality, with these local animal dances the ratio shifts toward fun. In contrast the Stomp Dance projects more seriousness than do either the other local dances or the intertribal dances from the Plains. One choice a group can make is to take especially spiritual music out of public view, as the Eastern Band of Cherokees have done with their Stomp Dances. Their large powwows attract more nonlocal tourists than do powwows in the Piedmont and Coastal Plains, tourists whose main destination may be the very busy Smoky Mountains National Park. Fragile before the powwow arrived, the Stomp Dance has been revitalized as part of renewed involvement with regional culture. This revival drew on the Oklahoma Cherokees for music to supplement the modest amount retained by the Eastern Cherokees, but, as Cherokee Hoop dancer Eddie Swimmer told me, did so only after a critical mass of interested Eastern Cherokee had been assembled by their interest in the powwow.[39]

The Eastern Cherokees now arrange Stomp Dance evenings as intimate affairs for themselves and invited visitors only. In terms of public versus private use, the Haliwa-Saponi Robin Dance and other Woodlands dances mark the other end of a continuum, since this local repertoire has become part of their powwow. The Occaneechi-Saponis are charting a middle course as they assemble a nonpowwow repertoire – some songs are private (including their Stomp Dances) and others see ceremonial use in public contexts. Lawrence Dunmore spearheads this effort. He was given songs by a member of Canada's Cayuga, which absorbed parts of the Saponi nation during the eighteenth century. Dunmore shared one of those songs at the dedication ceremonies for the Occaneechi village being reconstructed on the eighteenth-century Hillsborough site. His delivery of this simple song was very moving – even though only he understood the words. The message was that a specifically tribal ceremony could be marked with tribal music.

Dunmore also composes songs himself and in collaboration with others. He translated into Tutelo the text of "Mahk Jchi," recorded on compact disc by Ulali.[40] One member of that virtuosic, close-harmony female trio, (Northern) Tuscarora Pura Fé Crescioni, moved to North Carolina, sparked the North Carolina hand drum revival, and participates in some Occaneechi events, though her involvement has been limited by Ulali's cramped concert and festival schedule. "Mahk Jchi" has become both one of Ulali's signature tunes and a staple of the emerging Occaneechi repertoire. Lynette Jeffries told me that recent performances of it included one by Ulali in Italy – some crowd members knew the song well enough to sing along, Pura Fé had told her – and one by John Jeffries at the dedication of a park on Occaneechi Mountain, which he can see from his front porch.[41]

The way the Occaneechi are building a local repertory today, through modern gifts of songs from groups with whom they share a past as well as through creativity in which sharing looms large, is not so different from how the Haliwa-Saponi local repertoire came together. Dalton Lynch told me that their Alligator Dance came from the Seminoles, from Florida, whereas their Welcome Dance came from Chickahominy, from across the state line in Virginia. Is it reaching too far to consider this process parallel to the more widespread sharing of powwow music? Do such adoptions clarify boundaries of community identity by allowing closeup savoring of differences in song styles? Or might this practice indicate that a longtime function of music among Indians has been to articulate and reinforce the value of sharing between communities?

In 1955 James Howard defined Pan-Indianism as "the process by which sociocultural entities such as the Seneca, Delaware, Creek, Yuchi, Ponca, and Comanche are losing their tribal distinctiveness and in its place are developing a nontribal 'Indian' culture." Much later William Powers troped that "tribalism, a tendency toward maintaining tribal distinction, becomes indicative of traditional cultural identity and continuity in culture, while intertribalism, the tendency toward exchanging cultural traits between tribes and between the Euroamerican society, becomes indicative of modernity, social identity, and cultural change."[42]

These generalizations may make sense in the abstract, but they fit awkwardly on the Plains and simply don't work for North Carolina. In the return to widespread cultivation of public expressive culture in this region, powwow music and dance often remain the *only* Indian music and dance. Further, where powwow culture exists alongside regionally derived song and dance in the mid-Atlantic states, the powwow usually preceded (and stimulated) the revival of specifically tribal cultures. The powwow also marked a critical juncture in many communities' public reemergence. For example, John Jeffries wears Woodlands-style regalia today but is proud to have his older set of Plains-style regalia in the tribal museum in Clarksville, Virginia, because, he says, it was with the powwow that "they first witnessed the Occaneechi people coming back."[43]

The powwow was not "borrowed" by mid-Atlantic Indian communities; it was given to them and thus belongs not to some distant or overarching entity but, rather, to each Indian group simultaneously. It is not Pan-Indian; it is community specific many times over. This gift allows these many groups to perform shared values as embodied in shared materials and events, valuable in terms of both ideology and practicality in these small populations. When communities have retained or now seek out a tribal or pan-Woodlands repertoire, this music complements powwow music on a small scale. The Haliwa-Saponi powwow changed during early years so that the function of the local repertoire shrunk while the Occaneechi-Saponi local repertoire grew. The balance between repertoire types converged, attaining in both cases an equilibrium between prominent Plains-style multitribal music and a modest but important array of local songs and dances. At the same time, some North Carolina Indian composers portray precisely this balance of national and local within individual songs that never contradict Plains style but have texts in their own languages and may evoke Woodlands music subtly, as in the Tuscarora Flag Song.

In a study of powwows among Coastal North Carolina's Waccamaw-Sioux, Patricia Barker Lerch and Susan Bullers found a direct correlation between concern with traditional values and concern with cultivation of that community's powwow.[44] My consultants from various North Carolina Indian populations were unwilling to rank powwow music and local music in terms of either traditionality or overall value to community identity.

In any case "tribe" is not originally an Indian concept but, rather, an outsiders' caricature of group relationships in which variety and flux had long been the rule. The known history of *every* Piedmont and Coastal North Carolina Indian population is of jeopardy, amalgamation, dispersal, new alliances, and movement; the multitribal ancestral stocks described for the Haliwa-Saponis and Occaneechi-Saponis are representative. Current long-term places of residence were fixed gradually, as whites inexorably painted Indian populations into corners, into refuge areas of less desirable land. The idea of the tribe as a stable, bounded group has broad appeal: putative clarity and continuity of identity in the past implies the promise of those qualities being "recovered" in the future, offering succor in the unstable present. And these Indian communities are actually *becoming* "tribes" in the modern received sense because this model has practical appeal; federal and state governments want to know exactly to whom they should avoid providing services, and the communities who are designated as or wish to be called tribes desire coherence for any number of administrative reasons. But the mix of processes that have shaped and continue to shape mid-Atlantic Indian musical repertoires does not reflect the artificial clarity of the idea of the tribe but, rather, parallels the muddy actual history of populations acting out a dialectic between focused identity and the incessant realignment required for survival.

Is one type of North Carolina powwow more "traditional" or otherwise more useful than another? In a not-too-artificial sorting of these events, three types emerge: the large contest powwow, the small to medium-sized noncontest powwow arranged by an Indian community, and the small powwow for hire. I use the word *large* advisedly; that the Haliwa-Saponi contest powwow and the handful of other relatively old North Carolina powwows – notably those put on by the large urban Indian organizations – may have five or six drums attend makes them "large" only in regional context, of course. Many types of American festivals employ the contest format to impose order on and add suspense to long series of short songs or dances. The disadvantage of this for powwows is that they become less spiritual, according to numerous organizers. There tends to be less room for "specials," such as giveaways and social dances. But contests attract skilled dancers and thus larger crowds, making it easier to achieve a high energy level and for dancers to lose themselves in the attractive communion of flow. Haliwa-Saponi Linwood Watson and Dalton Lynch both pointed out to me that the sizeable Haliwa powwow retains a local feel because of both its focus on homecoming and the informality of publicizing the event.[45]

Most locally organized powwows, including those of the Occaneechi-SaponiS, remain what participants call traditional. Proponents of such events told me repeatedly that these tend to be more spiritual than contest powwows. To me the principal differences seemed more a consequence of size than of format (which, however, also tended to correlate with size). Time spent awarding prizes in contest powwows, and a bit more, is occupied in local "traditional" powwows by nondanced specials, such as flute playing, talking about crafts or wilderness survival skills, demonstrating primitive weapons (at which John Jeffries excels), or storytelling (which Lawrence Dunmore does so well). These specials, which offer a much-needed break to the dancers, who tend to be fewer than at contests, are fascinating to audiences. Such activities recall the old southeastern tribal fairs: "traditional" translates both as "noncontest" and as "more local through invoking local historical flavor." These changes of pace balance the lack of the suspense of competition, making the best smaller events just as much fun for audiences as the best large contests.[46]

Overall the powwows put on by the larger state-recognized Native communities are not all that different from those of smaller state-recognized groups and of the communities who do not yet have state recognition. In fact the many similarities between events – plus the enormous overlap in participants – of powwows of recognized and not-yet-recognized groups asserts a broader commonality than is formally acknowledged by the leaders of the recognized communities. Soon after learning in June 1999 that the North Carolina Commission of Indian Affairs had turned down the Occaneechi-Saponi petition for state recognition as a tribe (for the third time!), Occaneechi chairperson John Jeffries formally invited each member of the commission to the annual Occaneechi-Saponi powwow in Hillsborough, a gesture he has made repeatedly.

I asked Jeffries to spell out the implications of his invitation. Just as in song texts, a few words stand for much. He pointed out that the members of the commission go to many powwows, and that legislators, chiefs of recognized tribes, and Native Americans from elsewhere in the United States come to the Occaneechi-Saponi powwow. In fact he has heard that many of these visitors believe that this powwow is "one of the most traditional powwows they've been to." Jeffries continued: "What we're saying is that we're trying to follow tradition. So what I'm telling the Commission is that 'we would like for you to come to see what we're doing. There's no way that you can make a true decision sitting back. . . . You need to visit the community. . . . Come to our festival. See our people. See what we are doing. Anybody can hold a powwow. Boy scouts can hold a powwow. Non-Indians hold powwows. So come to *our* powwow and see what *we* are doing.'"[47]

For the tiny Occaneechi-Saponis to have achieved state recognition in the legally most straightforward way, they would have had to document how they fulfilled at least five of eight criteria set by the commission, criteria that emphasize continuities of blood – persisting family names, kinship relationships with recognized tribes, group genealogies – and of location as well as take into account earlier descriptions of individuals and communities as Indian. Expressive culture appears only in the seventh of the eight criteria: "documented traditions, customs, legends, etc. that signify the tribe's Indian heritage."[48]

There can be no doubt that the Occaneechi-Saponis possess plenty of expressive culture, but is it distinctively theirs, or even particularly Indian? Lawrence Dunmore learned much from his relatives: "the rattlesnake is an important symbol. . . . Grandfather had all these sayings, and there was a wealth of knowledge from grandmother. She made all the traditional foods. She knew all the plants, healing, all the [alcoholic] drinks."[49] And John Jeffries's knowledge of the outdoors and primitive weaponry is staggering in its scope. But a sort of circular reasoning could hold that little of this knowledge is either distinctively Indian today or just like anything we know of precontact Native expressive culture, simply because whites and blacks learned food ways, folk medicine, and so on from the Indians early on and then the expressive culture of all ethnic and racial groups changed in tandem over time. In addition, the fact that Indians needed to keep their heads low for several centuries to avoid persecution scarcely encouraged the retention of public Indianness. Expressive culture has had such a low profile in the criteria for state recognition because no community in the Piedmont or Coastal Plains has had any realistic chance to retain much.

The commission's bylaws charge it to help groups like the Occaneechis with their applications, yet the process remains antagonistic. This perpetuates centuries of factionalism among and within North Carolina Indian populations, factionalism that in recent times has perversely celebrated the value of community by endlessly arguing about who belongs to a particular one. The reasoning behind the commission's repeated denial of state recognition to the Occaneechis was as informal as it was legalistic: commission members supplemented their own statutes with strongly felt personal opinions of what "Indian" and "tribe" mean. Indeed, for *both* the members of the North Carolina Commission of Indian Affairs and the Occaneechi-Saponis, Indian and tribal identity reaches beyond the clumsy legal criteria for state recognition.

The final Occaneechi petition was in fact meticulous, and absolutely convincing to outsiders to the controversy who studied it, including me. The Occaneechis satisfied five (the minimum) or six of the eight official criteria – though not number seven, the only one that concerns expressive culture. In fact I doubt that any North Carolina Piedmont or Coastal Plains community could muster a convincing battery of documented traditions to do this. But while a critical mass of legends, songs, and so on has been lost, the values that imbued those cultural materials are alive and well in younger garb, in many a powwow. This cannot be proved in a legal sense but really is what matters.

The commission members were never sufficiently swayed by an unequivocal answering of the criteria set out carefully and legalistically by themselves. They needed something more, something both less and more tangible – to *believe* that the Occaneechi-Saponis were Indians in their hearts and as a community. John Jeffries felt that they would become convinced of this if they were to witness the Occaneechi community articulating shared traditional values in their powwow.

I would like to think that this played a part in what eventually happened. When the Occaneechi-Saponis finally did receive the legal imprimatur of state recognition, it was through a technicality: the commission missed a deadline to challenge a court ruling on a matter of legal procedure. Thus the commission did not openly admit that recognition was due on legal grounds but, rather, just let it happen. Since that day (February 4, 2002) the Occaneechi people have had new access to certain state committees and to commission services such as job listings, and they have been able to participate in programs restricted to state-recognized tribes (such as presentations about Indian life at the North Carolina Museum of History). There have been odd results too, such as a proliferation of phone calls to the tribal office about the possibility of an Occaneechi-Saponi casino (this does not arouse interest). But the most important development has been a thaw at the official level of tribal communications, a thaw long prepared by grass-roots diplomacy . . . at powwows.

NOTES

1. Chris Goertzen, "Powwows and Identity on the Piedmont and Coastal Plains of North Carolina," *Ethnomusicology* 45, no. 1 (2001): 58–88.

2. North Carolina Commission of Indian Affairs (NCCIA), *North Carolina Indians* (Raleigh: NCCIA, 1997).

3. Haliwa-Saponi Tribe, *Haliwa-Saponi Indian Tribe 32nd Annual Powwow* (powwow program) (N.p.: Haliwa-Saponi Tribe, 1997).

4. David Oxendine, "Racial Identity Development among Lumbee American Indian College Students on a Predominantly White Campus" (master's thesis, North Carolina State University, 1995).

5. Haliwa-Saponi Tribe, *Haliwa-Saponi Indian Tribe 32nd Annual Powwow.*

6. Dalton Lynch, interview with the author, April 1997, Warrenton, North Carolina.

7. See Theda Perdue, *Native Carolinians: The Indians of North Carolina* (Raleigh: Division of Archives and History, North Carolina Department of Cultural Resources, 1985), 66.

8. Frye Gaillard, "Cities Contradict Lumbees' Values," *Race Relations Reporter* 2 (1971): 8; Forest Hazel, "Black, White and 'Other': The Struggle for Recognition," in *Indians of the South: A Native American Resource Packet* (Durham NC: Institute for Southern Studies, 1985), 26–29; Gerald M. Sider, *Lumbee Indian Histories: Race, Ethnicity and Indian Identity in the Southern United States* (Cambridge: Cambridge University Press, 1993), 61.

9. Lawrence Dunmore, interview with the author, March 1997, Mebane, North Carolina.

10. John Jeffries, interviews with the author, April, May, and June 1997, Hillsborough, North Carolina.

11. These quotations appeared identically in numerous powwow programs, including Haliwa-Saponi Tribe, *Haliwa-Saponi Indian Tribe 32nd Annual Powwow*, 21–23; and Guilford Native American Association, *19th Annual Cultural Festival Powwow* (N.p.: Guilford Native American Association, 1995), 18–21.

12. Barre Toelken, "Ethnic Selection and Intensification in the Native American Powwow," in *Creative Ethnicity* (Logan: Utah State University Press, 1991), 137–56, 154.

13. Dunmore, interview, March 1997.

14. Lynette Jeffries, interview with the author, March 1997, Hillsborough, North Carolina; J. Jeffries, interview, April 1997; Dunmore, interview, March 1997.

15. Beth Velliquette, "Occaneechi 1 Step Closer to Recognition," *Chapel Hill Herald*, December 9, 1998, 12.

16. Dunmore, interview, March 1997.

17. J. Jeffries, interview, June 1997.

18. Hazel, "Black, White and 'Other,' " 27; Thomas E. Ross, *One Land, Three Peoples: A Geography of Robeson County, North Carolina* (Southern Pines NC: Karo Hollow, 1993); Thomas E. Ross, *American Indians in North Carolina: Geographic Interpretations* (Southern Pines NC: Karo Hollow, 1999).

19. John Lawson, *Lawson's History of North Carolina: Containing the Exact Description and Natural History of That Country, Together with the Present State Thereof and a Journal of a Thousand Miles Traveled through Several Nations of Indians, Giving a Particular Account of Their Customs, Manners, Etc. Etc.* (1714; reprint, Richmond: Garrett and Massie, 1951), 53–54; also see R. P. Stephen Davis Jr., Patrick C. Livingood, H. Trawick Ward, and

Vincas P. Steponaitis, *Excavating Occaneechi Town*, CD-ROM (Chapel Hill: University of North Carolina Press, for the Research Laboratories of Archaeology, 1998).

20. John Jeffries, remarks as powwow emcee, May 1996, Hillsborough, North Carolina.

21. Linwood Watson, interview with the author, April 1997, Warrenton, North Carolina.

22. Driver Pheasant Jr., interview with the author, May 1997, Cherokee, North Carolina.

23. J. Jeffries, interview, April 1997.

24. Thomas Beltrame and David V. McQueen, "Urban and Rural Drinking Patterns: The Special Case of the Lumbee," *International Journal of the Addictions* 14, no. 4 (1979): 533–48.

25. Derek Lowry, telephone interview with the author, April 1997. Also see the Lumbee sermons in Claude H. Snow Jr., "An Annotated Transcription of Eight Lumbee Indian Sermons in Upper Robeson County, North Carolina" (PhD diss., University of North Carolina, 1977).

26. Gaillard, "Cities Contradict Lumbees' Values," 6.

27. L. Watson, interview, April 1997; mother of Linwood Watson, interview with the author, April 1997, Warrenton, North Carolina.

28. Lynch, interview, April 1997.

29. John R. Finger describes an experiment one of his Eastern Band of Cherokee consultants made some years ago in connection with "chiefing," that is, being available by the side of the road for tourist photographs. Henry Lambert "worked one day wearing a warbonnet, the second dressed in modest Cherokee clothing and beadwork, and the third with flashy Plains attire again. The warbonnet and tepee of the Plains tribes brought him $80 the first day and $82 the third; Cherokee attire on the second netted him only $3" (*Cherokee Americans: The Eastern Band of Cherokees in the Twentieth Century* [Lincoln: University of Nebraska Press, 1991], 161–63). These tourists knew what "real" Indians looked like from their experiences with popular culture.

North Carolina powwow emcees may be community leaders, may be members who have gone away and then returned successful, or may be prestigious Indians from far away, some of whom embody a modern connection with pop culture. Apesanahkwat, the Menominee actor who played Lester Haines on TV's *Northern Exposure*, has emceed the Guilford Native powwow several times this decade.

30. Lynch, interview, April 1997.

31. J. Jeffries, remarks as powwow emcee, May 1996.

32. Lynch, interview, April 1997.

33. L. Watson, interview, April 1997.

34. Cherry Beasley, "Health," in Susan M. Presti, ed., *Public Policy and Native*

Americans in North Carolina: Issues for the '80s: Conference Proceedings (Raleigh: North Carolina Center for Public Policy Research, 1981), 26–44.

35. Jim Chavis, remarks as powwow emcee, May 1996, Hillsborough, North Carolina.

36. Blaine A. Brownell, "The Agrarian and Urban Ideals: Environment Images in Modern America," *Journal of Popular Culture* 5, no. 3 (1971): 567–87.

37. Bruno Nettl, *Blackfoot Musical Thought: Comparative Perspectives* (Kent OH: Kent University Press, 1989), 66.

38. Lowry, interview, April 1997.

39. Eddie Swimmer, interview with the author, May 1997, Cherokee, North Carolina.

40. Ulali, "Mahk Jchi," track 6 on *Mahk Jchi*, compact disk, Original Vision Records, n.d.

41. L. Jeffries, interview, April 1997.

42. James H. Howard, "Pan-Indian Culture of Oklahoma," *Scientific Monthly* 80 (1955): 215–20, quote at 215; William K. Powers, *War Dance: Plains Indian Musical Performance* (Tucson: University of Arizona Press, 1990), 11.

43. J. Jeffries, interview, May 1997.

44. Patricia Barker Lerch and Susan Bullers, "Powwows and Identity Markers: Traditional or Pan-Indian?" *Human Organization* 55, no. 4 (1996): 390–95.

45. L. Watson, interview, April 1997; Lynch, interview, April 1997.

46. The "specials" that surprised me most were tightly choreographed display dances by visiting troupes of "Aztec dancers." These small ensembles are extended families from Mexico who make a living at U.S. Latin American festivals and at powwows, sometimes under contract, sometimes as buskers through passing the hat or in a blanket dance. I've seen "Aztec Dancers" at powwows as small as one at Durham Technical College, which may have as few as a dozen North Carolina Indian dancers, and at ones large by local standards, such as the Guilford Native powwow, where "Aztecs" have been featured for more than ten years. Their dance outfits, modeled on pictures in centuries-old codices, emphasize bare skin and enormous feathered headdresses. Their purportedly ancient dances resemble ones I've seen at historic pageants put on by students at Mexican universities but do not recall any rural Indian dances of Mexico that I know.

"Aztec" can serve as shorthand for "Mexican Indian" in the United States. When Mexican immigrants – who often are Indians – marry U. S. Indians, the children are described as, for example, "Aztec-Lumbee" in Indian circles. However, a spokesperson for one "Aztec" troupe told me that the group was from Mexico City, and literally Aztec, though his mother – not part of the show – later, and to her son's marked displeasure, informed me that the family was Tarascan, originally from one of the villages bordering Lake P‡tzcuaro. The son had also announced that his group's dances represented unbroken tradition, passed down through the generations in his family, which seemed unlikely to me. On several occasions I timidly broached the topic of the traditionality of the "Aztec Dancers" in conversation with North Carolina Indians. Each time I was told that U.S. Indians leave the weighing of authenticity of the "Aztecs" to the "Aztecs," the transparent implication being that I ought to follow suit.

47. J. Jeffries, interview, April 1997.

48. North Carolina General statutes 143B-404 and 143B-505 created the North Carolina Commission of Indian Affairs and set out its duties, which include establishing "appropriate procedures for legal recognition by the State of presently unrecognized groups and tribes." The list of eight criteria for state recognition, written by members of the commission in 1979, became official in 1980. Both sets of criteria, as well as the thorough case for recognizing the Occaneechi-Saponi at the state level, can be easily accessed through the excellent Occaneechi-Saponi Web site, http://www.occaneechi-saponi.org. Most North Carolina tribes that already have state recognition now seek federal recognition, which does bring with it substantial financial, ideological, and political benefits.

49. Dunmore, interview, March 1997.

Contributors

PATRICIA C. ALBERS is professor of American Indian studies and anthropology at the University of Minnesota–Twin Cities. Her works include the classic anthology *The Hidden Half: Studies of Plains Indian Women* (University Press of America, 1983).

LISA ALDRED is associate professor in the Center for Native American Studies at Montana State University, in Bozeman. Her research centers on the commodification of Native spirituality by the New Age movement.

GRANT ARNDT earned a PhD in anthropology at the University of Chicago, where his doctoral research focused on the history of cultural performance by members of the Ho-Chunk Nation. He has previously published two articles on Native American urbanization in Chicago: "Relocation's Imagined Landscape and the Rise of Chicago's Native American Community," in *Native Chicago*, ed. Terry Straus (2002); and " 'Contrary to Our Way of Thinking': The Struggle for an American Indian Center in Chicago," *American Indian Culture and Research Journal* 22, no. 4 (1997). He has taught at the University of Iowa and is currently a visiting assistant professor at St. Olaf College in Northfield, Minnesota.

TOMMY ATTACHIE (Dane-zaa) is an elder and Dane-zaa songkeeper. He is the lead singer at all Dane-zaa ceremonials.

SAMUEL R. COOK is associate professor in the Center for Interdisciplinary Studies at Virginia Tech University, in Blacksburg. He is the author of *Monacans and Miners: Native American and Coal Mining Communities in Appalachia* (University of Nebraska Press, 2000).

GARY H. DUNHAM is director of the University of Nebraska Press and its longtime acquiring editor in Native Studies.

CLYDE ELLIS is associate professor of history at Elon College, in Elon, North Carolina. He is the author of *A Dancing People: Powwow Culture on the Southern Plains* (University Press of Kansas, 2003) and *To Change Them Forever: Indian Education At The Rainy Mountain Boarding School, 1893–1920* (University of Oklahoma Press, 1996). He is a coauthor, with Luke Eric Lassiter and Ralph Kotay, of *The Jesus Road: Kiowas, Christianity, and Indian Hymns* (University of Nebraska Press, 2002).

LORETTA FOWLER is professor of anthropology at the University of Oklahoma. She is the author of *Arapahoe Politics, 1851–1978: Symbols in Crises of Authority* (University of Nebraska Press, 1982); *Shared Symbols, Contested Meanings: Gros Ventre Culture and History, 1778–1984* (Cornell University Press, 1987); *The Arapaho* (Chelsea House, 1989); *Tribal Sovereignty and the Historical Imagination: Cheyenne-Arapaho Politics* (University of Nebraska Press, 2002); and *The Columbia Guide to American Indians of the Great Plains* (Columbia University Press, 2003).

DANIEL J. GELO is professor of anthropology and dean at the University of Texas at San Antonio. He has been conducting field research with Comanches and other Texas Indian people since 1982. Gelo edited *Comanche Vocabulary: Trilingual Edition* (University of Texas Press, 1995) and is a contributor to *Comanches in the New West, 1895–1908* (University of Texas Press, 1999).

BRIAN JOSEPH GILLEY is assistant professor of anthropology at the University of Vermont, in Burlington. He is the author of *Becoming Two-Spirit: The Search for Acceptance in Indian Country* (forthcoming from the University of Nebraska Press).

CHRIS GOERTZEN is associate professor of music history at the University of Southern Mississippi, in Hattiesburg. His books include *Fiddling for Norway: Revival and Identity* (University of Chicago Press, 1997) and (as coeditor) the European volume of the *Garland Encyclopedia of World Music*. He is working currently on a book examining the interaction of tradition and tourism as expressed in crafts and festivals in Oaxaca, Mexico.

DENNIS HASTINGS (Omaha) is the director of the Omaha Tribal Historical Research Project and a faculty member at Nebraska Indian Community College. He is a coauthor, with Robin Ridington, of *Blessing for a Long Time: The Sacred Pole of the Omaha Tribe* (University of Nebraska Press, 1997).

JASON BAIRD JACKSON is assistant professor of folklore at Indiana University, in Bloomington. He is the author of *Yuchi Ceremonial Life: Performance, Meaning and Tradition in a Contemporary Native American Community* (University of Nebraska Press, 2003).

JOHN L. JOHNS is a Vietnam veteran and former Monacan Tribal Council chief. He has been an active voice in the Monacan Nation's pursuit of federal recognition. He is currently studying pre-law at Georgia State University.

LUKE ERIC LASSITER is professor and director of the Graduate Humanities Program at Marshall University Graduate College. His books include *Invitation to Anthropology* (AltaMira, 2002) and *The Power of Kiowa Song: A Collaborative*

Ethnography (University of Arizona Press, 1998). He is a coauthor, with Clyde Ellis and Ralph Kotay, of *The Jesus Road: Kiowas, Christianity, and Indian Hymns* (University of Nebraska Press, 2002).

BEATRICE MEDICINE (Standing Rock Sioux) is a former professor of anthropology at Dartmouth College and at Stanford University. She retired from California State University–Northridge. She is the author of *Learning to Be an Anthropologist and Remaining "Native"* (University of Illinois Press, 2001).

ROBIN RIDINGTON is professor emeritus of anthropology at the University of British Columbia, in Vancouver. He is a coauthor, with Dennis Hastings, of *Blessing for a Long Time: The Sacred Pole of the Omaha Tribe* (University of Nebraska Press, 1997) and the author of *Trail to Heaven: Knowledge and Narrative in a Northern Native Community* (University of Iowa Press, 1988).

KATHLEEN GLENISTER ROBERTS is assistant professor of communication and rhetorical studies at Duquesne University, in Pittsburgh. She is the author of essays published in *Communication Theory*, *Text and Performance Quarterly*, *Communication Quarterly*, and other journals. Her current research projects concern ethnography, narrative, and the rhetoric and philosophy of intercultural communication.

R. D. THEISZ is professor of English and chair of humanities at Black Hills State University, in Spearfish, South Dakota. He is the author of *Sharing the Gift of Lakota Song* (Dog Soldier Press, 2003) and *Buckskin Tokens: Contemporary Lakota Oral Narratives* (Sinte Gleska College, 1974), and a coauthor, with Severt Young Bear, of *Standing in the Light: A Lakota Way of Seeing* (University of Nebraska Press, 1994).

RENAE WATCHMAN (Diné/Tsalagi) is a PhD candidate in the German Studies Department and the Graduate Program in Humanities at Stanford University. Her research interests include nineteenth-century travel literature, nineteenth-century representations of "the Other" in German literature, ethnography, philosophy, and Europeans' enduring interest in American Indians.

KARENNE WOOD has served for eight years as the Monacan Nation's director of social and economic development. She is also an accomplished and widely published poet whose works include *Markings on Earth* (2001). Wood works as a repatriation specialist for the Association for American Indian Affairs and has served as chair of the Virginia Council on Indians since 2003. She is currently a doctoral candidate in linguistic anthropology at the University of Virginia.

Index